WINNING
SEASONS

A Collection of Favorite Recipes

Published by

The Junior League of Tuscaloosa, Inc.
Tuscaloosa, Alabama

The purpose of the Junior League is exclusively educational and charitable and is to promote voluntarism, to develop the potential of its members for voluntary participation in community affairs, and to demonstrate the effectiveness of trained volunteers.

First printing 10,000 books   November 1979
Second printing 10,000 books   December 1979
Third printing 22,000 books   December 1980
Fourth printing 10,000 books   June 1984
Fifth printing 10,000 books   October 1994

To order copies of **Winning Seasons**, send check for $16.95 plus $2.75 shipping and handling. Alabama residents add $1.35 tax.

Winning Seasons
P. O. Box 1152
Tuscaloosa, Alabama 35403

International Standard Book Number: 0-918544-35-1

Printed in the USA by

WIMMER
The Wimmer Companies, Inc.
Memphis • Dallas

COOKBOOK COMMITTEE

Mrs. Peterson Cavert
Mrs. Allen Mattox

Mrs. Mark Bergaas
Mrs. Gene Bennett
Mrs. George Gordon
Mrs. Charles R. Pearce

Mrs. Carlos Shows
Mrs. Tony Smith
Mrs. William H. Tucker

Mrs. T. Griffin Stanley, Jr.

Mrs. Carl Adams, Jr.
Mrs. C. Rice Baxter
Mrs. Daniel M. Hoke
Mrs. H. Wayne Hutton
Mrs. Haskell Nevin
Mrs. James O. Parker

Mrs. Mickey M. Petty
Mrs. Ronald Phelps
Mrs. Terry H. Pickett
Mrs. Dennis Stanard
Mrs. Sidney Tarwater
Mrs. Wilfred Yeargan, Jr.

Illustrations by Mrs. Eric Lee Wilson

Acknowledgements: Dr. Sarah R. Jones; Patricia J. Seymour; Peggy Bishop, Tuscaloosa County Cooperative Extension Service; Dr. Cheryl W. Hutton, School of Home Economics, University of Alabama

The Junior Welfare Association of Tuscaloosa was organized in 1929 and became Junior League of Tuscaloosa in 1976. JWA published cookbooks in 1939 and 1957. Several of the favorite recipes from these two earlier volumes are included in **Winning Seasons.**

Proceeds from the sale of **Winning Seasons** will be used for community projects approved or sponsored by The Junior League of Tuscaloosa.

FOREWORD

Tuscaloosa and the Black Warrior River were named after the powerful and gigantic Choctaw Indian, Chief Tushkaloosa, "tushka" meaning warrior, and "lusa" meaning black. Situated at the southwest edge of Alabama's great coal and iron districts, the town of Tuscaloosa was incorporated in 1819 and soon became a great shipping and trading center. In 1826, Tuscaloosa became the state capital and held that title until 1846.

The University of Alabama opened in 1831 with an enrollment of thirty-five. In 1865, the Federal forces of Croxton's Raiders left the University and Tuscaloosa's industries in ashes. Slowly rebuilding, the school reopened in 1869 and today boasts an enrollment of over 17,000. The city has steadily grown to an estimated current population of 82,000 and has over 100 industries.

Tuscaloosa is lucky to be in an area where the seasons of the year are well defined. Spring is light-green, azalea-filled, daffodil-scented; summer is bright with sunshine, crepe myrtle, and gardenia. Fall is multicolored, sometimes spectacular red, yellow, and orange with oaks, mums, and marigolds; winter is brown, but dotted with camellias and spiced with pine. We are also in an agricultural area where we speak of summer as "squash, tomato, and pickling" season, and spring as "asparagus and strawberry" season. To the many local hunters, there are dove and deer seasons, duck, turkey, and squirrel seasons.

Also, being the home of the University of Alabama, Tuscaloosa is accustomed to living with and enjoying the football and basketball seasons. Alternate these with tennis, golf, swimming, and boating, and the number of seasons grows further.

This book takes advantage of all these interpretations and offers recipes, menu suggestions, and ideas to span each season of your year—whether it includes using fresh produce to best advantage, entertaining informally before or after football games, having the tennis group for lunch, or cooking your favorite hunter's latest trophy. You will find quick and easy dishes, gourmet ideas for fancy parties, advantageous ways to use kitchen helpers such as food processors and microwave ovens, and both traditional Southern fare and foods with foreign flavor. All are winning ideas for **Winning Seasons!**

A RECIPE THAT CANNOT FAIL

Take twelve fine, luscious full-grown months. See that they are thoroughly free from all memories of bitterness and jealousy. Separate them completely from all clinging particles of spite. Pick off all specks of pettiness. Have them as fresh and clean as when they first came from the storehouse of time. Cut these months into thirty parts. This portion will keep for only one year. Do not attempt to make the whole bunch up at one time, as so many people spoil the entire batch this way. Prepare only one day at a time, as follows:

Into each day put 12 parts of faith, 11 of patience, 10 of sincerity, 9 of cheer, 7 of confidence, 6 of rest, 5 of loyalty, 4 of hope, 3 of charity, 2 of prayer, and 1 well-selected resolution. Add to this one heaping teaspoonful of good spirits, a dash of fun, a pinch of gaiety, a sprinkling of play, and a heaping cup of good humor.

Pour into the whole a liberal amount of love and happiness and mix with mirth. Cook thoroughly into a fervent heat, garnish with laughter and a sprig of joy. Then serve with quietness, unselfishness, and courage, and a full successful year is a certainty.

—Ruth Barrick

TABLE OF CONTENTS

Appetizers
and
Beverages

BLEU CHEESE ROLL

1 (8-ounce) package cream cheese
4 ounces bleu cheese
1 teaspoon Worcestershire sauce
1 large sweet pickle, chopped

1 teaspoon garlic salt
½ cup ground walnuts
½ cup cut up parsley

Mix cream cheese, bleu cheese, Worcestershire sauce, pickle and garlic salt. Shape into 1 or 2 rolls and roll in nuts and parsley. Wrap in wax paper and refrigerate. Serve surrounded with your favorite crackers.

Mrs. E. S. "Brother" Harris, III (Frances Mathews)

CHICKEN CURRY CREAM CHEESE BALL

1 (8-ounce) package cream cheese
1 cup chicken, cooked and finely
   chopped
¾ cup almonds, toasted and
   finely chopped

⅓ cup mayonnaise
2 tablespoons chutney, chopped
1 tablespoon curry powder
¼ teaspoon salt
Flaked coconut or parsley

Mix cream cheese, chicken, almonds, mayonnaise, chutney, curry, and salt in large bowl and chill for several hours. Shape into ball. Roll in flaked coconut or parsley. Yield: 1 large cheese ball.

Mrs. Carl Adams, Jr. (Jean Anders)

DELICIOUS, QUICK, EASY CHEESE LOG

½ pound sharp cheddar cheese,
   grated
2 tablespoons minced onion
2 tablespoons minced green pepper
3 chopped stuffed olives
2 tablespoons chopped sweet pickle

1 hard-boiled egg, chopped
½ cup crushed saltine crackers
¼ cup mayonnaise
½ teaspoon salt

Combine cheese, onion, pepper, olives, pickle, egg, crackers, mayonnaise, and salt. Form into a log, loaf, or ball shape. Refrigerate.

Mrs. George Gordon (Jean Fargason)

OYSTER ROLL

2 (8-ounce) packages cream cheese
2 or 3 tablespoons mayonnaise
2 teaspoons Worcestershire sauce
1 or 2 pods garlic, pressed
½ small onion, pressed
⅛ teaspoon salt
2 (3½-ounce) cans smoked oysters

Cream enough mayonnaise into cheese to hold it together. Add Worcestershire sauce, garlic, and onion. Combine well. Spread about ½-inch thick on wax paper. Chop oysters and spread on top of cheese mixture. Roll as for jellyroll, using a knife to start it. Chill for 24 hours. Serve with toast rounds or crackers.

Mrs. James R. Shamblin (Patricia Terry)—Centre, AL

PINEAPPLE PEPPER CHEESE BALL

2 (8-ounce) packages cream cheese
1 (8-ounce) can crushed pineapple, drained
½ cup onion, chopped fine
¼ cup green pepper, chopped fine
1 cup pecans, chopped fine
1 tablespoon seasoned salt
1 teaspoon garlic powder
½ teaspoon onion powder

Let cheese soften at room temperature. Mix cream cheese, pineapple, onion, pepper, ½ cup of pecans, seasoned salt, garlic and onion powder. After mixing, place in refrigerator to firm, then roll into ball, covering with remaining pecans. Place cherry in center of ball for color.

Mrs. James William McFarland (Miriam Webster)

ROQUEFORT CHEESE BALL

2 (8-ounce) packages cream cheese
1 (3-ounce) package Roquefort cheese
1 (6-ounce) package sharp Nippy cheese
1 teaspoon Worcestershire sauce
⅛ teaspoon hot sauce
Paprika

Let cheeses stand until soft. Mix well cream cheese, Roquefort, sharp Nippy cheese, Worcestershire and hot sauce with hands. Make into two balls. Roll in paprika.

Mrs. Ted Hixon (Lucy McCaslan)

"THE BEST" CHEESE BALL

1 (5-ounce) jar Kraft Olde
  English cheese
1 (4-ounce) package bleu cheese
1 (8-ounce) package cream cheese
1 tablespoon Worcestershire sauce
⅛ teaspoon garlic powder

⅛ teaspoon Tabasco (more to
  taste)
¾ teaspoon salt
Red pepper to taste (lots)
1 cup pecans, chopped very fine
1 cup parsley, chopped

Let Olde English cheese, bleu cheese, and cream cheese come to room temperature. Blend well, then add Worcestershire sauce, garlic, Tabasco, salt, and red pepper. Blend thoroughly with hands. Divide cheese mixture into two portions and shape into balls; roll in mixture of chopped pecans and chopped parsley.

Variations: You may add nuts to cheese mixture and shape this into a Christmas tree and pat parsley on top for a festive touch. Add nuts and parsley to cheese, divide into 2 portions, shape into footballs and roll in paprika or red pepper, and stick in a toothpick that has a flag saying, "Our team is red hot!" Shape into hearts, bunnies, golf balls, tennis balls, whatever. Let your imagination run wild! And it tastes great, besides. Chill and serve with your choice of crackers. Freezes well.

Mrs. George Fields

AUNT ANN'S DIP

1 (8-ounce) carton French Onion
  dip
½ cup mayonnaise
2 tablespoons celery, finely
  chopped
2 tablespoons parsley, finely
  chopped

1 tablespoon lemon juice
1 tablespoon vinegar
1 clove garlic, crushed
1 (3-ounce) package cream
  cheese, softened

Combine onion dip, mayonnaise, celery, parsley, lemon juice, vinegar, garlic, and cream cheese, and mix well. Better after being refrigerated for a day or two. Makes 2 cups.

Mrs. James W. Eddings (Heidi Hoyt)

AVOCADO DIP

1 cup mashed avocado
1 (8-ounce) package cream cheese
3 tablespoons lemon juice
Dash of Worcestershire sauce

⅓ cup green onions, finely
 chopped (use some tops)
1 teaspoon salt

Gradually add avocado to cream cheese. Add lemon juice, Worcestershire sauce, onion, and salt. Mix until thoroughly blended.

Mrs. Carlos 'Sonny" Shows (Gloria Church)

AVOCADO-TOMATO DIP

1 pint (2 cups) sour cream
2 tablespoons mayonnaise
1 package Good Seasons Italian
 dressing mix (0.6-ounce)

2 diced avocados
2 diced tomatoes
Tabasco to taste
Salt and pepper to taste

Mix sour cream, mayonnaise, Italian dressing, avocados, tomatoes, Tabasco, salt, and pepper. Chill several hours. Serve with tortilla chips. Yield: About 8 cups.

Note: Recipe may be halved.

Mrs. Dennis Stanard (Beth Cowden)

CREAMY CARAWAY CHEESE DIP

¼ pound margarine or butter,
 softened
1 (8-ounce) package cream cheese
2 teaspoons paprika
2 teaspoons caraway seed
1 teaspoon dry mustard

1 tablespoon onion, finely
 chopped
¼ teaspoon salt
Freshly ground pepper
¾ cup sour cream

Cream butter in mixer. Add cream cheese, paprika, caraway seed, mustard, onion, salt, pepper, and sour cream. Refrigerate for 2 hours or until firm. Makes 2 cups.

Mrs. Howard Burchfield (Judy Forsyth)

DEVILED HAM DIP

1 (6¾-ounce) can Underwood
  deviled ham
1 (8-ounce) package softened
  cream cheese

½ to 1 teaspoon garlic powder
2 to 3 tablespoons Hellmann's
  mayonnaise

Soften cream cheese. Blend in deviled ham. Add garlic powder and enough mayonnaise to make it smooth. May add 1 ounce chopped pimiento, ½ tablespoon Worcestershire sauce, 2 tablespoons grated onion, 2 tablespoons pickle juice or catsup for more variety. A favorite with the menfolk!

Mrs. James L. Stephens (Janet Sherer)—Jacksonville, FL

DILL WEED DIP

⅔ cup mayonnaise
⅔ cup sour cream
1 tablespoon shredded green onion

1 tablespoon parsley
1 teaspoon dill weed
1 teaspoon Beau Monde seasoning

Mix mayonnaise, sour cream, onion, parsley, dill weed, and Beau Monde seasoning. Chill for 2-3 hours. Use as dip for raw vegetables.

Hint: Possible containers for dip are "limitless"—hollowed out large zucchini, cabbage, small pumpkin in the fall, eggplant, or a pineapple half with top attached.

Mrs. Fred "Brother" Fletcher (Erin Briggs)

EASY SHRIMP DIP

1 (8-ounce) package cream cheese
1 teaspoon onion powder
4 tablespoons catsup
6 tablespoons mayonnaise

1 teaspoon barbecue sauce
Pinch of salt
1 (4½-ounce) can shrimp,
  drained and chopped

Cream the cheese, add onion powder, catsup, mayonnaise, barbecue sauce, and salt. Mix well with mixer. Stir in shrimp and refrigerate at least 30 minutes before serving. Makes about 3 cups. Serve with crackers or chips. May add juice of ½ lemon for variation.

Mrs. Jimmy Hamner (Elizabeth "Libby" Bolling)

PINK CREAM CHEESE DIP

8 ounces cream cheese
2 tablespoons milk
2 tablespoons French dressing
⅓ cup catsup
1 tablespoon minced onion
¼ teaspoon salt

Combine cream cheese, milk, French dressing, catsup, onion, and salt in blender or food processor for a pretty and good pink dip. Makes 1 cup.

Mrs. Mark Bergaas (Mary Emmons)

BRANTLY'S CRABMEAT SPREAD

2 (6½-ounce) cans crabmeat, drained
½ cup Hellmann's mayonnaise
2 teaspoons horseradish (cream-style white prepared)
6 tablespoons lemon juice
2 tablespoons minced green onion
¼ teaspoon salt
¼ teaspoon pepper
Paprika

Remove cartilage pieces from crabmeat. Combine with Hellmann's, horseradish, lemon juice, onion, salt, and pepper. Cover; chill several hours. Sprinkle with paprika before serving with crackers. Yield: 2 cups.

Variations: Add ¼ cup catsup and 1 (8-ounce) package of cream cheese for a grand dip! May also serve hot and sprinkle the top with ½ cup toasted almonds.

Mrs. Jack McGuire, Jr. (Brantly Cochrane)

CRABMEAT MOLD

2 packages unflavored gelatin
¼ cup water
1 (10¾-ounce) can cream of shrimp soup
2 (3-ounce) packages cream cheese, softened in mixer
1 small onion, grated
1 tablespoon Worcestershire sauce
¼ teaspoon salt
1½ cups crabmeat
1 cup celery, chopped
1 cup mayonnaise
1½ tablespoons lemon juice
2 teaspoons Tabasco

Soften gelatin in water. Warm soup, add gelatin, stir until dissolved. Stir in cream cheese, onion, Worcestershire, salt, crabmeat, celery, mayonnaise, lemon juice, and Tabasco. Adjust seasoning. Pour into oiled 1-quart fish or ring mold. Refrigerate for at least 6 to 8 hours. Serve with crackers.

Bert Wear

DILLED SHRIMP SPREAD

1 (4½-ounce) can shrimp, drained
1 (8-ounce) package cream
  cheese, softened
1 tablespoon mayonnaise
¼ to ½ teaspoon garlic powder
1 teaspoon catsup

1½ teaspoons Worcestershire
  sauce
1 teaspoon lemon juice
2 tablespoons grated onion
1 teaspoon dill seed

Chop shrimp, reserving some whole ones for garnish. Combine cream cheese, mayonnaise, garlic powder, catsup, Worcestershire sauce, lemon juice, and onion; blend well. Add chopped shrimp; chill several hours or overnight. Shape as desired and garnish with whole shrimp and dill seed. Yield: 1 cup.

Mrs. Jack McGuire, Jr. (Brantly Cochrane)

EVERLASTING BRANDIED CHEESE SPREAD

1 pound sharp cheddar cheese,
  grated
4 ounces cream cheese (or other
  soft cheese)

1½ ounces olive oil
1 teaspoon caraway seed
1 teaspoon dry mustard
1½ ounces brandy or kirsch

Mix cheeses and olive oil. Blend well. Add caraway seed, mustard, and brandy or kirsch, and mix until smooth. Store in a sealable earthenware crock in refrigerator. Serve at room temperature. As spread is used, continue to add any grated leftover dry, hard (etc.) cheese you desire. May need additional mustard or brandy occasionally.

CHEDDAR PUFFS

½ cup (1 stick) butter or margarine
1 cup grated sharp cheddar cheese
  (4 ounces)

1¼ cups sifted flour
¼ teaspoon salt

Cream butter or margarine with cheese until smooth in a medium-size bowl. Blend in flour and salt, then knead lightly with hands to form a soft dough. Roll, a teaspoonful at a time, into balls; place on greased cookie sheets. Bake in hot oven (400 degrees) for 12 minutes, or until golden. Serve hot. Makes 3 dozen.

Mrs. Earl L. Carpenter (Betty Myrick)

LAYERED SEAFOOD COCKTAIL

Lettuce
1 pound medium shrimp, boiled
  and shelled
1 pound lump crabmeat

WHITE SAUCE:
½ cup mayonnaise
1 tablespoon Mr. Mustard
2 teaspoons lime juice
1 green onion, minced
¼ cup bell pepper, minced

CHILI SAUCE:
1 (12-ounce) bottle chili sauce
½ cup catsup
2 tablespoons lime juice
1 heaping teaspoon horseradish
Lemon slices

Mix mayonnaise, mustard, lime juice, onion, and pepper for the white sauce in a small bowl; cover with foil and refrigerate until chilled. Mix chili sauce, catsup, lime juice, and horseradish for the chili sauce; cover and refrigerate until chilled. Line 6 cocktail bowls with lettuce leaves. Layer the ingredients in this order: white sauce, crabmeat, chili sauce, and shrimp. Garnish each cocktail with a teaspoon of chili sauce and a lemon slice. Refrigerate until ready to serve. Yield: 6 medium cocktails.

Mrs. L. Page Stalcup, III (Rinna Cobb)—Mobile, AL

ARTICHOKE APPETIZERS

1 (6-ounce) box plain Melba toast
  rounds
2 (14-ounce) cans artichoke hearts

½ cup mayonnaise
½ cup grated Parmesan cheese

Slice artichoke hearts about ¼-inch thick. Place rounds on cookie sheet and top each with 1 artichoke slice. In separate bowl, mix mayonnaise and grated Parmesan cheese with spoon. Top each round and slice with 1 teaspoon of mayonnaise mixture. Bake at 350 degrees until lightly brown. Serve warm. Yield: About 4 dozen.

Hint: These may be prepared a few hours ahead and stored in refrigerator, BUT do not cook until ready to serve. These are always a big hit at parties. I've never had even one left over!

Mrs. Mickey M. Petty (Donna Davenport)

ASPARAGUS ROLL-UPS

20 slices white bread
1 (3-ounce) package bleu cheese
1 (8-ounce) package cream cheese
4 dashes Worcestershire sauce

20 asparagus spears (cooked, if fresh are used; or 2 15-ounce cans)
¾ cup melted butter

Trim crusts and use rolling pin to flatten the bread. Blend bleu cheese and cream cheese to workable consistency. Add Worcestershire sauce. Spread evenly on each slice of bread. Drain asparagus on paper towels. Roll one spear of asparagus in each slice of bread. Dip in butter to coat evenly, or brush butter over roll. Place on cookie sheet, side by side, seam side down. Bake at 350 degrees for 15-20 minutes, or until browned and crisp. Cut in thirds and serve hot. Serves 8-10.

Note: These can be frozen before cooking by placing on a cookie sheet until frozen and then placed in bags until ready to use. They keep well this way. When ready to serve, take out, slice into thirds and bake at 400 degrees for 10 minutes, then reduce heat to 350 degrees and bake for another 15-20 minutes. For variation, sprinkle bacon bits on asparagus before rolling up. They may also have Parmesan cheese sprinkled on top before baking. They make a great side dish, not cut but served whole.

Suzanne Augusta "Sissy" Herrod

BARBECUED SHRIMP (Appetizer)

½ teaspoon salt
½ teaspoon garlic powder
½ cup salad oil
¼ cup soy sauce
¼ cup lemon juice

3 tablespoons chopped parsley
2 teaspoons onion powder
½ teaspoon pepper
2 pounds large shrimp, peeled, uncooked

Combine salt, garlic, oil, soy sauce, lemon juice, parsley, onion, and pepper to make marinade, mixing well. Place shrimp in shallow dish and cover with marinade. Refrigerate about 3 hours. Put shrimp on shish-ka-bob skewers. Grill over fire for 4 minutes per side. (May broil in oven.)

Mrs. Jimmy Hamner (Elizabeth "Libby" Bolling)

CHEESE COOKIES

1 pound sharp cheddar cheese,
  grated very fine
2 sticks butter or margarine
2 cups flour

1 teaspoon salt
Red pepper to taste
1 cup pecans, chopped fine

Cream together cheese and butter. Add flour and knead. Add salt and red pepper. Add pecans and roll into sausage-like roll. Chill overnight and slice very thin. Bake at 350 degrees for 10 minutes. Do not brown.

Variation: Add ½ cup confectioners' sugar when you add the flour.

Mrs. Philip Lancaster (Margaret Haring)

CHEESE KRISPIES

1 pound sharp cheddar cheese,
  grated (room temperature)
2 cups plain flour
½ pound butter, melted

Dash salt
½ to 1 teaspoon red pepper
2 cups Rice Krispies

Sprinkle flour on cheese and pour on melted butter. Add salt and red pepper to taste. Add Rice Krispies to this mixture and knead together by hand until well blended. Roll into marble-size balls and place on ungreased cookie sheet. Flatten with fork and bake for 30 minutes at 300 degrees. Yield: About 150.

Mrs. Melford Espey, Jr. (Rebecca "Becky" Flowers)

CHEESE OLIVETTES

1 stick butter
½ pound sharp cheese, grated
⅓ teaspoon Tabasco

Dash garlic salt
1½ cups flour
Small stuffed olives

Have butter and cheese at room temperature. Add Tabasco and garlic salt. Blend with hands. Add flour gradually. Break off bit of pastry, flatten in palm of hand, center with olive, and roll in palms to cover olive completely. Use only enough to cover olive. Bake on baking sheet at 375 degrees about 15-20 minutes, until lightly colored and done.

Note: Dates are good done this way, too!

Mrs. William A. "Butch" Hughes (Betty Blondheim)

CHEESE ROLLS

2½ cups flour
1 cup soft butter

1 cup sour cream
3 cups grated cheddar cheese

Combine flour, butter, and sour cream to make dough. Chill, divided into 4 parts. Roll out dough like pie crust and put in cheese. Roll up like jellyroll. Cook on ungreased cookie sheet for 30 minutes at 350 degrees. Yield: 4 rolls.

Hint: Chill in foil if you are going to wait to cook.

Mrs. Hank Hawkins (Eugenia Partlow)

CHEESE STRAWS

1 stick of butter or margarine
1 pound New York State sharp
  cheese, grated

2 cups flour
¼ teaspoon cayenne pepper
Salt

Let butter and grated cheese be at room temperature. Blend butter and cheese until light and fluffy. Gradually add flour and cayenne pepper, beating well. (I use an electric mixer.) Put dough in a cookie press and shape on a cookie sheet. Sprinkle with salt. Bake at 350 degrees for about 10 minutes.

Mrs. George Fields

COCKTAIL PIZZAS

1 loaf Party Rye bread
1 (12-ounce) can tomato paste
½ pound salami or pepperoni,
  thinly sliced (approximately)

½ pound mozzarella cheese,
  sliced (approximately)
Dash oregano

Spread each slice of party rye with a generous amount of tomato paste. Next top with a slice of salami or pepperoni, then top with a slice of mozzarella cheese and a good dash of oregano. These may be made ahead and refrigerated or frozen. When ready to serve, run under broiler until the cheese is beginning to brown. These are great for teenage parties as well as cocktail parties. Always a big hit!

Mrs. Hilliard Fletcher (Betty Harlan)

FRITATA BITS

1 onion, finely chopped
1 clove garlic, minced
2 (6-ounce) jars artichoke hearts
4 eggs
¼ cup bread crumbs
¼ teaspoon salt
⅛ teaspoon pepper

⅛ teaspoon oregano
⅛ teaspoon hot sauce
½ pound (or 2 cups) grated
  cheddar cheese (sharp)
2 tablespoons parsley, chopped
Marinade from 1 jar of artichokes

Sauté onion and garlic about 5 minutes. Combine with chopped artichoke hearts. Beat eggs, bread crumbs, and spices. Stir in cheese, artichoke mixture, parsley, and marinade. Pour into 8 x 8-inch pan. Bake at 350 degrees for 30 minutes, or until brown. Serve warm or cold in bite-size chunks. Yield: 16-25 pieces.

Mrs. Henry S. Holman (Jan Frush)

KÄSEKUGELN (FRIED CHEESE BALLS)

2¾ cups Swiss cheese, grated
½ cup flour
2 eggs and 1 egg yolk, well beaten
1 teaspoon salt

½ teaspoon pepper
⅛ teaspoon nutmeg
Vegetable oil

In a mixing bowl, put eggs, salt, pepper, nutmeg. Add flour and cheese, alternately, until you create a heavy paste. If it is too wet, add a little more flour until it is stiff. Form into balls and drop in hot oil. Fry until golden.

Mrs. David Hefelfinger (Virginia Mauney)

PARTY MIX

1 (10-ounce) package frozen
  chopped broccoli
1 (3-ounce) package dried pastrami
1 (16-ounce) can tomatoes
2 heaping teaspoons chili powder

2 tablespoons Worcestershire
  sauce
4 beaten eggs
1 pound Velveeta cheese

Heat broccoli, meat, tomatoes, chili powder, and Worcestershire sauce. Add eggs and cook until thick. Transfer all to a double boiler and add Velveeta. Cook until thick. Serve in chafing dish with favorite bread, toast, or crackers.

Mrs. William J. Stack, Jr. (Leckie Kern)—Marietta, GA

MARINATED BROCCOLI

1 cup vinegar
1 tablespoon sugar
1 tablespoon dill seed
1 tablespoon Accent
1 teaspoon salt

1 teaspoon pepper
1 teaspoon garlic salt
1½ cups oil
3 bunches fresh broccoli, cut
  into flowerettes

Mix vinegar, sugar, dill seed, Accent, salt, pepper, and garlic salt well. Add oil and stir. Add broccoli and marinate 24 hours, turning several times. Use a non-metallic bowl with a seal-tight top for added convenience in mixing. Serves 60.

Mrs. John D. Cade (Virginia Duckworth)

CUCUMBER APPETIZERS

2 (3-ounce) packages chive cream
  cheese
¼ cup stuffed green olives,
  chopped

3 cucumbers

Either halve cucumbers lengthwise and scoop out seeds, or use corer to scoop out seeds. Fill hollows with cream cheese mixture, press halves together, wrap tightly in plastic wrap, and chill. Cut crosswise in ½-inch slices and serve.

Note: If not fresh cucumbers, peel to remove paraffin. They are pretty when scored lengthwise with the tines of a fork before slicing, if fresh.

Mrs. Lloyd Baker (Jan Heiliman)

MUSHROOM DELIGHT

11 ounces softened cream cheese
1 (4-ounce) can chopped
  mushrooms

1 (8-ounce) package Pillsbury
  Crescent rolls, rolled out
Egg white

Mix mushrooms and cream cheese. Spread mushroom and cream cheese mixture on top of flattened crescent rolls. Roll up in jellyroll fashion and slice. Brush egg white on top before baking. Bake for 10 minutes at 350 degrees.

Mrs. Adrian Goldstein (Betty Jo May)

MARINATED MUSHROOMS

1½ pounds button mushrooms
1 cup dry white wine
1 large lemon, thinly sliced
2 cups olive oil
8 green onion bulbs, minced
1 clove garlic, crushed and minced

1 tablespoon angostura
2 tablespoons salt
Several twists of the pepper mill
2 whole cloves
2 bay leaves
10-12 sprigs parsley, minced

Break the stems off the mushrooms and set aside or freeze to make soup. Wipe the caps with a clean, damp cloth. Combine wine, lemon, oil, onion, garlic, angostura, salt, pepper, cloves, and bay leaves in an enameled pot and boil 10 minutes. Remove pot from stove, add mushrooms, and allow mixture to cool. When cool, add parsley. Pour mixture into a big plastic bag, squeeze out all the air, and tie securely. Place in a pan in case the bag leaks and refrigerate for 48 hours, turning the bag whenever you think of it so the mushrooms get well soaked. To serve, drain (reserve the marinade to use over salads). Stick each mushroom with a toothpick and arrange in a suitable serving bowl. Serves 8 or more.

Mrs. J. C. "Bud" Miller (Presteen Sims)

MARINATED SHRIMP AND ARTICHOKES

2 (14-ounce) cans artichoke hearts
1½ pounds cooked, peeled
    medium shrimp
1 egg
¾ cup olive oil
¼ cup vegetable oil

½ cup wine vinegar
2 teaspoons dry mustard
2 tablespoons chives
2 tablespoons chopped scallions
1 teaspoon salt
¼ teaspoon pepper

Chill artichokes and shrimp. Drain and quarter artichokes and combine with shrimp. Beat together the egg, olive and vegetable oils, vinegar, mustard, chives, scallions, salt, and pepper. Pour over the shrimp and artichokes. Marinate overnight. Serve with toothpicks. Yields appetizers for 12.

Mrs. John C. Boles (Donna Waters)

SAUSAGE WHEELS

1 pound bulk sausage (room
    temperature)

2 recipes Regulation Pastry (See
    Index)

Roll out pie crust, and spread sausage out to the edges. Roll up, as in jelly-roll. Chill, slice thin, and bake in hot oven (400 degrees) on broiler pan for about 10 minutes. Makes 7 dozen.

Mrs. Tom Patton (Suse Donald)

SAUSAGE BALLS

1 pound sausage (hot or mild, or
  mixture of ½ pound of each)
1½ cups sharp cheddar cheese,
  grated

2 cups Bisquick
Dash hot sauce (not necessary
  with hot sausage)

Mix sausage, cheese, Bisquick, and hot sauce until well combined. Form into balls about 1½ inches in diameter. Place on ungreased cookie sheet. Bake at 350 degrees for 30 minutes. Serve hot. These freeze well. May put in oven frozen and bake 5 minutes longer.

Mrs. Carlos "Sonny" Shows (Gloria Church)

STELLA'S CHEESE STRAWS

3 cups flour
3 teaspoons baking powder
2 teaspoons salt
1 teaspoon red pepper
1 teaspoon paprika

1 teaspoon onion salt
1 cup butter or oleo, softened
1 pound sharp cheese, grated
9 tablespoons cold water

Sift flour, baking powder, salt, red pepper, paprika, and onion salt together into mixer bowl. Cut in butter and cheese with mixer. Sprinkle water over mixture and blend with fork. Use "star-shaped disc" on cookie press to form rows of cheese straws on ungreased cookie sheet. Bake at 325 degrees for 15 minutes, until slightly browned. Break into desired lengths. These freeze well. Yield: 12 dozen.

Hint: If you wish to use a food processor, mix the dough in thirds—1 cup flour mixture, 2 cups grated cheese, and ⅓ of the softened butter with 3 tablespoons cold water. DO NOT OVER PROCESS. Dough mixture will become too creamy.

Mrs. Thomas R. Wear, II

SPICY PECANS

2 pounds pecan halves
1 stick butter

Onion salt
Freshly ground pepper

Heat oven to 275 degrees. Melt butter in large iron skillet. Add pecans and toss to coat well. Sprinkle generously with onion salt and freshly ground pepper. Continue to toss gently for a few minutes. Put in oven and bake for about 20 minutes, or until pecans are crisp. Delicious served hot or at room temperature.

Mrs. Peterson Cavert (Mary Beth Wear)

SARDINE PASTRIES

1 stalk of celery, finely chopped
1 medium-size onion, finely
  chopped
¼ teaspoon Worcestershire sauce

⅛ teaspoon red pepper
¼ teaspoon lemon juice
1 (3¾-ounce) can of tiny
  sardines, drained

PASTRY:
1 (8-ounce) package cream cheese
¼ pound butter or margarine

Flour

Mix chopped celery and onion, Worcestershire sauce, red pepper, and lemon juice thoroughly. Add sardines and blend thoroughly. For pastry, cream together the cream cheese and butter or margarine. Add enough flour to make a stiff dough. Roll out very thin and cut in rounds with medium small cutter (size of a silver dollar). Place 1 teaspoon of sardine mixture on half of the pastry. Fold over; press edges together with fork. Bake on a cookie sheet until lightly brown in a 400-degree oven for about 10-12 minutes. Serve hot.

Note: These may be made ahead and refrigerated or frozen. They are delicious, and no one can guess what the filling is until you tell them! Men and women love these; I never have enough!

Mrs. George Fields

SHERRY STUFFED MUSHROOMS

12 large fresh mushrooms
¼ cup chopped onion
1½ cups bread crumbs (plus)*
1-1½ cups sour cream
½ cup sherry (plus)

1½-2 cups shrimp pieces
1 stick butter
Parsley, cayenne, salt, and
  pepper to taste

Stem mushrooms. Broil buttered caps. Chop stems. Add stems, onion, crumbs to melted butter in skillet and cook. Remove from skillet to large mixing bowl. Add shrimp, sour cream, sherry, and spices to taste. Spoon into upturned mushroom caps. Bake in a hot oven (400 degrees) for 5-10 minutes. Serves 4 to 6.

*Note: The reason for variance in quantity of some of the ingredients depends on the size of mushrooms.

Mrs. Ronald Sanders (Betsy McNair)

SOUTH CAROLINA'S LOW COUNTRY PICKLED SHRIMP

2½ pounds shrimp
Boiling water to cover shrimp
½ cup celery tops
½ cup pickling spices
3½ teaspoons salt
2 cups onions, thinly sliced

1¾ cups salad oil
¾ cup white vinegar
1½ teaspoons salt
2½ teaspoons celery seed
2½ tablespoons capers and juice
Dash of Tabasco (big)

Bring water to a boil. Drop in shrimp and add celery tops, pickling spices, and salt. Let come to a second boil and cook 5 minutes. Don't overcook. Drain and peel shrimp. Put in large casserole, alternating shrimp and onions. Combine oil, vinegar, salt, celery seed, capers and juice, and Tabasco; pour over shrimp mixture. Marinate at least 24 hours in refrigerator. Stir at least 3 times. This will keep at least a week in the refrigerator. Serve drained with crackers to 12 to 15.

Mrs. Joseph Rowland (Nancy Burch)

Note: This easily multiplies for 15 pounds of shrimp. Use 3 cups celery, 1 (1¼-ounce) box pickling spices, 4 tablespoons salt, 8 cups onions, 7½ cups salad oil, 4½ cups vinegar, 3 tablespoons salt, 4½ tablespoons celery seed, 1 bottle of capers and juice, and several big dashes of Tabasco. This does better if pickled 4 or 5 days, stirring several times each day. Serves 30 to 40.

Mrs. Harry Wright (Cissy James)

EASY CHAFING DISH SPECIAL (for Cocktail Parties)

2 tablespoons butter or
  margarine
¼ teaspoon dried marjoram
¼ teaspoon savory
¼ teaspoon thyme
¼ teaspoon rosemary

2 (4-ounce) cans Vienna sausage,
  cut in half, and liquid
1 (3-ounce) can whole button
  mushrooms
3 tablespoons dry red or white
  wine

In chafing dish, melt butter. Add marjoram, savory, thyme, and rosemary. Stir in Vienna sausages which have been cut in half and include jellied liquid. Add drained mushrooms and wine. Heat gently and serve at once. Provide cocktail picks.

Note: The dish can also be just as easy and a big hit if you substitute 4 (8-ounce) packages of miniature cocktail franks for the Vienna sausages and 1 cup bourbon for the wine. Add 1 cup dark brown sugar and 1 (14-ounce) bottle of catsup. Mix all and simmer for 1 to 2 hours.

Mrs. David M. Cochrane (Mary B. Tompkins)

"YOU WON'T BELIEVE IT" CRAB DIP

1 (6½-ounce) can white crabmeat, picked

1 (8-ounce) package cream cheese

1 stick *real* butter

In a saucepan, combine crabmeat, cream cheese, and butter. Heat and mix thoroughly. Transfer to hot chafing dish. Serve with kingsize Fritos. "This is so good, nobody believes the recipe!"

Hint: If recipe is doubled, only use 1½ sticks of butter.

Mrs. James P. Dill (Janet Younger)

CHEESE CLAM DUNK

6 or 7 (5-ounce) jars Old English cheese

2 (7½-ounce) cans drained minced clams, reserving juice to thin

½ green pepper, chopped

1 bunch green onions, chopped

Garlic salt to taste

Tabasco to taste

Paprika to taste

Worcestershire sauce to taste

Mix cheese, clams, pepper, onions, garlic, Tabasco, paprika, and Worcestershire sauce in top of a double boiler. Thoroughly heat. Transfer to a chafing or fondue dish to serve. Use Doritos to dunk with or anything else you wish. Fresh vegetables such as celery, carrots, cucumbers, etc., are delicious. This is tasty and easy, but must be thinned with clam juice as time goes on.

Mrs. Ronald C. Phelps (Margaret "Margie" Wood)

DRIED BEEF DIP

1 (8-ounce) package of cream cheese

2 tablespoons milk

1 (2½-ounce) jar Armour dried beef

¼ cup bell pepper, chopped

2 tablespoons dehydrated onion flakes

½ teaspoon garlic salt

¼ teaspoon pepper

½ cup sour cream

½ cup chopped pecans

2 tablespoons butter

½ teaspoon salt

Combine cream cheese, milk, dried beef, bell pepper, onion, garlic, and pepper. Blend well. Fold in sour cream and put into oven-proof dish. Crisp chopped pecans with butter and salt. Sprinkle nut mixture over other and heat 20 minutes at 350 degrees. Serve with Ritz crackers, Bugles, or whatever. Serves about 20 people hors d'oeuvres.

Mrs. Rufus L. Moore (Polly Shirley)

CRAB DIP FOR CHAFING DISH

1 (8-ounce) package cream cheese
2 (8-ounce) cartons sour cream
1 cup mayonnaise
2 teaspoons lemon juice

2 tablespoons Accent
1 tablespoon curry
1 pound lump crabmeat, picked

Mix cream cheese, sour cream, mayonnaise, lemon juice, Accent, and curry until smooth. Heat until warm. When ready to serve, fold in crabmeat. Makes about 1 quart.

Mrs. James M. Cain, Sr. (Rosalind Alexander)

HOT CHILI DIP

1 (15½-ounce) can chili with beans
1 (16-ounce) jar Cheez Whiz

3 tablespoons onion, finely
chopped

Heat and mix together chili, Cheez Whiz, and onion in a double boiler just long enough to separate cheese. Be sure not to heat for too long. Serve in chafing or fondue dish over low heat. Good served with Doritos. Could use new hot chili for variety.

Mrs. Glenn Powell (Caroline Chappell)

RATATOUILLE

2 medium eggplants, unpeeled
   and cut in ¼-inch slices
4 zucchini, cut in ¼-inch slices
1 teaspoon salt
8 tablespoons olive oil
   (approximately)

4 onions, thinly sliced
2 green peppers, thinly sliced
2 cloves garlic, chopped
4-5 juiced chopped tomatoes
Handful chopped parsley
Ground black pepper

Place eggplant and zucchini in colander and sprinkle with salt. Leave for about 30 minutes. Dry eggplant and zucchini. Sauté in 4 tablespoons hot olive oil until browned. This works better in a wok than a frying pan. Set aside. Sauté onions, green pepper, and garlic in 4 tablespoons olive oil until tender. Add eggplant and zucchini over onion mix. Add tomatoes, parsley, and pepper. Cover and cook gently until juices run. Uncover and cook until juices are almost evaporated, lifting gently from bottom to prevent scorching. Season with salt. Serve at room temperature as vegetable, or as hors d'oeuvre with crackers.

Mrs. Jack Davis (Dee Stewart)

SEAFOOD DIP FOR CHAFING DISH

½ pound butter
1 cup flour
1 (5.3-ounce) can evaporated milk
2 cups whole milk
2 tablespoons sherry
1 teaspoon paprika
1 teaspoon pepper
Salt to taste

1 pound crabmeat
2 pounds chopped cooked shrimp
1 (4-ounce) can mushrooms,
  chopped
1 bunch green onions, chopped
2 cups chopped parsley, (1 cup
  if dehydrated is used)

Make a cream sauce of butter, milks, and flour. Add sherry, paprika, pepper, and salt. When sauce is smooth, add crabmeat, shrimp, mushrooms, onions, and parsley. Serve hot from a chafing dish.

Mrs. John D. Cade (Virginia Duckworth)

MARY JANE SELDEN'S CLAM DIP

4 (7½-ounce) cans minced clams
3 (8-ounce) packages cream cheese

1 stick margarine
Dash of Worcestershire sauce

Melt cream cheese and margarine in double boiler. Add drained minced clams and Worcestershire sauce. Serve hot in chafing dish with Fritos.

Mrs. George S. Shirley (Betty Bailey)

HOT BROCCOLI DIP

2 (10-ounce) packages chopped
  broccoli
⅔ cup onion, finely chopped
⅔ cup celery, finely chopped
1 (2-ounce) can mushrooms,
  drained

1 (10¾-ounce) can cream of
  mushroom soup
2 (6-ounce) packages garlic cheese
Juice of ½ lemon
⅛ teaspoon garlic salt

Cook broccoli according to package directions; drain well. Sauté onions, celery, and mushrooms in a large skillet. When tender, add broccoli, soup, cheese, lemon juice, and garlic salt. Warm until cheese is melted. Serve in chafing or fondue dish. Serve with Fritos. Freezes well.

Mrs. Glenn Baxter (Ann Patton)

RUTH ANN NEILSON'S SPINACH DIP

2 (10-ounce) boxes frozen chopped spinach, cooked and drained, reserving ½ cup juice
1 stick margarine
4 tablespoons onion, chopped
4 tablespoons flour
1 (5.3-ounce) can evaporated milk
½ cup spinach juice
1 (6-ounce) package grated jalapeño cheese
Salt to taste
2 tablespoons Worcestershire sauce

Cook spinach, drain extra well, and reserve juice. Melt margarine in large skillet and sauté onion until soft. Add flour, milk, and spinach juice. Continue to cook and stir until thick. Add cheese and well-drained spinach, then add salt, Worcestershire sauce. Serve hot in chafing dish with large corn chips. May be frozen and heated in a double boiler.

Mrs. David M. Cochrane (Mary B. Tompkins)

GUACAMOLE

2 large ripe avocados, mashed
1 teaspoon lemon juice
1 teaspoon lime juice
½ (6-ounce) can green chilies, chopped very fine
4-6 green onions, chopped
1 teaspoon Nature's Seasons
1 large tomato, peeled and chopped fine
2 tablespoons mayonnaise
Salt to taste
Red pepper, a few shakes
⅛ teaspoon garlic powder

Peel and mash avocados. Combine lemon and lime juice and sprinkle over avocado. Add chilies, onions, Nature's Seasons, tomato, mayonnaise, salt, pepper, and garlic. Mix well and chill. For large amount, add 1 (8-ounce) carton of sour cream. Serves 10. Great with Fritos!

Mrs. William P. Patton (Pat Armstrong)

LILLIS ALLISON'S SEAFOOD SPREAD OR DIP

2 (8-ounce) packages cream cheese
2 (6½-ounce) cans crabmeat, picked
4 (4½-ounce) cans shrimp, cut up (or 2 pounds fresh cooked shrimp)
½ cup celery, cut fine
1 onion, cut fine
½ cup mayonnaise
½ cup sour cream
6 hard-boiled eggs, cut fine

Combine cream cheese, crabmeat, shrimp, celery, onion, mayonnaise, sour cream, and eggs. Can be served cold or hot in chafing dish. Serve with crackers and knife if used as spread. Serves 20.

Mrs. David M. Cochrane (Mary B. Tompkins)

ARTICHOKE AND BLEU CHEESE DIP

1 stick butter
1 (14-ounce) can artichoke hearts

1 (4-ounce) package bleu cheese
Lemon juice to taste

In skillet, melt butter and mix in artichoke hearts cut into eighths. Add bleu cheese and lemon juice. Serve in hot chafing dish with rye rounds.

Mrs. A. W. Struthers (Laura Richardson)

KATHLEEN'S CRAB DIP

3 (10¾-ounce) cans cream of
    mushroom soup
2 pounds fresh crabmeat
Juice of 1 lemon

½ pound sharp cheddar cheese,
    grated
1 tablespoon Worcestershire
    sauce

Heat soup; add *picked* crabmeat, lemon juice, cheese, and Worcestershire sauce. Serve hot in chafing dish with crisp toast points or crackers.

Mrs. Fred Maxwell (Kathleen Searcy)

SWEET 'N' SOUR MEATBALLS

6-8 pounds ground chuck
¼ cup parsley flakes
1 cup dried onion flakes

1 teaspoon sugar
2 (8-ounce) cans mushrooms,
    chopped

SAUCE:
¼ cup sugar
1 tablespoon cornstarch
¼ cup vinegar
¼ cup soy sauce

¼ cup Worcestershire sauce
1 teaspoon lemon juice
1 tablespoon water
1 cup catsup

Mix ground chuck, parsley, onion, sugar, and mushrooms together well and roll into balls in the size desired, depending on the use—cocktail or entrée. Bake at 350 degrees until done, approximately 20 minutes. Drain grease. Cook the sugar, cornstarch, vinegar, soy sauce, Worcestershire sauce, lemon juice, water, and catsup slowly until mixture thickens. Pour over meatballs. Sauce keeps forever. Meatballs freeze well with or without sauce. Serves about 40 for cocktails.

Note: Sauce may also be used on pork, chicken, or beef.

Donna Ratliff Perkinson

CHINESE MEATBALLS

1 pound ground chuck
1 beaten egg
3 tablespoons water
¼ cup seasoned bread crumbs
¼ cup milk

3 tablespoons minced onion
½ teaspoon salt
¼ teaspoon garlic salt
¼ teaspoon pepper
4 tablespoons butter

SAUCE:
⅓ cup soy sauce
⅔ cup water
1 teaspoon ginger

1 minced clove garlic
½ teaspoon dry mustard
2 tablespoons cornstarch

Combine ground chuck, egg, water, bread crumbs, milk, onions, salt, garlic salt, and pepper, then shape into small balls. Add butter to a large frying pan, and cook meatballs until evenly brown (10-15 minutes). Drain. Heat soy sauce, water, ginger, garlic, mustard, and cornstarch, and cook until mixture thickens. Add meatballs to sauce. Serve hot with toothpicks. Can be made the day before and reheated. Makes 30-40 meatballs.

Mrs. John C. Boles (Donna Waters)

SUGARED NUTS

1½ cups sugar
1 tablespoon light corn syrup
½ cup strong coffee

2½ cups mixed nut meats (I use pecans)

Combine sugar, corn syrup, and coffee in large saucepan. Cook to 240 degrees or soft ball stage. Remove from heat. Add nuts. Stir until syrup becomes creamy. Turn out onto greased cookie sheet. Working quickly, separate nuts with 2 forks. Cool.

Note: Delicious with coffee at holiday seasons. For variation, add ½ teaspoon cinnamon, 1 teaspoon vanilla and ½ teaspoon cloves.

Mrs. Gene Bennett (Belle Walter)

BLOODY QUEEN MARY

1 (46-ounce) can V-8 juice
8 ounces vodka
½ cup Lea & Perrins Worcestershire sauce
2 tablespoons Blue Plate barbecue
sauce

Juice of ¼ lemon
Good-sized pinch of celery seed
Dashes of Tabasco sauce (to
taste)

Mix V-8, vodka, Worcestershire, barbecue sauce, lemon juice, celery seed, and Tabasco. Pour over ice cubes (preferable to crushed ice). Makes 8-12 servings.

Don Barnes

BLOODY MARY MIX

1 tablespoon salt
1 tablespoon celery salt
10 dashes Tabasco (more if you
like it hot)
1 (5-ounce) bottle Lea & Perrins
Worcestershire sauce (no sub-
stitutes)

½ cup lemon juice (or juice of 6
lemons)
3 (46-ounce) cans V-8 juice

Into a glass gallon jug, put salt, celery salt, Tabasco, Lea & Perrins, lemon juice. Fill jug with V-8. Shake and chill. This will keep for 10 days if no vodka has been added. To make ahead for a crowd, use 5 cups vodka to a gallon of mix. Serve with celery stick "stirrer."

Mrs. George Wright (Stella Wellborn)

EASY FROZEN FRUIT DAIQUIRIS

1 (6-ounce) can frozen limeade
concentrate
6 ounces light rum
2 very ripe bananas, 1 pint ripe
strawberries, or 1½-2 cups
peeled and sliced ripe peaches

10-15 ice cubes

In blender container, put limeade concentrate and rum, and blend for 5 seconds. Then add fruit slowly and blend until puréed. Add ice cubes, one at a time, until desired slushiness and dilution. Keep in freezer. Makes 6-8 drinks.

Note: These are potent, so don't drink too many, although you'll want to!!

Mrs. Peterson Cavert (Mary Beth Wear)

PRESBYTERIAN PUNCH

6 cups water
4 cups sugar
1 (16-ounce) can frozen orange
 concentrate
1 (16-ounce) can water
1 (6-ounce) can frozen lemonade
 concentrate

1 (6-ounce) can water
1 (46-ounce) can pineapple juice
Juice of 2 lemons
3 mashed bananas
2 quarts ginger ale

Make a sugar syrup by boiling the 6 cups water and 4 cups sugar for 3 minutes. Add orange juice and lemonade concentrates, water, pineapple juice, lemon juice, and mashed bananas, and stir to combine well. Freeze. About ½ hour before serving, place frozen base in punch bowl and let thaw until slushy. Add ginger ale and serve. Makes 50-60 cups.

Note: This punch has been a real favorite for recital receptions and showers. A fifth of rum may be added with the ginger ale, but in that case, change the name!

Mrs. Mark Bergaas (Mary Emmons)

MY MOTHER'S ORANGE PUNCH

1 (46-ounce) can Hi-C orange drink
1 (46-ounce) can pineapple juice
2 (6-ounce) cans frozen orange
 juice concentrate
1 (6-ounce) can frozen lemonade
 concentrate

1 (6-ounce) can frozen limeade
 concentrate
1 (28-ounce) bottle chilled ginger
 ale

Combine juices in punch bowl. *Do not* add any water except to lightly rinse out frozen juice cans. Add ginger ale right before serving. Use ice ring or plenty of ice cubes. Serves 25.

Mrs. Joseph Rowland (Nancy Burch)

TRADER VIC'S TONGA PUNCH

½ scoop shaved ice
Juice of ½ lime
1½ ounces orange juice
¾ ounce lemon juice

1 dash grenadine
½ ounce curaçao
2 ounces light rum

Place ice; lime, orange, and lemon juice; grenadine; curaçao; and rum in blender. Blend and serve in 14-ounce chimney glass. Decorate with fresh mint and serve with long straw.

Mrs. Frank Mann (Faith McNamee)

TONIE'S TENNESSEE COOLER

½ gallon vanilla ice cream
¼ cup white crème de cacao

¾ cup Christian Brothers brandy

Soften ice cream; add crème de cacao and brandy and mix well. Place in original ice cream container or covered plastic container and freeze 8 hours. Serve in champagne glasses.

Note: May also be mixed in blender using the frozen ice cream and topped with nutmeg. Delicious after-dinner drink!

Mrs. John Pradat (Laura Parker)

"LIKE SCRATCH" EGG NOG PUNCH

½ gallon Pure Process Egg Nog
  Ice Cream (or any natural egg
  nog ice cream)*
2 quarts egg nog (any dairy brand
  is fine)

1 (13½-ounce) container frozen
  Cool Whip
2 cups bourbon (or more)
Nutmeg

Turn ice cream into punch bowl along with Cool Whip 30 minutes before party time. At the last minute, add liquid egg nog and bourbon. Stir, then sprinkle top with a few dashes of nutmeg. Have a cup and enjoy the party and the compliments!! Happy Holidays!

Note: Call plant or store and place order early, as they don't always have Egg Nog ice cream on hand.

Mrs. Allen Mattox (Harriet Marrs)

FROZEN WHISKEY SOUR

1 can frozen lemonade concentrate (any size)
1 can bourbon (same size as above)

2 cans water (same size can as
  frozen lemonade)

Mix together and put in freezer for 24 hours before serving, as it will take a long time to freeze. Serve in Old-Fashioned glasses with orange slice and cherry on top. This can be made with gin or vodka. Great summertime drink!

Mrs. George Wright (Stella Wellborn)

WHITE SANGRIA

Apples, cubed	1 bottle Sauterne
Cherries	½ cup brandy
Strawberries	½ cup sugar
Pineapple	20 ounces club soda

Soak apples, cherries, strawberries, and pineapple for 12 hours in Sauterne, brandy, and sugar. Just before serving, add club soda. Pour this mixture over ice and spoon some of the fruit mixture into each glass.

Mrs. William David Smith (Jane Bandy)

COFFEE PUNCH

1 gallon strong coffee	2 gallons milk
2 cups sugar	½ gallon vanilla ice cream
3 tablespoons vanilla	
3 (16-ounce) cans Hershey's chocolate syrup	

Make up coffee; add sugar, vanilla, and chocolate syrup. Divide mixture exactly between 2 punch bowls and add 1 gallon milk and 1 quart ice cream to each punch bowl. This is rich but very tasty. Serves a large crowd. Makes 3½ gallons.

Mrs. Sidney Tarwater (Susan Foster)

PUNCH

1 quart cranberry juice	1½ cups bourbon, vodka, or light rum
1 (10½-ounce) can pineapple juice	
1 cup orange juice	1 (48-ounce) bottle ginger ale or more
½ cup lemon juice	

Mix juices and refrigerate overnight. When ready to serve, add chilled liquor and ginger ale. Makes approximately 1 gallon.

Bert Wear

COFFEE LIQUEUR

2 quarts water, divided
6 cups sugar
2 ounces instant coffee (Taster's Choice)

7½ teaspoons pure vanilla extract
1 quart 180-proof pure grain alcohol

Boil 1 quart water. Add sugar, bring back to boil, and boil for 1 minute. Boil other quart water. Add instant coffee. Let both mixtures come to room temperature. Mix together and add vanilla and grain alcohol. Makes 3 quarts.

Donna Ratliff Perkinson

NANA'S SPICED TEA

6 teaspoons tea
16 cups water
2 teaspoons whole cloves
2 cups sugar

Juice of 3 lemons
Juice of 4 oranges
Grated rind of 1 lemon

Tie tea in thin cloth bag. Drop into boiling water with cloves and boil 4 minutes. Steep 4 minutes. Strain and pour over the sugar. Reheat, then add fruit juices and lemon rind. Serve plain or with a thin slice of lemon and a clove or two for each cup. After straining, the mixture may be reheated as desired without impairing the flavor. Makes 20 cups.

Mrs. Don Barnes (Sue Strickland)

FRUITED ICED TEA

2 cups granulated sugar
2 cups water
1 quart boiling water
8 small tea bags

2 quarts cold water
2 cups orange juice
¾ cup lemon juice

Boil sugar and 2 cups water for 5 minutes. In another pan, pour 1 quart boiling water over tea bags and brew for 5 minutes. Combine the two above mixtures. Add cold water, orange juice, and lemon juice. Mix well and pour into 1-gallon jug and refrigerate. Delicious with meals or alone all summer! Top with fresh sprig of mint before serving (optional).

Mrs. Mickey M. Petty (Donna Davenport)

WASSAIL

1 cup sugar
4 inches stick cinnamon
3 lemon slices
¼ cup water
6 cups dry red wine (claret or
   Bordeaux)

2 cups unsweetened pineapple
   juice
2 cups orange juice
1 cup dry sherry

In small saucepan, combine sugar, cinnamon, lemon slices, and water. Cook and stir for 3-5 minutes or until sugar dissolves. Strain to remove spices and fruit; keep warm. In large saucepan, heat *but do not boil* remaining ingredients. Combine with spiced syrup. Ladle into warm mugs. Garnish with additional lemon slices, if desired, and serve immediately. Makes 12 cups.

Mrs. J. C. "Bud" Miller (Presteen Sims)

HOT SPICED CIDER

1 gallon apple cider
1 teaspoon whole cloves

2 sticks cinnamon

Heat, but do not boil, cider, to which whole spices have been added. This is a good cold weather nighttime beverage, as it contains nothing to keep you awake.

Mrs. Peterson Cavert (Mary Beth Wear)

HONEY BUTTERED HOT WINE

2 cups Rhine wine
3 tablespoons Cointreau or
   Triple Sec
3 tablespoons honey

1 tablespoon sugar
4 teaspoons butter
4 lemon slices
4 cinnamon sticks

In medium saucepan, combine wine, liqueur, honey, and sugar. Heat to boiling. Pour into mugs. Top each with teaspoon butter. Garnish with lemon slice and cinnamon stick. Makes 4 servings. May be doubled.

Mrs. Dennis Stanard (Beth Cowden)

HOT BUTTERED RUM (MIX)

1 pound butter
1 pound brown sugar
1 quart vanilla ice cream

Dark rum
Nutmeg

Soften butter in bowl in warm oven. Add brown sugar and cream together. Slice ice cream and add to butter and brown sugar. Freeze. To serve, pour hot water into a mug with 1 ounce of dark rum, 2 teaspoons (or more) of mixture. Stir until frothy and add nutmeg on top. You can keep this in freezer and have on hand for a crowd in winter. Yield: 50 + servings.

Mrs. William V. Barkley (Carolyn Johnson)

HOT CHOCOLATE MIX

1 (8-quart) box powdered skim
  milk
1 (2-pound) box instant cocoa mix
1 (6- or 8-ounce) jar non-dairy
  coffee creamer

1 (1-pound) box confectioners'
  sugar, sifted
Dash salt

Mix together the powdered milk, cocoa mix, coffee creamer, confectioners' sugar, and salt. Store in airtight containers. Use 3 or 4 tablespoons per cup of boiling water. Good for children to give as gifts! Yield: 80 servings.

Mrs. James T. Cochrane (Sully Given)

SPICED TEA MIX

1 (1-pound, 2-ounce) jar Tang
1¼ cups sugar
¾ cup instant tea
1 teaspoon ground cinnamon
½ teaspoon ground cloves

½ teaspoon dried grated lemon
  rind
½ teaspoon dried grated orange
  rind
Dash salt

Mix together the Tang, sugar, tea, spices, rinds, and salt. Store in an airtight container. For 1 serving, use 1 heaping teaspoon mix per cup of boiling water or ⅓ cup mix per quart of boiling water. Good gift idea! placed in an "apothecary-type jar" with a ribbon tied around the top!!

Mrs. Bobby J. Babb (Peggy Meaders)

CRANBERRY PUNCH

1 gallon cranberry juice
2 (48-ounce) bottles ginger ale

1 quart vodka or light rum

Have all ingredients chilled. Combine in a large punch bowl the cranberry juice and liquor. At the last minute, add ginger ale. You may want to mix half at a time.

Note: Also excellent without the liquor—good color and not too sweet.

CRANBERRY TEA

1 pint cranberry juice
1 (20-ounce) can pineapple juice
½ cup light brown sugar
2 cups water

¼ teaspoon salt
½ tablespoon whole allspice
1 tablespoon whole cloves
3 cinnamon sticks, broken

Tie whole spices in cheesecloth bag. Mix juice, water, sugar, salt, and add spice bag Bring to a boil and then simmer until ready to use. Serve hot.

Mrs. Joseph Rowland (Nancy Burch)

Hint: Heat cranberry juice cocktail with a dash of ground allspice or whole allspice for a winter treat.

Soups

AVOCADO SOUP

3 ripe avocados
¾ cup heavy cream
2 (10½-ounce) cans chicken broth
  or about 3 cups homemade stock
1 tablespoon sherry

1 tablespoon grated orange rind
½ teaspoon powdered ginger
½ teaspoon salt
¼ teaspoon white pepper
¾ cup whipped cream

Purée avocado by pushing through sieve or in food processor fitted with steel blade. Measure 2½ cups avocado purée. Gradually stir in cream. Heat broth, take off heat, and add sherry. Gradually stir broth into the avocado mixture. Add orange rind, ginger, salt, and pepper. Chill and serve cold with a dollop of whipped cream. Minced ginger and avocado bits may be sprinkled on the whipped cream for garnish. Serves 8 to 10.

Mrs. David Hefelfinger (Virginia Mauney)

CHICKEN GUMBO SOUP

STOCK:

1 chicken carcass from baked hen
  or fryer (enough meat should be
  left on to yield about 1 cup)
5-6 cups water
1 small onion, cut in half

½ teaspoon salt
3 peppercorns
1 bay leaf
1 celery stalk with leaves

SOUP:

1 (28-ounce) can whole tomatoes
2 cups frozen or fresh okra
½ cup sliced celery
½ teaspoon salt
¹⁄₁₆-⅛ teaspoon chili powder
  (to taste)

¹⁄₁₆-⅛ teaspoon cayenne pepper
  (to taste)
¹⁄₁₆-⅛ teaspoon black pepper (to
  taste)
½ cup cooked rice
Chicken from carcass

Combine chicken carcass, water, onion, salt, peppercorns, bay leaf, and celery stalk in Dutch oven and simmer 1 hour. Strain off stock. Cool in refrigerator 3-4 hours and remove fat. Remove meat from chicken carcass and set aside. Reheat chicken stock and add tomatoes, okra, celery, salt, chili powder, cayenne pepper, and black pepper, and simmer 1 hour. Add rice and chicken. Heat and serve. Serves 6-8.

Mrs. A. J. "Lonnie" Strickland III (Kitty Langston)

CORN CHOWDER

¾ cup onion, chopped
¾ cup celery, cut diagonally in
  1-inch pieces
½ stick butter
1¾ cups milk
2 (10¾-ounce) cans cream of
  chicken soup, undiluted

1 (20-ounce) can Del Monte
  cream-style corn
½ teaspoon salt
½ teaspoon pepper
½ teaspoon sweet basil

Sauté onion and celery in butter. Add milk, soup, corn, salt, pepper, and basil. Heat well, but do not boil. Serves 6.

Note: When doubling recipe, use 1 can cream-style corn and 1 can family-style.

Mrs. Clarence Rice Baxter (Gin Jordan)

CREAM OF ASPARAGUS SOUP SURPRISE

1 (10¾-ounce) can cream of
  asparagus soup
½ cup heavy cream
10 canned asparagus tips, drained
2 slices bread, 2 days old

2 teaspoons anchovy paste
4 tablespoons butter
1 clove garlic, peeled and
  crushed

Mix soup and cream together with egg beater. Place on low heat. Place asparagus tips in saucepan with soup. Meanwhile, cut away and discard bread crusts. Spread bread with anchovy paste and cut into 1-inch squares. Melt butter in skillet and add garlic. Sauté bread cubes until golden. Pour soup into bowls, placing 5 asparagus tips in bottom of each bowl. Spoon anchovy croutons into soup. Serve immediately. Serves 2.

Mrs. Daniel Hoke (Gail Ford)

CREAM OF TOMATO AND PEA SOUP

2 cups cooked peas
1 (10¾-ounce) can tomato soup
2 cups cream

3 tablespoons sherry
Seasoning to taste

Purée peas in food processor with steel blade or push through sieve. Add tomato soup and cream to pea purée and heat slowly. Add sherry and seasoning to soup just before serving. Serves 6.

Mrs. Samuel Payne Wright (Frances Leapard)

CREAM OF SPINACH SOUP

2 tablespoons butter
3 tablespoons onion, diced
1 tablespoon flour
2 cups chicken broth
1½ cups cooked spinach
1-2 cups half and half

Sherry
Salt
Pepper
Nutmeg
Garlic salt

Sauté onion in butter until lightly browned and then stir in flour. Place spinach, chicken broth, and butter mixture in blender and process until smooth. Empty blender contents into saucepan. Add half and half and then bring to boil over low heat, stirring constantly. Add sherry, salt, pepper, nutmeg, and garlic salt to taste. Serve hot or cold. Garnish with sour cream if desired. Yield: 6 servings.

Mrs. E. L. Minges, Jr. (Valery Crichton)

CRÈME VICHYSSOISE

4 leeks with tops, sliced
3 cups potatoes, peeled and sliced
3 cups boiling water
4 chicken bouillon cubes
3 tablespoons butter

1 cup half and half
1 cup milk
1½ teaspoons salt
¼ teaspoon pepper

Cook leeks and potatoes in water for 10-15 minutes. Process in a blender or food processor fitted with steel blade, in batches if necessary, along with half and half, milk, salt, and pepper. Add butter and bouillon cubes and pour into a double boiler. Cook over hot water until very hot. Cool, chill. Serve *very* cold in chilled bowls.

Mrs. John D. Cade (Virginia Duckworth)

SHERRIED LOBSTER BISQUE

2 (10¾-ounce) cans cream of mushroom soup, undiluted
2 (10¾-ounce) cans condensed tomato soup, undiluted

⅔ cup dry sherry
1 cup light cream
2½ cups milk
1 (5-ounce) can lobster meat

In large kettle, combine cream of mushroom and tomato soups. Mix well. Stir in sherry, cream, and milk. Drain lobster meat and remove membrane. Add to soup. Bring just to boiling over medium heat, stirring occasionally. To serve, pour soup into tureen or soup cups. If desired, garnish with sliced green onion or parsley. Makes 10 servings.

Mrs. Willis Penfield (Freda Jungblut)

PARSLEY SOUP

½ cup onion, chopped
4 tablespoons butter, divided
4 cups chicken broth
2 big handfuls parsley

2 tablespoons flour
2 cups milk
Red pepper and salt to taste

Sauté onion in 2 tablespoons butter. Add chicken broth and simmer 10 minutes. Blend this in batches along with parsley in blender. In another pan, melt remaining butter and add flour. Cook for a minute. Add milk and stir until thick and creamy. Add parsley mixture to this. Also add red pepper and salt. Chill. Yield: 4 to 6 cups.

Note: Serve in glass mugs. Delicious!

Mrs. Gene Bennett (Belle Walter)

INELL'S SPLIT PEA SOUP

2½ quarts water
1 pound green split peas
1 medium onion, sliced
2 bay leaves
1 clove garlic, cut

1 teaspoon salt
1½ cups ham pieces*
1-2 hot peppers (or 3 shakes
    dried hot pepper) (optional)

Place water, peas, onion, bay leaves, garlic, salt, ham, and peppers in large pot. Bring to a boil. Cut heat to low and cook, covered, for 2-2½ hours. Stir occasionally. Yield: 8 servings.

*Hint: I usually use ham hocks for I feel they provide more flavor. If soup is used a second time or is reheated, more water can be added, for it becomes quite thick.

Suzanne Augusta Herrod

OYSTER STEW

2 cups milk
½ cup cream
¼ cup butter

1 pint oysters, with the liquor
1 teaspoon salt
Dash of pepper

Heat milk and cream to scalding. Just before serving, melt butter in saucepan. Add oysters with liquor, and cook gently, just until oyster edges curl. Add to scalded milk and cream. Season with salt and pepper. Serve immediately with oyster or other crackers. 2 servings.

Mrs. Christy B. Davidson (Sallie Holman)

JOY'S POTATO SOUP

1 large onion	1 carrot
¼ cup oleo	Celery tops
4 large or 5 medium potatoes	Parsley
2 quarts water (or 1 quart water and 1 quart chicken stock)	1 (5.33-ounce) can evaporated milk
4 chicken bouillon cubes	Bacon bits or Parmesan cheese for garnish
1 teaspoon salt	

Chop onion and sauté in oleo in Dutch oven until yellow and soft. Peel potatoes, slice ½-inch thick, and add to onion mixture. Add water, bouillon cubes, salt, celery tops, parsley, and scraped carrot. Cook until potatoes are soft. Remove carrot and celery and mash potatoes until pieces are pea-size. Grate carrot fine and return to soup. When ready to serve, add milk and heat through but do not boil. Can be served with bacon bits or Parmesan cheese sprinkled on top.

Note: Delicious with a corn muffin or warmed rye bread. Next day, blend smooth and serve cold.

Mrs. James A. Neville (Carole Gibson)

SQUASH SOUP

1 onion, sliced	2 cups cooked squash (fresh or canned)
1 stalk celery, chopped	
1 carrot, chopped	1 medium potato, chopped
4 tablespoons butter	2 teaspoons caraway seed
4 cups beef stock (or 4 bouillon cubes plus 4 cups water)	2 cups half and half
	Salt and pepper to taste

Sauté onion, celery, and carrot in butter until tender. Add stock, squash, potato, and caraway seed. Simmer until tender. Strain in food mill or whirl in blender. Add half and half and season. Serve hot or cold.

Mrs. Jack Davis (Dee Stewart)

WARM-UP SOUP

1 (10¾-ounce) can tomato soup, undiluted	1 cup water
	⅓ cup vodka
1 (10¾-ounce) can beef broth, undiluted	1 teaspoon Worcestershire sauce
	⅛ teaspoon Tabasco

Combine soups, water, vodka, Worcestershire, and Tabasco in saucepan. Heat just to boiling, stirring occasionally. Serve in mugs. Serves 4.

Mrs. Warren P. Davis (Linda del Gatto)

TURNIP GREEN SOUP

2 onions, chopped
4 tablespoons butter
2 cups cooked turnip greens or 2
(10-ounce) packages frozen,
with turnips
4 cups beef stock or 4 bouillon
cubes plus 4 cups water

¼ cup grits
1 teaspoon sugar
2 cups half and half
1 dash Tabasco
3 tablespoons butter
Salt and freshly ground pepper
to taste

Sauté onion in butter until tender. Add greens, stock, grits, and sugar. Simmer 30 minutes and purée through food mill. Add half and half and bring to a simmer. Season with Tabasco, butter, salt, and pepper just before serving.

Jack Davis

HOT AND SOUR SOUP

4 dried Chinese mushrooms or ¼
pound fresh mushrooms, sliced
4 cups chicken broth
½ cup thinly sliced lean pork
(optional)
⅓ cup bamboo shoots
2 bean curd cakes, cut in thin
slices (optional)
2 tablespoons white vinegar

1 tablespoon soy sauce
¼ teaspoon salt
Fresh ground black pepper to
taste
1 egg, slightly beaten
1 scallion, minced
1 tablespoon cornstarch, dissolved in 2 tablespoons water

Simmer mushrooms (and pork, if used) in broth 8-10 minutes. Add bamboo shoots and bean curd; simmer 5 minutes. Add vinegar, soy sauce, salt, and pepper (lots—it's supposed to be hot!) Stir in eggs until threads form. Add scallions. Add cornstarch mixture at end to thicken.

Mrs. Boyd Horn (Ruth Anderson)

EASY VEGETABLE GUMBO

4 cups water
1 envelope Lipton dry onion soup
mix (to make 32 ounces soup)
1 (1-pound) package McKenzie's
vegetable gumbo mixture

1 (16-ounce) can tomatoes (do
not drain)
2-3 tablespoons uncooked rice

Bring water to boil; add onion soup mix. Stir until soup comes to boil again. Add vegetables, tomatoes, and rice. Bring to boil and simmer for 30 minutes. Add more salt if desired. Yield: 6-8 servings.

Mrs. Carlos "Sonny" Shows (Gloria Church)

LENTIL SOUP WITH RED WINE

2 cups lentils	1 bay leaf
1 quart water	Pinch thyme
2 onions, chopped	Pinch marjoram
6 slices bacon, diced	2 potatoes, diced
4 cups beef stock	1 tablespoon tarragon vinegar
1¾ cups red wine, divided	Salt and pepper
1 ham bone	¼ cup chervil, finely minced
1 carrot, sliced	(optional)
2 stalks celery, diced	

Soak lentils in water for 12 hours. In large saucepan, sauté bacon and onion until onion is golden. Stir in the lentils and water in which they were soaked, beef stock, and 1¼ cups wine. Add ham bone, carrot, celery, bay leaf, thyme, and marjoram. Cover and simmer the soup for 45 minutes. Add potatoes and ½ cup wine and cook, covered, until potatoes disintegrate—45 minutes to 1 hour. Remove ham bone and bay leaf. Press soup through a sieve. Add vinegar and salt and pepper to taste. Reheat soup with chervil, although this last item is not a must.

Note: Terrific with salad, homemade bread and wine!

Karen LaMoreaux

ZUCCHINI CURRY SOUP

8 medium zucchini	4 cups chicken broth
2 medium onions, chopped	1½ cups half and half
½ to 1 tablespoon curry powder	Salt and pepper

Wash and snip ends of zucchini. Slice thickly. Place squash, onion, curry powder and broth in saucepan. Cover and simmer until zucchini is just tender. Cool a bit. Process in food processor fitted with steel blade or in blender with salt and pepper, in batches if necessary. Cool, add half and half. Serves 8.

Mrs. John D. Cade (Virginia Duckworth)

Hint: If a soup is too salty, add a few pieces of raw potato. Boil a few minutes, taste, and repeat the process if necessary.

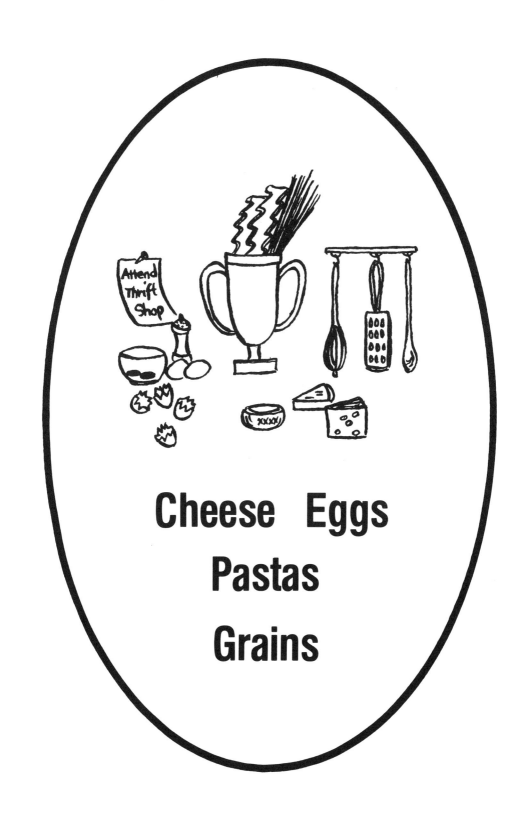

Cheese Eggs
Pastas
Grains

BACON AND CHEESE OVEN OMELET

12 slices bacon
6 (1-ounce) slices pasteurized
  process American cheese

8 eggs, beaten
1 cup milk

Preheat oven to 350 degrees. Cook bacon and drain. Curl one slice. Chop 4 slices of bacon and leave the others whole slices. Cut cheese slices into halves; arrange in bottom of a lightly-buttered 9-inch pie pan. Beat together eggs and milk with a fork and add chopped bacon. Pour over cheese and bake for about 30 minutes. Place bacon curl on top and arrange whole slices on top of omelet around the bacon curl. Bake 10 minutes longer. Let stand 5 minutes before cutting. Serves 5-6.

Mrs. Willis Penfield (Freda Jungblut)

CHEESE CLOUD

8 to 10 slices white bread
1 pound semi-sharp cheese,
  shredded
4 eggs

2 cups milk
Salt and pepper to taste
1 teaspoon dry mustard

Remove crust from bread, Spread half of cheese in bottom of a greased 7½ x 12-inch pan. Cover cheese with slices of bread. Cut to fit so that entire cheese layer is covered. Sprinkle remainder of cheese on top. Beat eggs with mixer; add milk, salt, pepper, and mustard. Pour over cheese and bread mixture. Cover and refrigerate several hours. Bake, covered, at 325 degrees for 45 minutes. Serves 6 to 8.
Optional: 2 cups chopped ham or sausage.

Mrs. George E. Hartley (Peggy Thompson)

WELSH RAREBIT

2 tablespoons melted butter
½ teaspoon salt
4½ teaspoons cornstarch
2 teaspoons Worcestershire sauce

2 teaspoons prepared mustard
1 (12-ounce) can beer
1 pound aged New York cheddar
  cheese, grated

Work salt, cornstarch, Worcestershire, and mustard into melted butter over medium heat. Gradually add beer, stirring constantly. Add cheese and continue stirring until mixture thickens. Serve over crisp toast.

Mrs. Ralph Redel (Jeanette Foster)

Old English cookbooks from the late 18th century refer to Welsh Rarebit as simply cheese melted on pieces of toast with no mention of today's version.

CHEESE-EGG-SAUSAGE BRUNCH TREAT

8 slices white bread
1½ pounds link sausage
1 dozen eggs
1 teaspoon dry mustard

2 cups milk
2 cups sharp cheddar cheese, grated

SAUCE:
1 (5.3-ounce) can evaporated milk
1 (10¾-ounce) can cream of
  mushroom soup

Day before serving, butter large (3-quart) casserole. Trim ends of bread and cut each slice into 4 squares. Line casserole dish with small squares. Cook and drain sausage. Cut into bite size pieces. Beat eggs; add sausage, mustard, milk, and cheese. Pour over bread squares in casserole dish. Cover and refrigerate overnight. Serves 8.

Next day, mix evaporated milk and mushroom soup. Spread over mixture; DO NOT MIX. Bake at 300 degrees for 1½ hours.

Hint: You may use 1½ cups chopped ham instead of the sausage. You may also try other breads such as whole wheat, rye, cracked wheat, or any other whole grain bread.

Mrs. Joe Brown Duckworth (Linda Wedgeworth)

CHEESE SOUFFLÉ

¼ cup butter
¼ cup flour
1½ cups milk
Salt, to taste
Worcestershire sauce, to taste

Cayenne pepper, to taste
8 ounces sharp cheddar cheese, grated
4 eggs, separated

Preheat oven to 375 degrees. Melt the butter over low heat; add flour, stirring with a whisk until blended. Meanwhile, bring milk to a boil and add all at once to butter-flour mixture, stirring vigorously with whisk. Season to taste with salt, Worcestershire sauce, and cayenne. Turn off heat and let mixture cool 3-4 minutes. Add cheese and stir until melted. Beat in egg yolks one at a time and cool. Beat the egg whites until "stiff but not dry." Cut and fold egg whites into the mixture. Turn into a 1½-quart soufflé dish (greased or ungreased). Bake 20-25 minutes. This leaves soufflé slightly creamy in middle. If you prefer it firmer, bake 30-40 minutes. Serves 4 to 6.

Mrs. Rick Byrd (Rene Nicol)

TRUFFLE CHEESE PUFF

2 eggs
½ cup flour
½ teaspoon salt
⅛ teaspoon pepper

½ cup grated cheese
½ stick butter
1 teaspoon thinly sliced truffle

In a bowl, lightly beat eggs; sift in flour, salt, pepper, and stir in cheese. In a 9-inch square pan, heat ½ stick butter in preheated 425-degree oven, and pour batter into pan. Sprinkle top with truffle and bake mixture for 15-20 minutes, until puffed and golden. Yield: 2 or 3 servings.

Mrs. Dudley Davis (Josephine Camp)

RAMEQUIN FORESTIÈRE

FILLING:

1 cup finely minced fresh
  mushrooms
1 tablespoon butter
1 teaspoon cooking oil

1 tablespoon minced shallots
1 tablespoon flour
4 tablespoons heavy cream
Salt and pepper

Preheat oven to 400 degrees. Sauté shallots and mushrooms in butter and oil until they begin to separate and brown. Lower heat and stir in flour. Remove from heat and pour in cream, then stir over moderate heat until thickened. Season with salt and pepper.

RAMEQUIN MIXTURE:

½ cup flour
2 cups cold milk
3½ tablespoons butter
½ teaspoon salt
⅛ teaspoon pepper

Pinch nutmeg
4 eggs
1⅓ cups grated Swiss cheese,
  divided

Place flour in saucepan. Gradually beat in milk with wire whisk. Stir constantly over medium high heat until mixture comes to a boil and thickens. Remove from heat and beat in butter, salt, pepper, nutmeg, and eggs, one at a time. Beat in 1 cup of cheese. Turn half of mixture into 9-inch lightly buttered baking dish. Spread filling on top, then cover with rest of mixture. Sprinkle remaining cheese on top. Bake in upper third of oven for 25 minutes. Serve immediately. Makes an excellent lunch when served with green salad, French bread, and dry white wine. Serves 4.

Mrs. Daniel M. Hoke (Gail Ford)

CREAMED EGGS ON ENGLISH MUFFINS

2 tablespoons butter or margarine
2 tablespoons flour
1 cup milk
4 hard-boiled eggs, cut into
   quarters

4 to 8 bacon slices, fried crisp
4 English muffins, split

Melt butter slowly in heavy saucepan. Add flour slowly to melted butter. Cook until bubbly. Remove from heat. Add milk gradually, until blended. Simmer, while stirring, until a medium sauce is achieved. Add egg quarters carefully. Toast English muffins. Spoon creamed eggs over split muffins. Sprinkle crumbled bacon over top. Yield: 4 servings.

Note: Serve with strawberries, pineapple, pears, apples, or mixture of fruit for a delicious brunch.

Mrs. William J. Gibson, Jr. (Susan Swaim)

EGGS BENEDICT

2 Holland rusks
2 large thin slices ham, grilled
2 eggs, soft poached
¾ cup Quick and Easy Hollandaise Sauce (See Index)

Parsley
Paprika
Truffle, thinly sliced

Cover Holland rusks with ham, then eggs, and top with Hollandaise sauce. Top each egg with a slice of truffle and garnish with sprig of parsley and sprinkle with paprika. Serve immediately. This is a serving for one and is easily multiplied.

Variation: Some people use English muffins and Canadian bacon as a variation.

Note: This is a classic dish reputed to have been created in the Vatican kitchen around 1760 for Pope Benedict XIII. Its excellence depends on the freshness and flavor of the various ingredients and also your ability to "bring the dish to a head" at the point of perfection of each of the ingredients.

Mrs. Allen Mattox (Harriet Marrs)

EGGS SOMERSET

4 English muffins, split and toasted
1½ cups (6 ounces) shredded Swiss cheese
2 tablespoons butter
2 tablespoons chopped green onion and tops
2 tablespoons flour
½ teaspoon salt
Dash nutmeg
1 cup half and half or milk
1 (6-ounce) package frozen crabmeat, thawed and drained
1 tablespoon dry sherry, optional
8 eggs, poached
4 slices bacon, cooked and crumbled

Sprinkle 3 tablespoons cheese on each toasted English muffin half. Set aside. Melt butter in a 1-quart saucepan; add onion and sauté 1 to 2 minutes. Stir in flour, salt, and nutmeg. Add half and half gradually, stirring to make a smooth sauce. Add crabmeat. Cook over medium heat, stirring occasionally, until thickened and bubbly. Cover and keep warm over low heat. As eggs are poaching, broil cheese-topped muffins until cheese is melted, about 3 minutes. For each serving, place 2 muffin halves on a plate. Top with 2 poached eggs. Spoon about ½ cup of the crab sauce over the eggs; sprinkle with crumbled bacon. Serve immediately. Makes 4 servings.

Note: As a variation, it is good without the eggs, also!

Mrs. William J. Stack (Leckie Kern)—Marietta, GA

MEXICAN SCRAMBLED EGGS

2 (14½-ounce) cans tamales (or 1 package frozen)
¾ cup margarine, divided
2 cups chopped onion
2 (8-ounce) cans tomato sauce
1 cup pitted black olives or stuffed olives
1 (2-ounce) jar mushrooms
Chili powder to taste
10 eggs, beaten
¼ teaspoon oregano
½ teaspoon garlic salt
3 cups shredded cheddar cheese

Butter 11½ x 7½-inch baking dish. Cut tamales in ¾-inch slices, spoon into baking dish, and place in 350-degree oven. Sauté onion in 4 tablespoons margarine for 6-8 minutes, stirring. Add tomato sauce, olives, mushrooms, and chili powder. Heat to boiling, and pour over tamales. Beat eggs with oregano and garlic salt. Melt remaining butter in skillet and cook eggs until soft scrambled. Spoon over mixture in casserole. Top with cheese. Bake 5 to 8 minutes, until eggs are set and cheese is melted. Serves 8.

Mrs. Thomas C. McMullen, Jr. (Deloris Madison)

TOASTED EGG CUPS

6 slices white bread
2 tablespoons melted butter
6 eggs, beaten
¼ cup milk

1 teaspoon salt
¼ cup shredded sharp cheese or
   cheddar cheese

Remove crusts from bread. Brush both sides of bread slices with butter. Gently press slices into 6 large custard cups. (Bread must be *very* fresh.) Combine beaten eggs, milk, salt, and cheese. Pour ⅓ cup egg mixture into each bread cup. Place custard cups (or use muffin tins) in a shallow-rimmed pan and bake at 350 degrees for 30 minutes. Serves 6.

Mrs. Wilfred W. Yeargan, Jr. (Mary Gail Williams)

PICKLED EGGS

1½ dozen hard-boiled eggs (small)
1 medium onion, sliced thin
1¾ cups vinegar
¾ cup water
3 tablespoons brown sugar
½ teaspoon salt

¼ teaspoon garlic salt
5 peppercorns
1 whole clove
Few dill seeds
Piece of ginger root

Set out two 1-quart screw-top jars. Prepare, peel, and cool eggs. Put onion slices into saucepan. Add the vinegar, water, sugar, salt, garlic salt, peppercorns, clove, dill seeds, ginger root. Set over medium heat and bring to a boil. Reduce heat, and simmer about 5 minutes. Put the eggs into the jars, and pour half of the vinegar mixture into each jar, being sure the eggs are covered. Cover jars, cool, and set in refrigerator. Before serving, let eggs pickle for several hours or overnight to acquire flavor. If desired, insert a whole clove into each egg. Will keep for several weeks if refrigerated.

Note: Ginger root may be frozen, and you can just slice some off while frozen. This recipe can be used whenever hard-boiled eggs are needed. They are especially good in salads with meat, seafood, potatoes, etc.

Eleanor Sutliff Fitts

To make perfect hard-boiled eggs: Use eggs that are at least 3 days old. Pierce shell with pin in large end, cover with water in a large saucepan, add 2 teaspoons salt, and bring to a boil slowly. When a full boil is reached, cover and remove from heat. Let stand 17 minutes, then run cold water over them. They should peel easily, but if not, chill them. Peeled hard-boiled eggs store well in a bowl of cold water in the refrigerator.

GREEN ONION SOUFFLÉ

1 tablespoon butter, softened
3 tablespoons grated Parmesan
cheese
2½ tablespoons butter
3 tablespoons flour
¾ cup hot milk
½ teaspoon salt
¼ teaspoon pepper
Pinch of freshly grated nutmeg
½ teaspoon dry mustard
½ teaspoon thyme

Dash cayenne pepper
3 eggs, separated
3 egg whites
¼ teaspoon cream of tartar
⅛ teaspoon salt
1½ cups cheese, grated (Swiss,
cheddar, or mixture of hard
ends)
1 cup green onions, chopped with
tops

Preheat oven to 350 degrees. Place inside oven a pan of water into which your soufflé dish will fit with the water level being 2 inches on the outside of the dish. Use softened butter to grease soufflé dish. Roll or dust Parmesan cheese around until dish is coated evenly, bottom and sides. If necessary, fit a wax paper collar around top of dish. Melt 2½ tablespoons butter in large saucepan. Add flour and cook, stirring, for about 2 minutes. Add hot milk all at once and stir vigorously with a wire whisk. Add salt, pepper, nutmeg, mustard, thyme, and cayenne, and cook for about 1 minute. Remove from heat. Beat in egg yolks, one at a time. Stir in onions. In a clean bowl (copper, if you have it), beat egg whites until foamy. Add salt and cream of tartar, and beat until they form stiff peaks. Put ¼ of egg whites in yolk mixture, and stir to blend. Put remainder of egg whites on top. Fold in rapidly, giving pan a quarter turn with each "fold." Turn soufflé mixture into prepared dish. Set in pan of water in hot oven. Don't let water boil. Bake for 1 hour and 15 minutes, or until top is brown and soufflé has pulled away from sides of dish very slightly. Serves 4-6.

Note: Good hot with sautéed mushrooms or mushroom sauce. Good leftover and cold for lunch. One (10-ounce) package frozen chopped spinach (thawed) may be substituted for onions.

Mrs. Peterson Cavert (Mary Beth Wear)

Hint: Soufflé Tips
1. *Do not open oven while cooking.*
2. *Cool cheese sauce before adding eggs.*
3. *To form a "top hat", use a teaspoon to draw a line 1 inch from the edge, toward the center, of the soufflé before cooking.*
4. *Must serve immediately.*
5. *One extra egg white will make soufflé hold shape better.*
6. *When adding the egg whites to the soufflé mixture, use an up and down folding-chopping movement, rather than a circular folding motion.*

CHICKEN SOUFFLÉ

3 tablespoons butter
3 tablespoons flour
½ cup light cream
½ cup chicken stock
4 large eggs, separated
½ teaspoon salt

⅛ teaspoon ground white pepper
2 cups finely chopped cooked
   chicken
1 teaspoon lemon juice
¼ teaspoon cream of tartar

Melt butter in a saucepan. Remove from heat and blend in flour. Stir and cook 1 minute. Remove from heat and add cream and chicken stock. Stir and cook over low heat until the sauce is smooth and is of medium thickness. Beat egg yolks until thick and lemon-colored, mix with a little of sauce, and add to the sauce along with salt, pepper, chicken, and lemon juice. Beat egg whites until they are foamy. Add cream of tartar and continue beating until the whites stand in soft, stiff peaks. Carefully fold into the mixture. Butter *only* the bottom of a 1½-quart soufflé dish and empty the mixture into it. Place the dish in a pan of hot tap water. Bake in a preheated slow oven (325 degrees) for 1½ hours or until the soufflé is well puffed and browned. Serve immediately, topped with Dilled Mushroom Sauce. A good garnish is Fried Bananas. (See Index.) Serves 4 to 6.

Dilled Mushroom Sauce:
2 tablespoons chopped onion
2 tablespoons butter
2 tablespoons flour
¼ teaspoon dillweed, crushed
¼ teaspoon salt

Dash of pepper
1 (3-ounce) can chopped,
   drained, mushrooms (sautéed
   fresh mushrooms may be used)
1¼ cups milk

Cook onion in butter until tender but not brown. Stir in flour, dillweed, salt, pepper, and mushrooms. Add milk all at once. Cook and stir until mixture thickens and bubbles.

Hints: Ham can be substituted in this soufflé, but use 1 cup of half and half instead of ½ cup light cream and ½ cup chicken stock. Top with mushroom sauce instead of Dilled Mushroom Sauce. I frequently cook and serve both of these soufflés in individual soufflé dishes.

Mrs. J. C. "Bud" Miller (Presteen Sims)

Hint: Extra egg whites may be frozen. Thawed, they beat to almost as great a volume as they do fresh.

CHEESE-SAUSAGE QUICHE

1 pound bulk sausage
½ cup onion, chopped
⅓ cup green pepper, chopped
½ cup sharp cheddar cheese, grated
1 tablespoon flour
2 eggs, beaten
1 cup evaporated milk
1 tablespoon parsley or 1 teaspoon dehydrated parsley flakes
¾ teaspoon seasoned salt
¼ teaspoon garlic salt
¼ teaspoon pepper
1 deep dish pie crust
1 (6- to 8-ounce) package sliced mozzarella cheese

Fry sausage and drain on paper towel. Sauté onion and green pepper in sausage grease for 3-4 minutes. Drain. Combine cheddar cheese and flour in large bowl. Stir in cooked sausage, green pepper, and onion. In another bowl, mix eggs, milk, and seasonings. Mix well. Put half of sausage mixture into pie shell. Layer half of mozzarella cheese slices. Cover with remaining sausage mixture. Pour egg-milk mixture over all of this. Bake on cookie sheet in 350-degree oven for 20 minutes. Take out and place remaining mozzarella cheese on top. Bake for 10 more minutes.

Note: This quiche has a pizza taste, and I serve it as a main dish with tossed salad. It can be frozen after baking and reheated in oven or microwave.

Mrs. Carlos "Sonny" Shows (Gloria Church)

Hint: Add an egg white to whipping cream if cream is too thin to whip.

EASY QUICHE

½ pound bacon
¼ pound Swiss cheese
3 eggs, beaten
2 cups milk
1 teaspoon salt
1/16 teaspoon pepper
1 unbaked pie crust

Fry bacon until crisp; drain and crumble into pie crust. Shred cheese; arrange over bacon. Beat eggs slightly with beater. Add milk and seasonings, and blend well. Pour over bacon and cheese. Bake in 400-degree oven for 30-40 minutes. Remove from oven while center appears soft. Cool for 5 minutes before serving. Serves 6.

Mrs. Roger C. Williams (Jo Ann Davenport)

QUICHE LORRAINE

1 (9-inch) unbaked pastry shell
12 slices bacon, cooked and
   blotted well
¼ pound Swiss cheese, grated
2 eggs
½ pint whipping cream

Pinch of nutmeg
Generous pinch of sugar
Pinch of cayenne
Pinch of black pepper
¼ teaspoon salt

Crumble bacon into small pieces into bottom of pastry; cover with cheese. Mix eggs, cream, nutmeg, sugar, cayenne, pepper, and salt with rotary beater just long enough to mix well. Pour over bacon and cheese. Bake 15 minutes at 400 degrees, then reduce heat to 300 degrees and bake 20 minutes longer. Serves 8.

Note: For a change, try Gruyère cheese and ¼ to ½ cup chopped ham. Prettiest when served in a 9-inch quiche dish and garnished with a sprig of parsley, if desired.

Mrs. Rufus L. Moore (Polly Shirley)

CRAB AND MUSHROOM QUICHE

4 eggs, well beaten
2 cups half and half
⅓ cup minced onion
1 teaspoon salt
⅛ teaspoon pepper
6 ounces frozen crabmeat, thawed

¾ pound fresh mushrooms,
   sautéed in butter
Butter
1 cup shredded mozzarella cheese
Chopped parsley
1 (9-inch) pie crust, unbaked

Combine eggs and the half and half, then add the onion, salt, and pepper; blend until smooth. Set aside. Drain crab on paper towels until very dry. Sauté mushrooms and sprinkle the crab, mushrooms, and cheese over bottom of pie shell. Pour in egg mixture and top with parsley. Bake at 425 degrees for 15 minutes. Reduce heat to 300 degrees and bake 30 additional minutes, until a knife inserted in center comes out clean. Let stand 15 minutes before serving. Serves 6 to 8.

Mrs. Wilfred W. Yeargan, Jr. (Mary Gail Williams)

Hint: Be sure and put a pan of water underneath an egg casserole while baking.

BAKED RICE

2 cups cold cooked rice
1 cup whole milk
1 egg, beaten well

½ pound sharp cheese, sliced
2 tablespoons melted butter
Salt and pepper

In a baking dish, mix rice, milk, egg, butter, salt and pepper. Put cheese on top and bake in 350-degree oven for 20 minutes. Serves 6.

Mrs. Harry Pritchett (Margaret "Sis" Partlow)

CHEESY WILD RICE SPINACH SUPREME

1 (6-ounce) package long grain
  and wild rice with seasonings
  (uncooked)
1 (4-ounce) can sliced mushrooms,
  drained (or ½ cup fresh
  mushrooms, sliced)
2 teaspoons prepared mustard
½ teaspoon salt

2¼ cups water
1 (10-ounce) package frozen
  chopped spinach
¾ cup chopped onion
1 tablespoon butter
1 (8-ounce) package cream
  cheese, cubed

Preheat oven to 375 degrees. Place wild rice, mushrooms, mustard, and salt in 2-quart casserole. Combine water, spinach, onion, and butter in saucepan and bring to a boil. Pour over rice mixture and stir. Cover tightly and bake for 30 minutes. Stir in cheese. Bake uncovered 10-15 minutes more. Makes 6 servings.

Mrs. John C. Boles (Donna Waters)

WILD RICE CASSEROLE

½ pound wild rice
1 cup chopped onion
1 cup chopped celery
1 stick butter

½ pound mild cheddar cheese,
  grated
1 (4-ounce) can mushrooms
1½ cups half and half

Boil rice according to directions. Sauté onion and celery in butter until tender. Mix with rice. Add cheese and mushrooms. Put into greased casserole. Pour half and half over rice mixture. Bake at 350 degrees for 30 minutes. Serves 10-12.

Mrs. Daniel Hoke (Gail Ford)

RICE AND GRAINS

½ cup long grain brown rice
½ cup wheat berries
¼ cup barley
¼ cup millet
¼ cup sunflower seed

¼ cup pumpkin seed
¼ cup garbanzo beans (optional)
¼ cup chopped pecans (optional)
Butter, soy sauce, chopped parsley,
   and mushrooms (All to taste)

Put all ingredients in large saucepan and cover well with water. Bring to a boil and cook a minute or two. Remove from heat, cover and let sit overnight. Reheat to serve and sprinkle with soy sauce. Add butter and chopped parsley and/or chopped mushrooms.

Note: All ingredients may be purchased at natural food stores.

RICE ITALIAN

¾ stick butter or oleo
1 green pepper, chopped
1 onion, chopped
1½ cups celery, chopped
1 cup raw rice
¼ teaspoon salt

¼ teaspoon pepper
2 (10½-ounce) cans consommé
   or bouillon
1 (4-ounce) can mushrooms
½ teaspoon Italian seasoning

Melt butter in pan. Add green pepper, onion, and celery. Cook until just wilted. Put vegetable and butter mixture in 2-quart casserole. Add rice, salt, pepper, bouillon, mushrooms, and Italian seasoning. Cook uncovered at 350 degrees for 1½ hours.

Mrs. Joe Starnes, III (Cynthia Emmengger)—Gadsden, AL

OVEN BROWN RICE

1 cup long grain rice (regular)
3 cups water

1 teaspoon salt

Put raw rice in a baking dish—not glass—that has a cover. Put in a 350-degree oven until brown, shaking several times to insure even browning. This will take 17-20 minutes. Bring water and salt to a boil. Carefully pour water over browned rice. Cover and bake for 20-25 minutes, or until liquid is absorbed. Remove from oven and let stand, covered, for 5 minutes before serving.

Note: Nutty flavor, nice separate grains.

Bert Wear

BRAZILIAN RICE

½ cup butter
2 tablespoons chopped onion
1 (10-ounce) package frozen
  chopped spinach
¼ pound sharp cheese, cubed
1 teaspoon instant bouillon
2 eggs, beaten

1 cup milk
1⅓ cups cooked rice
2 teaspoons salt
¼ teaspoon garlic powder
½ teaspoon oregano
¼ pound sharp cheese, cut in
  strips

Preheat oven to 350 degrees. Melt butter in heavy saucepan. Add onion and cook until tender. Add spinach, and cook in butter and onion until thawed. Add cheese and bouillon. Cook until cheese melts. Add eggs, milk, and rice, which have been mixed together. Add salt, garlic powder, and oregano. Bake in casserole at 350 degrees for 1 hour. Top with strips of cheese last 10 minutes. Serves 4.

Mrs. Robert Snow (Wilma Sanford)

BEST-EVER RICE CASSEROLE

1 cup raw long grain rice
1 stick of butter or margarine
  (sliced in chunks)
1 (10½-ounce) can onion soup
  with beef stock

¾ can of water
1 (4-ounce) can mushrooms
  (stems and pieces or sliced),
  plus liquid

Butter casserole. Add rice, butter, soup, water, mushrooms and liquid, and bake 45 minutes to 1 hour in 350-degree oven, stirring occasionally. May add 1 small jar chopped pimiento or 1 cup sliced green grapes or 1 cup chopped pecans tossed in last 10 minutes for a really super gourmet dish! Serves 4-6.

Note: Be it out in the woods camping or your finest dinner party, no one will turn this casserole down! Allen triples this one for a good dish to serve his scout troop and cooks it in a Dutch oven over a campfire. He adds only 2 sticks butter, even though he triples other ingredients. Great with any meat, especially wild game.

Mrs. Allen Mattox (Harriet Marrs)

FRIED ASSORTED RICE
(Main Dish for a light meal)

½ teaspoon monosodium
  glutamate (MSG)
2 eggs
½ teaspoon dry sherry
5 tablespoons peanut oil
2 tablespoons scallions, chopped

3½-4 cups cooked rice (cold)
½ cup diced ham or shrimp
½ cup parboiled sliced carrots
½ cup parboiled English peas
4 teaspoons soy sauce

If you are using a wok, preheat to 350 degrees. Beat the eggs with MSG and sherry. Set aside. Heat 2 tablespoons oil in wok or large fry pan. Pour in the egg and scramble very dry. Take the scrambled egg out and set aside. Put in pan another 3 tablespoons oil and brown the scallion. Add rice, ham, peas, carrots, soy sauce, salt, and finally the scrambled egg. Stir fry constantly 8-10 minutes, until ingredients are well blended and heated. Serves 4.

Maureen Cohen Koenemann

RICE AND GREEN CHILIES CASSEROLE

1 cup rice, uncooked
Salt and white pepper
¼ stick of butter or margarine
1 (4-ounce) can Pet green chilies,
  chopped

2 cups sour cream
½ pound Monterey Jack cheese
Salt and white pepper
½ cup grated sharp cheese

Cook rice until tender. Season with salt, pepper, and butter. Set aside. Combine sour cream and chilies (no need to drain chilies). Cut Monterey Jack cheese into slices. In a 1½-quart buttered casserole, alternate layers of rice, sour cream mixture, and cheese. Salt and pepper each layer. Repeat layers and top with grated cheese. Bake at 350 degrees for about 30 minutes. Serves 8 to 10.

Mrs. Dennis Stanard (Beth Cowden)

NOODLES DANDY

1 clove garlic, crushed (or 1
teaspoon garlic salt)
½ cup chopped onion
2 tablespoons butter
½ pound (1¾ cups) cooked cubed
ham
1 (8-ounce) carton large curd
cottage cheese

1 (10¾-ounce) can cream of
mushroom soup
½ cup milk
1 (4-ounce) can mushrooms
(pieces and stems)
½ pound noodles, cooked and
drained
¼ cup grated Parmesan cheese

Heat oven to 350 degrees. Sauté garlic and onion in butter. Add ham; brown slightly. Add cottage cheese, soup, milk, and mushrooms. Mix well. Combine ham mixture with noodles. Pour into buttered 2-quart casserole. Sprinkle with cheese. Bake 40-45 minutes, or until lightly browned.

Mrs. James L. Chancy, Jr. (Julia Williamson)

ITALIAN NOODLES

2 pounds ground chuck
1 clove garlic, crushed
2 (10¾-ounce) cans tomato soup
12 ounces cream cheese

1 (24-ounce) package egg noodles
5 to 6 green onions, chopped
2 cups sharp cheddar cheese,
grated

Roll chuck into very small meatballs. Brown in skillet. Add garlic to meat just before it is finished. Drain meatballs on paper towel. Heat soup over medium heat; add cream cheese and stir until cheese melts. Cook noodles as package directs. Butter lightly a 3-quart casserole. Drain noodles. Layer casserole with noodles, meatballs and chopped green onions (the green part as well as the white part). Add half of the grated cheddar. Pour half of the tomato mixture over this. Layer again (saving grated cheddar until last), pour on last half of tomato mixture, and top with the grated cheddar. Heat in a 350-degree oven until the cheese melts and casserole bubbles, about 30-35 minutes. Serves 8.

Mrs. Richard F. "Dick" Pride, Jr. (Sandra Wedgeworth)

MACARONI SUPREME

1 (8-ounce) package elbow
  macaroni
1 (10¾-ounce) can cream of
  mushroom soup
½ cup mayonnaise
¼ cup pimiento

¼ cup chopped onion
½ cup stuffed olives, chopped
1 cup mushrooms
1 pound sharp cheddar cheese,
  grated

Preheat oven to 350 degrees. Cook macaroni. Combine in a greased casserole with soup, mayonnaise, pimiento, onion, olives, mushrooms, and cheese. Bake at 350 degrees for 30-40 minutes. If it looks dry, cover with foil the last few minutes. Freezes well. Serves 8.

Mrs. John C. Boles (Donna Waters)

CAJUN SOUFFLÉ

2⅔ cups water
⅓ cup self-rising white corn
  meal mix
⅓ cup quick grits
⅛ teaspoon cayenne

2 cups shredded sharp cheddar
  cheese
4 eggs, separated
½ teaspoon cream of tartar
1 teaspoon salt

Combine water, corn meal mix and salt in a 3-quart saucepan; bring to a boil. Stir grits slowly into boiling mixture. Cover; lower heat and cook for 5-6 minutes, or until thick, stirring occasionally. Add cayenne and cheese; mix until cheese is melted. Cool 10 minutes, stir in beaten egg yolks. Heat oven to 350 degrees. Beat egg whites until foamy, add cream of tartar, and continue beating until stiff peaks form. Fold into grits mixture. Pour into 2-quart soufflé dish. Bake about 55 minutes. Serve immediately. Good with shrimp creole.

NOODLES WITH PESTO SAUCE

6 ounces noodles
3 tablespoons butter
1 tablespoon olive oil
¼ teaspoon crushed garlic
3 tablespoons chopped parsley

1 teaspoon dried basil leaves
½ teaspoon dried marjoram
  leaves
Parmesan to taste

Cook noodles in salted water. Melt butter. Combine with olive oil, garlic, parsley, basil and marjoram. Pour over cooked noodles and toss. Sprinkle with Parmesan. Makes 6 servings.

Charlotte Blackmon Marshall

GARLIC CHEESE GRITS

½ cup quick grits
1½ cups water
½ teaspoon salt
½ stick oleo

½ (6-ounce) roll garlic cheese
2 eggs
½ cup milk (approximately)

Heat oven to 350 degrees. Cook grits in water with salt in saucepan until thick. Melt oleo and cheese over low heat. Beat egg and put in measuring cup. Add milk to make 1 cup. Combine grits, cheese mix, and egg mix in 1-quart casserole. Mix well. Bake 35-40 minutes. Serves 4.

Note: Doubles easily for 8. Can be made ahead of time and refrigerated before cooking. Good brunch addition.

Mrs. Larry McGehee (Betsy Boden)—Martin, TN

QUICK AND EASY QUICHE LORRAINE

3 eggs, lightly beaten
1 cup half and half
5 slices bacon, crisply cooked
   and crumbled
¼ cup finely minced onion

1 cup grated Swiss cheese
¼ teaspoon salt
⅛ teaspoon pepper
1 (9-inch) unbaked pie shell

Preheat oven to 375 degrees. Combine eggs, half and half, crumbled bacon, onion, cheese, salt, and pepper and pour into pie shell. Bake for 35-40 minutes, or until knife inserted in center comes out clean. Serves 6 to 8.

Note: You can use bought frozen pie shells, but homemade is easy and tastes much better. For variation, use Gruyère cheese or a combination of Swiss and Gruyère.

Mrs. Rick Byrd (Rene Nicol)

**Poultry
and
Game**

CELESTIAL CHICKEN

6 chicken breasts, split
1 cup flour
1 cup cracker crumbs

½ cup sesame seed
3 eggs, beaten

SAUCE:
1 (10¾-ounce) can cream of
  chicken soup

2 tablespoons flour
½ stick butter

Bone chicken and cut into small pieces. Dip chicken into eggs; cover with flour, cracker crumbs and sesame seed mixture. Fry on medium temperature until golden brown. Bring soup, flour, and butter to a boil; simmer for about 7 minutes and add water to thin. Pour over chicken and serve with rice. Serves 4.

Mrs. Boyd Horn, Jr. (Ruth Anderson)

CHICKEN BREAST CORDON BLEU

4 large chicken breasts, split,
  boned, and skinned
Salt and pepper to taste
4 thin slices boiled ham, halved
4 slices natural Swiss cheese,
  halved
1 egg

2 to 3 tablespoons water
½ cup fine bread crumbs
½ cup all-purpose flour
½ cup grated Parmesan cheese
Melted butter or margarine
Hot salad oil

Place each half of chicken breast on wax paper; carefully flatten to ¼-inch thickness, using a meat mallet or rolling pin. Sprinkle chicken with salt and pepper. Place ½ slice of ham and cheese on each half of chicken breast; tuck in sides and roll up jellyroll fashion. Secure with toothpick or tie securely. Combine egg and water; beat well. Combine bread crumbs, flour, and Parmesan cheese. Dip each piece of chicken in egg; then coat with bread crumb mixture. Brown in mixture of butter and oil. (Reserve pan drippings for use in Creamy Sauce.) Serve with Creamy Sauce. Yield: 8 servings.

CREAMY SAUCE:
2 tablespoons all-purpose flour
Reserved pan drippings

¾ cup chicken broth
¼ cup dry white wine

Blend flour into pan drippings; cook over low heat until bubbly. Gradually blend in broth and wine. Cook, stirring constantly, until smooth and thickened. Yield: 1 cup.

CHICKEN BREASTS WITH VEGETABLES AND CREAM

2 skinned, boned chicken breasts
½ teaspoon lemon juice
Salt and pepper
5 tablespoons butter

1 or 2 tender celery stalks, diced
1 medium white onion, diced
1 medium carrot, diced
⅛ teaspoon salt

Rub the chicken breasts with drops of lemon juice and sprinkle lightly with salt and pepper. Heat the butter in a heavy 10-inch covered casserole. Add the diced vegetables and ⅛ teaspoon salt. Cook about 10 minutes, until tender but not browned. Quickly roll the breasts in the butter and vegetables, lay a 10-inch round of buttered wax paper over them, cover casserole, and place in a 400-degree hot oven. After 6 minutes, test chicken. It should be springy to the touch. Remove the breasts to a warm platter and cover while making sauce.

SAUCE:
¼ cup white or brown stock (or
  canned beef bouillon)
¼ cup port, Madeira, or dry
  white vermouth
1 cup whipping cream

Salt and pepper
Lemon juice as needed
2 tablespoons fresh minced
  parsley

Pour the stock or bouillon and wine into the casserole with the cooking butter and vegetables. Boil down quickly over high heat until liquid is syrupy. Stir in the cream and boil down again over high heat, until cream has thickened slightly. Cut off heat, taste carefully for seasoning, and add drops of lemon juice to taste. Pour the sauce over the breasts, sprinkle with parsley, and serve immediately. Yield: 4 servings.

Mr. J. C. "Bud" Miller (Presteen Sims)

POPPY SEED CHICKEN

2 cups boiled and boned chicken
  breast
1 cup sour cream
2 (10¾-ounce) cans cream of
  chicken soup

1 stick of butter, melted
2 tablespoons poppy seed
1 stack Ritz crackers, crushed

Place chicken chunks in baking dish. Combine sour cream and chicken soup. Pour over chicken. Sprinkle Ritz crackers over soup mixture. Melt butter and pour over crackers. Sprinkle with poppy seed. Bake 30-40 minutes at 350 degrees. Serves 4.

Mrs. Tony Smith (Susan Shirley)

CHICKEN AND YELLOW RICE

6 to 8 chicken breast halves
1 box (2 small packages) Uncle
  Ben's yellow rice
1 medium onion
2 (10¾-ounce) cans cream of
  celery soup

1 (10¾-ounce) can cream of
  chicken soup
1½ cups grated cheddar cheese
  (sharp)

Boil chicken, cool, and remove bones. Cook rice as package directs. Chop onion. Heat all cans of soup, adding 1½ cans water. Stir until smooth. Butter 3-quart casserole lightly. Add cooked rice. Place chicken on top of rice. Place chopped onion on top of chicken. Pour soup mixture over all. Top with grated cheese. Heat in 350-degree oven for about 30-35 minutes.

Note: Omit chicken and 1 can celery soup for great side dish.

Mrs. Richard F. Pride, Jr. (Sandra Wedgeworth)

CHICKEN CONTINENTAL

6 chicken breast halves (or your
  favorite pieces)
⅓ cup seasoned flour
¼ cup butter
1 (10¾-ounce) can cream of
  chicken soup
2½ tablespoons onion, grated

1 teaspoon salt
Dash of pepper
1 tablespoon parsley, chopped
½ teaspoon celery flakes
⅛ teaspoon thyme
1⅓ cup water
1⅓ cup Minute rice

Roll chicken in flour; brown in butter. Remove chicken and set aside. Stir soup, seasonings, and water into drippings. Cook and stir to a boil. Spread rice (uncooked) in a 1½-quart casserole. Pour all but ⅓ cup of soup mixture over rice. Stir to moisten. Top with chicken and rest of soup mixture. Bake covered at 375 degrees for 30 minutes, or until chicken is tender.

Note: For special occasions, this chicken may be cooked and diced (3 cups) and 2 chicken bouillon cubes may be added to 2⅔ cups of water and the soup. Then add 2 cups sour cream to soup mixture. Pour half of mixture into casserole, add 1½ cups rice, 1½ cups chicken, and ¼ cup sliced pitted ripe olives. Repeat the process with another layer of the soup mixture, rice, chicken, and olives. Cover and bake at 375 degrees for 20 minutes. Stir gently and bake 10 minutes longer, or until rice is tender. Remove casserole and sprinkle with paprika. Serves 8 to 10.

Mrs. Timothy Parker, Jr. (Cathy Jackman)

CHICKEN DIVAN

6 chicken breasts
2 (10-ounce) packages frozen broccoli
Margarine
2 (10¾-ounce) cans cream of chicken soup (may use cream of mushroom and/or cream of celery soup)
½ to 1 cup mayonnaise
1 tablespoon lemon juice
1 teaspoon Worcestershire sauce
¾ cup grated sharp American cheese
1 cup bread crumbs
1 tablespoon melted margarine

Boil chicken breasts slowly until done; bone. Cook broccoli according to package instructions. Grease generously a 13½ x 8¾-inch casserole dish. Arrange broccoli spears on bottom, then place chicken on top. Combine soup, mayonnaise, lemon juice, and Worcestershire sauce; pour over chicken and broccoli. Sprinkle cheese over the top. Toss bread crumbs with melted margarine; sprinkle over all. Bake at 350 degrees for 35 minutes. Serves 6.

Hints: For special occasions, add ¼ cup of sherry to sauce before pouring on top and sprinkle bread crumbs with paprika. Can also add ½ teaspoon curry powder. This dish is delicious with ham or turkey substituted for chicken.

Mrs. James William McFarland (Miriam Webster)

SIMON & GARFUNKEL CHICKEN

3 chicken breasts—skinned, boned, and halved
1 stick butter
Salt and pepper to taste
6 slices mozzarella cheese
Flour
1 egg, beaten
Bread crumbs
2 tablespoons chopped parsley
¼ teaspoon sage
¼ teaspoon rosemary
¼ teaspoon thyme
¼ cup dry white wine

Preheat oven to 350 degrees. Flatten chicken between sheets of wax paper; spread with half the butter (½ stick). Season with salt and pepper. Place 1 slice cheese on each piece of chicken. Roll and tuck ends. Coat lightly with flour, dip in egg, roll in bread crumbs, and arrange in baking dish. Melt remaining butter, and add parsley, sage, rosemary, and thyme. Bake for 30 minutes, basting with butter mixture. Pour wine over chicken; bake 20 minutes longer. Serves 6.

Mrs. John Russell, III (Walton Callen)—Aliceville, AL

CHICKEN À LA EARL

8 chicken breast halves, cooked
2 bell peppers, chopped
2 red onions, chopped
2 zucchini squash, cut and cubed
2 (4-ounce) cans mushrooms
3 or 4 carrots, grated
1 clove garlic, minced
Margarine or oil
2 (15½-ounce) cans tomato sauce
with seasonings

1 (11½-ounce) can jalapeño
peppers with oil
1 (10-ounce) package of 10
frozen tortillas, (flour)
2 cups sharp cheddar cheese
2 cups Monterey Jack cheese
1 head lettuce
2 to 3 tomatoes, sliced
1 (8-ounce) carton sour cream
Ripe olives

Cook chicken breasts in favorite seasonings. Sauté peppers, onions, squash, mushrooms, carrots, and garlic in margarine or oil. Add 1 can of the tomato sauce with seasonings and jalapeño peppers to vegetable mixture. Bone the chicken and add to the sauce. Stir in 1½ cups of cheddar and 1½ cups of Monterey Jack cheese. Cook tortillas according to package directions. Fill tortillas with chicken mixture, roll and place in a 13½ x 9 x 2-inch baking dish. Pour the remaining can of tomato sauce over tortillas. Sprinkle on remaining cheese. Bake in preheated 325-degree oven until bubbly, about 20-30 minutes. Serve at once over a bed of lettuce and tomato. Top with sour cream and chopped ripe olives.

Note: You will never know enchiladas can be so good until you try this!

Peggy Bishop—Tuscaloosa County Home Agent

LAZY DAY CHICKEN

9 boned chicken breast halves
⅓ cup all-purpose flour
1 (1⅞-ounce) package dried onion
soup mix
1 (10¾-ounce) can cream of
chicken soup, undiluted
1 (3-ounce) can mushroom slices

⅓ cup sherry, plus liquid from
mushrooms to make 1 full
soup can
½ cup rice
2 carrots, sliced
2 stalks celery, sliced
Paprika

Butter 15 x 10 x 1-inch pan. Dress chicken in flour and put in pan. Sprinkle with dry soup and place mushrooms, rice, carrots, and celery over chicken. Combine soup and liquids, pour over chicken, and top with paprika. Cover with foil and bake at 350 degrees for 1 hour.

Edna Ledyard—Selma, AL

COMPANY CHICKEN CASSEROLE

1½ cups uncooked Minute rice
¼ cup margarine
½ cup celery, diced
1 (2½-ounce) jar sliced mushrooms
2 (10¾-ounce) cans soup (any combination of cream of mushroom, cream of celery, or cream of chicken)
1 (6-ounce) can water chestnuts, sliced
1 (1.75-ounce) package Lipton onion soup mix
4 to 6 chicken breast
1 cup water

Sprinkle dry rice into bottom of large, well greased, flat baking dish. Sauté celery and mushrooms in margarine in small pan. In large bowl, combine cans of soup, mushrooms, celery, margarine, and water chestnuts. Shake the unopened envelope of onion soup mix to mix well. Add half of envelope to soup mixture in bowl. Stir well. Pour mixture over dry rice. Place chicken breasts, skin side up, over soup. Pour water over all this. Sprinkle other half of dry onion soup mix onto chicken. *Cover with lid.* Bake at 350 degrees for 1½ hours. Yield: 4 to 6 servings.

Mrs. Carlos "Sonny" Shows (Gloria Church)

CHICKEN PARMESAN

1½ cups Progresso Italian bread crumbs
½ cup Parmesan cheese
1 tablespoon salt
1 teaspoon pepper
6 chicken breast halves, skinned and boned
2 sticks butter or margarine, melted

Combine bread crumbs, cheese, salt, and pepper. Dip chicken in melted butter and then in crumbs, being careful to coat the breasts heavily. Place breasts, meat side up, in a baking dish and bake in a 350-degree oven for 30-35 minutes, uncovered. Do not turn the chicken.

Note: The chicken breasts may be prepared the day before and refrigerated, then baked. This freezes well before or after baking. To reheat after thawing, bake in a 325-degree oven until hot. Men can eat more than one.

Optional additions to cheese-crumb mixture are ¼ cup finely chopped almonds, 1 tablespoon minced parsley, and 1 tablespoon sesame seed.

Mrs. Walter Sansing (Mary Beth Lippeatt)

CURRY FRUIT AND CHICKEN

1 (30-ounce) can peaches
1 (15¼-ounce) can pineapple
8 chicken breast halves, skinned
  and boned
3 tablespoons cornstarch
¼ cup butter
3 medium onions

3-4 teaspoons curry powder
1 (10½-ounce) can chicken broth
1½ teaspoons salt
¼ teaspoon ginger
3 cups cooked long grain rice
Condiments: chutney, raisins,
  almonds, coconut

Drain peaches and pineapple, reserving ½ cup of each juice. Slice chicken crosswise into chunks; toss in cornstarch. Melt butter in large skillet. Add chicken, onions, and curry. Cook over medium heat for about 10 minutes. Stir in reserved fruit liquid, undiluted chicken broth, salt and ginger. Cook until it begins to boil and thickens. Pour into 2-quart baking dish. Add peaches and pineapple. Cover and refrigerate until ready to cook. Bake uncovered at 350 degrees for 45 minutes, or until bubbly. Serve over rice with condiments on the side.

Mrs. Timothy Parker, Jr. (Cathy Jackman)

CHICKEN WITH HONEY

2 tablespoons butter
2 tablespoons vegetable oil
6 chicken breast halves
Salt and pepper
2 medium onions, chopped
1 clove garlic, chopped
1 cup ground almonds

1 tablespoon basil
½ teaspoon pepper
½ cup honey
1½ cups chicken broth
2 tablespoons cornstarch
Juice of 1 lemon

Heat butter and oil in skillet and brown chicken breasts. Season them with salt and pepper. Remove from skillet to casserole dish. In same skillet, sauté onion and garlic until tender. Add almonds, basil, pepper, honey. Simmer until well mixed. Combine broth and cornstarch and add to onion mixture with lemon juice. Turn heat to high and stir until sauce thickens. Pour sauce over chicken, cover, and bake at 350 degrees for 1 hour. Or make ahead of time and refrigerate, then increase baking time by 15 minutes.

Hint: White wine, ½ to 1 cup, can be added for variation.

Mrs. Robert J. Kubiszyn (Lori Disque)

CHICKEN PRINTANIER (Springtime Chicken)

6 chicken breast halves, skinned
1 pound fresh asparagus, washed and trimmed (split lengthwise if fat)
1 ounce bleu cheese
½ cup Chablis
1 (10¾-ounce) can cream of chicken soup
Pepper

Grease casserole dish and put in chicken. Mix soup, cheese, wine, and pepper. Pour over chicken. Bake 30 minutes at 350 degrees. Remove, add asparagus, and cover tightly. Bake 30 minutes more. Serves 6.

Mrs. Tom Patton (Suse Donald)

CHINESE CHICKEN

10 chicken breast halves
1½ cups Sauterne wine
1 teaspoon pepper
1½ teaspoons minced onion
1 teaspoon powdered ginger
4 pods crushed garlic
1½ cups soy sauce
1 teaspoon salt (scant)
1 teaspoon thyme
2 teaspoons oregano
3 cups chicken stock
Flour

Use only the chicken breast—skinned, boned, and cut in small pieces. Combine wine, pepper, onion, ginger, garlic, soy sauce, salt, thyme, oregano, and stock. Marinate chicken in this mixture for at least 24 hours. Then drain the chicken and dust with flour. Fry until crispy brown.

Mrs. Michael McFerrin (Sherry Romaine)

GRAN'S SHERRY-TOMATO CHICKEN

3 whole chicken breasts
½ cup flour
1½ teaspoons salt
¼ teaspoon white pepper
3 tablespoons corn oil
½ cup onion, chopped
¾ cup peeled chopped tomatoes
¼ cup dry sherry
1 cup chicken broth
2 tablespoons minced parsley

Cut breasts in half, skin and bone them. Dip in mixture of flour, salt, and pepper. Heat oil in a skillet; brown the breasts in oil on both sides. Remove. Sauté the onions until brown. Stir in the tomatoes, sherry, and broth. Return breasts, cover, and cook over low heat for 25 minutes or until tender. Sprinkle with parsley and taste for seasoning. Serves 6.

Mrs. Harry A. Wright (Cissy James)

ROLLED CHICKEN BREASTS

12 boned chicken breast halves
1 package chipped beef (4 ounces)
1 (10¾-ounce) can cream of
    mushroom or cream of celery
    soup

1 (8-ounce) carton sour cream
12 slices bacon (12 to 16 ounces)

Roll up each chicken breast, wrap it in a slice of bacon, and secure with a toothpick. Line a 8 x 12 x 2-inch Pyrex dish with a layer of chipped beef. Lay rolled chicken on top of beef. Combine mushroom soup and sour cream and pour over chicken. (Can be refrigerated until ready to cook.) Bake at 350 degrees for 1½ hours or until tender. Terrific for lunch before the game!

Variation: Add 1/8 cup sherry to sour cream and soup mixture before cooking. If serving over rice, you may want more gravy, so use 2 cans mushroom soup.

Mrs. Russell Gibson (Sandee McRee)

EASY BUT FANCY CHICKEN BREASTS

6 boned chicken breasts (use
    whole or halved)
Salt and pepper to taste
1 (10¾-ounce) can cream of
    mushroom soup (undiluted)

1 cup white wine
1 cup sour cream

Place chicken breasts in baking dish. Salt and pepper to taste. Bake at 375 degrees for 30 minutes. Remove from oven and baste well with mixture of soup, wine and sour cream. Return to oven and bake for 30 minutes more, basting periodically until sauce is used. Serves 6 or 12.

Hint: If more than 6 breasts are cooked, or if you double recipe, don't double sauce.

Mrs. Robert N. Rice, Jr. (Carolyn Burchfield)

SOY CHICKEN

1 (2-2¼ pound) chicken
1 (5-ounce) bottle soy sauce
6 tablespoons butter, melted

2 tablespoons prepared mustard
2 tablespoons grated onion
Dash hot sauce (more to taste)

Combine soy sauce, butter, mustard, onion, and hot sauce. Cut up chicken and marinate in sauce several hours or longer. Cook over charcoal for 45-50 minutes, basting with sauce.

Mrs. Joseph S. Rowland (Nancy Burch)

PECHUGAS DE POLLO CON REJAS

6 small chicken breasts
Salt and pepper
¼ cup butter
¼ cup peanut or safflower oil
1 large onion, thinly sliced
1 (4-ounce) can chilies, unchopped
½ teaspoon salt

2 (4-ounce) cans chopped chilies
⅔ cup milk
½ teaspoon salt
2 cups thick sour cream
1 cup sharp cheddar cheese,
  grated

Bone chicken, salt and pepper it, and sauté until lightly brown; set aside. Save fat and sauté onion, whole chilies; set aside. Blend chopped chilies with milk, salt, until smooth; add sour cream and blend. Arrange chicken in casserole dish, put onion and strip chilies on top of chicken, then pour sour cream sauce over it. Sprinkle grated cheese on top. Bake at 350 degrees for 30 minutes.

Mrs. Boyd Horn, Jr. (Ruth Anderson)

EMERGENCY CHICKEN BREASTS

4 skinned, boned chicken breast
  halves
½ stick butter

Salt
Pepper
Paprika

Dry chicken breasts. Sprinkle heavily with paprika, less generously with salt and pepper, both sides. Heat butter over medium heat in skillet. When foam from butter subsides, add chicken breasts. Cook until brown on bottom; turn and brown top. Should take 7 minutes or less. Breasts are done when firm to touch instead of squishy. Serve with a little of the butter spooned over each.

Hints: Freeze boned chicken breast halves in packages of 2 or 3. They thaw rapidly in salt water, about 30 minutes to 1 hour, so are perfect for unexpected dinner guests or days when dinner gets pushed aside for other activities. These can be fancied up for guests. After removing from skillet, keep warm and warm mushrooms, artichoke hearts, or water chestnuts, almonds, etc., in butter and serve with chicken. Allow 2 halves per generous serving.

Mrs. Peterson Cavert (Mary Beth Wear)

CHICKEN AND SAUSAGE JAMBALAYA

1 baking hen (4-6 pounds)
2 quarts water
2 large onions, cut up
1 large bell pepper, cut up
2 cloves garlic
1 teaspoon seasoned salt
½ teaspoon red cayenne pepper
Ground chicken skin
1 cup cooking oil
2 pounds smoked sausage, cut in bite-size pieces
3 medium onions
2 large bell peppers
3 cloves garlic
3 ribs celery
6 teaspoons seasoned salt

1 teaspoon Kitchen Bouquet liquid
1 teaspoon paprika
1 teaspoon cayenne red pepper
½ small bottle Louisiana red hot sauce (not Tabasco)
1 teaspoon Accent
1 (28-ounce) can whole tomatoes
1 (10-ounce) package frozen lima beans
1 bunch green onions (tops and bulbs), finely chopped
½ cup fresh parsley, finely chopped (or ½ cup dehydrated parsley flakes)
6 cups Uncle Ben's converted rice
6 pints chicken stock

Cut and then boil the hen in two quarts water, seasoned with the onions, bell pepper, garlic, seasoned salt, and cayenne pepper. When chicken is tender, remove the skin, grind, and save it, plus 6 pints stock. Bone the chicken. Heat the cooking oil in a large pot, and brown the ground chicken skin. Leave the browned skin in the pot, and add sausage. When sausage has been cooked, remove it. Add and sauté onions, bell peppers, garlic and celery. Add seasoned salt, Kitchen Bouquet, paprika, red cayenne pepper, Louisiana red-hot sauce (NOT Tabasco) and Accent. Add tomatoes, lima beans, and the cooked sausage, then cook for 30 minutes, or until the lima beans begin getting tender. Add six pints chicken stock and/or water. Do not add water if you have enough stock. Bring to a hard boil on a high fire; add chicken, green onions, and parsley. MAY BE MADE TO THIS POINT AND FROZEN WITH RICE ADDED BEFORE USE. Bring to a boil again, and add rice slowly. KEEP STIRRING. Bring mixture to a boil again, then reduce heat to a very low setting and cover the pot. The rice should be cooked within 20-25 minutes. You now, hopefully, have prepared a tasty Cajun jambalaya. You talk about good! MAN, THAT'S GOOD, YAH!!!!

NOTES:
1. *You may substitute any number of different meats, including seafood, and make a wide variety of jambalayas.*
2. *Use a large, heavy metal pot—a cast iron black pot works best.*
3. *Jambalaya should be stirred often while it's cooking, but once the rice has been added, you should never stir in a circular motion. Rather, begin at the edge of the pot, go down to the bottom, then move the spoon towards the middle of the pot and lift. Follow this procedure around the entire pot.*

4. When using meat other than pork, always add about 50% more oil than this recipe calls for.
5. Always bring the mixture to a hard boil before adding rice. Bring it back to a hard boil after adding the rice.
6. After the rice is brought to a hard boil, reduce your heat to a very low setting and cover the pot.
7. All game makes good jambalaya. However, if you're cooking with venison, I recommend mixing it with an equal amount of pork.

Mrs. Gordon Miller, Jr. (Leslie Johnson) (edited)
and Lester LeBlanc, a professional Cajun cook—Baton Rouge, LA

CURRIED CHICKEN CASSEROLE

2 whole chicken breasts
6 chicken thighs
1 (10-ounce) package frozen broccoli (cooked until tender)
2 (10¾-ounce) cans cream of chicken soup

¾ cup mayonnaise
2 teaspoons lemon juice
1 teaspoon curry powder
¾ (6 ounces of 8-ounce) package Pepperidge Farm herb dressing
1 stick butter or margarine, melted

Cook chicken until tender. Take off bone in large pieces. Place in shallow baking dish and cover with broccoli. In another bowl, mix soup, mayonnaise, lemon juice and curry powder; pour over chicken and broccoli mixture. Sprinkle with herb dressing and pour melted butter over top. Bake 30 minutes at 350 degrees. Serves 10.

Mrs. Lloyd W. Wagner, Jr. (Martha Savage)

MARINATED CHICKEN AND RICE

8 chicken breast halves
2 teaspoons salt
½ teaspoon pepper
1 teaspoon Accent

1 (8-ounce) bottle Kraft Low-Cal Italian dressing
1½ cups uncooked rice
Water

Place breasts in a shallow baking pan. Season with salt, pepper, and Accent, and pour the Italian dressing over the breasts. Marinate for 2 hours. Broil, 5-7 inches from the heat for 20 minutes. Turn; broil 15-20 minutes longer or until browned. Remove from the heat and drain the remaining liquid into a measuring cup. Cover the breasts with foil to keep warm. Add enough water to the liquid to make 3 cups. Pour into a large saucepan and bring to a boil. Add 1½ cups rice; cover and simmer 17 minutes. Fluff up. Serve breasts over rice.

Mrs. L. Page Stalcup, III (Rinna Cobb)—Mobile, AL

BRUNSWICK STEW

3 pounds chicken
2 large onions, diced (2 cups)
½ pound ham, cut in small pieces
3 pints tomatoes, diced (fresh or
  canned)
1 pint lima beans
4 large Irish potatoes, diced
  (4 cups)

1 pint grated corn
1 tablespoon salt
¼ teaspoon pepper
Small pod red pepper (optional)
Tabasco to taste
½ cup Worcestershire sauce
3 ounces butter

Cut up chicken and put in a large pan with 3 quarts of water, onions, and ham. Simmer gently for 2 hours. Remove chicken, pull meat from bones and return meat to liquid. Add tomatoes, lima beans, potatoes, corn, salt, pepper, small pod of red pepper, Tabasco, and Worcestershire sauce. Cover and simmer gently for 1 more hour, stirring frequently to prevent scorching. Add butter and serve hot. Yield: 12 servings.

Hint: Some people add 2 cups of carrots, 1 cup green pepper, and 2 cups of celery in addition to above vegetables. Use fresh vegetables when in season.

Mrs. J. C. "Bud" Miller (Presteen Sims)

CHICKEN, BROCCOLI AND RICE CASSEROLE

½ stick butter
⅓ cup onion, chopped
½ cup celery, chopped
1 (10-ounce) package frozen
  chopped broccoli
1 (10¾-ounce) can cream of
  mushroom soup

1 cup raw instant rice
1 soup can milk
½ tablespoon sugar
1 small Cheez Whiz
1 cup cubed cooked chicken
1 tablespoon chopped pimiento
  for color (optional)

Melt butter, add onions and celery, and let simmer while preparing remaining ingredients. Drop broccoli in boiling salted water long enough to separate (do not cook); drain. Mix soup, rice, milk, sugar, Cheez Whiz, broccoli, and chicken in large bowl; add celery and onions. Pour in a 6½ x 9-inch buttered Pyrex dish. Cook 40 minutes, covered, at 350 degrees. Uncover for about 10-15 minutes, until set. Serves 4.

Hint: Serve as main dish or omit chicken for side dish. Can substitute shrimp or crab for chicken.

Mrs. John T. Webb (Jane Mills)

CHICKEN FOR SALAD

4-5 pounds chicken or chicken
  parts (legs, thighs, breasts)
1 onion
2 stalks celery with leaves
1 tablespoon salt

1 bay leaf
1 carrot, cut into 3-inch lengths
½ teaspoon mixed peppercorns
  and whole cloves

Put chicken or chicken parts in large kettle and cover with water. Add onion, celery, salt, bay leaf, carrot, peppercorns, and cloves. Bring to a boil and boil until tender. (Length of time will depend on what parts you are using. For a whole stewing chicken, 3-4 hours; for breasts, about 1 hour.) Add water if and when necessary. This gives tasty chicken and tasty stock for use in your chicken salad or casserole.

Mrs. Peterson Cavert (Mary Beth Wear)

CRISPY GOLDEN FRIED CHICKEN

1 (2- to 3-pound) broiler-fryer
  chicken, cut up
1 tablespoon salt
1 quart cold water
1½ cups all-purpose flour
1 tablespoon paprika

2 teaspoons salt
1 teaspoon black pepper
2 eggs, beaten
2 tablespoons milk
Salad or vegetable oil

Rinse chicken pieces in a mixture of 1 tablespoon salt and 1 quart water; drain chicken and chill 1 hour, if time permits. Combine flour, paprika, salt, and pepper in a brown paper bag. Place chicken in egg and milk mixture and let stand while oil heats to 350 to 375 degrees. Place chicken pieces in sack and shake vigorously, holding top securely. Cook chicken 10 to 15 minutes in deep fat or until browned; drain well on paper towels and paper bags. Yield: 4 servings.

Hints: You may use buttermilk instead of the egg mixture. Never buy pre-cut chickens, as they lose a great deal of flavor and moistness after they are cut. Buy small chickens for better flavor. Fresh, never-frozen chickens are also better whenever possible. Be sure to remove outside skin. They fry crisper and are better for you skinned any way you plan to cook. Always place dark pieces in center of skillet or on to cook first, because they take longer to cook. Let chicken drain for at least 1 minute before placing on serving platter.

Mrs. Allen Mattox (Harriet Marrs)

CHICKEN PIE WITH BISCUIT TOPPING

1 (5- to 6-pound) hen, cut up
2 teaspoons salt
6 tablespoons flour
2 cups flour

3 teaspoons baking powder
1 teaspoon salt
½ cup shortening
¾ cup milk

Simmer hen until meat begins to come loose from bones. Remove chicken from broth and remove skin and bone. Take out about 1 cup of broth and set aside to cool. Boil remaining broth down to about 2 cups. Mix flour into reserved cup of broth and, stirring constantly, slowly pour flour mixture into boiling broth. Place meat in large casserole; pour thickened broth over chicken and heat to boiling in 350-degree oven. Sift flour, baking powder, and salt together in mixing bowl. Cut shortening into flour. Make a hole in the center of mixture and add milk. Mix lightly, toss lightly on floured board, roll to ½-inch thickness and cut biscuits. Drop biscuits on top of hot casserole; turn oven to 425 degrees, brown, and serve.

Mrs. William H. Darden (Caroline Sullivan)

CHICKEN AND ARTICHOKE HEARTS CASSEROLE

3 (3-pound) fryers
1 pound margarine
1 cup sifted flour
7 cups milk
¼ pound cheddar cheese
5 ounces Gruyère cheese
1 (8-ounce) can tomato sauce
2 small buds garlic

2 teaspoons Accent
1 tablespoon salt
½-1 tablespoon cayenne pepper
  (according to how hot you
  like it)
5 (6-ounce) cans mushrooms
5 (14-ounce) cans artichoke
  hearts

Boil chickens until well done and season. Cool and bone; cut or tear into large pieces. Make a cream sauce the consistency of custard by melting margarine in a deep saucepan, adding flour and cooking until well blended. Add milk, stirring constantly to prevent lumping. In a small pan, melt grated cheese with tomato sauce. Add to this sauce the crushed garlic, Accent, salt, and pepper. Combine cheese sauce with cream sauce. Arrange artichoke hearts, chicken, and mushrooms in shallow, buttered 3-quart casserole and pour sauce over. Bake in 350-degree oven for 35 minutes. Makes two 3-quart casseroles; serves 30.

Note: Delicious served over Chinese noodles. Freezes well.

Ann Putzel and Mary McKenzie—Selma, AL

CHICKEN TETRAZZINI

4 pounds chicken breast, cooked as in "Chicken for Salad", and shredded
6 ribs celery, chopped
2 large onions, chopped
1 bell pepper (red or green), cut into ¼-inch dice
½ pound fresh mushrooms, sliced
3 tablespoons butter or margarine
2 cups chicken stock (or more)
1 tablespoon Worcestershire sauce
Black or red pepper to taste

½ pound cheddar cheese, grated
1 (10¾-ounce) can cream of mushroom or cream of celery soup
½ pound spaghetti, cooked just until tender (in stock if possible)
1 small bottle of stuffed olives, sliced (optional)
1 cup broken pecan meats (optional)
Buttered bread crumbs mixed with Parmesan cheese

Cook celery, onion, and bell pepper in butter until tender. Add mushrooms and cook for a short time. Add 2 cups stock, Worcestershire sauce, and pepper. Add soup and cheese; stir well. Add chicken. Correct seasoning. Add spaghetti. Put in 9 x 13-inch baking dish. Add more stock if it seems dry. Top with optional pecans and crumbs mixed with cheese. Bake at 350 degrees for 1 hour. Yield: 16-20 generous servings.

Note: This can be made a day ahead and refrigerated. Let it come almost to room temperature before putting in hot oven, to avoid breaking dish. Super good!!

Elizabeth Overton Cravens

SWEET AND SOUR CHICKEN

2 fryers, cut up
1 package (2.75-ounce box) Lipton onion soup mix
1 (10-ounce) jar apricot preserves (may use apricot-pineapple or pineapple preserves)

1 (8-ounce) jar Russian dressing

Preheat oven to 350 degrees. In a large shallow baking pan, place chicken skin side up in a single layer. Mix onion soup, preserves, and Russian dressing together and pour over chicken. Bake, uncovered, for 1 hour and 15 minutes, or until fork can be inserted with ease, basting occasionally. Pour all the sauce over the chicken when serving. Serves 8.

Mrs. G. Locke Galbraith (Suellen Ridgely)

HACIENDA CHICKEN

3 tablespoons butter
½ cup onion, chopped
1 (16-ounce) can tomatoes
1 cup water
½ cup green pepper, chopped
1 (2½-ounce) can sliced
  mushrooms and liquid
1 whole clove

1 tablespoon parsley, chopped
1 tablespoon salt
½ teaspoon pepper
1 teaspoon paprika
1 chicken, cut up
1 cup rice
½ cup Spanish green olives

Melt butter in heavy (or electric) skillet. Add onion and cook until lightly browned. Add tomatoes, water, green pepper, mushrooms and liquid, clove, parsley, salt, and pepper. Cut chicken into serving pieces and add to ingredients in skillet. Cover. Bring to boil, reduce heat, and simmer for 1 hour. Add rice and olives and continue cooking until rice is done and chicken is tender, approximately 1 more hour. Serves 6.

Mrs. Carl W. Albright, Jr. (Rainer Lamar)

CORNISH CURRY

1 (1-pound, 1-ounce) can whole
  apricots
2 fresh or frozen Rock Cornish hens
¼ cup softened butter
1 (6-ounce) package curry rice
¼ cup melted butter
½ cup sliced onion

½ cup chopped celery
2 tablespoons flour
1 teaspoon curry powder
1 cup water
2 chicken bouillon cubes
¼ cup medium pitted ripe olives
Parsley

Drain apricots, and reserve ½ cup syrup. Thaw frozen hens; remove giblets. Split hens, and place in a 13 x 9-inch baking pan or dish, skin side up. Brush with butter. Bake in preheated 350-degree oven for 1 hour to 1¼ hours or until fork tender, basting occasionally with remaining butter. Bake rice in 1½-quart covered casserole according to package directions (while hens are baking). Place melted butter in saucepan; sauté onions and celery in butter until almost tender. Stir in flour and curry powder; remove from heat. Stir in water and reserved apricot syrup gradually. Add bouillon cubes, and cook, stirring constantly, until mixture thickens and cubes melt. Cook for 2 minutes longer. Add apricots and olives; heat to serving temperature. Arrange rice, hens, apricots and olives on heated platter. Spoon some sauce over all. Garnish with parsley; serve with remaining sauce. Yield: 4 servings.

Mrs. Haskell Nevin (Sister Woodfin)

CHICKEN MEDITERRANEAN

1 tablespoon flour
1 cut-up chicken
1 tablespoon paprika
1 medium onion
1 green pepper cut in rings
1 (2 to 2½-ounce) can sliced
   mushrooms, drained

¼ cup soy sauce
2 tablespoons vinegar
1 clove garlic, crushed
⅛ teaspoon oregano, crushed

Preheat oven to 350 degrees. Shake flour in 10 x 16-inch Brown-In-Bag and place in 2-inch deep roasting pan. Wash and pat dry chicken pieces. Sprinkle paprika evenly over chicken and place in bag. Combine onion, green pepper, mushrooms, soy sauce, vinegar, garlic, and oregano and pour over chicken. Tie bag and make slits in it for steam to escape. Bake 1 hour or until tender. Thicken sauce if desired.

Mrs. Hank Leland (Lindsey James)

MUDDER'S MUSTARD CHICKEN

Chicken pieces (your favorite)
1 stick butter or margarine
Salt and pepper to taste

Prepared mustard
2 cups water

Sauté chicken pieces in butter in electric skillet. Salt and pepper to taste. Cover both sides of each chicken piece with prepared mustard. Add 2 cups water to skillet. Simmer one hour, covered, or until chicken is done. Add more water as needed. This makes delicious gravy.

Mrs. Thomas W. Moore (Stella Hillard)

CHICKEN AND RICE

Chicken pieces of your choice
1 cup raw rice
1 (10¾-ounce) can cream of
   mushroom soup

1 (10¾-ounce) can cream of
   celery soup
1 (10½-ounce) can onion soup

Place chicken in a large 2½- or 3-quart casserole. Mix rice, mushroom soup, celery soup, and onion soup together and pour over top of chicken. Bake covered at 350 degrees for 1½ hours; uncover last few minutes to brown.

Mrs. Sam P. Faucett, III (Leslie Wood)

EDITH'S CHICKEN AND RICE CASSEROLE

2 (10¾-ounce) cans cream of
  chicken soup
1 cup light cream
1 cup grated sharp cheese
1½ tablespoons minced onion
1 tablespoon prepared mustard
¼ teaspoon rosemary

½ teaspoon pepper
4 cups cooked rice
1 (1-pound, 4-ounce) can carrots
  and peas (tiny)
3 cups cooked chicken, cubed
1 (3½-ounce) can French fried
  onion rings

Blend soup with cream; cook over low heat until hot, being careful not to boil. Stir in cheese, minced onion, mustard, rosemary, and pepper; remove from heat. Alternately combine rice, carrots and peas, chicken, and sauce into layers in a lightly buttered 3-quart casserole. Sprinkle onion rings on top. Bake at 350 degrees, uncovered, 15 or 20 minutes, until mixture is bubbly. Serves 10.

Mrs. Maurice Tidwell

MRS. McMILLIAN'S TURKEY AND SHRIMP
IN CHAFING DISH

1 medium-size turkey, cooked and
  cut up, reserving stock
3 pounds shrimp, cooked and
  cleaned
½ pound butter
1 bunch spring onions, chopped
  tops and all
½ cup finely chopped parsley

3 small cloves of garlic, chopped
2 (4-ounce) cans mushrooms,
  diced, reserving liquid
8 tablespoons flour
1 pint of turkey stock and
  mushroom liquid
1 pint heavy cream
Salt and pepper to taste

Cook turkey and cut up; cook shrimp and clean. In a skillet, melt butter, add onions, parsley, garlic, and mushrooms. Cook until just tender. Transfer to a double boiler. Stir in flour, add stock and mushroom liquid, then the cream. Cook, stirring constantly, until desired thickness; add salt and pepper, then turkey and whole shrimp. Serve from chafing dish, in pastry shells, or on toast. Serves 15.

Mrs. David M. Cochrane (Mary B. Tompkins)

CHICKEN SQUARES

3 cups diced cooked chicken or
turkey
⅓ cup diced celery
1 small chopped onion
2 cups bread crumbs

4 beaten eggs
2 teaspoons poultry seasoning
¼ teaspoon salt
2 cups chicken broth

SAUCE:
1 (10¾-ounce) can cream of
mushroom or chicken soup

⅓ cup milk

Mix chicken or turkey, celery, onion, and bread crumbs; add eggs, poultry seasoning, salt, and chicken broth. Pour into a buttered 9 x 15-inch casserole. Bake at 350 degrees for 55 minutes or until lightly brown. Meanwhile, heat milk to a boil, add soup, and mix well. When chicken is brown, cut into squares, serve and spoon sauce over squares.

Hint: May substitute one 8-ounce package of herb seasoned stuffing mix for bread crumbs. You may also add ½ cup of broken pecans to the top of the chicken, and add 1 cup of sour cream and ¼ cup chopped pimiento to the sauce. Good dish for company.

Mrs. John G. Hogue (Peggy Hinton)

HOT CHICKEN SALAD

1 cup mayonnaise
½ teaspoon salt
1 cup diced celery
2 cups diced cooked chicken
1 cup sliced water chestnuts
2 tablespoons lemon juice

2 tablespoons grated onion
½ cup sliced almonds
1 cup sliced mushrooms
1 cup crushed potato chips
½ cup grated sharp cheddar
cheese

Mix mayonnaise, salt, celery, chicken, chestnuts, lemon juice, onion, almonds, and mushrooms; place in buttered casserole. Top with potato chips and cheddar cheese. Bake ½ hour at 350 degrees. Serves 4.

Variations: 1 can cream of chicken soup, 2 hard-boiled eggs (chopped), ½ cup chopped pecans, and 1 tablespoon Worcestershire sauce may be added if desired.

Mrs. Louis Payne (Catherine "Woodie" Murphy)

CAMP STEW

1 hen; cooked, boned, and cut in bite-size pieces
2½ pounds round steak, cooked tender and cut in bite-size pieces
1½ pounds lean pork, cooked tender and cut in bite-size pieces
6½ pounds potatoes, peeled and cut in large pieces
2½ pounds sliced onion
2 (16-ounce) cans tomatoes
1 (14-ounce) bottle catsup
Salt and pepper
1 stick butter or margarine

Add chicken, steak, pork, potatoes, onions, tomatoes, catsup, salt, pepper and butter, and cook until vegetables are tender. Stir often to prevent sticking. Serves a hungry crowd—at least 12.

Mrs. Ralph Clements (Ima Carl Turner)

ROSCOE'S BARBECUED CHICKEN

10 chicken halves

SAUCE:
1 large jar Durkee's Sauce
6 lemons, sliced
1 cup vinegar
2 sticks oleo
2 tablespoons dry mustard
2 tablespoons sugar
2 tablespoons salt

Cook chicken on grill for 10 minutes on each side. Meanwhile, have mixed Durkee's Sauce, lemons, vinegar, oleo, mustard, sugar, and salt. Cook until oleo melts, then start basting chicken with sauce. Cook 1½ to 2 hours, very slowly. Men love to cook this one!

Mrs. William Roscoe Johnson, III (Corella Rawls)

TURKEY AND RICE ORIENTALE

⅔ cup uncooked rice
3 tablespoons butter or margarine
Dash of garlic powder
3 tablespoons flour
1½ cups turkey broth
2 teaspoons soy sauce
Salt and pepper
2 cups slivered, cooked turkey

Cook rice in boiling salted water until tender. Save. Melt butter in skillet, add garlic and blend in the flour. Cook several minutes, then gradually add the broth, stirring until thickened. Add soy sauce and salt and pepper. Add turkey and serve over rice. Serves 4.

Mrs. Jack Echols (Connie Sue Morgan)

LONDON CHICKEN

24 pieces of chicken
½ cup butter or margarine
¾ pound sliced mushrooms (may use 6- or 8-ounce size can mushrooms)
2 (10¾-ounce) cans cream of chicken soup (undiluted)

1 (10¾-ounce) can mushroom soup (undiluted)
Pinch of thyme (optional)
Pinch of poultry seasoning (optional)
¼ cup white Rhine wine (more to taste)

Brown chicken in butter in large skillet. Remove and sauté fresh mushrooms. Place chicken in a large casserole. Mix cream of chicken and mushroom soups, thyme, and poultry seasoning. Pour over chicken. Cover with mushrooms. Refrigerate. When ready to bake, add wine, cover, and bake at 350 degrees for 1½ hours. Easy for working mothers and so-o-o... delicious! Serves 12. (May be cut in half).

Mrs. Allen Mattox (Harriet Marrs)

COQ AU VIN

2 small chickens, cut up
Seasoned flour
½ cup butter or margarine
3 tablespoons cognac
1 cup bouillon
12 very small onions
12 small fresh mushrooms
1 (16-ounce) can tiny baby carrots

1 cup Burgundy wine
1 bay leaf
⅓ teaspoon thyme
¼ teaspoon marjoram
Garlic salt
Parsley, fresh sprigs

Flour chicken, brown in butter, add cognac, and flame. Add bouillon, onions, mushrooms, carrots, wine, bay leaf, thyme, marjoram, and garlic. Cover and cook slowly for 2 hours. (I use my electric skillet.) Looks beautiful piled on a large silver tray. Serve garnished with parsley sprigs and new potatoes. Serves 8-10.

Mrs. Allen Mattox (Harriet Marrs)

FRIED DIXIE CHICKEN

1 (2- to 3-pound) broiler-fryer
chicken, cut up
Salt and pepper
2 cups all-purpose flour

1 teaspoon red pepper
1 egg, slightly beaten
½ cup milk
Hot oil

Season chicken with salt and pepper. Combine flour and red pepper; set aside. Combine egg and milk; dip chicken in egg mixture; then dredge in flour mixture, coating well. Heat 1 inch of oil in a skillet; place chicken in skillet. Cover and cook over medium heat about 30 minutes or until golden brown, turning occasionally. Drain on paper towels. Yield: 4 servings.

CREAM GRAVY:
4 tablespoons drippings
4 tablespoons all-purpose flour

2½ to 3 cups hot milk
Salt and pepper

Pour off all except 4 tablespoons drippings in which chicken was fried; place skillet over medium heat; add flour and stir until browned. Gradually add hot milk. Cook, stirring constantly, until thickened. Add salt and pepper to taste. Serve hot. Yield: About 2 cups.

Note: In the true Southern style, fried chicken is invariably served with rice, biscuits, and cream gravy.

SAUTÉED CHICKEN LIVERS (AND VARIATIONS)

1 pound chicken livers
Salt
Pepper

Flour
2 tablespoons butter
1 tablespoon vegetable oil

Season livers and coat with flour. Heat butter and oil until it crackles; add livers and sauté (medium high heat) for 2 minutes on each side, or longer if you prefer them well done.

Variations: To butter and oil add a few drops Worcestershire sauce, 2 teaspoons lemon juice and 1 small clove garlic, minced. Or to butter and oil add 1 tablespoon onion juice and 2 tablespoons lemon juice; and, after frying livers, add ¼ pound sautéed, fresh mushrooms. Or serve on toast points garnished with toasted almonds. Serves 4.

Mrs. Allen Mattox (Harriet Marrs)

WILD DUCK MARINADE AND DUCK-KABOBS

Duck breast, fillet and cut into
  1-inch cubes (count ½ breast
  per person)
1 (16-ounce) bottle Wishbone
  Italian dressing
1-2 cups Worcestershire sauce
Accent

Seasoned Salt
Pepper
1 pound bacon slices, cut in half
  (optional)
Tomatoes, cut into wedges
Bell peppers, cut into wedges
Onions, cut into wedges

Sprinkle duck breasts, after they are cut into 1-inch cubes, heavily with Accent, seasoned salt, and pepper. Mix Italian dressing and Worcestershire sauce until the marinade is a very dark color. Allow meat to marinate, covered tightly, at room temperature for approximately 4 hours or in refrigerator overnight. Make sure meat is covered in sauce, and stir a few times during that time period. When ready to assemble the kabobs, wrap each piece of duck with a small piece of bacon and place alternately on skewers with tomatoes, onions, and bell peppers. Grill outside if possible, or cook under broiler. Baste with marinade while cooking. Cook approximately 5 minutes per side for a total of 20-25 minutes over hot coals.

Note: This brings raves whichever way you choose to cook. We have never had anyone turn this one down, even if they have always disliked other wild game or duck recipes! Serve with French Bread and "Best Ever Rice Casserole" (See Index), and you have a super dinner!

Allen Mattox

WILD DUCK

2 (2-2½ pound) wild ducks
6 bacon slices
1 (6-ounce) can frozen orange
  juice concentrate, thawed
1 clove garlic, chopped
¾ teaspoon dry mustard

1 teaspoon ground ginger
½ teaspoon salt
⅓ cup sherry (or to taste)
1 tablespoon cornstarch
1 cup water

Clean ducks; tie legs and wings close to body. Place in shallow pan, breast side up, and lay strips of bacon over ducks. Roast at 425 degrees for 20 minutes. Combine undiluted orange juice, garlic, mustard, ginger, and salt in small saucepan. Heat to boiling, then add sherry. Pour over bird and continue to cook until tender at 325 degreess. Mix cornstarch with water and add to sauce after baking is completed. Time depends on age of ducks. Ducks are done when meat will pull loose from the bone.

Mrs. Robert L. McCurley, Jr. (Martha Dawson)

BREAKFAST QUAIL OR DOVES

12 quail or doves, or mixture	Flour
Salt	Bacon drippings or butter
Pepper	Worcestershire sauce
Egg	Milk or water

Split birds where legs join ribs. Salt, pepper, dip in egg, and generously flour pieces. Preheat ¼ inch of cooking oil in a heavy cast iron skillet or Dutch oven on medium heat. Fry until golden brown for about 10-15 minutes, usually turning once. Remove birds; drain on paper towels. Brown equal amounts of flour and pan drippings in skillet, stirring constantly to prevent lumping. Add 1 cup water or milk very gradually to 2 tablespoons of the flour you are adding. Cook until thickened. Make enough to cover game; correct the seasonings with salt, pepper, and Worcestershire sauce. Add game and simmer, tightly covered, 1 hour or longer. Serve over grits with homemade biscuits, - - - a dish fit for the king! Serves 4 (allow 2-3 birds per person).

Variation: May simmer in crockpot all night on Low.

Mrs. Allen Mattox (Harriet Marrs)

SMOTHERED QUAIL

6 quail or 12 doves (breasts)	2 cups chicken broth
6 tablespoons butter (*not*	½ cup sherry
margarine)	Salt and pepper to taste
3 tablespoons flour	Cooked rice

Season quail or doves with salt and pepper. Brown in a heavy skillet in butter. Remove quail to baking dish. Add flour to butter in skillet and stir well. Slowly add chicken broth, sherry, salt, and pepper to taste. Blend well and pour over quail. Cover baking dish and bake at 350 degrees for 1 hour, or until done. Serve with rice. Serves 3 to 4.

Variation: Sauce can be added in the middle of the baking time. Remove the birds and make sauce of the juice of 4 lemons, 3 tablespoons Durkee's dressing, and 1 tablespoon of Worcestershire sauce. Mix thoroughly and return the birds for 30 more minutes.

Mrs. William A. Miller (Jessica Frazier)

ROASTED WILD TURKEY

1 (8- to 10-pound) dressed wild turkey

DRESSING:

1 package Uncle Ben's half wild rice with herbs	⅛ teaspoon thyme
½ pound hot sausage	¼ cup parsley, chopped
1 cup celery, chopped	1 cup slivered almonds
1 cup onion, chopped	Salt and pepper to taste
Salt and pepper to taste	2 strips bacon

Prepare rice according to package directions and set aside. Brown sausage; when partially done, add onions and celery to brown. Add salt, pepper, and thyme. Combine rice, parsley, and almonds and mix with sausage mixture. Meanwhile, wash the dressed turkey inside and out. Sprinkle inside and out with salt and pepper. Stuff the turkey with dressing. Put the strips of bacon over the turkey. Place the turkey on rack in roasting pan and roast in 325-degree oven for 25 minutes per pound—3½ to 4 hours—basting with juices occasionally. Serves 8-10.

Note: A wild turkey has a wonderful full flavor that leaves domestic turkey's taste very bland. It deserves a rich dressing, and this one is even good cold.

Mrs. Joe Lee Hutt (Joanna Cravey)

ROAST DUCK

4 ducks	4 ribs celery
4 apples	1 stick margarine
4 onions	½ cup flour

SAUCE:

1 cup orange juice	3 onions, finely chopped
2 cups tomato juice	3 carrots, diced
1 cup beef broth	¼ cup parsley, chopped

Salt duck. Put onion, apple, and celery inside each duck. Steam 1 hour. Then melt margarine and mix in flour to make a paste. Spread paste on breast of duck. Heat oven to 500 degrees and put ducks in for 15 minutes, or until brown. Meanwhile, combine orange juice, tomato juice, broth, chopped onions, carrots, and parsley, and boil for 15 minutes. Turn ducks breast down in roaster, pour sauce over ducks, cover, and cook for 2 hours at 350 degrees. Serve with rice. Serves 8.

Mrs. Joe Sewell (Willie Veal)

SMOKED WILD TURKEY

1 (10- to 20-pound) turkey
10-20 pounds charcoal (1 pound
   per hour cooking time required)
Hickory chips, soaked
Seasoned salt

Thyme
Poultry seasoning
Butter, melted
1-2 cups wine
2 lemons, sliced

Weight	Charcoal	Water	Time
8 to 12 pounds	10 pounds	6 quarts	8 to 10 hours
13 to 16 pounds	12 pounds	7 quarts	10 to 12 hours
17 to 20 pounds	15 pounds	8 quarts	12 to 14 hours

Fill the bottom of smoker with charcoal, based on above chart. Light the entire amount of charcoal and let it stop flaming. Then place hickory chips on top of charcoal. Put pan of water on above charcoal, based on chart. Pour in wine of your choice and slice lemons and drop into water. Cover turkey *generously* all over with seasoned salt, then add thyme to taste and poultry seasoning to taste. You may inject, with a large syringe, melted butter and additional seasoned salt, thyme, and poultry seasoning into carcass. This really adds to the flavor and makes the meat very moist. Place turkey on the rack and seal smoker. I let this go all night, based on the number of hours on chart, and check early the next morning. The meat is thoroughly done when leg and wing (if left on) move freely.

Allen Mattox

DANCY DOVES

8-10 doves
½ stick margarine
½ cup celery, chopped
½ cup onion, chopped
Salt

Pepper
2 cubes chicken bouillon
1 cup boiling water
White wine (optional)

Salt and pepper doves. Brown in melted margarine on all sides. Place in casserole dish and cover with celery and onions. Dissolve bouillon cubes in water and pour over doves. Cover and place in 325-degree oven. Bake 1 hour 15 minutes. A little white wine may be added the last 15 minutes, but it isn't necessary. Yield: 4 servings.

Mrs. James G. Lee, III (Becky Thomson)

"STUFFED" DUCK WITH HOT SPICED APPLESAUCE

2 ducks, cleaned and washed

STUFFING:

2 onions, chopped
6 stalks celery, chopped
½ cup green stuffed olives,
  chopped

1 (2-ounce) can mushrooms,
  sliced
1 stick margarine, melted
1 cup sherry or other wine

APPLESAUCE:

1 (16-ounce) can applesauce
¼ cup brown sugar

1 teaspoon cinnamon

Mix onions, celery, olives, mushrooms, margarine, and wine. Fill duck cavities with stuffing and lay some around ducks. Bake in a covered casserole or baking bag (to eliminate basting) for 1 hour at 300 degrees. May sit in oven with heat cut off for another hour. Mix applesauce, brown sugar, and cinnamon in a small saucepan until thoroughly heated just before serving time. Serve the hot spicy applesauce with the duck.

Mrs. Paul W. Bryant, Jr. (Cherry Hicks)

BAKED DOVES

9 doves
Salt and pepper to taste
¾ stick margarine

¼ lemon
½ cup sherry
¼ cup water

Salt and pepper doves; brown in margarine. Remove doves to casserole. Squeeze lemon juice into skillet with margarine; add sherry and water. Stir well and pour over doves in casserole. Cover and bake 1½ hours at 325 degrees. This recipe works equally well with quail. Yield: 3-4 servings.

Note: For 30 to 36 doves, use the following amounts:
    3 sticks margarine
    Juice from 1-2 lemons, depending on size
    1½ to 2 cups sherry
    1 cup water
For 50 to 60 doves, use the following amounts:
    3½-4 sticks margarine
    Juice from 3 lemons
    2⅔ cups sherry
    2 cups water

Mrs. Jerre R. White (Jackie Cunningham)

DUCK GUMBO

STOCK:

2 large ducks
4 quarts water
1 onion, chopped
2 ribs celery, chopped

1 tablespoon salt
1 teaspoon pepper
1 bay leaf

METHOD FOR STOCK: Simmer ducks in water with onion, celery, and seasoning for 2 to 3 hours, until tender. Time will vary with size and age of ducks. Remove ducks from stock; strain stock and reserve. When ducks have cooled, bone and chop meat into bite-size pieces. It is best to do this the day before making the Gumbo.

GUMBO:

1 cup corn oil
1 cup flour
1 cup onion, chopped
1 cup green onion with tops, chopped
4 ribs celery, chopped
2 cloves garlic, minced finely or put through press
1 tablespoon salt
1 tablespoon pepper

½ teaspoon Tabasco
1 (8-ounce) can tomato sauce
1 (10-ounce) package frozen okra (optional)
2 tablespoons Worcestershire sauce
1 cup chopped parsley
1 pound smoked sausage, cut into bite-size pieces

METHOD FOR GUMBO: In a heavy black skillet, *slowly* brown the flour in oil until it is walnut-colored (about 1 hour), stirring constantly to prevent flour from burning. When roux is desired dark color, add chopped onions, celery, and garlic. Cook over medium heat for 5 minutes, stirring occasionally. Add hot stock, a little at a time, stirring until smooth. Add salt, pepper, Tabasco, tomato sauce, okra, and Worcestershire sauce. Add cut-up duck. Simmer for about 1 hour. Add chopped parsley and smoked sausage and simmer 30 more minutes. Serve in bowls over rice.

Mrs. Jerre R. White (Jackie Cunningham)

QUAIL IN WHITE WINE SAUCE

6 to 8 quail (or chicken breast
   halves or "pulley bones")
½ stick butter or oleo
1 onion, finely chopped
¼ cup flour

1½ cups chicken stock or
   canned chicken broth
½ cup white wine
Salt and pepper

Salt and pepper quail. Lightly brown in butter or oleo. Remove quail and put in baking dish. Sauté onion in drippings. Add flour and stir for about 2 minutes. Add chicken stock and wine. Stir. Pour sauce over quail. Cover and bake at 275 degrees for 1 hour and 15 minutes. Serves 4.

Mrs. Peterson Cavert (Mary Beth Wear)

DOVES (COUNTRY STYLE)

12-15 dove breasts
Salt
Pepper

Flour
1½ sticks butter

Preheat oven to 350 degrees. Salt, pepper and flour birds generously. Place birds in Dutch oven; add enough water to come about half-way on breasts. Place on top of stove on high heat. Let come to full boil. Add butter. Remove from stove, cover and cook in oven at 350 degrees for 1 hour. Serve with white or wild rice. Makes its own gravy. Serves 4 to 6.

Maureen Cohen Koenemann

MARINATED VENISON LOIN

½ cup olive oil
¼ cup lemon juice
½ cup red wine
1 teaspoon salt
1 teaspoon marjoram

1 teaspoon oregano
½ teaspoon pepper
1 clove garlic, minced
½ cup onion, chopped
¼ cup parsley, chopped

Mix oil, lemon juice, wine, salt, marjoram, oregano, pepper, garlic, onion, and parsley in pan that will hold and marinate the loin—a bread pan, depending on size of loin. Marinate for 6-8 hours. Barbecue the loin on the grill or roast as you would a beef tenderloin.

Note: The loin is the delicacy!

Mrs. Joe Lee Hutt (Joanna Cravey)

QUICK VENISON CHILI

1 pound ground venison	1 teaspoon oregano
½ pound sausage	½ teaspoon thyme
1 large onion, chopped	1 bay leaf
1 large clove of garlic, minced	1 (12-ounce) can beer
32 ounces tomato sauce	32 ounces red kidney beans,
2 or more (to taste) tablespoons	drained
chili powder	Salt and pepper

Brown venison and sausage in a heavy iron skillet or Dutch oven. Remove meat and sauté onions and garlic in grease. Mix meat, onion, garlic, tomato sauce, chili powder, oregano, thyme, bay leaf, beer, and kidney beans. Simmer, tightly covered, for 1 hour or more, stirring occasionally. Correct seasonings with salt and pepper. Cook until well thickened and rich in flavor. This is great cooked over a campfire in a heavy dutch oven and will fill lots of hungry mouths!

Note: This makes a tasty sauce for frankfurters. Place grilled franks in bun and top with chili and a spoonful of chopped raw onion.

Allen Mattox

"RAINEY'S" VENISON

1 venison roast	Garlic buttons
1 lemon, cut in half	

MARINADE:

Juice of 1 lemon	1 teaspoon rosemary
1 teaspoon salt	1 cup port or burgundy
½ teaspoon white pepper	
½ teaspoon monosodium	
glutamate (Accent)	

Trim *all* fat and fiber from cut of venison. Rub well with cut lemon. Stick with garlic buttons (number depends on size) deep into flesh. Using proportions above, mix enough marinade to cover venison. Mix lemon, salt, pepper, Accent, rosemary, wine; cover venison, and marinate overnight. Drain, saving marinade. Bake in 250- to 300-degree oven for 30-45 minutes per pound. Baste every 15 minutes for last hour of baking.

Note: Delicious hot, but great cold, sliced paper thin. Better if you get husband to smoke it! Smoking seems to take away all the "wild" flavor most people object to; therefore, we love to smoke all venison.

Mrs. Ernest "Rainey" Collins (Louise "Bebe" Williams)

SMOKED VENISON

10-20 pounds of venison
  (hindquarter or whatever)
10-20 pounds of charcoal
Hickory chips, soaked in water
Seasoned salt
Garlic salt

Accent
Savory
Thyme
½ pound bacon strips
1-2 cups wine

Weight	Charcoal	Water	Time
8 to 12 pounds	10 to 15 pounds	7 quarts	10 to 14 hours
13 to 30 pounds	15 to 20 pounds	8 quarts	14 to 16 hours

Fill bottom of smoker with charcoal, based on chart. Light the charcoal and let the flames die down. Then add hickory chips to charcoal. Put pan of water on, following the chart, and add wine of your choice to the water. Remove *all fat* and *extra fibers* and cover venison *generously* with seasoned salt, garlic salt, and Accent. Then sprinkle on the savory and thyme, and lay bacon on top of venison. Place venison on rack and seal smoker. I let this go all night, usually, and sometimes baste last 2 hours with barbecue sauce. Everyone swears this is roast beef or barbecued beef until they are shown the mark where the bullet went in, if I happen to be cooking that portion!

Allen Mattox

VENISON STEAK AND GRAVY

1½ to 2 pounds venison round
  steak, cut into 5 or 6 pieces
Salt and pepper to taste
¾ to 1 cup flour
Vegetable or corn oil
3 small onions, chopped
3 garlic cloves, minced finely or
  pressed

3 cups water
3 beef bouillon cubes
1 teaspoon salt
½ tablespoon onion salt
½ tablespoon garlic salt

Tenderize meat with mallet. Cut into serving size pieces, salt and pepper lightly and roll in flour. Use only as much cooking oil as it requires to cover the bottom of the size skillet used and brown venison steaks on both sides. Remove meat from skillet. Add chopped onion and garlic cloves to remaining oil in skillet and sauté until tender. Add water to skillet, scraping sides and bottom to loosen bits of flour left from the steaks. Drop in bouillon cubes and dissolve. Add salt, onion, and garlic salt and stir well. Return venison steaks to gravy, cover, and simmer slowly for 1 hour.

Mrs. Jerre R. White (Jackie Cunningham)

VENISON AND NOODLE STROGANOFF

1½ pounds ground venison
¼ cup margarine
½ cup onion, finely chopped
1 clove garlic, pressed or
  minced finely
½ pound fresh mushrooms,
  thickly sliced or 1 (4-ounce) can
  sliced mushrooms, drained
2 tablespoons flour
1 (8-ounce) can tomato sauce

¼ cup Burgundy
1 (10½-ounce) can beef bouillon,
  undiluted
1 teaspoon salt
¼ teaspoon pepper
¼ to ½ cup Parmesan cheese
1 cup (8-ounce carton) sour
  cream
6 ounces medium noodles

Brown ground venison in large skillet; remove to a bowl and drain all grease from skillet. Melt margarine and sauté onion, garlic, and mushrooms until onion is golden, about 3-5 minutes. Return ground venison to skillet with onion mixture and remove from heat. Stir in flour, tomato sauce, Burgundy, bouillon, salt, and pepper. Simmer 20-30 minutes, until mixture has thickened. Remove from heat and blend in sour cream. Cook noodles according to package directions. In lightly greased 2-quart casserole, layer half the noodles and cover with half the meat mixture. Repeat layers. Sprinkle with Parmesan cheese. Bake, uncovered, 25 minutes at 375 degrees.

Mrs. Jerre R. White (Jackie Cunningham)

VENISON ROAST

Venison roast
Buttermilk

Bacon
Salt and pepper

Marinate roast overnight in buttermilk. Remove meat from buttermilk, wipe it off, and put into a roasting pan. Season with salt and pepper and cover with several strips of bacon. Roast at 350 degrees until meat thermometer reads 140 degrees, medium rare.

Mrs. Max McCord, Jr. (Martha Nabers)

Main Dishes
and Sauces

GRILLED TENDERLOIN

2 pounds beef tenderloin
¼ cup margarine
½ cup olive oil
½ cup red wine
¼ cup white vinegar
Juice of 1 lime

½ teaspoon oregano
¼ teaspoon salt
¼ teaspoon black pepper
Dash of granulated garlic
1 (4-ounce) can sliced
    mushrooms

Combine margarine, olive oil, wine, vinegar, lime, oregano, salt, pepper, and garlic in saucepan; simmer 2-3 minutes. Marinate tenderloin in sauce for 1 hour. Grill for 40 minutes, basting often with sauce. When removed from grill, slice into filets. Add mushrooms to remaining sauce and spoon over meat. Garnish platter with parsley. Comment: A delightful way to please men by serving grilled steak in a beautiful style. Serves 4.

Mrs. Frank E. Spell (Bell Searcy)

TOMATO POT ROAST

1 (3- to 4-pound) chuck roast
Dash of garlic salt
1 teaspoon salt
1 teaspoon pepper
Flour
2 tablespoons bacon grease
1 envelope dry onion soup mix
    (2.75-ounce box)
1 cup water (or more)

3-4 potatoes, peeled and halved
    or quartered
6-8 carrots, peeled and halved or
    quartered
2 (15-ounce) cans Hunt's special
    tomato sauce with mushrooms
2 tablespoons Worcestershire
    sauce (or more)

Sprinkle roast with garlic salt, salt, and pepper. Roll in flour. Brown on all sides in hot fat. Place in a Dutch oven; add onion soup mix and water. Cook 1½ hours or longer, covered, on simmer or low, adding water as needed. Then add potatoes, carrots, tomato sauce, and Worcestershire sauce. Cook slowly for another hour. Serves 6.

Variations: As garnish, you may use parsley on the potatoes and carrots for a side dish. When in a hurry, just put all together and cook for 2½ hours.

Mrs. William V. Barkley (Carolyn Johnson)

PEPPER STEAK

1½ pounds round or sirloin steak, about 1 inch thick
¼ cup salad oil
1 cup water
½ teaspoon garlic salt
¼ teaspoon ginger
1 medium onion, cut into slices
2 medium green peppers, cut into strips
Rice
1 tablespoon cornstarch
½ teaspoon sugar
2 tablespoons soy sauce
1 medium tomato

Trim fat from meat; cut meat into 2½ x 1 x ¼-inch strips. Heat oil in large skillet. Add meat and sauté, turning frequently, until brown, about 5 minutes. Stir in water, garlic salt, ginger, and onion. Heat to boiling; reduce heat. Cover and simmer 15 minutes for round steak, 7 to 10 minutes for sirloin. Add green pepper strips during last 5 minutes of simmering. While meat simmers, cook rice.
Blend cornstarch, sugar and soy sauce; stir into meat mixture. Cook, stirring constantly, until mixture thickens and boils. Boil and stir 1 minute. Cut tomato into eighths and place on meat mixture. Cover; cook over low heat just until tomatoes are heated through. Serve with rice. Serves 4.

Mrs. Warren P. Davis (Linda del Gatto)

OLD WORLD SAUERBRATEN

1 (4-pound) rump roast
1 cup water
1 cup vinegar
2 teaspoons salt
½ teaspoon pepper
½ cup brown sugar, divided
1 medium onion, sliced
3 bay leaves
1 teaspoon peppercorns
1 tablespoon butter
¼ cup raisins
6 gingersnaps, crushed
1 cup sour cream

Wipe meat with damp cloth. Place in glass bowl. Bring to a boil the water, vinegar, salt, pepper, ¼ cup brown sugar, onion, bay leaves, and peppercorns. Pour over meat and cool. Cover and chill *24 to 48 hours.* Turn meat occasionally. Melt butter. Brown meat 5 minutes on each side. Add marinade; bring to a boil. Cover, and reduce to simmer. Cook until tender (2½ to 3 hours). Remove meat; strain liquid into saucepan. Add remaining brown sugar, raisins, and gingersnaps. Cook until thick, stirring constantly. Add some hot mixture to sour cream and mix well. Stir into remaining hot mixture. Heat. Pour over sliced meat. Serves 8 to 10.

Mrs. Robert N. Rice, Jr. (Carolyn Burchfield)

PAPRIKA BEEF ROLL

2 round steaks totaling 3 pounds	1 tablespoon boiling water
Salt	1 egg
Pepper	Stuffed olives
Paprika	Flour
¼ pound mushrooms, sliced	¼ cup butter or bacon drippings
1 large onion, sliced thin	6 whole mushrooms
¼ cup pimiento, chopped	3 small onions
½ cup fine bread crumbs	1 cup red wine
½ cup melted butter	Shredded carrots (optional)

Pound round steaks until thin. Rub in salt, pepper, and plenty of paprika. Overlap steaks on meat board, making 1 large steak. Spread steaks with a layer of mushrooms, then layer of onions and pimiento. Cover with bread crumbs. With beater, combine melted butter, boiling water, and egg. Immediately dribble this mixture over bread crumbs. Arrange stuffed olives in a row on long side of steak. Begin roll of meat around olives. Tie roll firmly. Flour outside. Brown in butter or bacon drippings in roaster or earthenware baker. Sprinkle lightly with salt, pepper, and paprika. Place whole mushrooms and small onions in roaster and add wine. Roast meat in 350-degree oven for about 2 hours. Serve hot or cold. Serves 6. (Shredded carrots may be added in roll.)

Mrs. Max Bailey (Mary Julia Knight)

PEPPER STEAK WITH TOMATOES AND MUSHROOMS

2 pounds round steak, cut in julienne strips	½ cup barbecue sauce
1 tablespoon fat	½ cup water
2 cups (1 pound) tomatoes, crushed	1 teaspoon salt
1 cup chopped onion	½ teaspoon basil, crushed
½ cup (4 ounces) sliced mushrooms, drained	2 medium green peppers
	Biscuits or rice

Brown meat in a large skillet. Stir in the tomatoes, onion, mushrooms, barbecue sauce, water, salt, and basil. Cover and simmer for 1 hour or until meat is tender. Cut green pepper into julienne strips and stir into meat mixture. While hot, turn this into a 2-quart casserole if skillet is not oven-proof. Arrange biscuits on top around the edge. Bake in 450-degree oven for 10-15 minutes, or until biscuits are golden brown. This can be served over hot rice without the biscuits. Serves 8.

Mrs. Charles P. Allison (Sherry Hafemuster)

SIRLOIN KABOBS

¾ cup soy sauce
1 cup corn oil
1 cup Burgundy wine
1 (6-ounce) can orange juice
  concentrate
½ teaspoon garlic powder
¼ cup prepared mustard
1 teaspoon ginger
¼ cup Worcestershire sauce

5 pounds sirloin tip roast, cut in
  1-inch cubes
3 or 4 green peppers, cut into
  strips
3 or 4 onions, cut into wedges
1½ to 2 pints fresh mushrooms
1½ to 2 pints cherry tomatoes
  (or tomatoes cut in wedges)

Combine soy sauce, oil, wine, orange juice, garlic, mustard, ginger, and Worcestershire sauce. Pour marinade over cubed sirloin in a large container that can be sealed. Refrigerate 24 hours. Mix or stir every so often. Place meat, green peppers, onions, mushrooms, and cherry tomatoes alternately on skewers. Cook over low fire. May baste with marinade during cooking. Serves 8-10.

Hint: To keep peppers and mushrooms from splitting when skewering, dip in very hot water for a minute.

Peggy Bishop—Tuscaloosa County Home Agent

COMPANY BEEF STEW

2 pounds lean beef, chopped into
  small cubes
1 (28-ounce) can stewed tomatoes
1 (4-ounce) can mushrooms
2 teaspoons tarragon
2 teaspoons sweet basil
Salt and pepper

2 cups celery or more, cut in
  1-inch lengths
2 cups carrots or more, cut in
  1-inch lengths
1 green pepper, sliced
2 tablespoons dehydrated onion
  flakes

Brown meat after dusting in flour. Remove from pan, place into casserole. Put juice from tomatoes and mushrooms in pan of meat drippings. Stir to thicken liquid. Pour over meat. Add tomatoes and mushrooms. Cover and place in oven for 1 hour at 350 degrees. Add tarragon, sweet basil, salt, pepper, celery, carrots, green pepper, and onion flakes. Cover and continue cooking for 1½ hours, or until vegetables are as tender as you like. Sometimes I add more tomato juice. Serves 8-10.

Note: This is delicious and a little different than ordinary stew!

Mrs. Ronald C. Phelps (Margaret "Margie" Wood)

HOME-CURED CORNED BEEF

8 quarts water (approximately)
Enough Kosher salt to make a
brine that will float an egg
(about 5 cups)
1 (5- to 8-pound) beef brisket or
eye of round roast
2 tablespoons pickling spice (or 1
teaspoon each of whole black
pepper, whole cloves, and
bay leaves)

1 teaspoon thyme leaves
3-6 cloves garlic
1½ teaspoons granular potassium
nitrate (saltpeter)—available
at drugstores

Use a plastic or earthenware bowl. Make the brine. Add the brisket or
roast and other ingredients. Weight the meat to be sure it is covered with
the brine. (I use a plate.) Cover and refrigerate for about 2 weeks, turning
the brisket every 3 days.

Mrs. Peterson Cavert (Mary Beth Wear)

CORNED BEEF

1 (5- to 8-pound) corned beef,
home-cured or purchased
1 bay leaf
1 onion, sliced
1 teaspoon whole peppercorns
1 carrot, cut into 3-inch lengths

2 ribs celery, cut into 3-inch
lengths
2 cloves garlic
Water
(No salt)

Put corned beef in kettle and cover with water. Add bay leaf, onion, peppercorns, carrot, celery, and garlic. Cover, bring to a boil, and boil for 2
to 3 hours, or until tender. Remove meat from broth and cut off excess fat.
If serving hot, remove from broth 30 minutes before serving and let firm up
before slicing. Cook cabbage or corn-on-the-cob in broth. Or chill. Slice
across the grain into very thin slices. Delicious. Serves 12 (approximately).

Mrs. Peterson Cavert (Mary Beth Wear)

ROUND STEAK SOUTHERN STYLE

2 pounds round steak
Flour
2 tablespoons oil
1 large onion, chopped
1 (10-ounce) package collard
    greens, thawed (or spinach)

¼ teaspoon instant minced garlic
1 teaspoon salt
½ teaspoon cracked pepper
1 can pitted ripe olives, drained
3 medium tomatoes, quartered
⅓ cup Parmesan cheese

Dredge round steak in flour. In large skillet, brown meat well in oil over medium heat, allowing about 20-25 minutes to develop rich color. Sprinkle onion over meat; distribute greens evenly atop onion. Sprinkle garlic, salt, and pepper over greens. Top with olives. Bake tightly covered at 325 degrees for 1½ to 2 hours, until meat is "fork" tender. Circle tomato wedges around edge of pan and sprinkle with cheese. Cover and return to oven. Bake an additional 15 minutes, until tomatoes are heated through. Serves 6.

Mrs. Ralph Quarles (Kat Pritchett)

Hint: Use 1 teaspoon salt to season 1 pound of meat.

BARBECUED CHUCK ROAST

1 (3 to 5 pound) chuck roast
1 teaspoon tenderizer
½ cup wine vinegar
¼ cup catsup
2 tablespoons cooking oil
2 tablespoons soy sauce

1 tablespoon Worcestershire sauce
1 teaspoon prepared mustard
1 teaspoon salt
¼ teaspoon pepper
¼ teaspoon garlic powder

Sprinkle both sides of meat with tenderizer, following manufacturer's directions. Place meat in Pyrex dish. Combine vinegar, catsup, oil, soy sauce, Worcestershire sauce, mustard, salt, pepper, and garlic powder. Mix well. Pour over meat. Marinate for 3 or 4 hours, turning several times. Marinade should be used to baste roast while cooking. Cook the roast on the grill, close to the flame 15 minutes on each side. Then raise grill and cook roast slowly for 1½ hours or until done. Serves 6 to 8.

Mrs. Wayne L. Williams (Nancy Tate)

STANDING RIB

3 ribs standing roast
Salt (approximately 1 teaspoon
   per pound of meat)

Paprika
Flour

Place meat in a roasting pan and season with salt and paprika. Dredge well with flour, and place in a very hot oven (550 degrees) for 20 minutes. Reduce the heat to 350 degrees and continue roasting, basting frequently. Allow 15 minutes per pound for rare, 20 for medium, and 30 for well done.

Note: This recipe was originally submitted under the name of Mrs. George Brownell, Birmingham, Alabama, in the Junior Welfare Association Cookbook, published in 1939.

Mrs. Albert Baernstein (Sis Wiesel)

BARBECUED BEEF

3 pounds round bone chuck roast
1 large onion, finely chopped
½ cup wine vinegar
2 tablespoons sugar
1 teaspoon salt

½ cup celery, finely sliced
2 teaspoons horseradish
1 (14-ounce) bottle catsup
½ cup water

Trim meat and cut in 3-inch pieces. Combine meat with remaining ingredients. Simmer, covered, for 2 hours or cook in crockpot for 8 hours. Mash with a potato masher to shred fine. Serve on hamburger buns.

Mrs. Charles P. Allison (Sherry Hafemuster)

NEVER-FAIL ROAST

Eye of round roast (or any other
   roast of your choice)
Kitchen Bouquet

Salt and pepper
1 stick of butter

Preheat oven to 500 degrees. This cooks any size roast brown on the outside and pink on the inside. Put roast in pan and coat with Kitchen Bouquet. Sprinkle with salt and pepper. Cover the top of roast with pats of butter. Place in preheated oven uncovered for 5 minutes per pound. DO NOT OPEN OVEN DOOR. When roast has cooked for 5 minutes per pound, turn off oven and leave for 2 hours. Don't open oven door until the end of this time. When this is done, you'll have a beautiful roast and plenty of au jus gravy.

Mrs. Charles R. Pearce (Liz Cunningham)

BEEF RAGOUT WITH WALNUTS

1½ pounds chuck or shoulder cut
   in 1½-inch cubes
2 tablespoons drippings or oil
   and butter
2 tablespoons flour
2 onions, sliced

1 cup red wine
1½ cups beef stock
*Bouquet garni
2 cloves garlic, crushed
Salt and pepper

GARNISH:
½ bunch celery cut in ½-inch
   slices (cut diagonally)
2 tablespoons sweet butter
¾ cup walnut halves

Pared rind of 1 orange, cut in
   needle-like strips
Salt and pepper

In heavy casserole, heat drippings and on high heat, brown meat and re-move from pan. Add onions, reduce heat to medium, and brown onions. Add flour to onions and brown well. Add meat, wine, stock, bouquet garnis, garlic, salt, and pepper, and bring to a boil. Cover casserole and cook on top of stove on a simmer or in oven at 350 degrees for 1½ hours, or until very tender. If sauce is not thick and rich, remove cover for last 30 minutes of cooking until sauce reduces. Taste for seasoning. Before serving, with a vegetable peeler, peel orange rind and boil for 5 minutes. Drain and cut peel in thin strips. Sauté celery in butter 2-3 minutes, add walnuts, salt, and pepper, and cook 4-5 minutes more. To serve, place beef in a dish, mix orange rind with celery and walnuts, and sprinkle on top of beef. Serves 4.

Note: This can be cooked 3 days ahead of time and refrigerated, or it can be frozen. The wine may be omitted, if desired.

HOW TO MAKE A BOUQUET GARNI (Great gift idea!): Place in center of 4-inch cheesecloth squares: ½ teaspoon of rosemary, marjoram, parsley, bay leaves, thyme. Bring corners of cloth together and tie with rick rack.

Cornelia Minges—New York caterer

BEEF STROGANOFF

½ cup chopped onion
½ cup mushrooms
4 tablespoons margarine
2 pounds round steak
½ cup beef bouillon
½ cup Burgundy wine

1 cup sour cream
2 tablespoons flour
1 tablespoon Worcestershire
  sauce
1 teaspoon salt
Dash pepper

Sauté onions and mushrooms in margarine. Cut beef in 1-inch strips and brown on both sides in skillet with onions and mushrooms. Push beef and vegetables to one side, add wine and bouillon. Bring to a boil and add sour cream mixed with flour. Simmer, covered, for 15 minutes. Before serving, add Worcestershire sauce, salt, and pepper. Serve over noodles or hot rice. Serves 6.

Variation: Substitute 2 pounds ground chuck for round steak.

Mrs. Charles P. Allison (Sherry Hafemuster)

CABBAGE ROLLS

1 large head of cabbage
  (approximately 3 pounds)
¾ cup long grain rice, cooked
1 small onion, chopped
¼ cup margarine
1½ to 2 pounds ground beef or
  chuck or round
3 eggs, slightly beaten
1½ to 2 teaspoons salt

¼ to ½ teaspoon pepper
¼ teaspoon garlic powder
2 teaspoons oregano
2 tablespoons parsley flakes
3 or 4 pork ribs (optional)
1 (10¾-ounce) can tomato soup
1 soup can of water
1 (16-ounce) can of tomatoes
2 tablespoons vinegar

Cut the core out of the cabbage and discard. Separate leaves and steam just long enough to make limber; then trim large veins lengthwise until leaves lie flat. Cook rice and let cool. Sauté onion in margarine and set aside. Combine ground beef, eggs, salt, pepper, garlic powder, oregano, and parsley; add rice and onions. Divide mixture equally among cabbage leaves, tuck ends in and roll like butcher's wrap. Place seam side down in large boiler or Dutch oven. Place pork ribs on top of cabbage rolls if desired. Combine tomato soup, water, tomatoes, and vinegar. Pour over cabbage rolls. Simmer covered 2 hours or more. Great for freezing and reheating later as an instant meal when time runs short. Children and all love this recipe! Serves 6-8.

Mrs. Larry Satterwhite—Birmingham, AL

CHEDDAR-FILLED BEEF ROLLS

1½ pounds ground beef
¼ cup dry bread crumbs
2 tablespoons bottled barbecue
   sauce
1 egg
½ teaspoon salt

1 cup shredded sharp cheddar
   cheese
¼ cup dry bread crumbs
¼ cup chopped green pepper
   (more if you like)
2 tablespoons water

Combine beef, bread crumbs, barbecue sauce, egg, and salt. Pat into
14 x 8-inch rectangle on foil or wax paper. Combine cheddar cheese,
bread crumbs, green pepper, and water. Spread over meat mixture. Roll
up, jellyroll fashion. Chill, then cut into 6 to 8 slices. Bake at 350 degrees
for 25-30 minutes.

Mrs. A. G. Williams (Martha Millar)

EGGPLANT MOUSSAKA

1½ pounds ground beef
3 tablespoons chopped onion
1 cup tomato sauce
2 tablespoons minced parsley
1 cup water
⅛ teaspoon ground cinnamon
Salt and pepper to taste
3 medium eggplants
Hot olive oil

2 cups shredded mozzarella
   cheese, divided
½ cup plus 2 tablespoons all-
   purpose flour
½ cup melted butter
1 (13-ounce) can evaporated milk
1 cup water
1 teaspoon ground nutmeg
2 eggs, well beaten

Combine beef and onion; sauté until beef is not red. Pour off fat. Add
tomato sauce, parsley, water, cinnamon, salt, and pepper; cover and simmer 45 minutes.

Peel eggplants and slice into ¼-inch slices. Sauté in oil until tender;
drain and cool. Arrange slices in a lightly greased 13 x 9 x 2-inch casserole;
top with meat mixture and sprinkle with one cup cheese.

Combine flour and butter in a medium saucepan. Cook over low heat one
minute. Add milk and one cup water; cook, stirring constantly until
smooth and thickened. Salt to taste. Remove from heat and add nutmeg,
eggs, and remaining cheese. Pour over meat mixture and bake at 350
degrees 45-50 minutes, until brown. Cool slightly before cutting into
squares. Serves 6 to 8.

Lew Worsham Voltz

ITALIAN MEAT LOAF

2 regular size slices rye bread
2 slices white bread
1 cup beef broth
1 pound lean ground beef
1 small onion, minced
2 teaspoons fresh parsley, minced
3 teaspoons grated Parmesan
  cheese

1 egg, beaten
½ teaspoon salt
¼ teaspoon coarse pepper
½ teaspoon oregano
2 slices bacon

SAUCE:
1 (8-ounce) can tomato sauce
½ teaspoon oregano
½-1 teaspoon Worcestershire sauce

2-3 drops Tabasco sauce
Salt
Pepper

Crumble rye and white bread into a large bowl. Pour broth over and allow to soak until liquid is absorbed. Mash with fork; add beef, onion, parsley, cheese, egg, salt, pepper, and oregano. Beat vigorously with a wooden spoon. Turn into oiled loaf baking dish and place bacon over top. Bake at 350 degrees for 30 minutes. Meanwhile, for the sauce, add to the tomato sauce the oregano. Worcestershire sauce, Tabasco, salt, and pepper, and heat thoroughly while stirring. Pour over the meat loaf at the end of first 30 minutes of baking, then bake an additional 35 minutes.

Mrs. Adrian Goldstein (Betty Jo May)

CHILI BAKE

2 pounds ground beef
1 onion, chopped
1 bell pepper, chopped
1 (28-ounce) can tomatoes

1 (15-ounce) can kidney beans
Salt
Pepper
Chili powder

Brown beef, onion, and bell pepper. Add canned tomatoes and kidney beans. Season to taste.

TOPPING:
1 cup self-rising corn meal
1 beaten egg
3 tablespoons melted shortening

½ cup milk
1 teaspoon sugar
½ cup self-rising flour

Mix corn meal, egg, shortening, milk, sugar, and flour. Drop by spoonfuls onto casserole. Bake at 400 degrees for 25 minutes. Serves 8.

Mrs. Eric Wilson (Margaret Marshall)

PUNCH AND JUDY CHILI

3 tablespoons butter or olive oil
1 large onion, minced
2 cloves garlic, minced
¾ pound chopped beef (or ground)
½ pound chopped pork (approximately 2 pork chops)
2 cups water
1⅓ cups canned tomatoes
1 green pepper, minced

½ teaspoon celery seed
¼ teaspoon cayenne
1 teaspoon cumin seed, crushed
1 small bay leaf
2 tablespoons chili powder
½ teaspoon basil
1½ teaspoons salt
1 (15-ounce) can kidney beans

Heat the butter in a skillet. Add the onions and garlic and sauté until golden brown. Add the meat and brown. Transfer the meat mixture to a large saucepan and add water, tomatoes, pepper, celery seed, cayenne, cumin, bay leaf, chili powder, basil, and salt. Bring to a boil, then reduce the heat and simmer, uncovered, until the sauce is as thick as desired, or about 3 hours. If desired, add one can of kidney beans just before serving. Freezes well; freeze prior to adding beans. Makes 4 servings.

Ruth Tisdale Wilder

CHILI CHEESE FANTASTIC

1 pound lean ground beef
1 medium onion, chopped
1 (1.25-ounce) envelope chili mix
1 (10¾-ounce) can condensed tomato soup
½ cup water
2 eggs, slightly beaten
1 cup milk

1 (6-ounce) package crushed corn chips
1 cup Monterey Jack cheese, shredded
1 cup sour cream
½ cup natural cheddar cheese, shredded

In large skillet cook ground beef and onion until meat is brown and onion is tender. Drain off excess fat. Add chili mix, tomato soup, and water. Simmer 5 minutes. Blend egg and milk into meat mixture. Cook and stir until thick and bubbly. Stir in corn chips and Monterey Jack cheese. Pour into 2-quart casserole. Bake uncovered at 350 degrees for 30 minutes. Spread top of casserole with sour cream; sprinkle with cheddar cheese. Return to oven for 3 to 5 minutes or until cheese melts. Serves 6.

Mrs. Tim Parker, Jr. (Cathy Jackman)

LASAGNE
(Favorite of Charlie Boswell)

2 pounds ground beef
1 medium onion, chopped
1 clove garlic, crushed
1 teaspoon chopped parsley
2 tablespoons sugar
1 teaspoon basil
1 teaspoon Italian herb seasoning
1 teaspoon salt
¼ teaspoon pepper
¾ cup sliced mushrooms
¼ cup chopped ripe olives

2 tablespoons salad oil
2 (16-ounce) cans whole peeled
  tomatoes
1 (15-ounce) can tomato sauce
1 (12-ounce) can tomato paste
¾ pound lasagne noodles
1 (16-ounce) carton ricotta cheese
  or cottage cheese
2 eggs, beaten
¾ pound mozzarella cheese, sliced
¾ cup grated Parmesan cheese

In large heavy pan saute beef, onion, garlic, and parsley Drain. Add sugar, basil, Italian seasoning, salt, and pepper. Mix; then add tomatoes, tomato paste, tomato sauce, mushrooms, and olives. Bring to a boil and simmer an hour or more. Cook lasagne noodles according to directions on package. Drain well. Mix together ricotta cheese and beaten eggs. In 13 x 9 x 2-inch baking dish, spread 1 cup sauce over bottom. Then alternate layers of criss-crossed noodles, ricotta cheese mixture, and meat sauce. Repeat layers. Sprinkle Parmesan cheese on top. Cover tightly and cook at 375 degrees for 30 to 40 minutes. Let cool for 10 minutes before serving. This can be re-frigerated and baked later in the day, but allow 15 minutes more baking time. This also freezes well. Serves 8-10.

Variation: Substitute 1 pound sausage for 1 pound ground beef.

Mrs. Charles A. Boswell

BEEF CORNWHEELS

1½ pounds ground beef
1½ teaspoons salt
⅛ teaspoon pepper
⅛ teaspoon thyme
½ cup cracker crumbs
⅓ cup finely chopped onion

⅔ cup milk
1 (12-ounce) can whole kernel
  corn, drained (optional)
½ cup grated cheddar cheese
2 teaspoons chopped pimiento
¼ cup catsup

Combine beef, salt, pepper, thyme, crackers, onion, and milk. Roll out or pat out on wax paper into 12-inch square. Combine corn, cheese, and pimiento. Spread over meat mixture. Roll as a jellyroll, sealing edges. Place on a rack in an open roasting pan. Bake at 350 degrees for 30 minutes. Brush catsup over loaf and continue baking 30 minutes more. Serves 6.

Mrs. Dudley Davis (Josephine Camp)

MULTI-PURPOSE MEAT SAUCE

2 pounds ground meat, browned
  and drained
2 (16-ounce) cans stewed tomatoes
2 tablespoons Worcestershire sauce
Seasoned salt and pepper to taste
½ cup chopped bell pepper
  (optional)

2 medium onions, chopped
1 (10-ounce) can tomato soup
½ cup Heinz catsup
1 (6-ounce) can sliced mushrooms, drained

Add meat, tomatoes, Worcestershire sauce, seasoned salt, pepper, bell pepper, onions, soup, catsup, and mushrooms to a heavy 3-quart saucepan and simmer 3 hours. Add water if needed to achieve desired thickness.

Note: I prepare this recipe in triple quantity to take to the beach for a week, or to freeze ahead for busy weeks. Can be used for tacos, spaghetti, sloppy joes, pizza, lasagna, chili, tamale pie. I freeze in 1-quart containers. Just right for my family of five.

Mrs. Wilfred W. Yeargan, Jr. (Mary Gail Williams)

STUFFED CABBAGE

1 large head cabbage
1½ pounds ground beef
1 small onion, chopped
¼ cup green bell pepper, chopped
2 eggs, beaten
½ cup cooked long-grain rice
1 teaspoon salt

⅛ teaspoon pepper
⅛ teaspoon marjoram
Butter or margarine
1 (16-ounce) can stewed tomatoes
½ cup water
1 tablespoon vinegar
1 tablespoon sugar

Cut out and discard core of cabbage. Remove large outside leaves; reserve. Working from the bottom, use a sharp paring knife to hollow out cabbage, leaving a shell about ½ inch thick. Place cabbage shell and leaves in a large bowl; add boiling water to cover; let stand 10 minutes. Drain. Thoroughly combine beef, onion, bell pepper, eggs, rice, salt, pepper, and marjoram. Fill cabbage shell, mounding mixture on top. Dot with butter. Press softened outside leaves around stuffed cabbage shell. Tie with soft cord or secure with toothpicks to hold shape. Place in a Dutch oven. Combine tomatoes, water, vinegar, and sugar. Pour around cabbage. Cover. Bake at 325 degrees for 2½ hours. Serves 6.

Mrs. Melford Espey, Jr. (Rebecca "Becky" Flowers)

SPECIAL SPAGHETTI

2 tablespoons olive oil
1 medium onion, chopped
2 cloves garlic, minced
1½ to 2 pounds ground meat, either beef or mixture of beef, veal, pork
2 (1-pound) cans tomatoes
1 (8-ounce) can tomato sauce
1 (6-ounce) can tomato paste

1 (8-ounce) can mushrooms
¼ cup chopped parsley
1½ teaspoons oregano
½ teaspoon thyme
Salt and pepper to taste
2 bay leaves
Spaghetti, 1 pound or more if desired, cooked according to directions

Brown onion and garlic in oil. Add meat and brown. Add tomatoes, tomato sauce, tomato paste, mushrooms, parsley, oregano, thyme, salt, pepper, and bay leaves and simmer at least 2½ hours, one of those hours uncovered. The longer the cooking time, the better! Serve over spaghetti. May pour ¼ cup melted margarine over cooked and drained spaghetti. Serves 6-8.

Mrs. Joe Lee Hutt (Joanna Cravey)

CHINESE HASH

1 pound ground chuck
2 medium onions, chopped
1 cup celery, chopped
2 tablespoons oil
1 (10¾-ounce) can cream of chicken soup (undiluted)
1 (10¾-ounce) can cream of mushroom soup (undiluted)

1½ cups warm water
½ cup uncooked rice
2 tablespoons soy sauce (up to ¼ cup, depending on taste)
1 (3-ounce) can Chinese noodles
1 (3-ounce) can French fried onion rings

Brown ground chuck, onions, and celery in oil. Mix well chicken soup, mushroom soup, water, rice, soy sauce, and Chinese noodles. Add to other ingredients. Bake in 9 x 12-inch casserole covered for 30 minutes at 350 degrees. Uncover and cook for 35 minutes more. Cover top with French fried onions and bake for 15 minutes more. Serve as is or over rice. For variation add 1 (6-ounce) can water chestnuts and ½ pound fresh mushrooms (or a 4-ounce can sliced mushrooms). Men who do not usually like casserole dishes really go for this! Serves 6 to 8.

Mrs. Ronald W. Laycock (Debby Barton)

SWEET AND SOUR BEEF

2 pounds ground beef
1 large onion, chopped
1 tablespoon vinegar
¼ cup brown sugar
1 teaspoon mustard

1 (6-ounce) can tomato paste
1 pint tomato juice
1 cup water
2 teaspoons salt

Brown meat and onions together. Drain and add vinegar, brown sugar, mustard, tomato paste and juice, water, and salt. Bring to a boil; reduce heat and cook slowly for 2 hours. Serve on toasted buns or in split Pita Bread (See Index).

Mrs. Winfrey Sanderson (Annette Harrison)

TACO SALAD

4 cups shredded lettuce
½ cup sliced green onions with
 tops
1 pound ground chuck
¼ cup chopped onions

1 (15-ounce) can chili beans or
 kidney beans, drained
1 (4-ounce) can taco sauce
8 ounces cheddar cheese,
 shredded

Toss lettuce and green onions in large bowl. Refrigerate. Brown meat in skillet. Add chopped onion and cook until tender. Stir in beans and taco sauce. Simmer 15 minutes. Spread hot meat mixture over lettuce in bowl. Sprinkle with cheese. Serve without stirring or tossing. 4 servings.

Mrs. Thomas R. Wear, II

TORTILLA CASSEROLE

2 pounds ground beef
1 (10-ounce) can enchilada sauce
1 (10¾-ounce) can cream of
 mushroom soup
1 (10½-ounce) can beef consomme

1 pound grated cheddar cheese
1 (8-ounce) package tortillas, cut
 bite size
1 large onion, chopped

Brown ground meat, onion, then drain grease. Add enchilada sauce, mushroom soup, and consomme. Heat to boiling. In 9 x 13-inch baking dish, alternate layers of tortillas, meat mixture, and cheese. Bake 30 minutes at 350 degrees. Serves 7 to 10.

Mrs. Richard L. Chaffin (Royce Woodley)

GROUNDMEAT UPSIDE-DOWN DINNER

1½ cups onion rings
1 pound ground beef
⅓ green bell pepper, diced
Salt to taste
¼ teaspoon pepper
1½ teaspoons chili powder
2 cups canned tomatoes

1 cup buttermilk
½ teaspoon soda
1 egg, beaten
2¼ teaspoons sugar
½ teaspoon salt
¾ cup corn meal
1½ tablespoons cooking oil

In skillet brown onion rings, ground beef, and green pepper with salt, pepper, and chili powder. Add tomatoes and bring to a boil. Pour mixture into a 2-quart casserole. Make topping by combining buttermilk, soda, beaten egg, sugar, and salt. Add corn meal a little at a time and then add the oil. Pour topping over mixture and bake at 450 degrees for 25-30 minutes. Serves 4.

Mrs. William M. "Billy" Curtis (Peggy Rice)

BEEF NOODLE CASSEROLE

1 (8-ounce) package wide egg
    noodles
2 pounds ground chuck
½ cup bell pepper, chopped
6 green onions, chopped
Salt to taste
1 (15-ounce) can tomatoes

1 (6-ounce) can tomato sauce
½ teaspoon garlic powder
1 (8-ounce) package cream
    cheese
½ cup sour cream
½ cup cottage cheese
½ cup cheddar cheese

Cook and drain noodles according to package directions. Brown the ground chuck. Add bell pepper, onions, and salt to taste. Cook until tender. Add tomatoes, tomato sauce, garlic powder, cream cheese, sour cream, cooked noodles, and cottage cheese. Place in a 3-quart casserole dish and top with cheddar cheese. Bake 30 minutes at 350 degrees. Serves 10.

Mrs. Rufus L. Moore (Polly Shirley)

MEXICAN TORTE

1 (13¾-ounce) package hot roll
  mix
1 pound ground beef
1 (1.25-ounce) package taco
  seasoning
1 cup chopped onion

1 (10-ounce) package chopped
  frozen spinach
1 cup cottage cheese
Salt and pepper to taste
1 egg, beaten with 1 teaspoon
  water

Prepare hot roll mix according to package directions. Brown hamburger and onion; drain well. Mix hamburger and taco seasoning. Cook spinach and squeeze dry. Mix with cottage cheese and season to taste. Divide roll dough into 3 parts and roll each in a circle to fit spring-form pan. Grease bottom and sides of pan and fit in dough round. Top with meat mixture and add second dough round. Top with spinach-cheese mixture and top with final dough round. Let rise about 1 hour. Score top with very sharp knife into six sections. Brush with egg wash and bake at 350 degrees for 45 to 50 minutes. Serves 6.

Mrs. Mark Bergaas (Mary Emmons)

QUICK LASAGNE

1 (5-ounce) package egg noodles
1½ to 2 pounds ground beef
1 heaping teaspoon salt
¼ teaspoon pepper
½ teaspoon garlic salt
1 (15-ounce) can tomato sauce

1 cup creamed cottage cheese
1 cup sour cream
1 cup chopped green onion
  (about 3 bunches)
1 cup shredded mozzarella cheese
  (or sharp cheese)

Cook noodles; drain. Brown meat; add salt, pepper, garlic, and tomato sauce. Simmer 5 minutes. Combine cottage cheese, sour cream, onion, and noodles in a large mixing bowl. Alternate layers of noodles and meat in 2-quart casserole. Start with noodle layer; end with meat layer (4 layers in all). Sprinkle cheese on top. Bake at 250 degrees for 25 minutes. Yield: 4-5 servings.

Mrs. Thomas C. McMullen, Jr. (Deloris Madison)

WESTERN CASSEROLE

1 (5-ounce) package large noodles
1 large onion, chopped
1 bell pepper, chopped
½ cup celery, chopped
4 tablespoons oleo
1 pound ground beef
1 (8-ounce) can tomato sauce

1 (14½-ounce) can tomato juice
¼ teaspoon salt
¼ teaspoon chili powder
1 (12-ounce) can niblet corn
1 medium can ripe olives
1 cup grated cheddar cheese

Cook noodles according to package directions. Sauté onion, bell pepper, and celery in oleo. Brown meat in this skillet and return onion, pepper, and celery. Add tomato sauce, tomato juice, salt, chili powder, corn, and olives. Mix with noodles. Place in 2-quart casserole. Press in cheese. Bake at 350 degrees for 20-30 minutes, until cheese melts. Serves 6 to 8.

Mrs. Paul Guthrie, Jr. (Donna Gortney)

ALMOND BEEF IMPERIAL

2 pounds ground beef
2 tablespoons drippings
1 teaspoon salt
2 cups chopped celery
¼ cup chopped green pepper
½ cup chopped onion
1 (2-ounce) jar pimiento
1 (4-ounce) can mushrooms
  (stems and pieces)

1 (10¾-ounce) can cream of
  mushroom soup
¼ cup soy sauce
½ cup water
1 (8-ounce) package noodles,
  cooked
1 cup sour cream
Almonds for topping

Brown meat in drippings. Add salt, celery, pepper, onions, pimiento, mushrooms and liquid, soup, soy sauce, and water. Cover tightly and simmer until tender. Combine noodles and sour cream with meat mixture. Place in greased casserole. Top with almonds. Bake at 325 degrees for 30 minutes. Serves 8.

Mrs. Edwin L. Minges (Pearl Mangum)

BEEF CORN BREAD

1 cup corn meal
1 cup milk
1 (16-ounce) can cream style corn
2 eggs, well beaten
½ teaspoon soda
¾ teaspoon salt

¼ cup bacon drippings
½ pound ground beef, sautéed
1 large onion, chopped
½ pound cheese, grated
2 jalapeño peppers, chopped

Mix corn meal, milk, corn, eggs, soda, salt, and bacon drippings. Grease large skillet or casserole dish. Pour ½ batter into skillet and sprinkle with beef, onion, cheese, and peppers. Pour remaining batter over top. Bake at 350 degrees for 1 hour. To freeze: prepare, freeze, and then bake. Serves 6 to 8.

Mrs. Haskell Nevin (Sister Woodfin)

SOUTH OF THE BORDER SPAGHETTI

1 large onion, diced
1 large bell pepper, diced
1 (28-ounce) can tomatoes
1 (28-ounce) can water
1 teaspoon salt

½ teaspoon pepper
2 tablespoons Mexene chili powder
1 pound ground round steak
8 ounces spaghetti
1 tablespoon salt

Dice onion and bell pepper into small pieces and cook until golden brown in bacon grease. Add meat and cook until brown. Add salt, pepper, and Mexene. Next add tomatoes and water. Let simmer slowly, stirring occasionally. Cook 30 to 45 minutes or longer. Serve over spaghetti. Serves 6.

Mrs. Ward McFarland (Frances Morrow)

BEEF-RICE ORIENTAL

1 small garlic button, minced
3 tablespoons salad oil
1½ cups diced cooked beef (or any
  left over ham, chicken, or
  shrimp)
1⅓ cups Minute rice

⅛ teaspoon pepper
2 cups hot water
1½ cups shredded lettuce,
  spinach, or escarole
2 tablespoons soy sauce

Sauté garlic in oil. Add meat, rice, pepper, and hot water, and mix just enough to moisten rice. Bring quickly to a boil over high heat. Cover and remove from heat. Let stand 5 minutes. Just before serving, add shredded lettuce and soy sauce and toss lightly. Make this in a 10-inch iron skillet.

Mrs. Carl W. Albright, Jr. (Rainer Lamar)

BOEUF BOURGUIGNONNE

4 slices bacon
3 pounds lean boneless beef, cut
  in bite-size pieces
½ can beef bouillon
1 tablespoon tomato paste
½ teaspoon leaf thyme
1 teaspoon salt
Freshly ground black pepper
1 bay leaf

2 cloves garlic, minced
2-3 cups good dry red wine
12-18 small boiling onions
½-¾ pound fresh mushrooms or
  canned
Flour and water to make a paste
Chopped parsley (optional)
¼ cup brandy (optional)

Simmer bacon in water 10 minutes; drain and dry well. (This eliminates smoky flavor.) Cut in ½-inch pieces. Place in heavy casserole. Brown beef in bacon fat (with a little oil if needed). Transfer to casserole and deglaze skillet with wine. Add beef bouillon, tomato paste, thyme, salt, pepper, bay leaf, and garlic. Pour enough wine to barely cover meat. Place casserole over direct heat, bring to a simmer, cover, and bake at 300 degrees for 3-4 hours, or until meat is tender, basting occasionally. If liquid cooks down, add more wine, bouillon, or mushroom liquid.

Vegetables: Peel onions (blanching for 1 minute makes this easier), and simmer in beef broth (bouillon cube in water will work) until tender. Reserve liquid. Slice or quarter mushrooms if large and sauté in butter. When meat is done, drain off gravy and add to it any leftover liquid from mushrooms or onions. Boil down about 5 minutes and add a flour-water paste gradually to thicken. Combine vegetables and meat and pour gravy over all. Sprinkle chopped parsley over top of all if desired. Flambé at the last minute with brandy. Serves 6-8.

Mrs. Robert L. McCurley, Jr. (Martha Dawson)

BEEF TENDER ON GRILL

1 beef tender (filet)
Salt

Pepper
Garlic salt

Build fire in grill with lid on one side of grill. Add hickory chips. Allow fire to burn down. Sprinkle tender with salt, pepper and garlic salt. Smoke tender on low fire for 40 minutes for rare beef.

Mrs. Lee Pake (Betty Gilpin)

CURRIED BEEF AND RICE

2 tablespoons green spring onions
1 pound fresh mushrooms or 1
  (8-ounce) can mushrooms
2 tablespoons butter
2 tablespoons flour
½ cup half and half or cream
Salt and pepper to taste
Sherry
½ cup sour cream

1 (3-ounce) package cream cheese
2 cups cooked roast beef or more
1 (10-ounce) package frozen
  chopped spinach, cooked
1 (6-ounce) package Uncle Ben's
  wild rice, cooked
1 teaspoon curry powder
Paprika

Sauté onions and mushrooms in butter. Add flour. Add half and half or cream, salt and pepper. Thin with a little sherry. Add sour cream and cream cheese, then beef. Add cooked chopped spinach. Cook Uncle Ben's rice according to directions on package. Mix all together, add curry powder, and put in large casserole dish. Sprinkle with paprika. Heat at 325 degrees about 30 minutes. Serves 8.

Note: Good company or luncheon dish!

Mrs. Gene Bennett (Belle Walter)

JEAN COBB'S QUICK CHOW MEIN

¼ cup margarine
1 pound cubed pork
1 medium onion, chopped
2 cups celery, diced
1½ cups water
2 teaspoons salt
1 (12-ounce) can bean sprouts

1 (6-ounce) can mushrooms
1 (6-ounce) can water chestnuts
2 tablespoons cornstarch
2 tablespoons soy sauce
2 tablespoons water
2 tablespoons sugar

Brown meat in margarine. Add onions and cook until transparent. Add celery, water, and salt. Let come to a boil. Cover and simmer 25 minutes. Add drained bean sprouts, mushrooms, and water chestnuts. In a small bowl, mix together the cornstarch, soy sauce, water, and sugar. Add to meat mixture and cook until thick. Serve over hot rice or warm chow mein noodles. Serves 4.

Mrs. L. Page Stalcup, III (Rinna Cobb)—Mobile, AL

PORK CHOP CASSEROLE

4 thick pork chops
6 tablespoons rice (raw)
1 onion, sliced thin
1 tomato, sliced thin
4 slices green pepper

Salt to taste
Pepper to taste
Dash of marjoram
Dash of thyme
1 (10½-ounce) can consommé

Brown pork chops and place on top of raw rice in casserole. Add pork chop drippings. Place slices of onion, tomato, and green pepper on each chop. Salt and pepper each chop and sprinkle with herbs. Pour consommé on top, cover, and bake at 350 degrees for 1 hour.

Mrs. Edward M. Streit (Eleanor Gage)

OVEN PORK CHOPS

6 pork chops, ½ to ¾ inch thick
1 tablespoon oil
Salt and pepper
1 (10¾-ounce) can cream of
    chicken soup (undiluted)

3 tablespoons catsup
1 tablespoon Worcestershire sauce
1 medium onion, sliced

Brown pork chops in oil, and season to taste with salt and pepper. Place drained chops in 2-quart casserole dish. Combine cream of chicken soup, catsup, Worcestershire sauce, and onion, then pour over pork chops. Cover and place in 350-degree oven for 45 minutes. Serves 6.

Mrs. Carlos "Sonny" Shows (Gloria Church)

TRADER VIC'S CHA SUI (Barbecued Pork)

2 pounds pork tenderloin
3 ounces bourbon or dark rum
1½ teaspoons salt
3 tablespoons sugar

3 tablespoons soy sauce
Chinese mustard and catsup or
    cocktail sauce

Cut pork tenderloin into 2 long strips. Mix bourbon, salt, sugar, and soy sauce into a paste and rub into the meat. Let stand for an hour or two so the flavor penetrates the meat, then barbecue or broil slowly for 1 hour. When cool, cut into thin diagonal slices and serve with Chinese mustard and catsup or cocktail sauce. Serves 4.

Mrs. Frank Mann (Faith McNamee)

HERBED PORK CHOPS BRAISED IN WHITE WINE

1 teaspoon dried sage leaves, crumbled
1 teaspoon dried rosemary leaves, crumbled
1 teaspoon finely chopped garlic
1 teaspoon salt
Pinch of freshly ground pepper
4 pork chops (preferably center-cut and about 1 inch thick)

2 tablespoons butter
1 tablespoon olive oil
¾ cup dry white wine (try apple wine for a different flavor)
1 tablespoon finely chopped fresh parsley (preferably the Italian kind)

If possible, buy whole sage and rosemary leaves and crumble with a mortar and pestle. Combine the sage, rosemary, garlic, salt, and pepper (the garlic may be chopped and combined with the other ingredients all in one step in a food processor), and press a little of this mixture into both sides of each pork chop. In a heavy 10- to 12-inch skillet, melt the butter with the olive oil over moderate heat. When the foam subsides, place the chops in the hot fat and brown them for 2 or 3 minutes on each side, turning with tongs to preserve juiciness. When the chops are golden brown, remove them from the pan to a platter. Pour off all but a thin layer of fat from the pan, add ½ cup of the wine and bring it to a boil. Return the chops to the pan, cover, and reduce heat to the barest simmer. Basting with pan juices occasionally (add water if necessary), cook the chops for 25-30 minutes, or until they are tender. Transfer the chops to a heated serving platter and pour the remaining ¼ cup of wine into the pan. Boil it briskly over high heat, stirring and scraping in any browned bits that cling to the bottom and sides of the pan, until it has reduced to a few tablespoons of syrupy glaze. Remove from heat, taste for seasoning, stir in the parsley, and pour over the chops for serving.

Mark Bergaas

KID'S SAUCY CHOPS

4 pork chops, ½-inch thick
2 tablespoons shortening, oil, or bacon drippings
Salt and pepper

1 (10¾-ounce) can cream of mushroom soup
¼ cup catsup (optional)
Onion slices (optional)

Preheat oven to 375 degrees. Heat oil in large skillet and brown chops on both sides on medium high heat. Put browned chops into casserole. Season them lightly with salt and pepper. Pour soup over meat. Cover and bake for 40 minutes. You may add ¼ cup catsup and a slice of onion on top of each chop as you place in oven to bake.

Mrs. Ralph Quarles (Kat Pritchett)

ROAST LOIN OF PORK WITH SHERRY SAUCE

1 (10-pound) pork loin, boned
  and trimmed
4 teaspoons salt
1 teaspoon pepper
1 teaspoon sugar

¼ teaspoon cayenne
2 teaspoons sage
Chablis or Sauterne
Boiling water

Rub loin with salt, pepper, sugar, and cayenne. Put in 450-degree oven for 10 minutes. Reduce temperature to 300 degrees. Sprinkle with sage, pour wine over meat, and bake 30 minutes per pound. Baste with more wine. Save gravy and pour off fat. Add boiling water (2 tablespoons) to pan and scrape up brown bits. Add enough boiling water to make 1½ cups of gravy.

SHERRY SAUCE:
2 tablespoons butter or margarine
2 tablespoons chives
1½ cups gravy (without fat)
2 tablespoons freshly squeezed
  lemon juice

¼ cup sherry (cooking)
Cornstarch (if desired)

Melt butter and sauté chives. Add gravy, then lemon juice and bring to a boil. Stir in sherry and reheat. May be thickened with cornstarch at the end. Makes 2 cups. Serve the sauce in heated gravy boat accompanying pork. Serves 8.

Mrs. Tom Patton (Suse Donald)

SPANISH PORK CHOPS

4 to 6 center-cut pork chops,
  ½-inch thick
Vegetable or salad oil
1 teaspoon salt
½ teaspoon chili powder
½ teaspoon pepper

½ cup chopped onion
⅓ cup bell pepper
½ cup long grain rice
1 (28-ounce) can tomatoes
1 cup grated cheddar cheese

Brown pork chops in oil in skillet. Drain and sprinkle with mixture of salt, chili powder, and pepper. Top with onion, bell pepper, and rice. Pour tomatoes over all. Simmer 1 hour. Add cheese and simmer until it melts. Serves 4.

Mrs. James L. Stephens (Janet Sherer)—Jacksonville, FL

PORK CHOP AND POTATO CASSEROLE

4 medium potatoes
2 large onions
4 medium-thick pork chops (more
   if you have heavy eaters)

Salt and pepper to taste
Milk - regular

Peel and thinly slice potatoes and onions. Place a layer of potatoes in bottom of dish (13x9x2-inch); salt and pepper layer. Next, place a layer of onions; salt and pepper layer. Arrange on top of the two layers the pork chops that have been seasoned with salt and pepper on both sides. Carefully pour milk into dish until it is about ½ inch deep in dish. Cover dish with foil, sealing around edges, and bake, covered, at 325 degrees for 1¼ hours. Uncover and bake 15 minutes more to brown chops. Serves 4.

Note: Important to slice the onions and potatoes thinly in order for them to cook thoroughly in the length of time stated. All that is needed to accompany this casserole is a vegetable or salad, since the meat and potatoes are cooking together. Most men love this combination!

Mrs. Dom Elmore (Susan Rogers)

ORANGE PORK CHOPS

8 pork chops, medium thick
1 stick butter
Salt and pepper

2 cups orange juice
2 tablespoons orange marmalade
   (if desired)

Brown both sides of pork chops in butter in hot electric skillet. Salt and pepper to taste. Pour orange juice over chops. Cover and simmer until done (usually about 1 hour, but time varies with thickness of chops). Add more juice if necessary, and 2 tablespoons of orange marmalade for added flavor, if desired. This makes a delicious gravy for rice. Serves 4.

Mrs. Thomas W. Moore (Stella Hillard)

COUNTRY HAM—GRANDMOTHER'S METHOD

1 (10-12 pound) country ham

Two days before serving, soak ham 24 hours in cold water. Next day at 7 p.m. have oven at 500 degrees. Put ham in covered roaster with 5 cups water. Put this in oven and immediately turn oven to 350 degrees. Leave 15 minutes. Turn oven back to 500 degrees. When oven heat reaches 500 degrees, leave for 15 minutes. Turn oven off and in the morning the ham is done. NEVER OPEN THE DOOR WHILE HAM IS BAKING.

Mrs. Peterson Cavert (Mary Beth Wear)

HAM PIE WITH CHEESE BISCUIT TOPPING

3 tablespoons onion, chopped
4 tablespoons green pepper,
  chopped
4 tablespoons butter or margarine
6 tablespoons flour
1(10¾-ounce) can cream of
  chicken soup
CHEESE BISCUIT TOPPING:
1 cup biscuit mix
½ cup sharp cheese, grated

1⅓ cups milk
2 cups diced ham
2 hard-boiled eggs, sliced
1 tablespoon lemon juice

⅓ cup milk

In a large skillet, cook onion and pepper in butter until soft, not brown. Add flour, heat, and mix thoroughly. Add soup and milk, and stir over medium heat until thick and smooth. Add ham, eggs, and lemon juice, and turn to low while making biscuits. Mix together the biscuit mix and cheese, then add the milk and stir just until all the flour is blended. Turn out onto a floured surface, roll, and cut into biscuits. Pour ham mixture into a large buttered casserole and top with biscuits. Bake at 450 degrees for 15 minutes, then reduce to 400 degrees, and cook until biscuits are brown. Cover loosely if browning too fast to be cooked thoroughly. Delicious! Serves 6.

Mrs. Larry Satterwhite—Birmingham, AL

HAM LOAF

2½ pounds raw pork (no fat),
  ground
3½ pounds raw cured ham,
  ground

1 cup cracker meal
4 eggs
½ teaspoon salt

SAUCE:
½ cup vinegar
2 tablespoons dry mustard

1 cup water
1 cup light brown sugar

Mix pork, ham, cracker meal, eggs, and salt with hands. Form into 2 loaves. Make flat on top. Cover with foil. Bake loaves at 350 degrees for 30 minutes and pour off excess grease. Continue cooking for 1½ hours, basting with sauce. Remove foil for last 10 minutes. For sauce, mix vinegar, mustard, water, and sugar in saucepan and simmer until slightly syrupy. Serves 6-8.

Comments: The loaves freeze quite well. Instead of loaves, make small balls and cook in large skillet until done. Serve in chafing dish with sauce.

Mrs. Daniel M. Hoke (Gail Ford)

BET BET'S CRÊPES

1 cup butter or Mazola margarine
1 cup flour
4 cups milk (2 cups hot water,
   2 cups evaporated milk)
1 teaspoon salt

⅛ teaspoon cayenne
2 cups finely diced ham
2 cups finely diced Swiss cheese
Crêpes (See Index)
Parmesan cheese

Melt butter over low heat in 4-quart saucepan. Blend in flour, stirring until mixture is smooth and bubbly, about 1 minute. Remove from heat. Slowly stir in warm milk. Stir until mixture is smooth. Return boiler to heat and *stir constantly* until mixture thickens and comes to boil. Boil 1 minute. If by some misfortune your sauce is lumpy, you may throw it in a glass blender and blend the lumps out, then return it to the heat. This should not happen if you slowly add *warm milk* to the warm flour and butter mixture. Add salt and cayenne. To this thick white sauce, add 1½ cups cooked ham and 1½ cups Swiss cheese, saving ½ cup of each for garnish. Stir. Cheese will melt and sauce will become very thick. You may cover this and set aside to use immediately, or you may refrigerate it for use in a day or so.

Make crêpes in 4- to 5-inch pan. Spread with ham-cheese mixture. Roll and place rolled side down, smooth side up on greased cookie sheet or shallow pan. Brush with melted butter. Garnish with ham and cheese bits by sprinkling on top. Seal with aluminum foil and freeze or place in refrigerator. Remove foil and dust with Parmesan cheese before baking. Bake at 375 degrees for 10-12 minutes if not frozen; 12-18 minutes if frozen.

Mrs. Edward "Flash" Florey, Jr. (Betty Finklea)

HAM AND BROCCOLI CASSEROLE

1 cup cooked rice
1 (10-ounce) package frozen
   chopped broccoli, cooked
6 tablespoons butter or margarine
1 whole onion, chopped
2 cups milk

1 tablespoon seasoned salt
½ teaspoon garlic powder
3 tablespoons flour
2 cups chopped ham
1½ cups cheddar cheese, grated
1 cup bread crumbs, crushed fine

Put rice in greased casserole dish; cover with broccoli. In saucepan, melt butter and sauté onion. Turn to low and add milk, seasoned salt, garlic powder, and flour. Add chopped ham and heat 2-3 minutes. Pour over broccoli, then cover with cheese and bread crumbs. Cook at 300 to 350 degrees for 30-45 minutes. Serves 8.

Mrs. James William McFarland (Miriam Webster)

HAM AND ASPARAGUS CASSEROLE

2 (8¼-ounce) cans asparagus tips	½ cup chopped onion
2 cups chopped ham	3 cups milk
3 hard-boiled eggs, sliced	½ cup Parmesan cheese
½ cup margarine	Salt and pepper to taste
½ cup flour	Pulled bread crumbs

Put two layers of asparagus, ham, and sliced eggs in casserole. Melt margarine, add flour, and cook over low heat until smooth. Add onion and cook until soft, not brown, stirring constantly. Add milk *slowly* and continue stirring until mixture begins to thicken. Add cheese and stir until melted. Add salt and pepper to taste. Pour this over casserole and top with pulled bread crumbs. Bake at 350 degrees for 30 minutes, or until bubbly. Yield: 4-6 servings.

Note: Easy and can be made ahead of time and refrigerated. Great for luncheon with congealed salad and rolls.

Mrs. Charles R. Pearce (Elizabeth Cunningham)

BAKED HAM

1 (10- to 12-pound) uncooked ham	1 cup brown sugar
2 to 3 sticks cinnamon	1 tablespoon dry mustard
1 tablespoon whole cloves	Pineapple juice
1 cup vinegar	1 (14-ounce) can sliced pineapple
1 cup white sugar	¼ cup vinegar
3 cloves garlic or 1 button (optional)	¾ cup water

Place ham in kettle large enough to completely cover with water. Pour boiling water over the ham and add cinnamon, cloves, vinegar, sugar, and garlic. Let remain in kettle over very slow heat for approximately 3¼ hours. Do not let the liquid boil; keep heat just high enough to see bubbles coming up in the liquid. Turn off heat, and let ham stand in liquid and seasonings for at least 4 hours or overnight. Take ham from liquid, remove skin and surplus fat. Blend brown sugar, dry mustard, with enough pineapple juice to make a paste. Pat this over top and sides of ham. Place in baking pan; add pineapple slices for garnish. Then add vinegar (or pineapple juice) and water to pan. Bake at 350 degrees for 1 to 2 hours, basting frequently. Save basting drippings, dilute with a little water, and spoon over ham slices after cutting.

Mrs. Carlos "Sonny" Shows (Gloria Church)

HAM JUBILEE

5 pounds boned cooked ham
1½ tablespoons cornstarch
⅓ cup sugar
¼ teaspoon cinnamon
⅛ teaspoon cloves
2 tablespoons concentrated orange
  juice

1 (16-ounce) can pitted Bing
  cherries, drained (reserve juice)
¾ cup Bing cherry juice
¾ cup sweet vermouth

Bake ham uncovered at 300 degrees for 2 hours. Lay a tent of foil over top while baking. Combine cornstarch, sugar, cinnamon, cloves, orange juice, cherry juice, and vermouth. Simmer for 2 minutes, then add cherries. Baste ham with part of the sauce. Serve ham sliced with the balance of the warmed sauce.

Mrs. David M. Cochrane (Mary B. Tompkins)

PAKE MEATBALLS

1 pound ground pork
¼ cup minced mushrooms
1 (5- to 6-ounce) can water chestnuts
2 tablespoons soy sauce
1 tablespoon sherry
½ teaspoon salt

½ teaspoon sugar
½ teaspoon MSG, Accent
¼ teaspoon garlic powder
1 egg, beaten
2 tablespoons cornstarch
Oil for frying

Mix pork with mushrooms and water chestnuts; add soy sauce, sherry, salt, sugar, MSG, and garlic powder, then beaten egg, and mix thoroughly. Sprinkle meat mixture with cornstarch and shape into balls about 1 inch in diameter. Fry in deep fat until golden brown. Drain. Serve on toothpicks and serve very hot, with Chinese mustard and catsup or cocktail sauce. Makes 30 to 35 meatballs.

Mrs. Frank Mann (Faith McNamee)

BARBECUED LEG OF LAMB

1 leg of lamb, approximately 6
  pounds

1 recipe Superb Barbecue Sauce
  (See Index)

Sear lamb on all sides over hot coals. Then put hood of cooker down and cook 1½-2 hours, or 10-12 minutes per pound, basting the last 30 minutes with sauce. Serve with additional sauce, heated.

Note: This makes a medium rare roast, pink and juicy, and is a nice change from mint or curry with lamb. Leftovers make great sandwiches, served with barbecue sauce on a bun.

Mrs. Peterson Cavert (Mary Beth Wear)

JEWELED FRANKS

4 franks
2 tablespoons sweet pickle relish
2 tablespoons onion, chopped
  fine

½ cup sour cream
2 tablespoons prepared mustard
½ cup shredded cheese
Hotdog caddies or buns

Heat franks according to package directions. Mix relish, onions, sour cream, and mustard. Place frank on hotdog caddie (great new idea for hotdogs or whatever—does not fall apart at the bottom) or buns. Spread sour cream mixture on frank. Sprinkle with cheese and place under broiler until cheese melts. Serves 2 to 4.

Note: Easy to multiply!

Peggy Bishop—Tuscaloosa County Home Agent

BARBECUE FRANKS

2 tablespoons prepared mustard
2 (8-ounce) cans tomato sauce
  (2 cups)
½ cup dark corn syrup
⅓ cup vinegar
⅓ cup onion, minced

2 tablespoons Worcestershire
  sauce
½ teaspoon celery seed
¼ to ½ teaspoon hot pepper sauce
1 pound (8-10) frankfurters,
  scored diagonally

In a large skillet, blend mustard and tomato sauce. Add corn syrup, vinegar, onion, Worcestershire sauce, celery seed, and hot pepper sauce. Cook over medium heat until mixture boils; reduce heat and simmer gently 30 minutes. Add franks and cook until hot and plumped, 7-8 minutes. Serve over rice. Serves 5 to 6.

Mrs. William R. Shamblin (Sandra Bryant)

LEG OF LAMB

1 leg of lamb
Flour
1 teaspoon ginger
2 tablespoons salt

¼ teaspoon pepper
1 chopped onion
2 tablespoons lard or shortening

SAUCE:
1 tablespoon Worcestershire sauce
1 tablespoon chili sauce
¼ teaspoon sugar

1 cup boiling water
1 tablespoon butter
3-4 slices pineapple

Dredge lamb with flour, ginger, salt, and pepper. Fry onion in lard until transparent. Discard onion and sear lamb in lard. Combine Worcestershire sauce, chili sauce, sugar, boiling water and butter to make sauce. Bake lamb in 300 to 325-degree oven for 35 minutes per pound, basting with sauce. One hour before it is done, place 3 or 4 pineapple slices on top of lamb and continue basting.

Hint: In order to remove skin from leg, place in hot oven for 10 to 15 minutes.

(This recipe originally appeared in The JWA Sampler, published in 1957, under the name Donalda Shelton).

Mrs. A. G. Williams (Martha Millar)

VEAL PARMESAN

1½ pounds veal, thinly cut
Parmesan cheese
Salt and pepper to taste
2 tablespoons Wesson oil
2 beef bouillon cubes, melted in
   a cup of water

⅓ cup of sherry
1 tablespoon butter or oleo
1 tablespoon flour
2 teaspoons vinegar

Cut veal in 3-inch squares or small pieces. Pound thin and dredge with Parmesan cheese, salt, and pepper. Brown slowly in oil in skillet. Add bouillon and sherry. Cover and simmer 15 minutes. Make a paste with melted butter and flour and thicken gravy. Add vinegar and serve at once on rice. Serves 6.

Mrs. Robert A. Drew (Jackie Atchison)

SAUSAGE CASSEROLE

1½ to 2 pounds bulk pork sausage
(can use 1 pound hot and
1 pound mild)
1 cup onion, chopped
1 cup green pepper, chopped
Margarine
1 cup celery, chopped

1 cup toasted slivered almonds
2 envelopes of Lipton's Chicken
Noodle soup mix (4.0-ounce
box)
½ cup wild rice or brown rice,
raw
5 cups water

Sauté and crumble sausage; drain. Sauté onion and green pepper until soft in margarine. Mix the sausage, onion, green pepper with celery, almonds, soup, and rice, then add the water. Pour into a casserole and bake, covered, 1½ hours at 375 degrees, stirring every now and then. Serves 8-10.

Note: Good with mushroom gravy.

Mrs. Charles S. Watson

PIZZA

2 pounds sausage
1 (13¾-ounce) box Pillsbury Hot
Roll mix (See Note)
1 (15-ounce) can spaghetti sauce
with meat
1 (15-ounce) can tomato sauce
with tomato bits
1½ cups chopped bell pepper

1½ cups chopped onion
3 (3-ounce) cans chopped
mushrooms
1 (3½-ounce) package sliced
pepperoni
1½ cups shredded mozzarella
cheese

Brown sausage. Pour into colander to drain all grease and wipe out grease in skillet with paper towel. Return meat to skillet. Add spaghetti sauce and tomato sauce. Warm. Grease three 12-inch pizza pans. Dissolve package of yeast (included in roll mix) in 1 cup warm water. Stir in roll mix to make dough. Divide dough into 3 parts and press each part into a pizza pan. Top with layer of meat mixture, then add pepperoni, bell pepper, onion, and mushrooms. Start cooking at 425 degrees, then raise temperature to 450 degrees after about 10 minutes. Cook another 10 minutes, or until crust browns lightly and filling bubbles. Top with shredded cheese just before removing from the oven. Yield: 3 pizzas.

Note: May use Crust for Pizza (See Index), if desired.

Mrs. Thomas C. McMullen, Jr. (Deloris Madison)

MOCK PIZZA

4 split English muffins
1 (15½-ounce) jar "thick and
  zesty" spaghetti sauce
1 pound sausage

1 package pepperoni slices
  (3½-ounce)
1 (6-ounce) package mozzarella
  cheese slices

Cook sausage until thoroughly done. Drain on paper towel. Spread muffins with spaghetti sauce. Top with crumbled sausage, pepperoni, and cheese. Bake on cookie sheet in 350-degree oven until hot and bubbly. Yield: 8 servings.

Mrs. Howard Garrison (Ashley Smith)

WHITE SAUCES

2 cups milk
2 tablespoons butter
3 tablespoons flour

Salt and pepper to taste
½ teaspoon dry mustard
  (optional)

I. Béchamel
Heat milk to barely simmer. Melt butter in heavy saucepan. Add flour and stir with a wooden spoon for 2 minutes. Add hot milk and stir with a wire whisk to blend smoothly. Bring to a slow boil and boil 2 minutes, stirring constantly. Add ¼ to ½ teaspoon salt, pepper, and mustard, if used. If not used immediately, put a pat of butter on the top of the sauce to prevent crust from forming. This makes a sauce of medium thickness. For a thinner sauce, reduce butter to 1 tablespoon and flour to 1½ tablespoons. For a thicker sauce, use 4 tablespoons butter and 5 tablespoons flour.

II. Veloute'
Make the same as béchamel, but substitute stock (meat, fish, chicken, or vegetable water) for milk, and taste before adding salt, pepper, or mustard.

III. Mornay
Use either preceding recipe and add 1 cup of Swiss cheese, grated, after sauce has come back to a boil. Stir until cheese is melted and sauce is heated through.

Hint: Use a thin white sauce for soups, a medium white sauce for scalloped dishes and cheese sauces, and a thick sauce as a base for croquettes and soufflés.

MARIE'S BARBECUE SAUCE

1 pint vinegar
1 pint catsup
1 pound butter
Juice of 2 lemons
3 tablespoons Worcestershire sauce

1 tablespoon chili powder
½ pound brown sugar
Salt and pepper to taste

In a 1-quart saucepan, combine vinegar, catsup, butter, lemon juice, Worcestershire sauce, chili powder, sugar, salt, and pepper. Bring to a boil over medium heat; turn heat to low and simmer for 10 minutes. If you want to use the sauce on pork or for oven barbecuing, it is best to leave out the butter. It is just as tasty. Makes 1½ pints.

Mrs. Dean Covington (Brenda Wood)

SOUTHERN BARBECUE SAUCE

¼ cup molasses
¼ cup catsup
¼ cup vinegar

¼ cup prepared mustard
¼ cup Worcestershire sauce
⅛ teaspoon cayenne pepper

Mix together the molasses, catsup, vinegar, mustard, Worcestershire sauce, and cayenne. Makes 1¼ cups. Doubles easily.

Mrs. Glenn Powell (Caroline Chappell)

THE ALLEN FAMILY'S
HORSERADISH BARBECUE SAUCE

1 (6-ounce) jar horseradish mustard
⅔ cup or fill jar with vinegar and shake to get mustard out
1 cup water
⅛ teaspoon garlic salt (or 1 clove garlic)

⅛ teaspoon salt
⅛ teaspoon pepper
1 stick of butter or margarine, melted

Mix mustard, vinegar, water, garlic, salt, pepper, and butter thoroughly over medium heat. Store in refrigerator. Delicious on chicken.

Mrs. Allen Mattox (Harriet Marrs)

SUPERB BARBECUE SAUCE

¼ cup vinegar
½ cup water
2 tablespoons sugar
1 tablespoon prepared mustard
½ teaspoon pepper
1½ teaspoons salt
¼ teaspoon cayenne pepper

1 lemon, ends cut off, cut into 2 thick slices
1 medium onion, sliced
½ stick oleo
1½ cups catsup
4 tablespoons Worcestershire sauce

In large saucepan, mix vinegar, water, sugar, mustard, pepper, salt, cayenne, lemon, onion, and oleo. Bring to a boil and simmer 20 minutes. Add catsup and Worcestershire sauce. Bring to a boil. Remove from heat. Especially good on lamb, chicken, pork chops. Baste last half hour of cooking on grill and/or serve at table with meat. Makes about 1 pint.

Mrs. Peterson Cavert (Mary Beth Wear)

BARBECUE SAUCE

1 pound butter
2 tablespoons dry mustard
6 tablespoons Durkee's Sauce
⅓ cup vinegar
⅓ cup lemon juice

8 teaspoons salt
2 tablespoons brown sugar
3 tablespoons Worcestershire sauce
1 tablespoon black pepper

Slowly melt all butter. Add mustard, Durkee's, vinegar, lemon juice, salt, brown sugar, Worcestershire sauce, and pepper. Mix well. Heat when ready to serve.

Mrs. Tommy Whitfield (Carolyn Flanagan)

BROTHER'S BARBECUE SAUCE

½ cup catsup
½ cup chili sauce
1 tablespoon mustard
½-1 teaspoon Tabasco

1 tablespoon Worcestershire sauce
¼ cup brown sugar
¼ cup lemon juice
½ cup water

Combine in a saucepan the catsup, chili sauce, mustard, Tabasco, Worcestershire sauce, brown sugar, lemon juice, and water. Simmer 10 minutes. Quick, easy, and delicious.

Mrs. George Gordon (Jean Fargason)

LEMON BUTTER

¼ cup freshly squeezed lemon
  juice
1 stick cold butter

Dash of salt
Dash of pepper

Using enamel, stainless steel, or glass saucepan, boil lemon juice with salt and pepper until it is reduced by ⅔. Cut butter into 8 pieces, Off heat, whisk in 2 pieces of butter. Then return to low heat and add butter one piece at a time, beating after each addition. Remove from heat.

To warm when serving, add 2 tablespoons hot water from cooking vegetables, or hot fish or chicken stock (depending on what you are serving it with). Fantastic over fresh asparagus!

Mrs. Peterson Cavert (Mary Beth Wear)

BAKED HAM GLAZE

1 (8-ounce) can pineapple
¼ cup brown sugar
2 tablespoons vinegar

¼ teaspoon dry mustard
Dash of cinnamon

In a small saucepan, mix the pineapple, sugar, vinegar, dry mustard, and cinnamon. Boil for 5 minutes. Glaze ham last 30 minutes of baking.

Mrs. Frank Pilsch (Sharon Snyder)

JEZEBEL SAUCE

1 (10-ounce) jar apple jelly
1 (10-ounce) jar pineapple
  preserves

1 (5-ounce) jar horseradish
1 (5-ounce) jar mustard
  (optional)

Mix jelly, preserves, horseradish, and mustard together in blender or with a fork. Serve with ham. Absolutely delicious!! Makes about 30 ounces.

Mrs. Don Barnes (Sue Strickland)

QUICK HORSERADISH SAUCE

1 cup mayonnaise
½ cup prepared horseradish

1 teaspoon prepared mustard

Mix mayonnaise, horseradish, and mustard together with French whisk. I couldn't eat a roast or steak without this sauce!

Mrs. Richard F. Pride (Sandra Wedgeworth)

JUTES FOSTER'S BIG BOY SAUCE

2 (14-ounce) bottles catsup
1 (12-ounce) bottle chili sauce
⅓ cup prepared mustard
2 tablespoons pepper
1 tablespoon dry mustard
1½ cups brown sugar, packed
1½ cups wine vinegar
1 cup fresh lemon juice

½ cup thick steak sauce
Tabasco to taste
¼ cup Lea & Perrins Worcestershire sauce
1 tablespoon soy sauce
2 tablespoons salad oil
1 cup beer

Mix catsup, chili sauce, mustard, pepper, dry mustard, brown sugar, vinegar, lemon juice, steak sauce, Tabasco, Worcestershire sauce, soy sauce, oil, and beer together well. Sauce keeps well in refrigerator. To use, alternate layers of meat and sauce. Cover and heat well before serving. Sauce is good with *all* meats, especially venison. Casseroles can be made ahead and frozen.

Hint: Put the wine vinegar in the catsup and chili bottles, shake well, and you will get all of the catsup and chili sauce out of the bottles.

Mrs. Thomas W. Moore (Stella Hillard)

HORSERADISH SAUCE

1 cup mayonnaise
2 hard-boiled eggs, chopped
2 tablespoons lemon juice
½ teaspoon dried parsley flakes
¼ teaspoon garlic salt

¼ teaspoon celery salt
¼ teaspoon onion salt
1 teaspoon Worcestershire sauce
3 tablespoons horseradish

Blend mayonnaise, eggs, lemon juice, parsley, garlic salt, celery salt, onion salt, Worcestershire sauce, and horseradish. Serve over hot string beans or other vegetables. This will keep several days in refrigerator.

Mrs. James G. Lee II (Becky Thomson)

CRANBERRY-HORSERADISH SAUCE

1 (1-pound) can whole berry
   cranberry sauce

1 tablespoon prepared horseradish, or more to taste

Put cranberry sauce in a bowl and work well with fork. Add horseradish and beat to blend well. Good with cold turkey and roast pork.

FREDDIE WINSTEAD'S REMOULADE SAUCE

2 hard-boiled egg yolks, finely
  grated
¼ cup yellow horseradish mustard
2 tablespoons catsup
¼-½ teaspoon red pepper
1½ teaspoons salt
1 tablespoon paprika

2 cloves garlic, finely chopped
¼ cup tarragon vinegar (do not
  substitute)
½ cup green onions with tops,
  finely chopped
¼ cup salad oil

Mix together the egg yolks, mustard, catsup, pepper, salt, paprika, garlic, vinegar, onions, and oil and refrigerate for a day. The older it gets, the better it gets. Makes 1 cup.

Mrs. Jack McGuire, Jr. (Brantly Cochrane)

GREEN ONION SAUCE

1 bunch young green onions,
  chopped
2 tablespoons butter

Salt
Paprika
Worcestershire sauce

Sauté onions in butter for about 5 minutes. Season with salt and paprika. Add a good dash of Worcestershire. Bring to a boil and serve. Great over steak!

Mrs. Peterson Cavert (Mary Beth Wear)

FOR MARINATING BEEF TENDERLOINS
24 HOURS AHEAD OF COOKING

1½ cups Wesson oil
¾ cup soy sauce
¼ cup Worcestershire sauce
2 tablespoons dried mustard
2½ teaspoons salt

1 tablespoon coarse pepper
  seasoning
¼ cup wine vinegar
1½ teaspoons dried parsley
⅓ cup lemon juice

Mix oil, soy sauce, Worcestershire sauce, mustard, salt, pepper, vinegar, parsley, lemon juice, and pour over tenderloins. Marinate tenderloins for 24 hours. Cook tenderloins for 30 minutes at 350 degrees without sauce, or grill over coals if desired.

Mrs. George Shirley (Betty Bailey)

MEAT MARINADE

1½ cups salad oil
¾ cup soy sauce
¼ cup Worcestershire sauce
2 tablespoons dry mustard
2¼ teaspoons salt

1⅓ cups lemon juice
1 tablespoon pepper
½ teaspoon parsley, fresh
  or dried
½ cup wine vinegar

Mix oil, soy sauce, Worcestershire sauce, mustard, salt, lemon juice, pepper, and vinegar. Store covered in refrigerator. Great for all beef, pork, and chicken. Good for any vegetables on shishkabobs. Keeps well after marinating. Makes approximately 1 quart.

Mrs. William E. "Brother" Oliver (Sue Kelly)

BASTING SAUCE FOR GRILLED PORK CHOPS

2 tablespoons butter
½ cup soy sauce
1 lemon
½ teaspoon onion salt
Freshly ground pepper, generous
  dash

¼ teaspoon Tabasco, or to taste
Bourbon or sherry to taste
  (optional)

In small saucepan, mix butter, soy sauce, lemon (cut in half, squeeze juice in, and drop shells in), onion salt, pepper, Tabasco, and bourbon or sherry. Boil 5 minutes. Baste pork chops often the last half hour of cooking on grill, keeping sauce hot, if possible. Enough for four 1-inch chops.

Mrs. Peterson Cavert (Mary Beth Wear)

SEASONED SALT

2 tablespoons celery salt
2 tablespoons garlic salt
2 tablespoons onion salt
1½ teaspoons paprika

1¼ teaspoons chili powder
½ teaspoon black pepper (scant)
⅛ teaspoon cayenne pepper

Mix the celery, garlic, and onion salt, paprika, chili powder, black pepper, and cayenne pepper, and sift together three or four times. Put in a jar with a tight lid, preferably one with inside shaker top. This may be multiplied, using these same proportions, as many times as your jar or bottle will hold. This is a good general purpose blend, especially good for all meat dishes.

Hint: Makes a nice gift for any cook!

Mrs. Allen Mattox (Harriet Marrs)

MUSHROOM SAUCE

½ pound fresh mushrooms, finely
sliced or chopped
4 tablespoons butter, divided
1½ cups stock or tinned beef
broth (not consommé), divided

½ cup sliced onion
½ cup dry red wine
2 teaspoons flour
Salt
Paprika

In a medium-size skillet, melt 2 tablespoons butter over medium heat. When foam from butter subsides, add mushrooms. Sauté mushrooms for 2 minutes. Add ½ cup stock. Cover and simmer over low heat for 10 minutes. In another pan, sauté onion in 2 tablespoons butter. Add 1 cup stock and wine to onion, cover and simmer for 10 minutes. Mix flour with 2 tablespoons of the onion stock, and blend it back into onion mixture. Simmer until mixture is thickened, then remove from heat. Stir in mushroom mixture. Add salt and paprika to taste. Serve with steak or roast beef.

QUICK AND EASY HOLLANDAISE

2 egg yolks
1 stick *cold* butter or oleo

2-3 tablespoons lemon juice

In small pan, place 2 slightly beaten egg yolks, 1 stick cold butter or oleo, and 2 to 3 tablespoons lemon juice. *Do not cut up butter.* Cook over very *low* heat, stirring constantly until butter is melted and sauce is slightly thick. Serves 4-6.

Mrs. Charles R. Pearce (Elizabeth Cunningham)

MOCK HOLLANDAISE

1 cup mayonnaise
Juice of 1 medium lemon

1 tablespoon melted butter

Mix all ingredients together slowly with French whisk. Couldn't be easier, and tastes good! Makes 1½ cups.

Mrs. Richard F. Pride, Jr. (Sandra Wedgeworth)

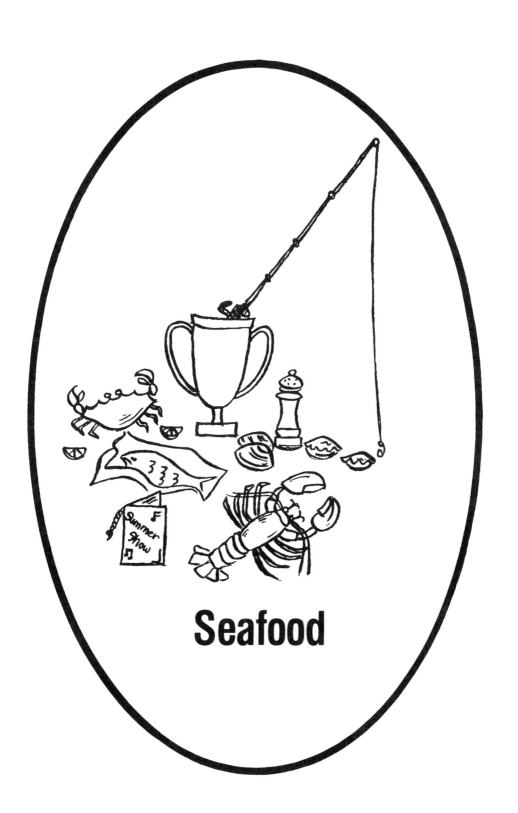

Seafood

SHRIMP AND CHEESE CASSEROLE

6 slices white bread
½ pound Old English cheese
(usually comes sliced)
1 pound prepared shrimp (ready
to eat)

¼ cup butter, melted
3 whole eggs, beaten
½ teaspoon dry mustard
Salt to taste
1 pint milk

Break bread in pieces about size of a quarter. Break cheese into bite-size pieces. Arrange shrimp, bread, and cheese in several layers in greased casserole. Pour margarine or butter over this mixture. Beat eggs. Add mustard and salt to eggs, then add milk. Mix together and pour this over ingredients in casserole. Let stand a minimum of 3 hours, *preferably overnight* in refrigerator, covered.

Bake 1 hour in 350-degree oven, covered. Serves 4.

Note: Naturally, if you slightly increase the amount of shrimp, you improve the dish. When doubling the recipe, use 3 pounds of shrimp and use a 3-quart casserole.

Mrs. Julian Reed (Peggy Ethridge)

SHRIMP AND AVOCADO MOUSSE

1 envelope unflavored gelatin
⅓ cup cold water
¾ cup boiling water
1½ teaspoons salt (approximately)
¼ teaspoon curry powder, or to
taste
2 teaspoons Worcestershire sauce
Few drops Tabasco
½ pound cooked shrimp; peeled,
deveined and chopped

Grated rind of 1 lemon
1 tablespoon lemon juice
2 tablespoons chopped chives
2 medium-size ripe avocados,
peeled and puréed (about
2 cups)
¾ cup heavy cream, whipped
½ cup mayonnaise
Vegetable oil

Sprinkle gelatin over cold water to soften. Combine with boiling water and stir until dissolved. Cool slightly. Stir in salt, curry, Worcestershire sauce, Tabasco, lemon rind, lemon juice, chives, and avocados. Refrigerate. When the mixture has begun to set, fold in the whipped cream and mayonnaise. Taste for seasoning. Brush a 6-cup mold with oil; turn upside down to allow any surplus to drain. Spoon the mousse into mold and refrigerate several hours. Serves 8 to 10.

Hint: Avocados most easily puréed in bowl of electric food processor with steel blade.

Mrs. Glynn "Sonny" Hewett (Jean Mosley)

SHRIMP ÉTOUFFÉE

1 medium onion, finely chopped
2 green onions, finely chopped
3-4 cloves garlic, minced
¼ cup celery, finely chopped
½ cup butter or margarine
2 tablespoons flour
2½ cups water
1 (10½-ounce) can tomato purée
2 bay leaves

1 tablespoon Worcestershire sauce
1 teaspoon salt
½ teaspoon sugar
½ teaspoon whole thyme, crushed
⅛ teaspoon pepper
1 pound (3 cups) cleaned raw
   shrimp (2 pounds in shell)
2 eggs, hard-boiled and
   quartered

Sauté onions, green onions, garlic, and celery in butter until tender. Add flour, cook and stir until lightly browned. Add water, tomato purée, bay leaves, Worcestershire sauce, salt, sugar, thyme, and pepper. Simmer uncovered, stirring occasionally, for 25 minutes, or until almost desired consistency. Add shrimp and cook 15 minutes more. Garnish with eggs. Serve over rice. Serves 4 to 6.

Mrs. Earl L. Carpenter (Betty Myrick)

SHRIMP PIE

Small amount of oil
¼ cup celery, minced
1 bunch green onions, chopped
   fine
½ small green pepper, minced
3 cups boiled and cleaned shrimp
Salt
Pepper
Tabasco

3 cups cooked long grain rice
1¼ cups water
1 (10¾-ounce) can condensed
   cream of mushroom soup
1 bay leaf
Worcestershire sauce
Paprika
Crumbled egg yolk (optional)
Pimiento, chopped (optional)

Sauté in oil the celery, onions, and green pepper about 5 minutes. Add shrimp and sauté 5 minutes. Salt and pepper to taste, and add a few dashes Tabasco. Mix with cooked rice; add water, mushroom soup, bay leaf. Add a few dashes Worcestershire sauce. Taste for salt and pepper. Pour entire mixture into a greased 2-quart baking dish. Sprinkle with paprika. Bake at 350 degrees for about 30 minutes, until mixture is thoroughly heated. May be garnished with crumbled egg yolk and pimiento. Serves 6 to 8.

Mrs. Glynn "Sonny" Hewett (Jean Mosley)

SHRIMP CREOLE

3 tablespoons cooking oil
2 tablespoons flour
1 clove garlic
1 (1-pound) can tomatoes
1 (8-ounce) can tomato sauce
1½ teaspoons salt
1 teaspoon sugar

½ teaspoon chili powder
1 tablespoon Worcestershire
   sauce
Dash Tabasco sauce
1 green bell pepper, chopped
1 medium onion, chopped
2 pounds shrimp

Cook shrimp by boiling in shrimp and crab boil; peel and clean. Mix together the oil, flour, garlic, tomatoes, tomato sauce, salt, sugar, chili powder, Worcestershire sauce, Tabasco, bell pepper, and onion. Cook uncovered in dutch oven over low heat for 1 to 1½ hours. Add shrimp to the mixture at the last 20 minutes of cooking time. Serve over rice. Serves 6 to 8.

Mrs. William H. Tucker (Harriet Belle Little)

Freeze shrimp in water. Tastes fresh when used up to 5 months later!

SHRIMP IN BEER

1 (3-ounce) box shrimp boil
½ cup salt
1 (2¼-ounce) box mustard seed
1 (1½-ounce) box celery seed
1 tablespoon black peppercorns
1 teaspoon red pepper

2 lemons, sliced
4 (12-ounce) cans beer
1 cup vinegar
8 pounds fresh shrimp
   (heads off)

Combine shrimp boil, salt, mustard seed, celery seed, black peppercorns, red pepper, lemons, beer, and vinegar, and bring to a boil. Drop in shrimp and return to a boil. Boil 3 to 5 minutes, until pink and tender. Serve hot(!) with Cross and Blackwell seafood sauce with horseradish added. Toss salad and French bread and you're ready for dinner. Makes 8 1-pound servings.

Note: This recipe multiples well. If doing 16 pounds, reserve pot liquor for second boiling. Also reserve some liquid for storage if any shrimp happen to be left over, which I doubt!

Mrs. Allen Mattox (Harriet Marrs)

SHRIMP AND WILD RICE

1 tablespoon to ¼ cup green
   pepper, thinly sliced
2 tablespoons to ½ cup onion,
   grated
2 tablespoons to ½ cup mushrooms, sliced (optional)
2 tablespoons to ¼ cup butter
   (depending on amount of above)
1 tablespoon Worcestershire sauce
½ tablespoon mustard

Few drops of Tabasco
1 pound shrimp, cooked and
   cleaned
1 (10¾-ounce) can cream of
   mushroom soup
¼ teaspoon pepper
½ cup cheddar cheese, grated
   (optional)
2 cups cooked long grain and
   wild rice

Sauté pepper, onion, and mushrooms in butter until soft. Add Worcestershire, mustard, Tabasco, shrimp, soup, pepper, cheese, and cooked
rice. Bake in a buttered casserole in a moderate oven (325 to 350 degrees)
until bubbly. Serve hot in casserole or in a chafing dish. Serves 4.

Mrs. T. Griffin Stanley, Sr.—Hampton, SC

SHRIMP WITH SPINACH NOODLES

3 pounds cooked shrimp
1 (5-ounce) package green
   spinach noodles

8 medium-size spring onions

SAUCE:

8 ounces sour cream
1 cup mayonnaise
1 (10¾-ounce) can cream of
   mushroom soup

2 tablespoons mustard
2 slightly beaten eggs
1 cup grated sharp cheese

Cook noodles in 1 quart water plus 1 teaspoon oil. Chop tops and bottoms
of onions. Add to cooked noodles while still hot. Drain if necessary. In
greased 2-quart casserole, layer noodles, shrimp, and sauce. Make 2
layers. Top with extra cheese. Bake at 350 degrees for 30 minutes. Serves 8
to 10.

Note: Freezes well.

Mrs. E. Calhoun Wilson (Gene Henderson)

SHRIMP REMOULADE

½ cup olive or salad oil
1 teaspoon salt
2½ tablespoons paprika
¼ to ¾ teaspoon cayenne pepper
2 garlic cloves, minced
⅓ cup tarragon vinegar

⅓ cup horseradish mustard
2 tablespoons catsup
½ cup chopped green onions
   with tops
3 cups cleaned or canned cooked
   shrimp (2 pounds with shell)

Combine oil, salt, paprika, cayenne pepper, garlic, vinegar, mustard, catsup, and onions. Mix well. Gently add shrimp. Chill shrimp in sauce 4 or 5 hours or overnight. Drain shrimp and serve on lettuce. Garnish with tomato wedges or quartered hard-boiled eggs. Serve extra sauce on the side. Serves 6.

Mrs. Robert Dugins (Melville Neilson)

Hint: For 1 cup cooked shelled shrimp, buy ¾ pound raw shrimp without heads. Allow ¾ to 1 pound per person when buying shrimp to serve as main dish.

WINKIE'S SHRIMP CASSEROLE

2 pounds cooked shrimp
6 slices bread, toasted for
   crumbs
½ cup slivered almonds
Margarine
3 hard-boiled eggs

2 (10¾-ounce) cans cream of
   mushroom soup, undiluted
1 cup mayonnaise
1 (2-ounce) jar cut pimiento
2 tablespoons Worcestershire sauce
(No salt added to this!)

Grate bread crumbs. Mix half of bread crumbs with half of almonds in margarine, reserving the remainder for topping. Mash eggs. Mix the shrimp, bread crumbs, almonds, eggs, soup, mayonnaise, pimiento, and Worcestershire sauce and put into buttered casserole. Top with reserved crumbs and almonds. Bake in 325-degree oven for 20 minutes. Serve over fluffy rice. Good and easy! Serves 6.

Mrs. Charles K. Beauchamp (Winkie Clarkson)

TIPSY SHRIMP

2¼ pounds shrimp
1 (10-ounce) package frozen
  English peas

2 (2-ounce) can mushrooms
¾ cup ripe olives, chopped
¾ cup almonds, slivered

SAUCE:
6 tablespoons melted butter
6 tablespoons flour

1½ cups cream
1½ cups wine

Cook shrimp and peas separately, but just for a few minutes each. Don't overcook. Combine with mushrooms, olives, and almonds. For sauce, blend butter and flour, then add cream and wine and cook until thick. Mix with shrimp mixture and put in deep casserole. Sprinkle with bread crumbs and butter. Bake at 350 degrees for 35-40 minutes. Serves 4.

Mrs. Joseph Rowland (Nancy Burch)

CREAMED SHRIMP

2 small cans shrimp
1 small onion, chopped
¼ cup celery, chopped
¼ cup green pepper, chopped

Salt and pepper to taste
1½ cups medium white sauce
Buttered bread crumbs

Combine shrimp, onion, celery, pepper, and season with salt and pepper. Add white sauce. Pour into greased casserole. Top with buttered bread crumbs. Bake at 350 degrees for 45 minutes. Serve over rice. Serves 6.

Note: Good with fruit salad.

Mrs. Paul W. Bryant, Jr. (Cherry Hicks)

SHRIMP NANTUA

5 pounds cooked, shelled shrimp
¾ stick butter
2 tablespoons flour
1 tablespoon tomato paste

2½ cups heavy cream
Salt and cayenne pepper to taste
1½ cups seeded, diced tomatoes

Sauté shrimp sprinkled with flour in melted butter. Mix tomato paste with a little cream, then add the rest of the cream to shrimp. Add tomato cream to shrimp and simmer, stirring, until thickened. Add cayenne and salt. At last minute, add tomatoes. Serve with rice. Serves 10.

Mrs. David Hefelfinger (Virginia Mauney)

SHRIMP CURRY

⅓ cup butter
3 tablespoons flour
1 to 2 tablespoons curry powder
  (or to taste)
¼ teaspoon paprika
½ teaspoon salt
⅛ teaspoon nutmeg

2 cups light cream
3 cups cleaned and cooked
  shrimp
1-2 teaspoons ginger
1 tablespoon lemon juice
⅛ teaspoon Worcestershire sauce

CONDIMENTS:
Chutney, raisins, chopped peanuts, chopped almonds, chopped green onions, bacon crumbs, grated boiled eggs, grated coconut.

Melt butter; blend in flour, curry, paprika, salt, and nutmeg. Add cream gradually, cooking until it thickens, stirring constantly. Blend in shrimp, ginger, lemon, and Worcestershire. Serve with rice and condiments. Serves 4.

Frances Wells Brooker

SHRIMP SKILLET DINNER

1 cup sliced celery
⅓ cup chopped green pepper
¼ cup chopped onion
1 (16-ounce) bottle Kraft French
  dressing

1 tablespoon flour
3 cups cooked rice
1 pound cooked, peeled shrimp

Cook celery, green pepper, onion in small amount of dressing until tender. Stir in flour, mix in remaining dressing, add rice and shrimp. Cover, heat five minutes. Serves 4.

Mrs. Lee Pake (Betty Gilpin)

WHITNEY ECHOLS' FRIED SHRIMP

Shrimp
Salt
Pepper
1 egg, beaten

2 to 3 tablespoons whole milk
Cracker meal
Flour
Oil

Clean raw shrimp, leave tail on, and split down black line. Remove vein. Clean, wash, and dry. Sprinkle salt and pepper on shrimp to taste. Dip in egg beaten with milk, then dredge in flour, dip back in egg mixture, and dredge in cracker meal. Fry in deep hot fat.

Mrs. David M. Cochrane (Mary B. Tompkins)

CRAB AND ASPARAGUS CASSEROLE

1 pound fresh white lump
  crabmeat

4 (10½-ounce) cans green
  asparagus (reserve juice)

CREAM SAUCE:
3 tablespoons margarine
3 tablespoons cornstarch
1 cup milk
1 cup asparagus juice
4 tablespoons mayonnaise (not
  homemade)
¼ teaspoon garlic salt
Salt and pepper to taste

Dash of Tabasco
Dash of Accent
1 tablespoon Worcestershire
  sauce
1 teaspoon lemon juice
1 jigger sherry
Grated sharp cheddar cheese

Pick crabmeat and drain asparagus *well.* Place asparagus in greased casserole and cover with crabmeat. Make cream sauce by blending margarine and cornstarch until smooth in a saucepan. While stirring, gradually add milk and asparagus juice. Cook until good consistency. Fold in mayonnaise, garlic, salt, pepper, Tabasco, Accent, Worcestershire sauce, lemon juice, and sherry. Pour sauce over the top of crab and sprinkle with grated sharp cheddar cheese. Bake at 325 degrees until hot and cheese is melted.

Hint: You may make this casserole ahead of time except for grated sharp cheese, and refrigerate until 30 minutes prior to serving. Place in 325-degree oven until hot and bubbly, then sprinkle cheese on top and place back in oven just a minute, until cheese melts (about 20-25 minutes, total time).

Mrs. David M. Cochrane (Mary B. Tompkins)

CRABMEAT DIVAN

1 (10-ounce) package frozen
  broccoli
1 (6½-ounce) can king crabmeat,
  drained
⅓ cup mayonnaise

1½ teaspoons lemon juice
½ teaspoon mustard
1 teaspoon grated onion
¼ cup grated cheese

Preheat oven to 350 degrees. Cook broccoli according to package directions; drain. Arrange on heat-proof platter and cover with crabmeat. For sauce, mix mayonnaise, lemon juice, mustard, and onion. Spoon over crab. Top with cheese. Bake 20 minutes. Serves 4.

Mrs. Roger C. Williams (Jo Ann Davenport)

CRAB IMPERIAL

1 pound crabmeat, fresh lump
½ medium green pepper,
  chopped fine
1 medium onion, chopped fine
¼ cup celery, chopped fine
2 tablespoons melted butter
1 teaspoon parsley flakes
Juice of ½ lemon

½-1 teaspoon salt
1 teaspoon Worcestershire sauce
2-3 drops Tabasco
½ cup Miracle Whip (*do not*
  substitute)
2 tablespoons regular
  mayonnaise
Paprika for top

Remove any shell from crab. Sauté in a large skillet the chopped vegetables in butter for just a few minutes (until limp). Combine in the same skillet the parsley, lemon juice, salt, Worcestershire sauce, Tabasco, Miracle Whip, and mayonnaise. Remove from heat and combine crab lightly—toss, but *don't crush* crab. Place in well-greased individual shells; sprinkle with paprika. Bake at 350 degrees for 20-25 minutes. Serves 6.

Mrs. George Gordon (Jean Fargason)

CRABMEAT WITH SHERRY

2 tablespoons butter
¾ cup warm milk
4 tablespoons flour
½ teaspoon salt
Pepper

1 (6½-ounce) can fresh crabmeat
1 pint box fresh mushrooms
2 tablespoons butter
¼ cup sherry

Make cream sauce adding warmed milk to melted butter, flour, salt, and pepper. Add crabmeat. Sauté mushrooms in butter, then add to creamed crabmeat. Last, add ¼ cup of sherry. Put in buttered casserole and bake for 30 minutes in a 450-degree oven. Serves 4.

Mrs. Laurence S. Woodley (Bee Bagwell)

HOT CRAB SALAD

1 pound flaked crabmeat
1 bell pepper, minced
1 small onion, minced
1 cup mayonnaise
½ teaspoon salt

⅛ teaspoon pepper
1 teaspoon Worcestershire sauce
1 cup bread crumbs
¼ cup buttered bread crumbs

This recipe can be made in baking shells, individual casserole dishes, or one large casserole. Combine crabmeat, bell pepper, onion, mayonnaise, salt, pepper, Worcestershire, and 1 cup bread crumbs, and place in greased shells or casserole(s). Top with buttered bread crumbs. Bake at 375 degrees for 10-15 minutes for shells, 25 minutes for individual casseroles, and 35-40 minutes for a large casserole. Serves 8.

Mrs. Robert H. Davis (Doris Herold)

CRAB À LA SUISSE

4 tablespoons margarine
4 tablespoons flour
¼ teaspoon garlic salt
2 cups milk
Salt to taste

½ pound Swiss cheese, cut up
1 pound fresh lump crabmeat
Dash Tabasco sauce
½ cup grated Parmesan cheese

Melt margarine. Add flour and garlic. Mix well. Slowly add milk. Cook and stir until thick. Add salt, Swiss cheese, crabmeat, and Tabasco. Mix well. Pour into 2-quart casserole dish and sprinkle with Parmesan cheese. Bake at 350 degrees for 30 minutes. May be served on English muffin or large seashells. Serves 6.

Mrs. Randolph Fowler (Shirley Jones)

COQUILLES ST. JACQUES

⅓ cup dry white wine
2 tablespoons chopped green onions
½ pound scallops, cut into small pieces
1 cup fresh mushrooms, sliced
3 tablespoons butter

3 tablespoons flour
½ teaspoon salt
1½ cups light cream
2 tablespoons parsley, chopped
10 cooked crêpes (See Index)
½ cup grated Swiss cheese

In saucepan, combine wine, onion, scallops, and mushrooms. Cover and simmer 5 minutes. Meanwhile, melt butter in skillet. Stir in flour and salt. Pour in light cream; cook, stirring constantly, until thickened. Add parsley, then scallop-mushroom mixture. Fill cooked crêpes in shallow baking dish; fold over. Sprinkle with cheese. Heat in 350-degree oven for 10-15 minutes, until cheese melts. Makes 10 crêpes.

Mrs. Joseph Vengrouskie (Mary L. Lunsford)

SEAFOOD CRÊPES

½ cup chopped shallots or green onions
1 cup sliced fresh mushrooms
2½ sticks butter
3 tablespoons flour
½ cup white wine
1 quart light cream
3 or 4 egg yolks

Salt and pepper
½ pound cooked lobster meat
½ pound cooked shrimp (pieces)
½ pound crabmeat
½ cup drained, sliced water chestnuts
2 teaspoons cognac
12 crêpes

Sauté shallots or green onions and mushrooms in 1½ sticks butter. Add flour and cook 2-3 minutes. Gradually add wine and cream and simmer 8-10 minutes. Remove from fire and stir in beaten egg yolks, adding enough to make a sauce of medium consistency. Season to taste. Sauté lobster, shrimp, crabmeat, and water chestnuts in 1 stick butter 4-5 minutes. Add cognac and ignite. After cognac burns out, add half of the sauce to the seafood mixture. Divide this onto the crêpes and roll up. Cover crêpes with the remainder of the sauce. Serves 6.

Note: Any combination of seafoods may be used.

Mrs. J. C. "Bud" Miller (Presteen Sims)

FILLETS IN CREAMY WINE SAUCE

1 tablespoon butter
2 tablespoons minced green onion
1 pound sole or flounder fillets,
  cut into serving pieces
1½ cups sliced fresh mushrooms
¾ cup dry white wine, such as
  Sauterne

2 tablespoons flour
¼ cup heavy cream
1 teaspoon salt
⅛ teaspoon white pepper
½ teaspoon lemon juice
¾ cup shredded Swiss cheese

Melt butter in 12 x 8 x 2-inch baking dish and add minced green onion. Arrange fillets over onions and cover with sliced/chopped mushrooms. Pour wine over top. Bake at 350 degrees until fish flakes readily with a fork, approximately 10-15 minutes, depending on thickness of fillets. In a 1-quart casserole, combine flour, cream, salt, and pepper until smooth. Carefully drain hot liquid from fish into cream mixture and stir well. Heat until sauce thickens. Add lemon juice and stir. Pour sauce over fish and sprinkle shredded Swiss cheese on top. Heat in oven until cheese has melted. Garnish with parsley sprigs. Serves 4.

Allan F. Stanley—Varnville, SC

SCALLOPS THERMIDOR

1 pound scallops
1 (4-ounce) can mushrooms and
  liquid
4 or 5 fresh chopped scallions
¼ cup butter
¼ cup flour
1 cup milk
1 teaspoon salt

½ teaspoon powdered mustard
⅛ teaspoon cayenne pepper
2 tablespoons chopped parsley
  (fresh or dried)
2 tablespoons white wine
Grated Parmesan cheese
Paprika

Cut large scallops in half. Drain mushrooms, reserving liquid. Melt butter. Add scallops, mushrooms, and scallions. Sauté about 5 minutes. Remove from butter. Blend flour into butter. Add milk and mushroom liquid gradually and cook until thickened, stirring constantly. Add salt, mustard, cayenne pepper. Blend. Add scallops, mushrooms, parsley, and wine. Place in well-greased individual shells or ramekins. Sprinkle with Parmesan cheese and paprika. Bake in 400-degree oven for 10-15 minutes, or until brown. Serves 4.

Mrs. W. McKay DeLoach (Marilyn Williams)

BETTY'S SEAFOOD CASSEROLE SUPREME

1 (14-ounce) can artichoke hearts
2½ pounds cleaned shrimp
1 pound lump crabmeat
2 tablespoons butter, melted
3 tablespoons flour
½ teaspoon prepared mustard
½ teaspoon curry powder
½ teaspoon paprika
1 cup cream or half and half

1 cup whole milk
Red pepper and salt to taste
1 tablespoon Worcestershire
  sauce
1 tablespoon catsup (heaping)
2 tablespoons lemon juice
2 tablespoons sherry
1½ cups grated New York cheese

Layer artichoke hearts, shrimp, and crabmeat in casserole. Make sauce of butter, flour, mustard, curry, paprika, cream, whole milk, pepper, salt, Worcestershire sauce, catsup, lemon juice, and sherry. Pour over shrimp and crab. Top with cheese and bake at 400 degrees for 20 minutes. Serves 10.

Mrs. William F. Barnes, Jr. (Diane Manderson)

ESCALLOPED OYSTERS

1 pint oysters, drained and rinsed
2 cups bread or saltine cracker
  crumbs

½ stick butter
½ cup milk
Salt and pepper to taste

Make alternate layers of oysters, bread or cracker crumbs, and butter until a 9 x 13-inch baking dish is filled. Pour warmed milk over layers; add salt and lots of pepper. Put crumbs and remaining butter on top, then bake at 350 degrees for about ½ hour.

Hint: Half and half milk is better than regular milk.

Note: This recipe was originally submitted under the name of Mrs. Battle Searcy, Sr., in the Junior Welfare Association Cookbook, published in 1939.

Mrs. Albert Baernstein (Sis Wiesel)

TRIPLE SEAFOOD BAKE

1 cup half and half
1 cup milk
⅓ cup sherry
1 (10¾-ounce) can mushroom soup
2 cups long grain rice
1 (5-ounce) can lobster, drained
1 (4½-ounce) can shrimp, drained
and split
1 (7½-ounce) can minced clams,
drained

1 (3-ounce) can mushrooms,
drained or ½ cup sliced fresh
1 (5-ounce) can water chestnuts,
drained and sliced
1 tablespoon dried parsley flakes
¼ teaspoon minced garlic
2 tablespoons toasted sliced
almonds
2 tablespoons butter

Stir half and half, milk, and sherry into soup. Add uncooked rice, lobster, shrimp, clams, mushrooms, chestnuts, parsley flakes and garlic. Sprinkle with almonds and dot with butter. Bake at 350 degrees for 50 minutes. Serves 4 to 6.

Mrs. Richard Shelby (Annette Nevin)

FISH FILLET SUPREME

2 or 3 pounds of fish fillet
(catfish, bass, trout, or salt
water fish)
1 stick of butter (*not* margarine)
Juice of 1 lemon, large to medium
size
⅛ teaspoon onion powder (or 1
tablespoon finely chopped green
onion tops)

1 teaspoon salt (½ teaspoon for
salt water fish)
⅛ teaspoon pepper
1 tablespoon Sauterne (optional)
or Worcestershire sauce (use
one but not both)
1 teaspoon paprika
1 tablespoon Parmesan cheese
(freshly grated is delicious)

Place butter in shallow baking dish or broiling pan bottom. Put into 400- to 450-degree oven until butter is browned but not burned. This is what makes the fish so good. Place fillets, fleshy side down, in hot butter and return to oven for 10-15 minutes. Then turn fillet over and baste with butter and juice. Sprinkle each fillet with lemon juice, dry Sauterne, cheese, salt, pepper, onion powder, and paprika. Place in oven for about 5-6 minutes, or until done. Place under broiler and broil quickly. Baste fillets with sauce. This is delicious with a tossed salad and hot French bread. Serves 4.

Mrs. Edward "Flash" Florey, Jr. (Betty Finklea)

SEAFARER'S BAKE

9 lasagna noodles (about ½ pound)
1 (10-ounce) package frozen chopped spinach, thawed
1 large onion, chopped
2 tablespoons vegetable oil
1 (3-ounce) package cream cheese, at room temperature
1 cup creamy cottage cheese
1 egg, beaten
1 teaspoon Italian herb seasoning
Salt and pepper

1 (10¾-ounce) can condensed cream of celery soup
⅓ cup milk
½ pound cooked shrimp
1 pound fish fillets, cubed
3 tablespoons grated Parmesan cheese
2 tablespoons fine seasoned bread crumbs
⅓ cup shredded sharp cheddar cheese
Butter or margarine

Cook and drain noodles according to package directions. Arrange three noodles in bottom of greased oblong 2-quart baking dish. Press thawed spinach in a strainer to remove all moisture. Cook onion in hot oil until soft. Blend in spinach, cream cheese, cottage cheese, egg and herb seasoning; add salt and pepper to taste. Spread about ⅓ of this mixture over noodles in dish. Combine soup, milk, shrimp and fish; spread about ⅓ of mixture over cheese layer. Repeat layers. Mix Parmesan cheese and bread crumbs; sprinkle on top. Bake in oven at 350 degrees for 45 minutes. Top with cheddar cheese and dot with butter; bake 5 minutes more. Let stand about 20 minutes before cutting in squares to serve. Makes 6 to 8 servings. *Note: This dish takes a little time to put together but is so good you won't mind the effort. Serve raw vegetable relishes and bread sticks to round out the meal. And don't forget this recipe when company is coming or you need something special for a covered-dish supper or buffet. Just double the ingredients and add artichoke hearts or black olives for glamour.*

Allan F. Stanley—Varnville, SC

SALMON PIE

1 envelope unflavored gelatin
1¼ cups water
2 (7¾-ounce) cans salmon, drained and flaked
¾ cup chopped celery
½ cup Hellmann's mayonnaise

¼ cup chopped parsley
2 tablespoons chopped capers
2 tablespoons lemon juice
1 teaspoon grated onion
1 teaspoon celery seed
1 baked (9-inch) pastry shell

Sprinkle gelatin over water. Heat, stirring, until dissolved. Chill until slightly thickened. Stir into thickened gelatin the salmon, celery, Hellmann's, parsley, capers, lemon juice, onion and celery seed. Turn into pastry shell. Chill until set. Serves 6 to 8.

Mrs. Dudley Davis (Josephine Camp)

SALMON BALLS

1 (15½-ounce) can salmon
1 egg
½ cup flour
1 heaping teaspoon baking powder

¼ cup salmon liquid
Salt and pepper to taste

Drain salmon, save liquid. Break salmon up in mixing bowl. Add egg and mix well. Add flour and mix well. Just before you get ready to cook the salmon, add baking powder to salmon liquid and beat with fork until foamy. Pour into salmon mixture, add salt and pepper, and mix well. Drop by spoonfuls into hot oil and do not overcrowd pan. Cook until lightly brown. Serves 6.

Mrs. Robert E. McCoy (Brenda Magruder)

BAKED SEAFOOD CASSEROLE

1 pound crabmeat
1 pound cooked and deveined
  shrimp
1 cup mayonnaise
½ cup green peppers, chopped
¼ cup onion, minced

1½ cups celery
1 teaspoon salt
1 tablespoon Worcestershire
  sauce
2 cups potato chips, crushed
Paprika

Mix together the crabmeat, shrimp, mayonnaise, green peppers, onion, celery, salt, and Worcestershire sauce. Pour into a 9 x 13-inch dish and completely cover with crushed potato chips. Sprinkle with paprika if desired. Bake at 400 degrees for 20 to 25 minutes. Serves 8.

Mrs. Glenn Baxter (Ann Patton)

TUNA CURRY

⅓ cup chopped onion
¼ cup chopped green pepper
1 clove garlic, minced
2 tablespoons butter
1 cup sour cream
1 teaspoon curry powder or more

Salt and pepper
1 (6½-,7-, or 9¼-ounce) can tuna
Raisins
Peanuts, chopped
Cashews, chopped
Shredded coconut

Cook onion, green pepper, and garlic in butter until tender but not brown. Stir in sour cream, curry, salt, and pepper. Drain tuna and break into bite-size pieces. Add and heat slowly, stirring often, just until hot. Serve over hot rice and pass condiments: raisins, peanuts, cashews, shredded coconut, etc. Serves 4.

Mrs. James Hodo Walburn (Dean Frank)

SEAFOOD GUMBO

ROUX:

2 cups plain flour

1 cup oil (peanut preferable)

Pour oil into hot skillet. When oil is hot, pour flour into it, stirring so it won't be lumpy. Reduce heat to medium-low to medium and brown the flour very *slowly*. Stir constantly; do not burn or let stick. This will take a pretty good while, approximately 1 hour, so be patient. You can tell when it's done by the odor and by the dark *brown* color.

GUMBO:

Roux (above)
3-4 medium onions, chopped fine
7 stalks celery, chopped fine
Garlic to taste (fresh or minced)
Butter
1 pound fresh okra, chopped, or
  1 (10-ounce) package frozen
  chopped okra
4 cans chicken stock (10½-ounce),
  or may use fresh

2 (28-ounce) cans tomatoes
Salt, Tabasco, Worcestershire
  sauce to taste
2 pounds peeled, raw shrimp
2 pounds crabmeat
Crab claws or bodies, if
  available
2 tablespoons filé
Hot steamed rice

Sauté onions, celery, garlic, in butter until soft. Add to roux and let simmer on back of stove while heating stock. (I also cook my okra in a little oil in a skillet before adding it to the gumbo. I let it get soft and mushy.) Heat stock in large soup pot. Add roux and stir until smooth. Add okra, tomatoes, salt, Tabasco, Worcestershire sauce, and simmer about 3 hours. Add shrimp, crabmeat, crab bodies and cook about 30 minutes. Remove from heat, add filé, and serve in large bowls over rice. Serves 8.

Hints:
1) *Do not boil gumbo to which filé has been added.*
2) *"Meme", of Bon Secour, Al., says, "NEVER add BLACK PEPPER".*
3) *1 pint of oysters plus liquid may be added with other seafood, if desired.*

Mrs. Thomas W. Moore (Stella Hillard)

Hint: Filé is the powdered sassafras leaf. It is used as a thickening agent. Filé is NEVER put in until just a minute before serving, after the gumbo is removed from the heat. To add while gumbo is cooking would make the gumbo stringy and unfit for use.

Salads
and
Salad
Dressings

PARTY GRAPEFRUIT SALAD

3 large grapefruit
2 (3-ounce) packages lemon
   gelatin

¾ cup boiling water
Lettuce leaves
Food coloring

Cut grapefruit in half long way (not as you cut for breakfast). Scoop out pulp and juice of 2 grapefruit, saving rind. Measure 3¼ cups of the pulp and juice, using third grapefruit to make this amount if needed. Pour boiling water over gelatin. Stir until dissolved. Stir the 3¼ cups grapefruit into the jello. Color the mixture red for Christmas and Valentine's Day or green for spring or summer. Pour the grapefruit mixture back into the four grapefruit rind halves. Refrigerate until congealed. When ready to serve, cut each half in half again. If gelatin mixture has sunk down, trim grapefruit down to the mixture. Serve on lettuce leaves with Dressing for Grapefruit Salad. Serves 8.

DRESSING FOR GRAPEFRUIT SALAD

3 tablespoons flour
½ cup sugar
3 egg yolks, well beaten
1 cup pineapple juice

12 marshmallows
½ pint whipping cream,
   whipped
1 cup slivered almonds

Combine flour, sugar, egg yolks, and pineapple juice in heavy saucepan. Cook over low heat, stirring constantly, until thickened. Remove from heat and add marshmallows, stirring well. Let mixture chill in refrigerator. Fold in whipped cream and almonds. Tint the dressing to go with the grapefruit salad, making it a lighter shade. Dressing is good over other fruit salads.

Mrs. Joseph Rowland (Nancy Burch)

CINNAMON-APPLESAUCE SALAD

½ cup hot water
⅓ cup cinnamon candy
1 (3-ounce) package lemon gelatin
1 cup crushed pineapple

¼ teaspoon salt
¼ teaspoon nutmeg
2 tablespoons lemon juice
1 (20-ounce) can applesauce

Dissolve candy in hot water and add to lemon gelatin. Add remaining ingredients. Pour into oiled mold and chill until set. Serves 8.

Mrs. Ward McFarland (Frances Morrow)

WATERCRESS SALAD

FOR EACH SERVING:

¼ to ⅓ bunch watercress
1 slice crisp bacon, crumbled
1 green onion or shallot, chopped

1 fresh raw mushroom, sliced
4 pecan halves, broken
1 tablespoon golden raisins

To one recipe of French Dressing (See Index) add:
½ teaspoon horseradish
1 teaspoon Worcestershire sauce

2 teaspoons sugar

Mix ingredients for dressing well. Pour over salads immediately before serving. May substitute spinach for watercress.

Mrs. Peterson Cavert (Mary Beth Wear)

COLD BUTTERBEAN SALAD

2 (10-ounce) packages frozen baby
  limas
1 cup Hellmann's mayonnaise
1 (12-ounce) can shoe peg corn,
  drained

1 bunch spring onions, chopped
  with tops

Cook beans according to package directions and drain. Add corn, onions, and mayonnaise and mix well. Chill. Serves 8. Good in summertime instead of potato salad.

Note: Doubles, triples, etc. easily. If doubling, don't quite double mayonnaise.

Mrs. George Wright (Stella Wellborn)

RUSSIAN FRUIT CREAM MOLD

1 (3-ounce) package lemon gelatin
1 cup juice from crushed
  pineapple, heated
1 cup mashed peaches

1 cup crushed pineapple
⅓ cup shredded coconut
1 (8-ounce) carton sour cream

Dissolve gelatin in hot juice. Add peaches, pineapple, coconut, and sour cream. Pour into mold and congeal. Yield: 8 servings.

Mrs. Robert McCurley (Martha Ann Dawson)

CAESAR SALAD

½ cup olive oil
2 garlic buds, squeezed
1 egg
2 tablespoons Worcestershire sauce
4 tablespoons lemon juice

Salt and pepper to taste
1 bunch Boston lettuce
1 pound fresh spinach
Parmesan cheese
Croutons

Two hours ahead of serving, mix in a cup the olive oil and squeezed garlic buds. In another cup, mix egg, Worcestershire sauce, lemon juice, salt and pepper. Refrigerate.

Toss together in large bowl the Boston lettuce and spinach. Let stand at room temperature for 1 hour. Pour one-half of olive oil mixture and one-half of lemon juice mixture over lettuce and spinach. Sprinkle heavily with Parmesan cheese. Sprinkle on salt to taste. Toss and add other half of dressing mixtures and more Parmesan cheese and salt. Top with croutons. Serves 6 to 8.

Mrs. Howard Garrison (Ashley Smith)

APRICOT CONGEALED SALAD

1 (3-ounce) box lemon gelatin
1 (3-ounce) box orange gelatin
1 (16-ounce) can apricots, chopped
1 (16-ounce) can crushed pineapple

2½ cups liquid reserved from
    canned fruit
¾ cup miniature marshmallows
½ cup pecans, broken

Drain apricots and pineapple and reserve liquid. Add water to make 2½ cups. Heat liquid to boiling point and use to dissolve gelatin. Let cool to room temperature. Add chopped fruit, pecans, and marshmallows. Turn into pan; chill. Cover with Topping for Apricot Congealed Salad.

TOPPING FOR APRICOT CONGEALED SALAD

2 tablespoons flour
½ cup granulated sugar
1 beaten egg

1 cup orange juice
2 tablespoons butter
1 cup whipped cream

Combine flour with sugar, then mix with slightly beaten egg. Add orange juice and butter. Cook over low heat, stirring, until thick. Remove and cool. Fold cooled mixture into whipped cream. Spread over salad and chill, or serve in dollops over fresh fruit salad. Serves 10-12.

Mrs. W. Lee Hudson (Jeannie Edwards)—Albany, GA

MOLDED ASPARAGUS SALAD

2 envelopes unflavored gelatin
1½ cups liquid (water, beef
  broth, bouillon cube, asparagus
  juice, consomme, etc.)
½ cup white vinegar
¾ cup sugar
1 (10½-ounce) can cut asparagus

1 (5-ounce) can water chestnuts,
  sliced thin
1 cup pimiento, cut into strips
1 cup celery, finely chopped
1 tablespoon onion, finely
  minced
2 tablespoons lemon juice

Dissolve gelatin in ½ cup liquid. Combine sugar and vinegar with 1 cup liquid and bring to a boil. Remove from heat. Add gelatin, onion, and lemon juice, and allow to cool. Add asparagus, water chestnuts, pimiento, and celery. Season to taste. Pour into 1½-quart mold or 8 x 8-inch square pan which has been greased slightly. Chill until firm. Serve on lettuce leaves with homemade mayonnaise. Yield: 8 to 9 servings.

Mrs. Charles A. Trost (Annie Orr)

TOMATO ASPIC

2 envelopes unflavored gelatin
¾ cup cold water
2 cups tomato juice
½ onion, diced
3 stalks celery, chopped
Few parsley flakes
½ teaspoon sugar
2 teaspoons salt

¼ teaspoon black pepper
Dash red pepper
Dash celery salt
1 teaspoon Worcestershire sauce
3 tablespoons tomato catsup
½ cup celery, chopped
½ cup bell pepper, chopped
½ cup stuffed olives, chopped

Soak gelatin in cold water for 3 minutes. Put tomato juice in boiler with sliced onion, celery, parsley flakes, sugar, salt, black pepper, red pepper, celery salt, Worcestershire sauce, and tomato catsup. Bring to a boil and let simmer a minute. Add gelatin, stir until dissolved, and strain. Refrigerate until it is partially congealed. Add bell pepper, celery, and stuffed olives. Pour into mold. Chill thoroughly. Yield: 6-8 servings.

Note: Artichoke hearts may be substituted for bell pepper, celery and olives.

Mrs. Joseph Vengrouskie (Mary Lucius Lunsford)

GRAPEFRUIT-MUSHROOM SALAD

1 ruby red grapefruit	1 large head Boston lettuce
½ cup sliced raw mushrooms	2 scallions, chopped with tops

Peel grapefruit, exposing inner pink flesh. Section, removing seeds and all membranes, and halve sections. Tear lettuce into salad bowl. Add grapefruit, mushrooms, and scallions. Pour French Dressing (See Index) over and toss. Good winter salad. Serves 4.

Mrs. Peterson Cavert (Mary Beth Wear)

COTTAGE CHEESE & FRUIT SALAD

1 (16-ounce) carton cottage cheese	1 (20-ounce) can chunk pineapple, drained
1 (3-ounce) package orange pineapple gelatin	1 (4½-ounce) Cool Whip
1 (11-ounce) can mandarin oranges, drained	

Sprinkle gelatin over cottage cheese. Add oranges and pineapple and mix well. Fold in Cool Whip. This will keep 3 or 4 days in refrigerator and flavor improves. If liquid forms, just stir. 10 servings.

Note: Use mayonnaise instead of Cool Whip for a different but delicious result.

Mrs. Robert Snow (Wilma Sanford)

FROZEN STRAWBERRY SALAD

1 pint strawberries, sliced (may use frozen)	2 (3-ounce) packages cream cheese
1 (10-ounce) package marshmallows, cut in small pieces (or miniature marshmallows)	⅔ cup mayonnaise
	1 cup whipping cream, whipped

Combine strawberries with marshmallows and let stand. Blend cream cheese and mayonnaise. Fold into whipped cream and then into berry mixture. Pour into pan or mold. Freeze until firm. Put in refrigerator about 30 minutes before serving. Serve on a bed of shredded lettuce. Yield: 10-12 servings.

Mrs. Joseph Rowland (Nancy Burch)

ONIONS FIRST SALAD

3 large onions
1 lemon
½ cup salad oil
¼ cup vinegar
2 tablespoons lemon juice

1 teaspoon savory
½ teaspoon salt
Tomatoes
Lettuce
Cucumbers

Cut the onions and lemon in paper-thin slices. Arrange in layers in small bowl with lemons on top. Combine salad oil, vinegar, lemon juice, savory, and salt. Pour over onion and lemon slices. Chill 8 hours or overnight, stirring occasionally. Drain and reserve dressing. Serve onions with tomatoes, lettuce, and cucumbers. Sprinkle onion dressing over all. The onions are delicious just by themselves. Yield: 4-6 servings.

Mrs. Joseph Rowland (Nancy Burch)

RUBY SALAD

1 cup diced beets and juice
1 envelope unflavored gelatin
¼ cup cold water
½ cup sugar

½ cup vinegar
½ teaspoon salt
1 teaspoon horseradish

Soften gelatin in cold water. Drain beets. Heat juice in saucepan with sugar, vinegar, and salt. Add gelatin and stir until dissolved. Chill until slightly thickened. Fold in beets. Chill until firm. Serves 4.

Mrs. Joseph Rowland (Nancy Burch)

MARINATED SAUERKRAUT

1 (16-ounce) can shredded sauerkraut, drained well
1 green pepper, chopped small
1 onion, chopped small
1 cup celery, chopped small

1 carrot, grated
½ cup vinegar
¼ cup oil
¾ cup sugar

Place sauerkraut, green pepper, onion, celery, and carrot in bowl and toss lightly. Mix vinegar, oil, and sugar and pour over vegetables to marinate. This salad goes well with chicken, beef, pork, barbecue, or even a grilled cheese sandwich. Keeps well in refrigerator for at least 2 weeks.

Mrs. James T. Cochrane (Sully Given)

PICKLED BEET SALAD

1 (1-pound) can sliced beets	3 or 4 small cloves
½ cup vinegar	1 small bay leaf
2 tablespoons sugar	1 small onion, sliced
½ teaspoon salt	

Drain beet liquid into saucepan, reserving beets, and add vinegar, sugar, salt, cloves, bay leaf, and onion. Bring to the boiling point. Reduce heat and simmer 5 minutes. Add beets and refrigerate overnight.

SALAD:

1 (3-ounce) package lemon gelatin	2 teaspoons grated onion
¾ teaspoon salt	Dash of pepper
1 cup boiling water	¾ cup drained diced pickled
¾ cup drained pickled beet	beets
liquid	¾ cup diced celery
1 teaspoon prepared horseradish	

Dissolve gelatin and salt in boiling water. Add beet juice, horseradish, onion, and pepper. Chill until very thick (egg white consistency). Fold in beets and celery. Pour into 1-quart mold or 5 individual molds.

Note: This salad is very good with wild game.

Mrs. Jerre R. White (Jackie Cunningham)

SUMMER FRUIT SALAD

1 cantaloupe, peeled and cut in ¾-inch cubes	1 cup blueberries
1 (20-ounce) can pineapple chunks in juice, undrained	1 cup grapes, halved
1 unpeeled apple, cubed	1 (6-ounce) can frozen orange juice concentrate, thawed and undiluted
2 peaches, peeled and cut in wedges	2 bananas, peeled and cut in ¼-inch slices
1 cup strawberries, halved	

Layer fruits in large bowl in order given, except bananas. Pour orange juice concentrate over. Cover and chill for 6-8 hours. Add bananas an hour before serving. Serves 10-12.

Optional additions: ½ honeydew melon, peeled and cut in ¾-inch cubes
½ cup fresh raspberries (add with bananas)

Bert Wear

SESAME BEAN SPROUT SALAD

½ pound fresh bean sprouts
1 (4-ounce) jar or can sliced
  pimientos, drained
¼ cup green onions, chopped
2 tablespoons sesame oil or
  safflower oil
2 tablespoons rice or wine vinegar
2 tablespoons soy sauce

2 tablespoons sesame seed,
  toasted
½ teaspoon garlic salt
½ teaspoon minced fresh ginger
½ teaspoon sugar
½ teaspoon freshly ground
  pepper

Rinse bean sprouts in cool water. Drain and place in large bowl. Thoroughly mix pimientos, onions, sesame oil, wine vinegar, soy sauce, sesame seed, garlic salt, ginger, sugar, and pepper. Pour over bean sprouts and toss. Cover and refrigerate at least 2 hours or overnight. Serves 4.

Rebekah Ball Embry

GREEN GAGE PLUM SALAD

1 (3-ounce) package lime gelatin
1½ cups boiling water
1 (16-ounce) can green gage
  plums, drained (reserve juice)
½ cup plum juice
⅛ teaspoon salt

1 teaspoon vinegar (cider)
Blanched, toasted almonds
1 (3-ounce) package cream
  cheese
½ teaspoon ground ginger

Dissolve gelatin in water. Add plum juice, salt, and vinegar. Cool. Pit the plums, leaving them whole, and place an almond in each. Place in bottom of mold. Pour ½ of the gelatin mixture over the plums and chill until firm. When the remaining gelatin begins to thicken, add the cream cheese and ginger (whipped together) to is and pour over the plums. Chill until firm. Yield: 8 servings.

A tart salad; good with game.

Mrs. William H. Ausmus (Elizabeth "Becki" Steward)

Lemon juice will keep sliced fruit and vegetables from turning brown. Toss apples, pears, avocados, bananas, peaches, mushrooms in lemon juice, or drop them in a bowl of water to which the juice of a lemon has been added. Lemons give more juice if dropped in boiling water for a minute.

VEGETABLE BOUQUET

1 (1-pound) can cut green beans, drained
1 (1-pound) can red kidney beans, drained
1 (7-ounce) can pitted ripe olives, drained
1 (1-pound) can artichoke hearts, drained
1 (4-ounce) jar pimiento, cut up
1 (8-ounce) can mushrooms, drained
1½ cups celery, cut diagonally
1 onion, cut in rings
¼ cup chopped parsley
¼ cup tarragon vinegar
½ cup oil
1½ teaspoons salt
1 tablespoon sugar
1 tablespoon fines herbes
¼ teaspoon Tabasco

Combine all ingredients and refrigerate overnight. Stir occasionally. Serves 10-12.

Note: Great wintertime salad!

Mrs. W. Van Brown

PEACH ASPIC

2 (3-ounce) packages of peach-flavored gelatin
1 envelope unflavored gelatin
1½ cups boiling water
1 cup orange juice
3 tablespoons lemon juice
1½ cups fresh mashed peaches
Grated rind of 1 lemon
Sugar

Dissolve both plain and peach-flavored gelatin in boiling water. Add orange juice, lemon juice, and lemon rind. Sweeten peaches to taste and add to gelatin mixture. Pour into a 6-cup ring mold and chill. Garnish with Dressing.

DRESSING:
1 (3-ounce) package cream cheese
2 tablespoons mayonnaise
1 peach, mashed

Whip the cream cheese and add remaining ingredients. Mix thoroughly. Place in center of aspic ring.

Mrs. A. J. Strickland, III (Kitty Langston)

CREAM CHEESE-BROCCOLI SALAD

2 (10-ounce) packages frozen
  chopped broccoli
1 teaspoon salt
1 cup beef consomme
2 envelopes unflavored gelatin
¼ cup cold water
1 (8-ounce) package cream cheese
3 teaspoons Tabasco
1 cup mayonnaise
2 tablespoons Worcestershire
  sauce
3 tablespoons lemon juice
½ teaspoon pepper
4 hard-boiled eggs, chopped

Cook broccoli with salt. Bring consomme to a boil. Soften gelatin in ¼ cup cold water, then dissolve in hot consomme. Crumble cream cheese into hot consomme. Stir until dissolved. Let cool. Add Tabasco, mayonnaise, Worcestershire, lemon juice, pepper, and chopped eggs. Stir well. Add other ingredients, mix. Pour into a greased 3-quart ring mold. Chill. Serves 12.

Ann Underwood

STELLA'S RICE SALAD

2 packages chicken Rice-a-Roni
¾ cup green pepper, chopped
8 green onions, chopped
16 stuffed olives, sliced
2 (6-ounce) jars marinated
  artichoke hearts, cut
⅔ cup Hellmann's mayonnaise
1 teaspoon curry powder
  (optional)

Cook rice according to directions on package, omitting oleo. Cool. Add pepper, olives, onions, and drained artichokes. Save marinade and mix with mayonnaise and curry powder. Add this to rice mixture. Toss and chill for at least 5 hours. Serves 8-10.

Mrs. Ralph Quarles (Kat Pritchett)

SLAW FOR A CROWD

5 medium cabbages
2 (28-ounce) cans tomatoes
2 cups vinegar
2 cups sugar
1 cup water
1 teaspoon black pepper
¼ cup salt
Dash Tabasco

Prepare cabbage (shred or cut). Mash tomatoes. Mix together in large non-metallic container. Add vinegar, sugar, water, pepper, salt, Tabasco. Mix well. Chill. Serves 40.

Mrs. Thomas R. Wear, II

ST. PATRICK'S DAY CONGEALED SALAD

½ (3-ounce) package lime gelatin
½ (3-ounce) package lemon gelatin
1 cup boiling water
1 (8-ounce) can crushed pineapple, drained
1 cup cottage cheese
½ cup mayonnaise
½ (5.33-ounce) can evaporated milk
1 heaping tablespoon horseradish
Pinch of salt
½ cup pecans, chopped
1½ tablespoons lemon juice
½ teaspoon green food color
Salad oil for greasing mold

Dissolve gelatin in boiling water and let cool. Add pineapple. In another bowl mix together the cottage cheese, mayonnaise, milk, horseradish, salt, pecans, lemon juice, and food color. Add gelatin mixture to above ingredients and pour into a 1-quart greased mold. Chill until set, about 4 hours. Serves 8 to 10.

Note: Another ½ tablespoon horseradish is necessary for those with zippy tastebuds and for men who usually do not eat congealed salads!!!

Mrs. Gordon Miller, Jr. (Leslie Johnson)

TOSSED FRESH SPINACH SALAD

1 pound fresh spinach, washed, dried, and torn
4 ounces water chestnuts, drained and sliced
2 hard-boiled eggs, sliced
5 slices bacon, crisply cooked and crumbled

DRESSING:
½ cup sugar
½ cup vinegar
1 cup oil
2 tablespoons Worcestershire sauce
⅓ cup catsup
1 small to medium onion

Toss spinach, water chestnuts, eggs, and bacon, and serve with dressing. For dressing, combine sugar, vinegar, oil, Worcestershire sauce, catsup, and onion in blender jar and blend well. The dressing is delicious on other greens and on fruits. It keeps indefinitely. Yield: 6 servings.

Optional: 4 ounces fresh mushrooms, sliced.

Mrs. Pettus Randall (Cathy Johnson)

CUCUMBER-LIME MOLD

2 (3-ounce) packages lime gelatin
1½ cups hot water
4 (3-ounce) packages cream
  cheese, softened
2 cups salad dressing (not
  mayonnaise)
2 teaspoons horseradish

½ teaspoon salt
4 tablespoons lemon juice
1½ cups diced cucumber (about
  1 large cucumber)
½ cup minced onion (or 2 tablespoons instant minced onion)

In large mixing bowl, dissolve gelatin in hot water. Add cream cheese, salad dressing, horseradish, and salt. Beat until smooth. Blend in lemon juice. Mixture may be strained at this point if too lumpy. Chill until thickened. Fold in cucumber and onion. Turn into 6-cup mold or dish. Chill. (Recipe may be halved.) Yield: 12-16 servings; it's very rich.

Mrs. Dennis Stanard (Beth Cowden)

ORANGE PEAR SALAD

1 (15-ounce) can pears
1 (3-ounce) package orange
  gelatin

1 (3-ounce) package cream
  cheese, softened
½ pint whipping cream

Drain pears and reserve juice. Boil juice, then add gelatin and dissolve. Refrigerate until partially set. Blend pears and cream cheese in blender. Add whipping cream and gelatin mixture. Blend well. Mold until firm.

Mrs. James W. Eddings (Heidi Hoyt)

WINTER FRUIT BOWL

4 medium grapefruit
1 cup sugar
½ cup orange marmalade

2 cups (½ pound) fresh or frozen
  whole cranberries
3 medium bananas

Peel, core, and section grapefruit, reserving juice. Set aside grapefruit. Add enough water to juice to measure 1 cup liquid. Combine liquid with sugar and marmalade. Heat to boiling, stirring to dissolve sugar. Add cranberries. Cook and stir until skins pop, 5 to 8 minutes. Remove from heat and cool. Add grapefruit, cover, and chill. Just before serving, slice bananas and stir into chilled grapefruit mixture. Yield: 10 servings.

Mrs. Max Bailey (Julie Knight)

VEGETABLE ASPIC

1 (10-ounce) can consomme
1 envelope unflavored gelatin
1 (16-ounce) can small whole
   green beans, drained (reserve
   liquid)

1 (8½-ounce) can artichoke
   hearts
4 hard-boiled eggs, diced
Worcestershire sauce
Lemon juice

Dissolve gelatin in warmed consomme diluted with liquid from beans. Season with lemon juice, Worcestershire sauce, salt, and pepper. Combine with green beans, artichoke hearts, and eggs. Pour into ring mold and congeal.

Mrs. William Manderson (Elizabeth Woollen)

TOMATOES WITH AVOCADO DRESSING

1 ripe avocado
⅓ cup mayonnaise
1 tablespoon lemon juice
1 tablespoon fresh onion juice
Dash Worcestershire sauce

Dash Tabasco
Salt to taste
3 ripe tomatoes
Salad greens
Chopped chives

Work avocado through a sieve or blend in a blender. Mix the purée with mayonnaise, lemon juice, onion juice, Worcestershire sauce, Tabasco, and salt. Peel tomatoes, cut into slices and arrange them on a bed of salad greens. Pour avocado dressing over the tomatoes and sprinkle with chopped chives. The avocado dressing is also good as a dip for fresh vegetables such as celery, cauliflower, squash, carrots, etc.

Mrs. Howard Burchfield, Jr. (Judy Forsyth)

SEVEN-UP SALAD

7 ounces 7-Up
2 cups miniature marshmallows
1 (3-ounce) package lime gelatin
1 (8-ounce) package cream cheese,
   at room temperature

2½ cups crushed pineapple
¾ cup chopped walnuts or
   pecans
⅔ cup mayonnaise
1 cup Cool Whip

Combine 7-Up and marshmallows in a saucepan. Heat until marshmallows are melted. Add gelatin and stir until dissolved. Pour over softened cream cheese and mix well. Add pineapple with juice and nuts. Refrigerate until partially thickened. Stir in mayonnaise and fold in Cool Whip. Pour into flat dish or mold. This can be served as a dessert or salad.

Mrs. Alex O. Gatewood (Diane Gainey)

GERMAN POTATO SALAD

8-10 slices bacon
6 medium potatoes, unpared
1 onion, chopped fine
1 teaspoon salt
⅛ teaspoon pepper
1 teaspoon dry mustard

¼ cup sugar
½ cup water
¼ to ½ cup vinegar
1 egg, slightly beaten
Onion rings (optional)
Crisp bacon (optional)

Cook bacon until crisp, reserving drippings. Crumble bacon. Boil potatoes until tender, remove skins while hot, and slice. Combine bacon, potatoes, and onion. To the bacon drippings, add salt, pepper, dry mustard, sugar, water, vinegar, and beaten egg. Cook mixture until the egg thickens. Pour it over the bacon-potato mixture and stir until the liquid is dissolved. Garnish, if desired, with onion rings and additional pieces of crisp bacon. If potatoes seem dry, add more vinegar, sugar, and water. Makes 8 servings.

Mrs. Wilfred Yeargan, Jr. (Mary Gail Williams)

Hint: Wash and freeze dill weed in small plastic bags in June. Use all year in green beans, potato salad, shrimp dishes. Other fresh herbs, such as basil, tarragon, and marjoram, also freeze well.

MARGARET BROWN'S STUFFED
FRESH TOMATO SALAD

6 medium tomatoes
1 (6-ounce) jar artichoke hearts,
  drained
1 (4-ounce) jar cocktail
  mushrooms, drained
1 (8-ounce) bottle Italian
  dressing

½ cup mayonnaise
⅓ cup sour cream
1 teaspoon curry powder
1 teaspoon lemon juice
1 tablespoon instant onions
Paprika
Seasoned salt and pepper

Scoop out tomatoes; sprinkle with seasoned salt and pepper. Turn upside down and drain for ½ hour or more. Marinate mushrooms and artichokes in Italian dressing for 1 hour. Place drained mushrooms and artichokes in the tomatoes. Combine mayonnaise, sour cream, curry, lemon juice, and onion and put on top. Sprinkle with paprika and serve on lettuce. Yield: 6 servings.

Hint: Save Italian Dressing to use on future salads.

Mrs. David M. Cochrane (Mary B. Tompkins)

RICE AND ENGLISH PEA SALAD

1⅓ cups raw Minute rice
1½ cups water
½ teaspoon salt
1 (10-ounce) box frozen English
  peas, cooked
¼ cup French dressing
¾ cup mayonnaise

1 tablespoon minced raw onion
¾ teaspoon curry powder
½ teaspoon salt
⅛ teaspoon pepper
½ teaspoon dry mustard
1 cup celery, diced

Cook rice in water and salt according to directions on box. Mix rice, peas, French dressing, mayonnaise, onion, curry powder, salt, pepper, and dry mustard together with refrigerate in bowl or 2-quart mold.

Mrs. Adrian Goldstein (Betty Jo May)

SWEET PEA SALAD

2 (17-ounce) cans LeSeur peas
4 ounces cheddar cheese, grated
½ small white onion, chopped fine
½ to ¾ cup mayonnaise

Pinch of salt
Paprika
2 hard-boiled eggs

Drain peas in colander. Mix peas, cheddar cheese, onion, mayonnaise, and salt; refrigerate overnight or for at least 2-3 hours. To serve: slice eggs and place on top of salad. Sprinkle paprika on top. Serves 8 to 10.

This is a good luncheon dish. Easy and has to be made ahead of time.

Mrs. William V. Barkley (Carolyn Johnson)

SOUR CREAM CUCUMBERS

½ teaspoon salt
1 tablespoon sugar
2 tablespoons cider vinegar
1 cup sour cream
2 tablespoons chopped chives

2 tablespoons chopped fresh dill
1 tablespoon celery seed
Few drops Tabasco
2 firm cucumbers, unpeeled

Dissolve salt and sugar in vinegar. Add sour cream. Stir until smooth. Add chives, dill, and celery seed. Slice cucumbers paper thin and combine with dressing. Chill one hour or more. Yield: 4 to 6 servings.

Mrs. Wilfred W. Yeargan, Jr. (Mary Gail Williams)

FROZEN SOUR CREAM FRUIT SALAD

2 (8-ounce) cartons sour cream
¾ cup sugar
Dash salt
2 tablespoons lemon juice
4 slices pineapple

6 cherries
⅓ cup pecans
1 banana
Cup cake liners

Mix together the sour cream, sugar, and salt. Then add lemon juice. Cut up the pineapple, cherries, pecans, and bananas, and add to the sour cream mixture. Put cup cake liners in muffin tins. Fill each liner about ¾ full. Freeze. When ready to serve, remove paper liners and serve on shell of lettuce. Makes 12-15.

Mrs. William Tucker (Harriet Belle Little)

SOUR CREAM FRUIT SLAW

1 2½-pound head cabbage, grated
2 large apples, grated
⅔ cup grated green pepper, drained
½ cup pineapple tidbits, drained

1 cup sour cream
1½ tablespoons mayonnaise
½ teaspoon salt
¼ teaspoon pepper

Combine cabbage, apple, green pepper, and pineapple. In separate bowl, combine remaining ingredients. Pour dressing over cabbage mixture and toss lightly. Garnish with additional pineapple and apple slices. If storing in refrigerator, seal. Yield: 6-8 servings.

Mrs. Jack Echols (Connie Sue Morgan)

CAULIFLOWER SALAD

1 cauliflower
1 onion
1 (2¾-ounce) bottle stuffed olives
1 cup oil
½ cup vinegar

1 teaspoon salt
1 head lettuce
1 (4-ounce) package Kraft bleu cheese

Cut up cauliflower and olives, and slice onions into thin rings. Place in large bowl. Mix oil, vinegar, and salt. Pour over vegetables in bowl, cover, and marinate in refrigerator for 4 hours or more. Immediately before serving, add lettuce and crumbled bleu cheese. Yield: 12 to 16 servings.

Mrs. E. S. "Brother" Harris, III (Frances Mathews)

PISTACHIO SALAD (OR DESSERT)

1 (3-ounce) package instant
    pistachio pudding mix
1 (20-ounce) can crushed pine-
    apple (do not drain)

2 cups miniature marshmallows
1 (9-ounce) container Cool Whip
Fresh strawberries or maraschino
    cherries for garnish (optional)

Place pineapple and juice in large bowl. Sprinkle with dry pudding mix. Add marshmallows and Cool Whip to pineapple mixture. Stir well and refrigerate. May top with fresh strawberries or maraschino cherries. Yield: 8-10 servings.

Mrs. Jimmy Hamner (Elizabeth Bolling)

CREOLE SALAD

1 (10-ounce) package elbow
    macaroni
2 tablespoons Italian dressing
1 teaspoon onion, grated
3 medium-sized tomatoes, peeled,
    chopped, and salted

1 (3-ounce) bottle stuffed olives,
    sliced
4 ounces cheddar cheese, grated
¾ cup mayonnaise
Dash of cayenne pepper

Cook macaroni according to package directions. Drain. Place in container. Sprinkle with Italian dressing and add onion. Let cool. Add tomatoes, olives, and cheese. Stir gently. Add mayonnaise and cayenne pepper. Keep refrigerated. Serves 4-6.

Mrs. David B. Ellis (Patricia Mitchell)

SUMMER VEGETABLE MOLD

1 cup celery, chopped
1 cucumber, chopped
1 green pepper, chopped
1 onion, chopped
1 tomato, chopped

1 teaspoon salt, or more to taste
1 envelope unflavored gelatin
3 tablespoons hot water
1 pint mayonnaise

Drain chopped celery, cucumber, green pepper, onion, and tomato in colander with salt for 1 hour. Dissolve gelatin in hot water. Mix all of this with mayonnaise. Mold. Serve with Melba toast or Triscuits. Or use as sandwich filling. Makes 12 sandwiches.

Mrs. Hugh Ragsdale, Jr. (Kate Webb)

TWENTY-FOUR HOUR SLAW

1 cup vinegar
½ cup sugar
2 teaspoons celery seed
1 teaspoon dry mustard
1 teaspoon salt
¼ teaspoon black pepper
1 cup salad oil

1 large head cabbage (which has
    been prepared for slaw)
2 medium onions, cut in rings
Optional: 1 green pepper, diced
    fine
6 stuffed olives, sliced

Let vinegar, sugar, celery seed, mustard, salt, and pepper come to a boil in a saucepan. Add salad oil. Remove from heat and pour over cabbage and onion. Cover tightly and let stand in refrigerator for at least 24 hours. (Will keep for a week in refrigerator.) Yield: 8 servings.

Mrs. John A. Russell, III (Walton Callen)—Aliceville, AL
Mrs. Wayne Guy (Becky Morton)

CAROLINE'S LAYERED SALAD

1 pound fresh spinach, torn
2 (10-ounce) packages frozen peas,
    thawed
1 head lettuce, torn
8 hard-boiled eggs, sliced
1 pound bacon, cooked and
    crumbled

4 ounces Swiss cheese, cut in
    strips or shredded
1 medium onion, sliced thin, or
    ½ cup chopped scallions with
    tops
1½ cups mayonnaise

Layer spinach, peas, lettuce, eggs, bacon, cheese, and onion, and seal with mayonnaise. Refrigerate overnight. Toss before serving. Serves 10.

Variations: Add 2 tomatoes, cut in wedges, before tossing. Layer ½ cup seasoned croutons or bread crumbs on top of cheese. Add 1 (8-ounce) can water chestnuts, sliced; add 1 cup chopped celery.

Mrs. T. Griffin Stanley, Jr. (Phyllis Miglarese)

FROZEN CRANBERRY SALAD

1 (1-pound) can whole berry
    cranberry sauce
1 (8-ounce) can crushed pineapple
    (do not drain)

1 (8-ounce) carton sour cream

Mix together and freeze in the cranberry can and another can equal size. When ready to serve, cut other end of can out and push salad out. Slice and serve on lettuce. Yield: 8 servings.

Joyce Green Rives

Freeze unwashed fresh cranberries in the plastic bag they came in. Use as you would fresh ones all year.

SPICED PEACH SALAD

2 (16-ounce) cans spiced peaches,
    cut in big chunks
2 cups peach juice
1 cup orange juice
¾ cup water
2 (3-ounce) packages lemon gelatin

1 cup chopped pecans (fairly
    large pieces)
1 cup seedless grapes or 1 cup
    pineapple chunks (both in
    season)

Dissolve gelatin in hot peach juice. Add orange juice and water. Refrigerate until syrupy. Add cut peaches, pecans, and grapes or pineapple. Place in ring mold or individual molds and refrigerate until congealed.

DRESSING:
½ pint whipped cream
2 tablespoons mayonnaise

½ cup orange juice

Whip cream, add mayonnaise and orange juice. Serves 12-16.

Mrs. Robert N. Rice, Jr. (Carolyn Burchfield)

TOMATO-GEL SALAD

1 envelope unflavored gelatin
½ cup water
1 (10¾-ounce) can condensed
tomato soup
2 (3-ounce) packages cream cheese
1 cup mayonnaise

1 tablespoon onion juice
2 tablespoons lemon juice
½ cup celery, chopped
½ cup bell pepper, chopped
½ cup stuffed olives, sliced
½ cup scallions, chopped

Soften gelatin in water for 3 minutes. Heat soup. Add gelatin and stir until dissolved. Add cream cheese and beat until smooth. Add mayonnaise, onion juice, lemon juice, celery, pepper, olives, scallions. Blend well. Pour into greased mold and refrigerate until firmly set. Yield: 12 servings.

Note: Two (7-ounce) cans water-pack tuna, crab, or shrimp may be added for a delicious main dish salad. May also serve as a spread with crackers.

Mrs. James R. Shamblin (Patricia Terry)—Centre, AL

CISSY'S CHRISTMAS SALAD

1 (3-ounce) package red raspberry
gelatin
1 (3-ounce) package lime gelatin
1 (21-ounce) can cherry pie filling
1 (8-ounce) can crushed pineapple
1 (3-ounce) package cream cheese,
softened

⅓ cup mayonnaise
1 (4½-ounce) carton frozen
whipped topping
Green food coloring
Red cherries

Dissolve red raspberry gelatin in 1 cup boiling water. Add cherry pie filling. Pour into 9 x 9 x 2-inch pan. Chill until partially set. Dissolve lime gelatin in 1 cup boiling water. Mix softened cream cheese with mayonnaise until smooth. Add lime gelatin. Stir in undrained pineapple. Fold in whipped topping and stir in food coloring. Spread on top of cherry mixture. Chill until set, cut into squares, and top with mayonnaise and red cherry.

Children like this.

Mrs. Harry Wright (Cissy James)

MRS. ATKINSON'S DELICIOUS SALAD

2 egg yolks
4 tablespoons vinegar
2 teaspoons sugar
½ pint cream, whipped
½ pound miniature marsh-
  mallows

1 (16-ounce) can chunk
  pineapple, drained
1 (16-ounce) can white cherries,
  drained
4 ounces shelled almonds

Beat egg yolks well. Add vinegar and sugar. Cook until thick, stirring all
the time. Let cool completely. Whip cream and mix with cooked mixture.
Add to this the marshmallows, pineapple, cherries, and almonds. Mix all
together. You may serve it then or refrigerate overnight. Serves 8.

Mrs. Don Barnes (Sue Strickland)

MAMA'S APRICOT SALAD

½ cup cold water
2½ envelopes unflavored gelatin
1 (16-ounce) can apricots
1 cup sugar

Juice of 2 lemons
1 (3-ounce) package cream
  cheese
1 cup whipping cream, whipped

Soak gelatin in cold water. Drain apricots and add sugar to apricot syrup.
Heat to boiling point and pour over gelatin. Reserve 1 cup of mixture and
set aside. Run apricots through sieve and add lemon juice and remaining
gelatin mixture. Set in refrigerator until congealed. Mash cheese until
smooth. Stir into cream that has been whipped. Then add 1 cup gelatin
mixture that you saved earlier. Mix well and pour over top. Set back in
refrigerator to congeal. Serves 8.

*Note: This was my grandmother's recipe, and no trip to Mama's was com-
plete without it.*

Mrs. Ronald W. Laycock (Deborah Barton)

*Hint: A pretty way to serve chicken salad is in a ring of cantaloupe or
honeydew, made by slicing whole melon crosswise and removing seeds.
Garnish with watercress or mint leaves.*

CHICKEN SALAD

1 hen (5 to 6 pounds)
3 cups chopped celery
1 cup chopped sweet pickles
3 dashes Tabasco sauce

3 tablespoons salad oil
2 tablespoons lemon juice
1 teaspoon salt

Stew hen and chop into pieces. Combine all ingredients; mix well. Chill. Yield: 6 servings.

Mrs. Frank E. Spell (Bell Searcy)

CHICKEN SALAD WITH RAISINS AND ALMONDS

1½ cups cold, cooked chicken
1 cup seedless raisins
Enough water to cover raisins
⅔ cup blanched almonds
½ cup light cream
Salt and pepper to taste

2 teaspoons lemon juice
1 tablespoon finely chopped
  onion
4 tablespoons mayonnaise
1 tablespoon chopped parsley

Cut the chicken into bite-sized pieces. Soak raisins in cold water for 15 minutes, bring to a boil and drain. Combine almonds, cream, salt, pepper, lemon juice, onion, and mix with mayonnaise. Add chicken and raisins. Toss. Sprinkle with parsley and serve. Serves 4.

Mrs. Earl L. Carpenter (Betty Myrick)

GRANDMA WHITSON'S CHICKEN SALAD

1 (5 to 6-pound) hen

1 cup celery

SAUCE:
4 eggs
4 cups finely ground cabbage
¾ cup sugar
6 tablespoons vinegar

1 stick butter
½ cup chicken broth
Salt and pepper to taste
1 teaspoon mustard

Simmer hen until meat comes loose from bones. Bone and grind chicken in food grinder. Grind celery. Beat eggs well. Add cabbage, sugar, vinegar, butter, broth, salt, pepper, and mustard. Cook until thickened, stirring constantly. Pour hot sauce over ground chicken. When cool, add celery. Pour a little extra vinegar over top of salad. Refrigerate overnight.

Mrs. William H. Darden (Caroline Sullivan)

CONGEALED CHICKEN SALAD

2 cups diced chicken (about 4
  chicken breasts)
1 envelope unflavored gelatin
1½ cups cold chicken broth
2 chicken bouillon cubes
¾ cup mayonnaise
1 cup sour cream
1 tablespoon lemon juice

Salt to taste
¾ teaspoon dillweed
⅛ teaspoon Tabasco
1 cup chopped celery
¾ cup sliced pimiento-stuffed
  olives
1 tablespoon minced onion

Cook chicken breasts seasoned with poultry seasoning, salt, and pepper in pressure cooker. Save broth and cool. Soften gelatin in 1½ cups broth. Add bouillon cubes and stir until dissolved in small saucepan over low heat. Combine mayonnaise, sour cream, lemon juice, salt, dill, and Tabasco in bowl. Stir in cubed chicken, broth mixture, celery, and onion. Congeal in dish. Garnish with olive slices. Best when made a day ahead.

Mrs. Daniel Propst (Dru Fulton)

TUNA NOODLE SALAD

1½ (6½-ounce) cans tuna fish
  (in oil)
1 medium bell pepper, chopped
  fine
2 hard-boiled eggs, grated
3 tablespoons sweet salad picklets

¼ cup stuffed sliced olives
1 small onion, grated
1 (5-ounce) package extra fine
  noodles, cooked by directions
Mayonnaise to taste

Mix all the above ingredients together. Add mayonnaise to taste. Mold in cup. Serve on lettuce. Yield: 6 servings.

Mrs. John G. Sumner (Diane Condon)

SHRIMP SALAD

3 cups cooked chopped shrimp
  (approximately 2 pounds)
1 cup diced celery
4 hard-boiled eggs, chopped
½ cup sliced stuffed olives
¼ cup sliced green onions

¼ cup chopped dill pickle
1 cup mayonnaise
2 tablespoons chili sauce
2 teaspoons prepared horseradish
1 teaspoon salt

Combine shrimp, celery, eggs, olives, onions, and dill pickle. Blend mayonnaise, chili sauce, horseradish, and salt. Add to shrimp mixture and toss lightly. Chill. Yield: 6-8 servings.

Mrs. Daniel M. Hoke (Gail Ford)

JOAN'S CHICKEN-RICE SALAD

⅓ cup bottled French dressing
⅔ cup mayonnaise
1 cup chopped celery
1½ cups cooked, cubed chicken
1 cup pineapple chunks or
   mandarin orange sections

3 cups cooked rice
Salt and pepper
½ cup chopped almonds,
   walnuts, or pecans

Mix all ingredients together. Chill thoroughly. Serve on bed of lettuce or in pineapple shells. (Quarter pineapple length-wise, cut out fruit and drain shells cut side down.) Serves 6-8.

Mrs. David Brown

STUFFED AVOCADO BOAT

4 avocados
1 cup cooked, diced chicken
1 cup diced apple
½ cup diced celery

½ cup chopped nuts
Mayonnaise or salad dressing
Stuffed olives, sliced
Dash of paprika

Cut avocados lengthwise. Remove pulp, seeds and refrigerate shells. Combine chicken, apple, celery and nuts with avocado pulp, using mayonnaise or salad dressing to suit your taste. Fill avocado shells with mixture. Garnish with olive slices and dash of paprika. Serve on lettuce with crackers or bread. Yield: 6-8 servings.

Mrs. A. E. Poole (Marion Daniel)

AVOCAT FRANCOISE

2 ripe avocados
1 lemon
2 hard-boiled eggs, chopped
6 ounces canned or frozen cooked
   shrimp

1 (4-ounce) can sliced mush-
   rooms, drained
Mayonnaise
Lettuce

Cut avocados in half and remove seeds. Cut lemon in half and rub inside of avocados with lemon. Mix eggs, shrimp, and mushrooms together. Add enough mayonnaise to shrimp mixture to moisten. Spoon shrimp mixture into avocado halves. Place avocado halves on lettuce leaves and serve. Serves 4.

Mrs. A. J. "Lonnie" Strickland, III (Kitty Langston)

NEW ORLEANS SEAFOOD DELIGHT

2 pounds fresh shrimp (medium)
1 (3-ounce) bag shrimp boil

1 pound crabmeat (fresh, if
  possible)

SAUCE:
1 cup Hellmann's mayonnaise
½ cup chili sauce
2 tablespoons oil and vinegar
  dressing
1 tablespoon grated onion

2 teaspoons lemon juice
2 teaspoons horseradish
½ teaspoon Worcestershire sauce
1 teaspoon salt
Dash black pepper

4-5 large avocados

Lemon juice

Cook shrimp and shell. In small bowl, mix Hellmann's, chili sauce, dressing, onion, lemon juice, horseradish, Worcestershire sauce, salt, and pepper into a sauce. Pour sauce over cooled shrimp and crumbled crabmeat. Cover and refrigerate 2½-3 hours. Cut avocados in half, remove pits, and brush surfaces with lemon juice. Spoon seafood into centers, heaping generously. Serve on lettuce. Serves 8.

Mrs. William H. Ausmus (Elizabeth "Becki" Steward)

MOLDED TUNA SALAD

1 teaspoon mustard
½ cup canned English peas,
  drained
2 hard-boiled eggs, chopped fine
2 (6½-ounce) cans tuna, drained
2 tablespoons onion, grated
1 cup mayonnaise

2 tablespoons lemon juice
¾ cup celery, chopped
2 tablespoons pimiento, chopped
Pinch of salt
2 envelopes unflavored gelatin
½ cup cold water

Combine all ingredients except gelatin and water. Dissolve gelatin in cold water and add to tuna mixture. Place in mold that has been greased with mayonnaise. Chill overnight. Serve on lettuce leaves. Serves 6.

Mrs. Randolph Fowler (Shirley Jones)

MOCK CRAB SALAD

2 cups cold cooked rice
1 (13-ounce) can white tuna,
   drained and flaked
1 (4-ounce) jar pimientos, diced
   (optional)
4 green onions, finely sliced (or
   1-2 tablespoons instant minced
   onion, rehydrated)

Mayonnaise
Onion and garlic powders
Salt and freshly ground pepper
Lettuce leaves
Parsley sprigs

Combine rice, tuna, pimientos, and green onions with mayonnaise to moisten in medium bowl. Add seasonings to taste and mix well. Serve on lettuce-lined salad plates and garnish with sprigs of parsley. Serves 6-8.

Note: For a spread, thin mixture with more mayonnaise and serve with crackers or an assortment of raw vegetables. A great way to use leftover rice.

Rebekah Ball Embry

TUNA MOUSSE

1 (3-ounce) package lemon gelatin
½ cup boiling water
1 cup Campbell's chicken gumbo
   soup
2 tablespoons minced onion
2 tablespoons minced celery

2 tablespoons minced bell pepper
½ cup mayonnaise
½ cup sour cream
2 cups tuna fish, drained
Paprika to taste

Mix lemon gelatin and water. After gelatin is cool, add the soup, onion, celery, bell pepper, mayonnaise, sour cream, tuna fish, and paprika. Pour into a 11 x 7-inch pan or any type mold. Can be made ahead of time. Serves 6.

Note: This is great for stuffing tomatoes!

Mrs. J. Stuart Patton (Cindy Fitch)

BAYLEY'S OF MOBILE WEST INDIES SALAD

1 medium onion, chopped fine
1 pound fresh lump crabmeat
Salt and pepper
4 ounces Wesson oil
3 ounces cider vinegar
4 ounces ice water

Divide chopped onion in half and spread one-half over bottom of large mixing bowl. Separate crabmeat lumps and place on top of onion in bowl, then add balance of onion on top of this. Now salt and pepper to taste (about 1 teaspoon each). Pour over all, first the Wesson oil, next the vinegar and last the ice water. Cover and place in refrigerator to marinate 2-12 hours. When ready to serve, toss lightly but do not stir. Do not subsitute any of the ingredients, as the result will not be the same. Delightful served as hors d'oeuvres with Premium saltines or party crackers of your choice.

Variation: Some people like to add 1 cup chopped celery mixed with onion for a variation.

Mrs. James Chancy (Christine Patton)

BLENDER MAYONNAISE

2 eggs
1 teaspoon dry mustard
1 teaspoon salt
1 teaspoon sugar
½ teaspoon paprika
¼ teaspoon celery salt
Dash cayenne
⅓ cup lemon juice
2 cups salad oil

Blend eggs, mustard, salt, sugar, paprika, celery salt, cayenne, lemon juice, and ¼ cup of the oil for 5 seconds. Add remaining oil in a steady stream while the motor runs.

Martha Moore Warner

BLEU CHEESE DRESSING

½ cup bleu cheese (1 Kraft Cold Pack)
½ cup buttermilk
½ cup mayonnaise
½ teaspoon garlic salt

Blend all ingredients well. Chill before serving. Makes 6 servings.

Mrs. Richard O. Jones (Cissie Roberts)

BUTTERMILK SALAD DRESSING

2 cups mayonnaise
2 cups sour cream
2 tablespoons finely minced onion
2 tablespoons finely chopped
  parsley
2 tablespoons chopped chives

½ teaspoon celery salt
½ teaspoon onion powder
1 teaspoon chervil
½ teaspoon pepper
1 teaspoon salt
2 cups buttermilk

Combine mayonnaise and sour cream. Add onion, parsley, chives, celery salt, onion powder, chervil, pepper, and salt. Blend well. Add buttermilk. Refrigerate at least 2 hours or overnight.

Note: "Instant" dried onion, parsley, and chives may be used. For a vegetable dip, reduce buttermilk by half.

CAROL'S CONFETTI FRENCH DRESSING

½ cup oil
⅓ cup vinegar
1½ teaspoons salt
⅓ cup sugar
1 tablespoon minced or 3 tablespoons grated onion
¼ teaspoon celery salt

2 tablespoons green pepper,
  chopped
2 tablespoons pimiento, chopped
½ teaspoon paprika
¼ teaspoon dry mustard
3 tablespoons catsup

Put all ingredients in blender container. Process on "chop" for 30 seconds.

Mrs. T. Griffin Stanley, Jr. (Phyllis Miglarese)

GRENADINE SALAD DRESSING

¼ cup sugar
⅓ cup light corn syrup
¼ cup white vinegar
2 or 3 tablespoons grenadine

1 teaspoon dry mustard
1 teaspoon salt
1 teaspoon grated onion
1 cup salad oil

Combine sugar, corn syrup, vinegar, grenadine, mustard, salt, and onion in a blender container. Blend. Add oil slowly. Mixture will thicken. Chill.

Note: This is good over any fruit salad. A particularly good and unusual one is of tossed dark greens, avocado chunks, grapefruit bits, and pomegranate seeds.

Mrs. James A. Neville (Carole Gibson)

MAYONNAISE

3 egg yolks
¾ teaspoon onion salt
½ teaspoon salt
1 teaspoon paprika
1 teaspoon dry mustard
¼ teaspoon white pepper

Several drops Tabasco
Juice of 1 lemon (2-3
   tablespoons)
2¼ cups safflower oil or corn oil
2 tablespoons boiling water

Have all ingredients at room temperature. To make with mixer: beat egg yolks until thick. Add onion salt, salt, paprika, mustard, pepper, Tabasco, and 1 tablespoon lemon juice; beat for 1 minute. Add oil, ¼ teaspoonful at a time, beating constantly, being sure egg yolks have absorbed the oil before you add more. When about ½ cup of the oil has been added, sauce will thicken. Then add 1 tablespoon of oil at a time, adding 1 teaspoonful lemon juice whenever sauce gets very thick. Beat well after each addition. Beat in boiling water. Correct seasoning.

To make in food processor: use plastic blade. Put egg yolks, onion salt, salt, paprika, mustard, pepper, Tabasco, lemon juice in work bowl. Process for about 10 seconds. Add ¼ cup oil through feed tube as machine is running, then add remaining oil. Process until thick. Turn out into bowl and add boiling water by hand (use whisk). Correct seasoning. Keep in covered bowl in refrigerator. Makes 2½ cups.

Mrs. Peterson Cavert (Mary Beth Wear)

GREEN GODDESS SALAD DRESSING

1 cup mayonnaise
½ cup commercial sour cream
¼ teaspoon garlic powder
2 green onions and tops, coarsely
   cut
¼ cup green pepper, coarsely cut

2 tablespoons freshly squeezed
   lemon juice
¼ cup parsley
¼ teaspoon black pepper
Dash Worcestershire sauce

Place in blender or food processor fitted with steel blade the mayonnaise, sour cream, garlic powder, onions, green pepper, lemon juice, parsley, pepper, and Worcestershire sauce. Process for 10 seconds (high speed on blender) until pale green and smooth. Makes 2 cups.

Note: Excellent and so easy!

Mrs. J. C. "Bud" Miller (Presteen Sims)

DRESSING FOR SLAW

1 pint mayonnaise
1 (8-ounce) carton sour cream
Juice of 1 lemon
1 teaspoon salt
1 tablespoon sugar

2 tablespoons vinegar
1 teaspoon mustard
Grated onion to taste
Optional: 2 teaspoons dill seed

Mix all ingredients and pour over cabbage. Makes about 3½ cups of dressing, enough for 2-3 heads of cabbage. Keeps well in refrigerator.

Mrs. Daniel Hoke (Gail Ford)

CREAMY DRESSING FOR SLAW

2 tablespoons sugar
1 teaspoon salt
½ teaspoon celery seed
2 tablespoons tarragon vinegar

1 teaspoon prepared mustard
  (Dijon)
½ cup mayonnaise

Mix sugar, salt, celery seed, vinegar, mustard, and mayonnaise together and pour over cabbage which has been sliced. This makes enough for 1 medium head of cabbage.

Mrs. David Hefelfinger (Virginia Mauney)

PIQUANT DRESSING

⅓ to ½ cup sugar
1 teaspoon salt
1 teaspon dry mustard
1 teaspoon paprika
¼ teaspoon celery salt
⅓ cup catsup

¼ cup vinegar
Juice of 1 lemon (approximately
  4 tablespoons)
10 drops Tabasco
¼ cup grated onion
¾ cup salad oil

Blend together the sugar, salt, dry mustard, paprika, and celery salt. Add catsup, vinegar, lemon juice, Tabasco, onion, and oil. Beat thoroughly. Chill. Shake again before serving. Keeps well in refrigerator for several weeks. Makes 1 pint.

Mrs. E. Calhoun Wilson (Gene Henderson)

POPPY SEED DRESSING

4 tablespoons mayonnaise   2 teaspoons lemon juice
2 tablespoons honey   ½-1 teaspoon poppy seed

Mix together the mayonnaise, honey, and lemon juice. Add poppy seed as desired. Refrigerate. Serve over watermelon and cantaloupe balls, and pineapple.

Mrs. Thomas A. Howard, Jr. (Patricia Roberts)

RUSSIAN DRESSING

1 pint mayonnaise   1 teaspoon chives, chopped
1 pint chili sauce   2 tablespoons vinegar
¼ cup pimiento, chopped   Dash paprika
2 hard-boiled eggs, chopped fine 1 teaspoon grated onion, or to
1 tablespoon parsley, chopped   taste

Stir together the mayonnaise and chili sauce. Add pimiento, eggs, parsley, chives, vinegar, paprika, and onion. Keeps well covered in refrigerator.

Mrs. Tommy Whitfield (Carolyn Flanagan)

ROQUEFORT DRESSING

2 cups mayonnaise   1 large clove garlic, crushed
1 (5.33-ounce) can evaporated   1 teaspoon celery salt
  milk   1 teaspoon sugar
¼ pound Roquefort cheese,
  softened

Combine in mixer bowl the mayonnaise, milk, cheese, garlic, celery salt, and sugar. Blend well. Keep in covered bowl in refrigerator.

Mrs. Lloyd W. Wagner, Jr. (Martha Savage)

MINT DRESSING

1¼ cups salad oil
⅓ cup white vinegar
⅓ cup lemon juice
2½ teaspoons seasoned salt

⅛ teaspoon pepper
3 tablespoons sugar
¼ cup finely chopped fresh mint

Combine oil, vinegar, lemon juice, seasoned salt, pepper, sugar, and mint into a jar with a tight-fitting lid. Shake to mix well. (You may use a blender.) Refrigerate until ready to use. Shake again before using. Makes 2 cups. Great for Melon Balls! Garnish with sprigs of mint.

Mrs. E. Allen Mattox (Harriet Marrs)

PATTI'S SALAD DRESSING

¾ cup vegetable oil
⅔ cup vinegar
1 cup chili sauce
1 cup sugar

1 tablespoon Worcestershire sauce
2 small onions, minced
Sprinkle of garlic salt
3-4 ounces bleu cheese, mashed

Combine in a small bowl the oil, vinegar, chili sauce, sugar, Worcestershire, onions, and garlic salt. Mix well. Blend in bleu cheese. Keeps well, covered, in refrigerator.

Mrs. T. Griffin Stanley (Phyllis Miglarese)

HEDGE HILL GARDEN LETTUCE DRESSING

2 hard-boiled eggs
¼ cup vinegar
¼ cup sugar

2-3 tablespoons whipping cream
¼ teaspoon salt

Dissolve the sugar in the vinegar while the eggs are boiling. Peel and separate eggs. Mash yolks with a fork and add cream as necessary to make a paste of medium consistency. Add vinegar-sugar mixture, salt, and finely crumbled egg whites. Serve over fresh garden lettuce. Good over spinach, too, with bacon crumbles.

Mrs. Ernest "Rainey" Collins (Louise "Bebe" Williams)

FRENCH DRESSING

1½ teaspoons salt
½ teaspoon black pepper
1 teaspoon paprika
1 teaspoon confectioners' sugar

½ teaspoon dry mustard
Several shakes of cayenne
⅓ cup wine vinegar
1 cup safflower or corn oil

Mix together the salt, pepper, paprika, confectioners' sugar, dry mustard, cayenne, and vinegar; then add oil. Shake before using. Keeps well in refrigerator.

Mrs. Peterson Cavert (Mary Beth Wear)

PARMESAN SALAD DRESSING

½ cup oil
¼ cup lemon juice
3 tablespoons Parmesan cheese

⅛ teaspoon garlic powder
⅛ teaspoon salt
¼ teaspoon sugar

Mix together oil, lemon juice, Parmesan cheese, garlic powder, salt, and sugar. This is very good on a spinach salad.

Mrs. Stuart Patton (Cindy Fitch)

SALAD DRESSING (FOR FRUIT SALAD)

⅓ cup sugar
1 teaspoon celery seed or poppy
   seed
1 teaspoon grated onion
1 teaspoon paprika

1 teaspoon salt
1 teaspoon dry mustard
4 tablespoons vinegar
1 cup cold Wesson oil

Mix sugar, celery seed, onion, paprika, salt and mustard with 1 table-spoon vinegar. Alternately mix in remainder of vinegar and oil with rotary egg beater. Excellent on cole slaw.

Note: This recipe was originally submitted under the name of Mrs. William McQueen in the Junior Welfare Association Cookbook published in 1939.

Mrs. Albert Baernstein (Sis Wiesel)

Vegetables

ARTICHOKES ALLA ROMANA

4 medium-size artichokes
⅓ cup olive oil
¼ cup water
4 garlic cloves (optional)
Juice of 1 lemon

1 teaspoon salt
½ teaspoon pepper
1 teaspoon mint flakes (or sprigs
 of fresh mint)

Remove stems and points of the artichokes and remove tough outer leaves. Cut into quarters, removing white fuzzy fiber or choke. Soak artichokes for a few minutes in water containing part of lemon juice. Wash and drain well. Place in a saucepan with sides down, with water, oil, lemon juice, mint, and garlic. Sprinkle with salt and pepper. Cover and let steam until tender (until leaves pull loose easily). Serve on side, and pour over them some of the oil in which they have been cooked. Serves 4.

Mrs. Michael McFerrin (Sherry Romaine)

ARTICHOKE BAKE

1 (14-ounce) can artichokes
1 (6-ounce) can water chestnuts
1 (10¾-ounce) can mushroom soup
¼ can milk
3 hard-boiled eggs

1 cup Spanish olives
1½ cups grated hoop cheese
1 cup bread crumbs
Butter

In 1-quart round casserole, slice artichokes in half to make a layer. Next, make a layer of sliced water chestnuts, sliced crosswise. Next, a layer of sliced hard-boiled eggs. Next, a layer of sliced olives. Repeat each layer. Mix milk and soup and pour over all ingredients. Top layers with hoop cheese. Top cheese with bread crumbs and dot with butter. Cook at 350 degrees for 20-30 minutes, until well heated. Yield: 4-6 servings.

Suzanne A. (Sissy) Herrod

FRIED BANANAS

6 bananas
Lemon juice

4 tablespoons butter
1 tablespoon sherry or Madeira

Peel bananas. Cut in half lengthwise or leave whole. Brush with lemon juice and cook in butter over low heat 3 to 4 minutes. Sprinkle with sherry or Madeira. Yield: 6 servings.

Mrs. J. C. "Bud" Miller (Presteen Sims)

ASPARAGUS—ARTICHOKE CASSEROLE

1 (14½-ounce) can asparagus
spears
1 (15-ounce) can hearts of
artichokes
1 (10¾-ounce) can cream of
mushroom soup

6-8 slices bread, toasted and cut
into cubes
1 stick butter or oleo, melted

Into baking dish, put 1 layer asparagus spears, then 1 layer hearts of artichokes which have been cut into thirds. Pour over this the soup. Cover casserole with bread squares. Pour melted butter or oleo over bread squares. Heat in 225- or 250-degree oven until bubbly. Serves 6-8.

Mrs. Chris Kyle (Bake Eatman)

FRESH ASPARAGUS

Choose fat, firm stalks of asparagus, with buds at tips tightly closed. Store upright in a plastic container with top or tall pitcher covered with plastic bag. Stand stalks on butt ends in about an inch of water. Will keep, refrigerated this way, for several days.

To cook, snap off butt ends. Peel stalks below buds to get rid of tough fibrous outer material. Tie spears in bundles of 8-10 with string, tips pointing same way. Bring a generous amount (5 quarts) of water to a boil in a kettle which will hold asparagus lying down. Add salt to water at the rate of ½ teaspoon per quart. Drop asparagus bundles into boiling water. Bring water back to a boil as rapidly as possible. Boil 5 minutes, then test the bottoms—or leave one spear loose. When it bends slightly or is tender, remove bundles to a folded towel and drain. If serving "naked", use napkin folded on serving platter. If "dressing" with sauce, move bundles to a bare platter. Cut strings and remove.

BRANDIED-SPICED PEACHES

1 (29-ounce) can peach halves
¼ cup sugar
1 tablespoon white vinegar

½ teaspoon whole cloves
5 or 6 sticks of cinnamon
¼ cup brandy

Drain peach halves, reserving syrup. Combine sugar, vinegar, cloves, cinnamon, and peach syrup in saucepan. Simmer for 5 minutes. Add peach halves and heat through. Cool. Stir in brandy. Store covered in refrigerator for 48 hours or longer before serving. Serves 4.

Mrs. Cayce Rumsey (Jan Sumners)

HOLIDAY ASPARAGUS

3 (12-14 ounce) cans asparagus
1 cup blanched, slivered toasted
  almonds, divided
½ pound fresh mushrooms
2 tablespoons butter
¼ cup onion, finely grated
2 tablespoons flour

2 cups hot milk, or use liquid
  from asparagus and add
  enough milk to make 2 cups
¼ teaspoon salt
½ teaspoon dry mustard
1 pound cheddar or Swiss cheese
Croutons (optional)

Sauté mushrooms in butter. Layer asparagus, ¾ cup almonds, and mushrooms twice in rather deep baking dish. Melt butter and cook onion in it for a minute, then add flour and cook, stirring, for about 2 minutes. Add hot liquid all at once and stir with a whisk until thick and smooth. Add cheese and stir until melted. Add salt and mustard and adjust seasoning. Pour cheese sauce over the layered mixture in baking dish. Top with ¼ cup almonds or croutons. Place in 300-degree oven for 45 minutes to 1 hour. Serve very hot. Yield: 8-10 servings.

Mrs. Peterson Cavert (Mary Beth Wear)

GOURMET GREEN BEAN CASSEROLE

1 cup fresh sliced mushrooms (or
  two 4-ounce cans, drained)
1 medium onion, sliced
½ cup butter
¾ cup sharp cheddar cheese
⅛ teaspoon Tabasco
2 teaspoons soy sauce

1 teaspoon salt
½ teaspoon black pepper
3 (10-ounce) packages frozen
  French-cut green beans
1 (5-ounce) can water chestnuts
½ to ¾ cup slivered almonds

Sauté onion and mushrooms in butter. Add grated cheese, Tabasco, soy sauce, salt and pepper. Simmer over boiling water and stir until cheese is melted. (If you are careful and use very low heat, you do not have to use a double boiler for this step.) Cook the green beans as directed on package until just tender. Drain. Mix with mushroom-cheese mixture and add water chestnuts which have been drained and sliced. Pour in 8 x 13-inch casserole and sprinkle with almonds. Bake 20 minutes at 375 degrees or until it bubbles through and through. Yield: 12-15 servings.

Mrs. Gary Loper (Nancy Tally)

SPICY GREEN BEAN BUNDLES

2 (1-pound) cans whole green
   beans
6 strips of bacon
Salt

Pepper
Red wine vinegar
Garlic powder
Toothpicks (12)

Cut bacon strips in half. Drain beans. Using 6 half strips of bacon per can, wrap beans in a packet with bacon and fasten with toothpick. Arrange on baking tray and sprinkle with salt, pepper, wine vinegar and garlic powder to taste. Cook at 350 degrees for about 1 hour, turning packets over for bacon to cook. Yield: 4-6 servings.

Mrs. Richard Thigpen (Mary Ann Anderson)

BEAN POT

1 (16-ounce) can lima beans
1 (16-ounce) can kidney beans
1 (40-ounce) can pork and beans
½ pound bacon, sliced and
   chopped

¼ teaspoon dry mustard
½ cup vinegar
2 medium onions, sliced
2 cloves garlic
1 cup brown sugar

Fry onions, bacon, and garlic. Heat vinegar and brown sugar until discolored. Mix beans, bacon mixture, and vinegar mixture and bake at 350 degrees for 1 hour. This can be made a day ahead, refrigerated, and then baked slowly (300 degrees) for 2-3 hours. Great for large crowds!

Mrs. Ronald Charles Phelps (Margaret Wood)

RED BEAN TOSS

1 (1-pound) can kidney beans
1 cup thinly sliced celery
⅓ cup chopped sweet pickle
¼ cup finely chopped onion
1 cup diced sharp cheddar cheese
½ teaspoon salt

½ teaspoon chili powder
½ teaspoon Worcestershire sauce
Few drops Tabasco sauce
½ cup mayonnaise
1 cup crushed Fritos

Drain beans and combine with celery, pickle, onion, and cheese. Blend seasonings with mayonnaise, add to bean mixture, and toss. Spoon into 1-quart baking dish. Sprinkle with Fritos. Bake at 450 degrees for 10 minutes. Garnish with green pepper rings (optional). Yield: 10 servings.

Mrs. Johnny Mack Hutt (Mary Elaine Leyden)

SWEET-SOUR GREEN BEANS

1 pound fresh green beans	½ cup water
Boiling salted water	⅓ cup cider vinegar
4 slices bacon	2 tablespoons sugar
1 medium onion, chopped	¼ teaspoon salt
2 teaspoons flour	⅛ teaspoon pepper

Trim ends of beans and cut in 2-inch pieces. Cook beans in boiling salt water to cover until crisp and tender, 6 to 8 minutes, and drain. Plunge into ice water. Drain and set aside.

In large skillet, cook bacon until crisp. Drain and crumble. Drain off all but 2 tablespoons drippings. Sauté onion until tender. Stir in flour; cook and stir until bubbly. Stir in water, vinegar, and sugar. Heat to boiling and continue to cook until slightly thickened. Add beans, tossing some. Sprinkle with salt, pepper, and bacon. Cook at 350 degrees until bubbly. Yield: 4 servings.

Note: May use 1-pound can of beans if fresh beans are not available.

Mrs. Alex O. Gatewood (Diane Gainey)

MB'S BAKED BEANS

1 (40-ounce) can pork and beans	1 tablespoon prepared mustard (Dijon-style)
1 (16-ounce) can green limas, drained	2 tablespoons Worcestershire
1 (15-ounce) can kidney beans, drained	2 tablespoons lemon juice
1 (15½-ounce) can pineapple chunks in juice, drained (reserve juice)	5 slices bacon, cut in 1-inch pieces
¾ cup catsup	1 large onion, cut into 12 wedges
⅓ cup brown sugar	⅓ cup pineapple juice (or more)
	1 green pepper, chopped (optional)

In a 3-quart baking dish, mix all beans, pineapple, catsup, brown sugar, mustard, Worcestershire sauce, lemon, bacon, onion, pepper, and pineapple juice. Stir well. Taste for seasoning. Add more pineapple juice if you like beans juicier. Bake, uncovered at 300 degrees for 3 hours, or put in a crockpot on Low for 5-6 hours. Serves 10-12.

Mrs. Peterson Cavert (Mary Beth Wear)

LIMA BEAN CASSEROLE

3 (16-ounce) cans lima beans
1 onion, chopped
1 (2-ounce) jar pimiento
1 (8-ounce) container sour
   cream

1 (10¾-ounce) can cream of
   celery soup
½ cup grated cheese
½ cup Ritz crackers
1 stick oleo

Drain lima beans well. Mix beans, onion, pimiento, sour cream, and celery soup together. Cover and let stand several hours or overnight. Put in casserole dish and top with grated cheese. Cover with crumbled Ritz crackers. Melt oleo and pour over crackers. Bake at 325 degrees for 35-45 minutes. Serves 8-10.

Mrs. Tommy Whitfield (Carolyn Flanagan)

FRESH BROCCOLI

Choose large, bright green stalks of broccoli with tightly closed green buds. Store wrapped in plastic wrap in refrigerator—will keep several days to a week if wrapped well.

To cook, peel stems below buds deep enough to expose whitish tender inside. Cut a cross in stem ends about 2 inches deep, halve entire stalk, or remove flowerettes and cut stem into 2-inch lengths. Put in saucepan with 2 teaspoons salt and about an inch of water. Bring to a boil and boil about 5 minutes, until broccoli turns a deep green. Cover and turn heat to low. Cook for another 7 minutes, then test stems with a fork. They should be crunchy-tender. Cook a while longer if not, but watch carefully. Remove to a folded towel to drain. Then put on a platter and add desired sauce, or serve undressed. Delicious with just a squeeze of lime. Also excellent served chilled with French dressing or in a green salad.

HEAVENLY BROCCOLI

2 (10-ounce) packages broccoli or
   2 bunches fresh
1 (4-ounce) container cream
   cheese and chives

1½ (10¾-ounce) cans cream of
   shrimp soup
2 teaspoons lemon juice
Butter

Cook broccoli and drain. Top with butter. Place in casserole. Mix soup with cream cheese and add lemon juice. Pour over broccoli. Heat until bubbly. Yield: 6-7 servings.

Mrs. William Manderson (Elizabeth Woollen)

GOLDEN BROCCOLI

3 (10-ounce) boxes frozen chopped
broccoli
1 (10¾-ounce) can mushroom soup
1 cup grated sharp cheese
2 tablespoons minced onion
2 eggs, well beaten

1 cup Kraft mayonnaise
Salt and pepper to taste
2 tablespoons butter
½ cup cheese cracker crumbs (or
saltine cracker crumbs)

Cook broccoli 5 minutes after it comes to a boil and drain well. To make sauce: mix soup. cheese, minced onion, eggs, mayonnaise, and seasonings with broccoli and pour into buttered 2-quart casserole dish. Dot with butter and sprinkle with finely-rolled cheese crackers. Bake at 350 degrees for about 30 minutes or until center bubbles. Serves 8-10.

Mrs. James M. Cain, Sr. (Rosalind Alexander)

PANNED BEETS

2 beets
2 tablespoons oil

Salt

Remove roots, tops and skins of beets. Slice, dice, or shred the vegetable. Heat oil in heavy skillet or saucepan. Add the vegetable, salt slightly, and toss until beets are coated with oil. When vegetable sizzles, turn down heat and stir just enough to prevent burning. Heat for a few minutes—time will depend on size of vegetable. The beets should be served crisp. Works well with other firm vegetables like squash, carrots, etc.

Mrs. Wayne Hutton (Cherie Whetstone)

PENNSYLVANIA CABBAGE AND APPLES

1 tablespoon salad oil or bacon
drippings
2 cups shredded red cabbage
(1 medium head)
1 cup cubed unpeeled apple
(1 medium)

2 tablespoons brown sugar
2 tablespoons vinegar
2 tablespoons water
½ teaspoon salt
Dash black pepper
¼ teaspoon caraway seed

Heat oil in large skillet; add remaining ingredients. Cover tightly and cook over low heat, stirring occasionally. For crisp cabbage (I like better), cook 15 minutes. For old-fashioned cabbage, cook 25 to 30 minutes. Garnish with raw, unpeeled apple rings if desired. Serves 4 to 6.

Mrs. Wayne Hutton (Cherie Whetstone)

CABBAGE AU GRATIN

4 cups shredded cabbage
2 tablespoons melted butter or
   margarine
1½ tablespoons flour

½ teaspoon salt
1 cup milk
1 cup grated cheddar cheese
2 cups bread crumbs, buttered

Boil cabbage about 5 minutes. Drain well. Combine butter, flour and salt in a saucepan. Blend in milk. Cook over low heat, stirring constantly, until smooth and thickened. Alternate layers of cabbage, cheese and sauce in a greased 1½-quart casserole. Sprinkle bread crumbs on top. Bake at 350 degrees for 25-30 minutes. Serves 6.

Mrs. Don Price (Gay Malone)

BUFFET CHEESE-SCALLOPED CARROTS

12 medium carrots, peeled and
   sliced
1 small onion, minced
¼ cup butter
¼ cup flour
1 teaspoon salt
1 teaspoon regular mustard

2 cups milk
⅛ teaspoon pepper
¼ teaspoon celery salt
½ pound sharp cheese slices
3 cups buttered French bread
   crumbs

Cook carrots in boiling salted water for 10 minutes. Drain. Cook onion in butter until clear. Stir in flour, salt, and mustard. Add milk. Cook, stirring constantly, until smooth and thick. Add pepper and celery salt. In 2-quart casserole, arrange layers of carrots and cheese until both are used up, ending with carrots. Pour sauce over carrots. Top with bread crumbs. Bake uncovered for 25 minutes at 350 degrees. Yield: 8 servings.

Note: This may be made ahead and refrigerated. In this case, bake about 40 minutes.

Mrs. Ralph R. Williams (Bea Hill)

CARROTS AU RUHM

1 (2-pound) bag of carrots
½ cup of sugar
1 stick of butter

½ cup dark or light rum
1 teaspoon salt

In a 3½ to 4-quart pan, boil your scraped carrots in salted water for about 20 minutes or less (just until tender). Drain the carrots and add sugar, butter, and rum. Return to heat and cook over high heat until all the liquid is evaporated.

Mrs. David Hefelfinger (Virginia Mauney)

CARROT LOAF

2 cups ground carrots
2 eggs
1 cup bread crumbs
2 cups milk

2 teaspoons salt
½ teaspoon pepper
4 tablespoons melted margarine

Preheat oven to 350 degrees. Mix all ingredients together and pour into a casserole. Bake for 1 hour or until firm. Serves 6.

Mrs. Wilbur Manderson (Ann Moore)

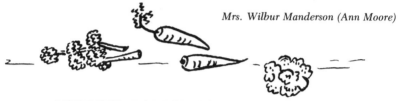

CURRIED BAKED CAULIFLOWER

1 large head or 2 (10-ounce)
    packages frozen cauliflower
½ teaspoon salt
1 (10¾-ounce) can cream of
    chicken soup

6 ounces shredded cheddar cheese
⅓ cup mayonnaise
1 teaspoon curry powder
¼ cup bread crumbs
2 tablespoons melted butter

Cook cauliflower with salt and drain. Mix soup, cheese, mayonnaise, and curry. Add to cauliflower. Turn into flat baking dish. Toss crumbs in melted butter and sprinkle on top. Bake uncovered at 350 degrees for 30 minutes. Serves 6 to 8.

Mrs. John C. Boles (Donna Waters)

TANGY MUSTARD CAULIFLOWER

1 medium head cauliflower
2 tablespoons water
½ cup mayonnaise

1 teaspoon finely chopped onion
1 teaspoon prepared mustard
½ cup shredded cheddar cheese

Place cauliflower in 1½-quart glass casserole. Add water and cover with glass lid or plastic wrap. Microwave on High for 8-9 minutes, or until done. Combine mayonnaise, onion, and mustard in small mixing bowl. Spoon sauce on top of cauliflower. Sprinkle with cheese. Microwave on Roast for 1½-2 minutes to heat topping.

Note: The cauliflower may be steamed until tender, frosted with topping and then baked at 350 degrees until topping is heated through and cheese is melted, 5-10 minutes.

Mrs. Wilbur Manderson (Ann Moore)

FRIED CORN

6 to 8 large (or 10 to 12 small)
ears corn
1 to 2 tablespoons sugar
½ to 1 teaspoon salt
⅔ stick margarine

Dash of Accent
½ to 1 cup cold water (some
corn requires more water than
other—keep adding until soft)

Preheat oven to 375 degrees. Grate (do not cut) corn from cob. Add seasoning and pour into heavy skillet in which margarine has been melted over low heat. Stir corn, adding water as it thickens. Continue stirring until soft consistency, cover and let simmer for 10-15 minutes, stirring occasionally. Pour into casserole and let bake in hot oven (375 to 400 degrees) until lightly browned.

Note: Some corn does not contain enough starch. If corn does not thicken, a little cornstarch mixed with water may be added.

Mrs. Carlos "Sonny" Shows (Gloria Church)

DILLED CARROTS

1 (12-ounce) package fresh baby
carrots
2 bouillon cubes

1 stick butter
2 teaspoons dill weed

Boil carrots in water with dissolved bouillon cubes until tender (about 7 minutes). Drain carrots. Place in a skillet with melted butter. Be sure butter coats all carrots. Sprinkle dill weed over carrots and shake to be sure dill is on all carrots. Place in serving dish and serve immediately. Yield: 6-8 servings.

Suzanne A. Herrod

CHEESY BROCCOLI

1 large chopped onion
½ stick oleo
3 (10-ounce) packages frozen
chopped broccoli
1½ (10¾-ounce) cans mushroom
soup

1½ rolls Kraft garlic cheese
¾ cup water chestnuts, chopped
or sliced
1 teaspoon Accent
¾ cup bread crumbs

Sauté onion in butter. Add broccoli and let thaw in pan. Add soup, cheese, water chestnuts, and Accent. Place in baking dish with crumbs on top. Bake at 300 degrees for 1 hour. Serves 6-8.

Mrs. Walter C. Densmore (Mary Kate Fuller)

APPLE AND ONION CASSEROLE

4 medium onions, sliced
3-4 hard, tart cooking apples
  (prefer York variety)

½ stick butter
Salt, pepper, sugar, cinnamon
Juice of 1 lemon

Preheat oven to 350 degrees. Parboil sliced onions for 10 minutes. Save ⅓ cup of the water. While onions are boiling, peel, core, and slice apples, dropping slices into a bowl of water to which lemon juice has been added. Layer in a casserole the drained apples and onions, dotting each layer with butter and sprinkling the onion layers with salt and pepper and the apple layers with sugar and cinnamon. Pour over the ⅓ cup cooking water. Bake in 350-degree oven for 45 minutes to 1 hour. Serves 6.

Note: This is especially good with any pork dish. Surprisingly, it has more of the apple taste than the onion taste. Optional garnishes for the top are crumbled bacon and/or buttered croutons.

Mrs. Peterson Cavert (Mary Beth Wear)

AUTUMN PUDDING

CASSEROLE:

3 cups cooked sweet potatoes,
  mashed
1 cup sugar
½ teaspoon salt

2 well-beaten eggs
½ stick margarine
½ cup milk
3 teaspoons vanilla

TOPPING:

1 cup brown sugar
⅓ cup flour

1 cup broken pecans
½ stick butter

Mix the ingredients for the casserole together and place in a 2½-quart casserole. Mix the ingredients for the topping together and spread over the casserole. Bake uncovered for 30 minutes at 350 degrees. Especially good for the holidays. Serves 4-6.

Variations:
I. *Reduce vanilla to 1 teaspoon, substitute orange juice for milk, add 1 tablespoon grated orange rind.*
II. *Reduce vanilla to 1 teaspoon. Add 1 (8¼-ounce) can drained crushed pineapple.*
III. *Add ½ teaspoon nutmeg and ½ teaspoon cinnamon.*
IV. *Add 1 cup coconut to either filling or topping.*

Mrs. Joe F. (Skip) Cannon (Diane Stansell)

CELERY SPECIAL

4 cups celery, cut in 1-inch slices
   or larger
1½ teaspoons salt
1 (5-ounce) can water chestnuts,
   sliced

1 (10¾-ounce) can cream of
   chicken soup
¼ cup pimiento, diced
¼ cup buttered bread crumbs
¼ cup slivered almonds

Combine celery, salt, and 2 quarts water in saucepan and boil 7-8 minutes. Drain. Add water chestnuts, soup, and pimiento and pour into greased 1½-quart casserole. Sprinkle with bread crumbs and almonds. Bake at 350 degrees for 30-35 minutes. Serves 6-8.

Mrs. Joseph Rowland (Nancy Burch)

BAKED CHILIES RELLENOS

1 (4-ounce) can whole green chilies
½ pound sharp cheddar cheese
2 eggs

2 cups milk
½ cup flour
1 teaspoon salt

In the bottom of a buttered casserole dish, arrange the chilies, cut in 2-inch squares. Cut the cheese into long fingers and put in a layer on top of chilies. Beat eggs slightly, then beat in milk, flour, and salt. Pour this mixture over cheese and bake at 350 degrees for 45-50 minutes or until custard is set. Serves 4.

Mrs. Robert H. Davis (Doris Herold)

CORN-CHEESE CASSEROLE

6 ears corn (or frozen corn)
½ cup minced onion
½ cup diced green pepper
4 eggs, lightly beaten
1½ cups milk

1 cup shredded cheddar cheese
1½ cups soft bread crumbs
¾ teaspoon salt
¼ teaspoon ground black pepper

Preheat oven to 350 degrees. Cut corn kernels from cobs (makes about 3 cups). In large bowl, combine corn with remaining ingredients and mix well. Pour into a buttered 2-quart casserole. Cover and bake for 30 minutes. Uncover and bake 30 minutes longer, or until golden brown and a knife inserted in center comes out clean.

Mrs. Terry H. Pickett (Gisela Vollprecht)

CORN-OKRA JAMBALAYA

¼ pound bacon
1 pound okra, sliced
2 medium onions, chopped
1 (1-pound) can tomatoes

3 ears corn, cut from ears
1½ teaspoons salt
Chinese noodles

Fry bacon until crisp. Remove from pan and drain on paper towel. In bacon fat, sauté onions and sliced okra. Cook to seal the okra, but do not brown. Add tomatoes. Cook 5 minutes. Add corn and salt. Cook 5 minutes more—must not be runny. Place in greased casserole. Sprinkle with Chinese noodles and crushed bacon. Bake at 350 degrees for 10 minutes. Serves 4-6.

Note: For the best Jambalaya, use fresh corn only.

Mrs. Glynn Hewett (Jean Mosley)

CORN PUDDING

6 tablespoons melted butter
2 tablespoons self-rising flour
4 beaten eggs
2 tablespoons sugar
1 teaspoon salt

2 cups fresh corn or 1 (10-ounce)
    package Tennessee brand
    frozen cream corn
1 cup milk

Preheat oven to 325 degrees. Blend butter, flour, salt, and sugar. Add beaten eggs. Stir in corn and then milk. Pour in casserole and bake for 45 minutes at 325 degrees. Serves 8.

Mrs. W. Lee Hudson (Jeannie Edwards)—Albany, GA

CRISP CORN PATTIES

2½ cups fresh corn (or one (20-
    ounce) can fancy cream-style
    corn)
2 eggs

2 tablespoons flour
1 tablespoon sugar
½ teaspoon salt
Butter for frying

If fresh corn is used, cut in thin layers from the top of the kernels and scrape the cob to extract the corn milk. Beat eggs and dry ingredients together until smooth and add to corn. Drop by spoonfuls into hot skillet containing a small amount of butter. Fry until crisp. Serves 4.

Mrs. Samuel Payne Wright (Frances Leapard)

SHOE PEG CORN CASSEROLE

1 (12-ounce) can white shoe peg
  corn
1 (16-ounce) can French-cut green
  beans
½ cup chopped celery
½ cup chopped bell pepper

½ cup chopped onion
½ cup grated sharp cheese
½ cup sour cream
1 (10¾-ounce) can cream of
  celery soup

TOPPING:
1½ cups Ritz cracker crumbs

1 stick butter

Drain corn and green beans. Mix corn, beans, celery, bell pepper, onion, cheese, sour cream, and celery soup. Salt and pepper to taste. Place in casserole. Melt butter and stir crumbs into butter. Use this mixture as topping on casserole. Bake at 350 degrees for 45 minutes. Serves 4-6.

Note: This may be fixed with ½ cup slivered almonds over it.

Mrs. Sam P. Faucett, III (Leslie Wood)

EGGPLANT SOUFFLÉ

1 large eggplant
½ stick butter
Salt/pepper to taste
2 eggs, beaten

¾ cup milk
8-10 saltines, crumbled
¼ cup chopped onion
1 cup grated cheese

Preheat oven to 350 degrees. Peel and boil eggplant until done. Mash with potato masher. Stir in butter while hot. Season with salt and pepper. Stir in eggs, milk, saltines and onions. Put into casserole and top with cheese. Bake at 350 degrees for 40 minutes. Serves 6-8.

Mrs. Robert Inman (Paulette Strong)

SHOESTRING EGGPLANT

1 small eggplant
1 egg
1 tablespoon water

1 cup cracker crumbs (saltine
  crackers)
Vegetable oil for frying

Peel eggplant. Slice eggplant in ½-inch thick slices. Cut each slice into ½-inch strips. Soak in iced, salted water for 30 minutes. Dry.
Dip slices into mixture of beaten egg and 1 tablespoon water. Roll in cracker crumbs. Shallow fry in hot oil as for French fried potatoes. Drain on absorbent paper and sprinkle with salt. Makes 6-8 servings.

Mrs. Carlos "Sonny" Shows (Gloria Church)

MARINATED FRUIT

1 (16-ounce) can peach halves,
  drained
1 (16-ounce) can pear halves,
  drained
1 (16-ounce) can apricot halves,
  drained
1 (20-ounce) can pineapple rings,
  drained

1 can spiced apple rings (red or
  green), drained
1 stick oleo
½ cup brown sugar
1 cup sherry
2 tablespoons flour

Make up the day before using. Cut large halves in half, and also pineapple rings. Arrange fruit in layers with apple rings on top in deep casserole dish. In a double boiler, melt and bring to a boil the oleo, brown sugar, sherry, and flour. Let thicken and pour over fruit. Refrigerate for 24 hours. Heat, uncovered at 350 degrees for 20-30 minutes, or until bubbling hot. Yield: 8-10 servings.

Note: May substitute juice from fruit or rum for part or all of sherry. May also add 2 to 3 teaspoons curry powder to sauce. Interesting additions: 1 (8-ounce) package chopped dates; 2 or 3 bananas, cut in slices; 1 (11-ounce) can mandarin oranges; ½ cup almonds or pecans. Delicious as a dessert served with sour cream on top.

Mrs. Richard Thigpen (Mary Ann Anderson)

FRESH MUSHROOMS

Choose white, firm mushrooms, the caps closed underneath so the gills are not visible. If possible, handpick each one. They should smell fresh and earthy. Store unwashed in refrigerator in a plastic bag. They will keep this way for several days. If not used by the third day, sauté them. They will keep for a week at least and can be added at the last minute to almost any dish calling for fresh mushrooms.

To sauté: Wash gently and drain on towel. Cut off ends of stems. Snap stems off caps. Slice stems crosswise. Slice caps or quarter, if small. Cook in batches of about ¼ pound. For each batch, heat 2 tablespoons butter and 1 tablespoon oil in skillet over medium high heat until foam from butter subsides. Add mushrooms and cook, shaking pan to turn mushrooms, for 4-5 minutes, or until they brown lightly.

STUFFED MUSHROOMS

40 mushrooms (1-2 inches in
 diameter)—or any size will do
½ cup grated Parmesan cheese
½ cup dry bread crumbs
¼ cup onion, finely chopped
 (green onion is good, too)
2 tablespoons fresh parsley

½ teaspoon salt
Pepper and hot pepper sauce to
 taste
½ teaspoon oregano
1 stick butter or margarine,
 melted

Wash and dry mushroom caps. Trim rough ends of stalk and chop finely. Add stems to cheese, bread crumbs, onion, parsley, and seasonings. Toss gently and stuff caps with mixture. Place in baking dish (any size will do, and it may take more than one). Spoon melted margarine or butter over each cap. Bake in 350-degree oven for 25 minutes. Can also be baked ahead of time for 20 minutes and then broiled for a few minutes to reheat. Serves 6-8. Good as cocktail "bites" or accompaniment to tenderloin or steak.

Note: Can't have too many of these—usually not enough! Left over stuffing may be refrigerated or frozen. Use at a later time on top of any casserole or as a spread for crackers or thin-sliced pumpernickel.

Mrs. Charles A. Trost (Annie Orr)

MUSHROOM SUPREME

1 pound whole mushrooms
2 tablespoons butter
2 beef bouillon cubes
½ cup hot water
½ stick butter
2 tablespoons flour

½ cup cream
⅛ teaspoon salt
Dash pepper
½ cup bread crumbs
½ to 1 cup Parmesan cheese

Sauté mushrooms in butter, and put in buttered baking dish. Dissolve beef cubes in water. Melt ½ stick butter and blend with flour. Add cream, salt, pepper, and beef broth. Pour over mushrooms. Top with cheese and bread crumb mixture before baking. Bake for 30 minutes at 350 degrees. Serves 4.

Note: Preparation—30 minutes, Baking—30 minutes. Easy to do ahead. Great for special dinner party.

Joyce Green Rives

MUSHROOMS ON TOAST

1 pound mushrooms	¼ teaspoon paprika
¼ cup softened butter	4 pieces of toast without crusts
2 teaspoons lemon juice	½ cup cream
1 tablespoon parsley	2 tablespoons sherry
½ teaspoon salt	

Heat oven to 375 degrees. Pull stems from mushrooms and reserve for another use. Cream butter, add lemon juice, parsley, salt, and paprika. Spread half of mixture on toast and place in baking dish. Spread remaining butter on caps of mushrooms. Place mushrooms on toast and pour cream on top. Cover baking dish and bake 20 minutes. Add sherry before serving. Makes 4 servings.

Guesna Bush

MY FAVORITE OKRA

Okra, small and medium pods, 12 per person

Wash but do not remove stem end. Boil vigorously 2 quarts water and 2 tablespoons salt. Add okra and boil exactly 3 minutes. Drain, rinse with cold water and chill. Serve cold. Eat with fingers (as you would an unhulled strawberry) after dipping in homemade Mayonnaise. (See Index)

Mrs. Jack Davis (Dee Stewart)

FRIED ONION RINGS

1 (12-ounce) can beer	Dash pepper
1½ cups flour	3 large yellow onions
½ teaspoon salt	Peanut oil
1 teaspoon sugar	

Mix flour and beer. Let stand at room temperature at least 3 hours. Add salt, sugar, pepper. Heat peanut oil (3 inches deep in frying pan) to 375 degrees (use a fat thermometer). Slice onions ¼-inch thick and separate slices into rings. Dip onion rings in batter and drop into hot oil. Fry, turning once, until golden brown. Drain on brown paper sack.

Notes: To make ahead for a group, heat oven to 200 degrees and keep fried rings inside on a brown paper covered cookie sheet. They will stay crisp for several hours. These freeze well. Reheat in 400-degree oven for about 5 minutes. This batter can be used for other vegetables, such as sliced zucchini, squash, green tomatoes—or shrimp, etc.

Mrs. Peterson Cavert (Mary Beth Wear)

FRIED OKRA

1 quart okra	2 teaspoons pepper
2 cups milk	2 cups salad oil
2 cups corn meal	2 teaspoons salt

Wash and slice okra ¼- to ½-inch thick. Place okra in a deep bowl, and cover with milk. Let stand 30 minutes; drain. Pour corn meal and pepper in a bag. Add okra and shake until thoroughly coated. Heat salad oil to 380 degrees in a large frying pan. Add okra to make a single layer. Turn only once during frying; do not stir. Remove okra when light brown and place on paper towels to drain. Sprinkle with salt. Place okra in a 13 x 9½ x 2-inch baking dish, and bake at 200 degrees for 30 minutes.

Mrs. Julian Reed (Peggy Ethridge)

BURGUNDY ONIONS

6 large yellow onions	Salt and pepper
3 tablespoons butter	1½ cups Burgundy

Cut onions into ¼-inch slices and separate into rings. Melt butter in large skillet. Add onions, toss to coat with butter, and sauté until they are tender and golden. Add Burgundy, salt and pepper; cover and simmer over lowered heat for about 15 minutes. Remove cover, raise heat, and cook until wine reduces almost to a glaze. Serves 6-8.

Note: Great with steak or roast. Reheated leftovers are good on hamburgers.

Mrs. Peterson Cavert (Mary Beth Wear)

Hint: Wrap onions in foil and bake with or instead of potatoes. Serve with butter, salt, and pepper.

CREAMED PEAS WITH WATER CHESTNUTS

1 stick oleo or butter	2 (10-ounce) packages of frozen
2 (10¾-ounce) cans cream of	green English peas
celery soup, undiluted	1 (6-ounce) can water chestnuts

Melt oleo in saucepan. Stir in cream of celery soup. Meanwhile, cook peas according to package directions; drain. Add peas to soup mixture. Quarter water chestnuts and add. Heat thoroughly and serve.

Mrs. Ray Moore, Jr. (Margie Mantel)

SCALLOPED ONIONS AND CHEESE

2 pounds small onions
Water
9½ tablespoons butter
½ cup flour
4 cups milk
1 teaspoon salt

2 teaspoons dry mustard
6 ounces grated cheddar cheese
1½ cups dry bread crumbs
1 (8-ounce) can sliced mush-
    rooms, drained (optional)

Peel onions and boil in small amount of water until almost tender (about 10 minutes), and drain. Melt 8 tablespoons butter; add flour to make a paste. Add milk, stir, and cook until thickened. Stir in mustard and cheese. Place onions in greased casserole; pour sauce over onions. Combine remaining butter and crumbs. Cover casserole with buttered crumbs. Bake at 350 degrees for about 20 minutes. Serves 8.

Note: This dish is particularly good with doves, quail, or duck. If using the mushrooms, sprinkle over the onions before covering with the cheese sauce. Recipe works well substituting other strong flavored vegetables such as cauliflower or broccoli for the onions.

Mrs. Jerre R. White (Jackie Cuningham)

CHARLESTON POTATOES

½ cup mayonnaise
½ cup sour cream
    (All mayonnaise or all sour
    cream may be used)
2 tablespoons paprika
2 tablespoons sweet pickle
    relish

2 tablespoons dried parsley
1 tablespoon minced onion
    (Spring onions are better)
½ teaspoon garlic salt
12 medium-sized new potatoes
    in jackets
1 stick whipped oleo

Mix mayonnaise, sour cream, paprika, relish, parsley, onion, and garlic salt. Put in covered jar and refrigerate several hours or overnight. Wash and boil potatoes until tender. Place hot potatoes in serving dish. Put whipped oleo on top (cut in several pieces). Pour mayonnaise-sour cream sauce over this. Freshly ground black pepper and sprigs of parsley may be added as a garnish. Serves 4 to 6.

Note: This dish is delicious with fowl or beef—especially steak and a salad. Men always love it! It's pretty and red. Potatoes may be cooked well ahead of time, with water drained off except for an inch or so in bottom of pan, and kept on simmer or reheated when time to serve. Sauce and oleo should be put on hot potatoes just before serving. The whipped oleo gives a fluffy effect.

Mrs. Ed "Flash" Florey, Jr. (Betty Finklea)

PEAS AND ARTICHOKES

2 (16-ounce) cans tiny peas
drained
1 (15-ounce) can artichoke hearts,
drained

½ stick butter or ¼ cup olive oil
1 tablespoon instant minced
onion
Salt and cracked pepper

Preheat oven to 375 degrees. Melt butter in saucepan and add instant onion and artichoke hearts. Turn the artichokes to coat well. Add salt and generous amount of pepper. In a shallow baking dish, make a bed of peas. Arrange the artichoke hearts on top, pouring the liquid over all. Cover and bake for 40 minutes. Serves 6.

Mrs. Earl L. Carpenter (Betty Myrick)

BAKED POTATO PUDDING

6 to 8 large Idaho potatoes
¼ cup grated onion
3 eggs, well beaten

1 cup hot milk
6 tablespoons melted butter
½ teaspoon salt

Preheat oven to 350 degrees. Peel and grate potatoes. Mix with onion, eggs, milk, butter, and salt. Beat well and pour into well-buttered shallow baking pan, about 8 x 12 inches. Bake for 1 hour and 30 minutes.

Mrs. Joe Tanner, Jr. (Carol DesRochers)

FRIED POTATO PORCUPINES

Baking potatoes (Idaho or russet),
preferably aged—approximately
1 per person

Peanut oil (2-3 inches deep in
frying pan)
Flour

Heat oil to 375 degrees. Grate potatoes coarsely (use grater blade in food processor). Put in colander and rinse thoroughly. Let drain and squeeze out most of the moisture. Put potatoes in bowl and add enough flour to make them stick together when you pick up a small amount (approximately 2 tablespoons flour to one potato). Drop potatoes into oil by bunches, about 2 tablespoons per handful. Fry, turning once, until golden brown. Drain on brown paper sack. Sprinkle with salt.

Note: These freeze well. Reheat in 400-degree oven for about 5 minutes. These are very crisp and crunchy. A perfect accompaniment for an informal steak dinner or hamburgers.

Bert Wear

PICKLED POTATOES

24 very small new potatoes (I use
  48 "large marble-sized" when
  I can buy them)
3 cups Wesson oil
1 cup tarragon vinegar
1 large onion, grated on large side
  of grater

Salt to taste (lots)
Whole black peppercorns to taste
⅛ teaspoon garlic powder
¼ teaspoon seasoned salt

Boil new potatoes in jackets until tender. Drain. Cook French Dressing made of Wesson oil, vinegar, onion, salt, whole peppercorns freshly cracked or coarsely ground, garlic powder, and seasoned salt. Bring to a full rolling boil, pour over potatoes and let stand several hours (3 or 4) before serving. May be reheated and served as a vegetable or served cold (mix dressing vigorously) as a salad. Serves 6-8.

Mrs. Allen Mattox (Harriet Marrs)

Hint: Wash parsley, drain well, remove twine or band, if any, and freeze in plastic bag. To use in cooking, snip off required amount with scissors. Thaws almost pretty enough to use as garnish.

POTATOES—RESTUFFED

6 medium potatoes
2 tablespoons salad oil
¼ cup butter
1 cup chopped onion
2 cloves garlic, crushed

½ cup sour cream
¼ teaspoon pepper
1 teaspoon salt
1 tablespoon chopped parsley

Wash and dry potatoes well; prick with fork. Rub skins with oil. Bake at 400 degrees for 1 hour.
In skillet, melt ¼ cup of butter. Sauté onion and garlic until tender. Set aside.
When potatoes are done, slice top (thin) lengthwise. Scoop out potatoes and mash until smooth. Add sautéed mixture (do not drain). Mix in sour cream, pepper, and salt. Beat well. Spoon filling back into potato skin and return tops. Put in the oven for 10 minutes before serving. Sprinkle with parsley. Yield: 6 servings.

Note: Great make ahead.

Mrs. Warren P. Davis (Linda del Gatto)

SOUR CREAM POTATOES

6 medium potatoes
2 cups shredded cheddar cheese
½ cup butter
2 cups sour cream

⅓ cup chopped green onions
Salt and pepper to taste
2 tablespoons butter

Boil (don't overcook) potatoes, cool, and then coarsely grate into greased baking dish. Melt butter, sour cream, and cheese. Add onions, salt, and pepper. Stir mixture with potatoes. Dot with butter. Bake at 350 degrees for 25 minutes. Serves 6-8.

Mrs. Billy Curtis (Peggy Rice)

CHIVE POTATO SOUFFLÉ

2 cups hot mashed potatoes
½ cup sour cream
3 tablespoons chopped chives

1½ tablespoons salt
3 eggs, separated

Beat egg whites until stiff, but moist. Set aside. Beat yolks until smooth and add to potato mixture. Fold in beaten egg whites, sour cream, and chives, and pour into a buttered 1½-quart casserole. Bake at 350 degrees for 45 minutes. Serves 4 to 6.

Mrs. Hank Leland (Lindsay James)

SPINACH CAROLYN

2 (10-ounce) packages frozen
spinach (or fresh if available),
cooked and drained
2 cups cottage cheese
4 eggs, well beaten
1 cup grated cheddar cheese (may
save ¼ cup to sprinkle on top
if desired, at very last)

Salt and pepper to taste
1 teaspoon caraway seed or
dried basil
1 to 2 cups Pepperidge Farm
Herbed dressing

Mix spinach, cottage cheese, beaten eggs, cheddar cheese, salt, pepper, and either caraway or basil gently and put into buttered baking dish. Sprinkle top with herbed dressing. Bake covered at 300 degrees for 45 minutes. Last 5 minutes of baking, sprinkle on last of cheddar cheese. Can be frozen prior to the day you wish to bake and add about 10 minutes to baking time, or bake until set. Serves 8 to 10.

Ruth G. Kirkpatrick

SPEEDY SPINACH

3 (10-ounce) packages frozen
  spinach
1 (1.37½-ounce) package Lipton
  Onion Soup mix

1 (8-ounce) carton sour cream
Bread crumbs
Parmesan cheese

Thaw and drain spinach and mix with onion soup mix and sour cream.
Put in greased casserole. Top with bread crumbs and Parmesan cheese.
Bake at 325 degrees for 30 minutes. Serves 6.

Mrs. Ronald Ray Turner (Carolyn Hamilton)

SPINACH NEW ORLEANS

4 (10-ounce) packages frozen
  spinach
1 (8-ounce) package cream cheese
Juice of 1 lemon
Rind of ¾ lemon, grated very fine

1½ cups bread crumbs
Salt and pepper to taste
Butter

Cook spinach according to package directions. Drain well. Place in mixing bowl with chopped cream cheese and mix well. Add lemon juice and
the lemon peel. Salt and pepper to taste. Place this mixture in a 2-quart
casserole dish. Cover lightly with bread crumbs. Dot with butter. Bake at
350 degrees for 25 minutes. Serves 8 to 10.

Suzanne A. Herrod

SPINACH TIMBALES

3 tablespoons butter or margarine
3 tablespoons flour
½ teaspoon salt
¼ teaspoon black pepper
1 cup milk
3 eggs, slightly beaten

1 tablespoon chopped onion
1 teaspoon lemon juice
1 teaspoon lemon rind
1 cup cooked, drained chopped
  spinach
Watercress or parsley

Melt butter in the upper part of a double boiler; gradually stir in flour,
salt, and pepper. Add milk, blending constantly with wire whisk, until
thick and smooth. Add eggs, onion, lemon juice, lemon rind, and spinach.
Mix well. Spoon into 6 well-greased baking cups. Place in a shallow baking pan filled with ½ inch of water. Bake at 350 degrees for 25-30
minutes or until firm. Invert on serving plate and garnish with watercress
or parsley. Yield: 6 servings.

Mrs. James F. Hughey (Jerry Hammack)

BUTTERNUT SQUASH CASSEROLE

3 cups mashed butternut squash,
 cooked with a pinch of salt
1 cup sugar
½ cup butter
⅓ cup milk
2 eggs
1 teaspoon vanilla

1 teaspoon nutmeg
1 teaspoon cinnamon
½ cup brown sugar
⅓ cup flour
1 cup nuts
⅓ cup melted butter

Mix squash, sugar, butter, milk, eggs, vanilla, nutmeg, and cinnamon; put in baking dish. Mix and sprinkle on top the brown sugar, flour, and nuts. Pour butter over the top. Bake at 350 degrees for 35-45 minutes.

Note: Pour this mixture into an unbaked pie shell, add topping, and you have a delicious squash pie. There is enough to make 2 pies with this recipe.

Mrs. Tim Parker, Jr. (Cathy Jackman)

SAMFORD UNIVERSITY'S SQUASH CROQUETTES

2 pounds yellow crook-neck
 squash, cooked, drained, and
 mashed
2 teaspoons salt
1 tablespoon sugar
1 teaspoon black pepper
½ cup onion, chopped fine
¼ cup margarine, melted

2 eggs, beaten
1 cup corn bread crumbs
 (approximately, depending on
 moisture in squash)
2 cups white bread crumbs
Vegetable oil
Butter or margarine (optional)

Mix squash, salt, sugar, pepper, onion, margarine, eggs, and corn bread crumbs. Form into croquettes. If they will not hold shape well, add a little more corn bread. Roll in white bread crumbs and fry in deep fat until brown. They freeze great! Serves 6-8.

To make a casserole, place in a buttered casserole and top with buttered white bread crumbs. Bake, uncovered, at 350 degrees for 45 minutes to 1 hour. Will appear light to touch and be brown on top and sides. Super!

Mrs. Allen Mattox (Harriet Marrs)

Hint: Buy green and red bell peppers and hot peppers in quantity when they are most plentiful in summer and least expensive. Chop and freeze in 1-cup packages. Good for cooking all winter, or for jelly or relish when you can't get to it in the summer. Prepare the nicest-shaped bell peppers for stuffing (remove top and core) and freeze in plastic container.

SQUASH À LA BAMA

1 pound squash
½ stick oleo
1 egg
½ cup mayonnaise
2 tablespoons onion, chopped
2 tablespoons green pepper, chopped

1 cup grated cheese
½ package cracker or bread crumbs
Chopped pimiento for color

Clean, slice, and boil squash until tender. Drain squash and mix with other ingredients. Bake in buttered casserole dish at 350 degrees for 30-35 minutes. Serves 6.

Mrs. George Gordon (Jean Fargason)

STUFFED SQUASH

8-10 medium squash, yellow or zucchini
½ cup chopped bell pepper
1 medium tomato, chopped
1 medium onion, chopped
2 slices bacon, fried and crumbled

½ cup grated cheddar cheese
½ teaspoon salt
Dash pepper
Butter

Wash squash and simmer in water for 8 minutes. Drain and cool slightly. Cut a thin slice from top of each and remove seeds and discard, or chop and add with remaining ingredients. Combine remaining ingredients except butter. Mix well and spoon into squash. Dot each with pat of butter. Bake at 400 degrees for 20 minutes.

Mrs. Hank Hawkins (Eugenia Partlow)

PARTY SQUASH

1 pound sliced squash
1 teaspoon sugar
½ cup mayonnaise
½ cup minced onion
¼ cup finely chopped green pepper
½ stick oleo
½ cup chopped pecans (optional)

1 egg, slightly beaten
½ cup grated cheese
¼ teaspoon salt
⅛ teaspoon pepper
1 cup bread crumbs
Butter
¼ cup chopped pimiento (optional)

Cook squash, drain, and mash. Add sugar, mayonnaise, onion, green pepper, oleo, egg, cheese, salt, and pepper. Put in a 2-quart casserole. Top with crumbs and dot with butter. Bake 35-40 minutes at 350 degrees. Yield: 8 servings.

Mrs. William W. Jessup (Pat Proctor)

YELLOW SQUASH WITH TOMATOES

4 large squash	Butter
2 large onions	Salt
2 large tomatoes	Bread crumbs

Slice ingredients thin and layer them in a greased 2-quart casserole. Alternate with 1 teaspoon butter and dash of salt on each layer. Cover top with bread crumbs and 2 tablespoons butter. Cover and bake at 350 degrees for 45 minutes. Serves 8.

Note: Zucchini can be substituted for yellow squash. Also good with 1 cup grated cheddar cheese added to top for last 15 minutes of baking time (uncovered).

Mrs. Frank Pilsch (Sharon Snyder)

SQUASH-BACON CASSEROLE

6 slices bacon, fried crisp	1 cup grated cheddar cheese
2 cups cooked yellow squash	(or more)
2 tablespoons bacon grease	½ cup fine buttered bread
1 tablespoon onion, chopped fine	crumbs
Salt and pepper to taste	

Mash cooked squash. Mix with bacon grease, onion, crumbled bacon, salt, pepper, and half of cheese. Pour into a buttered casserole dish. Cover with remainder of cheese and top with bread crumbs. Bake at 350 degrees until a rich golden brown, about 20 minutes. Serves 4.

Note: Eggplant may also be used.

Mrs. William V. Barkley (Carolyn Johnson)

BAKED TOMATOES

1 quart canned tomatoes, drained	½ cup sugar
1¼ cups toasted bread crumbs, divided	1 teaspoon salt
	3 tablespoons butter

Mash tomatoes: Mix 1 cup bread crumbs, sugar, salt, and butter into tomato pulp. Pour into buttered baking dish and cover with remaining bread crumbs. Bake at 300 degrees for 30 minutes. Serves 4.

Mrs. Samuel Payne Wright (Frances Leapard)

GREEN TOMATOES AU GRATIN

5 green tomatoes	Butter
Salt and pepper to taste	Cracker crumbs
¾ cup shredded cheddar cheese	

Cut tomatoes in half crosswise and remove cores. Slice halves into ⅓-inch slices and sprinkle with salt and pepper. Layer half of tomato slices in a shallow buttered baking dish, and sprinkle with half of cheese. Repeat layers. Dot with butter and cracker crumbs. Cover dish and bake at 400 degrees for 45 minutes. Uncover last 10 minutes to brown crumbs.

Mrs. Julian Reed (Peggy Ethridge)

SCALLOPED TOMATOES

2 cups onion	¼ teaspoon pepper
2 tablespoons butter	2 tablespoons brown sugar
2 teaspoons salt	2 cups canned tomatoes
½ teaspoon celery salt	1½ cups bread cubes

Slice onions thin and parboil about 5 minutes. Drain. Sauté bread cubes in butter. Add salt, celery salt, pepper, and sugar to onions and then mix with tomatoes. Pour into greased casserole dish. Top with bread crumbs. Bake uncovered at 350 degrees for 1 hour. Yield: 6 servings. Optional: Add 1 pound zucchini, sliced. Sauté with onion.

Mrs. Dwain R. Winstead (Louise Shepard)

ZUCCHINI PIZZAS

Large zucchini	Salt

FOR EACH SLICE OF ZUCCHINI:

1 tablespoon pizza sauce	2 tablespoons grated mozzarella,
1 teaspoon chopped black olives	Monterey Jack, or other white
1 teaspoon minced green onion	cheese

Preheat broiler, placing rack about 5 inches from heat source. Cut zucchini into slices ¼-inch thick. Salt lightly. Place slices on baking sheet and add in order the pizza sauce, black olives, green onion, and cheese. Broil until cheese is melted and bubbly, about 4 to 5 minutes. Zucchini should be crisp. Yield will depend on size of zucchini.

Rebekah Ball Embrey

Hint: Grate zucchini lengthwise into long strips and steam just until heated through. Serve as you would pasta with spaghetti sauce.

SPINACH ELEGANTE

2 (10-ounce) packages chopped spinach
1 (6-ounce) can mushroom crowns
6 tablespoons butter
1 tablespoon flour
½ cup milk

½ teaspoon salt
Dash of red pepper
1 (6-ounce) can mushroom pieces
1 (14-ounce) can artichoke bottoms

SOUR CREAM SAUCE:
½ cup sour cream
½ cup mayonnaise

2 tablespoons lemon juice

Cook spinach according to directions, drain, and mash. Sauté mushroom crowns in butter; remove and set aside. Add flour to melted butter and cook until bubbly. Blend in milk and stir until smooth. Add salt, pepper, mushroom pieces, and spinach. Put artichokes on the bottom of a buttered casserole and cover with spinach mixture. Mix sour cream sauce ingredients and pour over spinach. Arrange mushroom crowns over all. Heat through. Serves 6-8.

Mrs. William A. "Butch" Miller (Jessica Frazier)

TURNIP GREENS By Request of "Rainey"

I'm a "dump" cook, but here goes...

1 bunch turnip greens
1 slab salt pork size of hand
1 teaspoon salt
1 teaspoon sugar

1 teaspoon vinegar
¼ teaspoon Accent
Few drops pepper sauce
Water

Dice salt pork rather fine. While it is rendering (very low heat) in iron pot or deep-well cooker, wash and pick greens. When the meat is totally rendered, add greens. Cover with water. Cook covered until tender (hard to overcook for Southerners). Add seasoning and cook 20 minutes. Serve in bowls with "pot likker." Corn bread a must!!

Note: Peas may be cooked the same way, but omit the sugar and vinegar. Add medium onion stuck with whole cloves.

Mrs. Ernest "Rainey" Collins (Louise "Bebe" Williams)

VEGETABLES MORNAY

3 (10-ounce) packages frozen
  mixed vegetables
1⅓ cups water

¾ teaspoon salt
¼ teaspoon seasoned salt
3 tablespoons butter

SAUCE:
⅓ cup butter or margarine
4½ tablespoons all-purpose flour
¼ teaspoon nutmeg
¼ teaspoon leaf thyme
¾ teaspoon salt
Whole milk to make 3 cups when
  added to vegetable cooking
  liquid

½ cup grated Parmesan cheese
Buttered bread crumbs (or
  crushed Ritz crackers)

Place vegetables, water, salt, seasoned salt, and butter in a saucepan. Cover and heat to boiling. Simmer for 5 minutes. Drain vegetables, reserving cooking liquid. Put vegetables in casserole dish.

Preheat oven to 350 degrees. Melt butter and blend flour, nutmeg, thyme, and salt, stirring constantly for 2 minutes. Remove from heat and gradually stir in reserved vegetable liquid, with enough milk to make 3 cups. Stir over low heat until smooth and thick. Add cheese and pour over vegetables. Sprinkle with crushed crackers or bread crumbs. Bake in preheated oven for 30 minutes, or until bubbly. Serves 8-10.

Note: This casserole may be made the day before and refrigerated, adding bread crumbs at last minute.

Mrs. Tom Patton (Suse Donald)

BAKED ZUCCHINI

4 tablespoons olive oil, divided
1 medium onion, minced
6 medium zucchini, unpeeled,
  chopped
⅔ cup cooked rice

½ cup grated Swiss cheese
½ cup chopped parsley
1 large egg, beaten
Salt and pepper to taste
2 tablespoons bread crumbs

Heat 3 tablespoons olive oil in large skillet. Sauté onion until soft. Add zucchini and cook, covered, for 10 minutes over low heat, stirring occasionally. Remove from heat and allow to cool slightly. Combine rice, cheese, parsley, egg, salt and pepper. Add zucchini mixture and mix well. Place in greased 1½ quart baking dish. Bake, uncovered, in 375 degree oven for 20 minutes. Makes 6 servings.

Charlotte Blackmon Marshall

Bread

ALMOND RING

¼ cup butter
1 cup milk
2 packages yeast
2 eggs
½ cup sugar
1½ teaspoons salt

4½-5 cups flour
½ cup sugar
2½ tablespoons cinnamon
1 (8-ounce) can almond paste
¼ cup melted butter

TOPPING:
1 cup confectioners' sugar
2 tablespoons milk
¼ teaspoon vanilla

¼ teaspoon almond flavoring
Chopped or slivered toasted
almonds

Heat milk and butter until warm (115 degrees). Add yeast and beat until dissolved. Add eggs, sugar, and salt and beat again. Add flour, 2 cups at a time, making a soft dough. (This may be done in a mixer.) Place dough in greased bowl and turn to grease top. Cover loosely with plastic wrap and let rise until doubled in bulk. Punch dough down. Divide in half. Roll each half of dough into rectangle approximately 18 x 6 inches. Work almond paste until it is spreadable, adding milk if necessary to soften. Spread ½ on each rectangle. Brush with melted butter. Sprinkle with cinnamon and sugar, mixed. Sprinkle with almonds (optional). Roll from long side like jellyroll. Arrange on lightly buttered baking sheet in a circle. With sharp knife or scissors, cut from outside of circle ¾ of way to center every 1½ inch. Turn cut pieces on their sides. Cover and let rise until doubled, about 1 hour. Bake at 350 degrees until light brown, about 30 minutes. Carefully remove to a wire rack to cool, or serve warm. When cool, frost with topping made of confectioners' sugar, milk, and flavorings. Sprinkle with almonds. Yield: 2 rings.

Variations: Leave out almonds and almond paste. Use chopped pecans and/or raisins. Instead of putting roll in circle, cut into 1-inch pieces and let rise in muffin tin for sweet rolls. Makes about 3 dozen. Use grated orange rind instead of cinnamon in filling, and orange juice instead of milk in frosting. Omit almonds and flavorings. Form ring or rolls. Frost while hot. Delicious Christmas or Easter breakfast treat. Keep one, give one as a gift.

Mrs. Peterson Cavert (Mary Beth Wear)

Inexpensive thermometers which register from 100 to 400 degrees are available in most housewares departments. Use for yeast, candy-making and frying.

BUTTERMILK BREAD

3 tablespoons sugar
2½ teaspoons salt
⅓ cup butter or margarine
1 cup buttermilk, scalded (or 1 cup milk soured with 1 tablespoon vinegar)

1 cup warm water (115 degrees)
1 package active dry yeast
5¾ cups (approximately) flour
¼ teaspoon soda

Stir sugar, salt, and butter into buttermilk; cool to lukewarm. Place water in large warmed bowl. Add yeast and stir until dissolved. Add buttermilk mixture. Stir in 3 cups flour and soda; beat until smooth. Add remaining flour to make soft dough that has rough, dull appearance and is sticky. Stir until dough leaves side of bowl. Knead on floured surface until smooth and elastic with satiny appearance. Form into ball; press top of ball into greased bowl and turn over. Cover with cloth wrung out in hot water. Let rise in warm, draft-free place for about 1 hour, or until doubled in bulk. Punch dough down with fist; pull edges into center. Turn out onto lightly floured board, cover, and let rise for 5 minutes. Cut in 2 equal portions. Form each into loaf about 9 x 7 x 1 inches and place in greased 9-inch loaf pan. Let rise until doubled in bulk. Heat oven to 375 degrees. Place pans in oven about 2 inches apart to allow all sides of bread to bake. Bake for about 35 minutes or until done. Turn out onto rack. Brush top lightly with melted butter. Makes 2 loaves.

Ruth Tisdale Wilder

CHEESE PEPPER BREAD

1 package active dry yeast
¼ cup warm water (115 degrees)
2⅓ cups flour
2 tablespoons sugar
1 teaspoon salt

¼ teaspoon soda
1 cup dairy sour cream
1 egg
1 cup shredded cheddar cheese
½ teaspoon pepper

Grease two 1-pound coffee cans. In large bowl of mixer dissolve yeast in water. Add 1⅓ cups of flour, the sugar, salt, soda, sour cream, and egg. Blend ½ minute on low speed, scraping bowl constantly. Beat 2 minutes at high speed, scraping bowl occasionally. Stir in remaining flour, the cheese, and pepper thoroughly. Divide batter between the two cans. Let rise in warm place 50 minutes. (Batter will rise slightly but not double.) Heat oven to 350 degrees. Bake 40 minutes or until golden brown. Immediately remove from cans. Cool slightly before slicing. Makes 2 loaves.

Mrs. Haskell Nevin (Sister Woodfin)

CINNAMON SWIRL BREAD

1 package active dry yeast
¼ cup warm water (115 degrees)
2 cups milk, scalded
⅓ cup sugar

2 teaspoons salt
¼ cup shortening
6 cups flour

CINNAMON MIXTURE:
½ cup sugar
1 tablespoon cinnamon

3 teaspoons water

Dissolve yeast in warm water. Combine milk, sugar, salt, shortening. Cool to lukewarm. Stir in 2 cups of flour. Beat well. Add the yeast; mix. Add enough of the remaining flour to make a moderately stiff dough. Knead until smooth (about 9 minutes). Shape into a ball. Place in lightly-greased bowl. Cover. Let rise in warm place 1 hour and 15 minutes. Punch down. Roll dough into two 15 x 7-inch rectangles. Combine cinnamon mixture and pour half over each rectangle. Sprinkle 1½ teaspoons water over each. Roll into loaves. Place in 9 x 5 x 3-inch loaf pans. Cover and let rise until double (about 45-50 minutes). Bake in 350-degree oven for 30 minutes. Makes 2 loaves.

Mrs. James Allen Randall (Kathleen Powers)

DILLY CASSEROLE BREAD

1 package active dry yeast
¼ cup warm water (115 degrees)
1 cup creamed cottage cheese,
    heated to lukewarm
2 tablespoons sugar
1 tablespoon instant minced onion

1 tablespoon butter
2 teaspoons dill seed
1 teaspoon salt
¼ teaspoon soda
1 unbeaten egg
2¼-2½ cups all-purpose flour

TOPPING:
Butter, melted

Salt

Dissolve yeast in water. Combine in mixing bowl the cottage cheese, sugar, onion, butter, dill seed, salt, soda, egg, and yeast. Add flour to form a stiff dough, beating well after each addition. Cover and let rise in warm place (85-90 degrees) until light and double in size, about 50-60 minutes. Stir dough down. Turn into well-greased 8-inch round 1½-2 quart casserole. Let rise in warm place until light, 30 to 40 minutes. Bake at 350 degrees for 40-50 minutes, until golden brown. Brush top with melted butter and sprinkle with salt. Makes one large round loaf of bread.

Mrs. Allen Mattox (Harriet Marrs)

EARLY COLONIAL BREAD

½ cup yellow corn meal
⅓ cup brown sugar
1 tablespoon salt
2 cups boiling water
¼ cup cooking oil
2 packages dry yeast

½ cup warm water (115 degrees)
¾ cup stirred whole wheat flour
½ cup stirred rye flour
4¼ to 4½ cups sifted all-
purpose flour

Thoroughly combine the corn meal, brown sugar, salt, boiling water and oil. Let cool to lukewarm, about 30 minutes. Soften yeast in ½ cup warm water. Stir into the corn meal mixture. Add the whole wheat and rye flours; mix well. Stir in enough all-purpose flour to make a moderately stiff dough. Turn out on lightly floured surface and knead until smooth and elastic, 6 to 8 minutes. Place in a greased bowl, turning once to grease surface. Cover and let rise in warm place until double, 50 to 60 minutes. Punch down; turn out on lightly floured surface and divide in half. Cover and let rest 10 minutes. Shape into two loaves and place in greased 9 x 5 x 3-inch loaf pans. Let rise again until almost double, about 30 minutes. Bake in 375-degree oven for 45 minutes or until done. (Cap loosely with foil after first 25 minutes if bread browns too rapidly.) Remove from pans. Brush tops with melted oleo if desired. Cool on rack.

Mrs. Victor M. Friedman (Segail Irwin)

HONEY WHOLE WHEAT BREAD

4 cups warm water (115 degrees)
3 packages active dry yeast
½ cup honey
4 teaspoons salt
⅓ cup oil

1¾ cups non-fat dry milk
½ cup wheat germ or wheat
bran
10 cups (approximately) whole
wheat flour

Sprinkle yeast on warm water in large bowl. Stir to dissolve. Add honey, salt, oil, dry milk, wheat germ or bran, and enough flour to make stiff dough. Knead on floured board 8-10 minutes, using additional flour as needed to keep dough from sticking. Place in greased bowl, turning to grease top. Cover with plastic wrap and let rise until doubled. Punch dough down. Divide into thirds. Let rest while you butter 3 loaf pans. Form dough into loaves and place in loaf pans. Let rise until almost doubled. Preheat oven to 375 degrees and bake until loaves sound hollow when turned out of pans and tapped on bottom. If loaves start browning too much, place foil over tops. Cool on wire racks. Freezes well. Makes 3 loaves.

Mrs. Peterson Cavert (Mary Beth Wear)

IRISH SODA BREAD

2 cups unsifted unbleached flour
½ cup sugar
¾ teaspoon salt
1 teaspoon soda
2 packages yeast

4 cups unsifted whole wheat
    flour
½ cup wheat germ
1 stick oleo
2¾ cups buttermilk

In large mixing bowl, mix unbleached flour, sugar, salt, soda, and yeast. In small saucepan, over low heat, warm the buttermilk and oleo until oleo melts. Don't let get too warm. Pour oleo and buttermilk into large mixing bowl, and with large heavy spoon or mixer, beat until yeast is dissolved. Add whole wheat flour and wheat germ and knead until mixed. (Knead in bowl!) Grease large mixing bowl and turn dough in it until dough is greased. Cover with foil and let rise. (Foil reflects warmth and makes dough rise faster.) Punch dough down and divide into two round balls. Place each ball in greased 1½-quart round casserole. Brush tops with melted oleo. Cover with foil and let rise. Bake in 325-degree oven for 30-40 minutes, until brown on top. Remove to cooling racks and brush well with melted oleo. Freezes beautifully. Serve well-toasted and hot. This is the dark, nourishing bread so frequently served in Ireland.

Mrs. Bruce McEachin (Charlotte Cammack)

OATMEAL BREAD

4 cups boiling water
3 cups old-fashioned rolled oats
2 tablespoons or 2 packages yeast
7-8 cups unbleached flour, divided

2 tablespoons salt
¼ cup corn oil
½ cup molasses or honey

Pour boiling water over oats, stir, and let cool to 115 degrees. Add yeast and 2 cups flour; stir well. Let rise, uncovered, until doubled in bulk and top "evens out", about 2 hours. Add salt, oil, honey or molasses, and stir well. Add remainder of flour in 2-cup increments, stirring well after each addition. When dough becomes too stiff to stir, turn out on well-floured board and knead, using extra flour as needed, until smooth and elastic, about 10 minutes. Divide dough into thirds; let rest while you grease three loaf pans. Form each third into a loaf and place in pan. Let rise until doubled, about 1-1½ hours. Bake in a preheated 350-degree oven for 35-40 minutes, or until top is brown and bottom sounds hollow when tapped. Cool before slicing. Makes 3 loaves.

Hints: Regular all-purpose flour may be used. The weather and temperature will affect the amount of flour and rising times. This is good toast and sandwich bread and makes wonderful bread crumbs.

Mrs. Peterson Cavert (Mary Beth Wear)

WHITE BREAD

3½ cups boiling water
⅓ cup shortening
½ cup sugar
½ cup plus 1 tablespoon potato flakes
1 heaping tablespoon coarse salt

¼ cup lukewarm water (115 degrees)
1 teaspoon sugar
2 packages dry yeast
10-11 cups unbleached flour, unsifted

Pour boiling water over shortening, sugar, potato flakes, salt. Let cool to lukewarm (115 degrees). Dissolve yeast and teaspoon of sugar in lukewarm water. Allow to proof about 5 minutes (gets bubbly and expands). Add to potato mixture and stir. Add flour, 2 cups at a time, stirring after each addition. When dough becomes stiff enough to knead, turn out on well-floured board and knead until stiff and elastic, about 10 minutes, adding more flour if necessary. Put in greased bowl, turn to grease top. Let rise, covered, until doubled in bulk, about 1½ to 2 hours. Punch dough down and knead again, lightly. Form into 3 loaves and place in greased 8½-inch loaf pans. Let rise until doubled. Bake in preheated 350-degree oven 30 to 40 minutes, or until tops are brown and bottom sounds hollow when turned out of pans and tapped. If desired, brush tops with melted butter while hot. Makes 3 loaves.

Mrs. Peterson Cavert (Mary Beth Wear)

EASY BANANA NUT BREAD

¼ pound butter or margarine
⅔ cup sugar
2 eggs
1⅓ cups mashed bananas (3)

2 cups sifted flour
1 teaspoon baking soda
1½ teaspoons salt
½ cup chopped nuts

Melt butter over very low heat in a large saucepan. Remove from heat and stir in sugar, unbeaten eggs and bananas. Stir in flour sifted with soda and salt only until blended. Stir in nuts. Pour into greased loaf pan and bake 60 minutes at 350 degrees. Cool for 10 minutes inside pan. Let cool on rack completely before wrapping in foil. Yield: 1 loaf.

Mrs. Charles R. Pearce (Elizabeth Cunningham)

LIZ'S CORN BREAD DRESSING

1 recipe corn bread, crumbled
  (Recipe follows)
1 (8-ounce) package Pepperidge
  Farm herb stuffing mix
1 large onion, chopped
2½ cups celery, chopped
2 tablespoons parsley, chopped
1 teaspoon salt
1 teaspoon pepper

1 teaspoon paprika
1 tablespoon poultry seasoning
  (or ½ teaspoon each of sage,
  thyme, marjoram, and ¼ teaspoon each of coriander and
  allspice)
1 stick butter
6-8 cups turkey stock or tinned
  chicken broth

Cook vegetables in butter until tender. Add corn bread and stuffing mix. Stir in enough stock to moisten thoroughly. Bake at 350 degrees for 1 hour or more, until brown on top. Makes 3 quarts, approximately 12 servings.

Dressing freezes well. For a small family, make Thanksgiving and freeze half for Christmas dinner.

CORN BREAD:
4 cups corn meal (plain)
4 teaspoons baking powder
½ teaspoon soda

2 eggs
3 cups buttermilk
2 teaspoons salt

Preheat oven to 425 degrees. Combine ingredients. Turn into greased 9 x 13-inch baking dish. Bake for 20 minutes.

Elizabeth Overton Cravens

OATMEAL MUFFINS

1 cup quick cooking oatmeal
1 cup buttermilk
1 egg
⅓ cup melted shortening or oil
½ cup brown sugar, packed

1 cup flour
½ teaspoon salt
½ teaspoon soda
1 teaspoon baking powder

Mix oatmeal and buttermilk and let stand 45 minutes to 1 hour. Add egg; beat well. Add cooled shortening; mix well. Fold in dry ingredients. Bake at 400 degrees for 15-20 minutes in greased muffin pans. Let stand for a few minutes before removing from pan to firm up. These are very good for the bread or for dessert with jelly or honey. I usually serve them with a meatless meal such as macaroni and cheese, salad, vegetable, and muffins. Yield: 10-12 muffins.

Mrs. Carlos "Sonny" Shows (Gloria Church)

ONION BREAD

1 envelope dry onion soup mix
1 teaspoon salt
6 cups flour (approximately),
  divided

2 packages dry yeast
1 tablespoon melted oleo
2½ cups warm water (115
  degrees)

Mix well in a large bowl soup mix, salt, 2½ cups flour, and yeast. Add oleo and water and mix well. Add remaining flour to make a soft dough. Turn out onto floured board and knead about 3 minutes. Put dough in greased bowl, turn to grease top. Cover and let rise until double. Punch down with a spoon. Divide dough in half and put in two greased loaf pans. Cover and let rise until almost double in size. Heat oven to 350 degrees and bake loaves about 40 minutes. Makes 2 loaves.

Hint: To make a crusty top, before putting in oven, brush tops of loaves with 1 egg beaten with 1 tablespoon water.

Mrs. Glenn Powell (Caroline Chappell)

MOZZARELLA LOAF

12-inch loaf of French bread
1 pound mozzarella cheese
¼ cup grated Parmesan cheese

⅓ cup softened butter
½ teaspoon garlic salt
½ teaspoon oregano

Cut loaf into 1-inch thick slices. Cut mozzarella cheese into 12 slices, each ¼-inch thick. Combine Parmesan cheese, butter, garlic salt, and oregano. Spread on each slice of bread. Reshape loaf, alternating bread and cheese slices. Press together firmly and brush remaining butter mixture on outside of loaf. Bake at 400 degrees for 8 minutes.

Mrs. A. E. Poole (Marion Daniel)

BUTTERFLAKE CHEESE ROLLS

1 cup chopped black olives
4 slices bacon, cooked and
  crumbled
1 cup shredded cheddar cheese

1 green onion, chopped
¼ cup mayonnaise
2-3 drops Worcestershire sauce
1 dozen brown-'n'-serve rolls

Combine olives, bacon, cheese, onion, mayonnaise, and Worcestershire sauce. Pull rolls apart slightly and stuff each with cheese mixture. Place in muffin tins and bake at 375 degrees for 15 to 20 minutes.

Mrs. Ryan deGraffenried, Jr. (Jynx Bailey)

ALL-BRAN ROLLS

1 package yeast	½ cup shortening
1 cup warm water (115 degrees)	1 teaspoon salt
½ cup All-Bran	2 tablespoons sugar
1 egg	3½ cups flour, approximately

Sprinkle yeast on water, stir until dissolved. Add All-Bran, egg, shortening, salt, and sugar. Mix well. Add flour, 1 cup at a time. Beat vigorously by hand after each addition. When dough begins to leave the side of the bowl, cover and let stand until double. Punch dough down, roll on floured board, and shape into Parker House or whatever shape desired. These can be frozen at this point. When ready to use, take out desired number, place on greased cookie sheet. Let thaw and double in size—about 1½ hours. Preheat oven to 425 degrees. Bake for about 15 minutes.

Note: When frozen and kept very cold, these travel well. Let rise and bake at your destination.

Mrs. Jimmy Gamble—Tuscumbia, AL

EASY REFRIGERATOR ROLLS

2 cups water	2 tablespoons or 2 packages
1 cup sugar	active dry yeast
1 cup shortening or butter	2 eggs, beaten
1½ teaspoons salt	6 cups unbleached flour, unsifted

Bring water to boil. Pour over sugar, shortening, salt. Stir to dissolve. Cool to lukewarm (115 degrees). Add yeast; stir. Add beaten eggs. Stir in flour 2 cups at a time. Dough will be sticky. Cover. Refrigerate 8 hours or overnight. (Dough will keep at least a week in refrigerator.) To make out rolls: 2 hours before serving, roll ⅓ of dough at a time about ¼ inch thick on floured board. Make into desired shape; dip in melted butter, if desired, and put in buttered pan. Let rise 1 hour. Bake in preheated 350-degree oven 20-30 minutes, or until brown on top. To make ahead in the day or to freeze, take rolls out of oven after about 15 minutes when firm but not yet brown. Cool on wire rack. (Freeze if desired.) Finish baking at 350 degrees for 15 minutes or until brown. Yield: 5-6 dozen.

Mrs. Peterson Cavert (Mary Beth Wear)

PITA BREAD

1 tablespoon active dry yeast
2 tablespoons honey
2½ cups warm water (115 degrees)

6-7 cups flour (unbleached)
4 teaspoons salt

Dissolve yeast and honey in warm water; let stand about 10 minutes. In mixer bowl, combine yeast mixture, salt, and about 3 cups flour. Beat for 2 minutes. Stir in enough flour to make a stiff dough (3 cups). Knead until smooth and elastic, 8 to 10 minutes. Place in greased bowl, turning to grease top of dough. Let rise until doubled, about 1 hour. Heat oven to 450 degrees. Divide dough into 12 pieces and let rest about 10 minutes. Roll each piece into a 6-inch circle. Arrange on ungreased baking sheet (I can do 3 at a time). Bake on bottom rack for 10 minutes. Repeat until all dough is used. If tops are pale, broil for a minute. Watch!

To use, heat in a 300-degree oven for 5 minutes. Then cut into semi-circles (scissors work well). Using a sharp knife, make a "pocket" in each piece. Fill with taco fixings, hot pork and beans with wieners cut up in them, stir-fried pork and Chinese vegetables, etc. Even peanut butter and jelly is good!

Bert Wear

VERA'S BLIZZARD ROLLS

1 package active dry yeast
2 cups warm water
¼ cup sugar
½ teaspoon salt
1 egg

⅔ cup shortening, melted
4 cups self-rising flour
Grated cheese or bacon bits
(optional)

In a small bowl, dissolve the yeast in warm water. Mix the yeast mixture with the sugar, salt, egg, and shortening. After this is mixed well (preferably by hand), add flour, working in a little at a time, followed by optional ingredients if desired. Let the dough stand in refrigerator 1 hour before baking. Spoon mixture into greased muffin tins ½ full. Bake at 425 degrees for 12-15 minutes. This dough keeps very well for at least a week in a covered container in the refrigerator; just pinch desired amount off and bake. Yield: 4 dozen.

Variations: 1) Sprinkle uncooked rolls with cinnamon-sugar. 2) Put a ½-inch cube of cheese in each roll.

Mrs. Kenric Minges (Candace Speck)

SOUR CREAM CRESCENTS

1 cup sour cream
1½ packages dry yeast
⅓ cup warm water (115 degrees)
1 cup butter or margarine (2
   sticks), softened

½ cup sugar
½ teaspoon salt
4 cups sifted flour
2 eggs, well beaten

Heat sour cream in top of double boiler over simmering water until it becomes slightly yellow around edges (separation of cream does not affect product). Meanwhile, dissolve yeast in warm water. Put butter, sugar, and salt in large bowl. Pour heated sour cream over and stir until butter is melted. Cool slightly. Blend 1 cup of the flour into sour cream mixture, beating until smooth. Add yeast mixture and mix well. Add 1 cup of flour, beaten eggs, then remaining flour, beating well after each addition. Cover bowl and refrigerate 6 hours or overnight.

To shape: On floured surface, roll ¼ of dough at a time into a circle ¼-inch thick. Cut into 12 wedge-shaped pieces. Roll up each wedge, beginning at wide end, and place on greased baking sheet with point underneath, curved into crescent shape. Let stand, uncovered, 1 hour. Bake at 375 degrees for 15 minutes. These freeze well if you bake until firm but not brown. Cool, then freeze. Let come to room temperature again before browning. Yield: 4 dozen.

Mrs. Ernest "Rainey" Collins (Louise "Bebe" Williams)

SOUR DOUGH STARTER

2 cups plain flour
2 cups warm water in which
   potatoes have been cooked

1 package dry yeast

Dissolve yeast in potato water and add to flour. Mix well. Place mixture in a warm place overnight. In the morning, put 1 cup of mixture in a container with a tight cover and store in the refrigerator. This is your starter. Use the remaining batter for immediate baking. Do not use a container with metal parts. If you use a glass jar with a metal lid, put wax paper or plastic wrap over the mouth of the jar before putting on the lid.

Mrs. Jan Bates (Joan Bostick)

FEEDING AND GUIDELINES FOR SOUR DOUGH

1 cup plain flour   1 cup milk
⅓ cup sugar

Sift flour, measure, and sift again with sugar. Add milk slowly to make a smooth mixture. Add to the culture you have left (at least 1 cup). This feeding is necessary to keep culture active.

Guidelines for your culture:
1. Feed once a week.
2. Leave out of refrigerator on "feeding day" for 3 to 5 hours.
3. Do not use for 24 hours after feeding.
4. After 3rd week, you can feed culture with double the recipe each week or half the recipe each week.
5. Always have at least 1 cup of culture left.
6. Do not use a container with metal parts.

Mrs. Jan Bates (Joan Bostick)

SOUR DOUGH RYE BREAD

1 cup sour dough   2 tablespoons oil or melted
1 cup warm water (115 degrees)   butter
2 cups rye flour   3 tablespoons granulated sugar
1 package active dry yeast   4-5 cups unbleached flour
¼ cup warm water (115 degrees)   Corn meal
2 teaspoons salt   1 egg
1 tablespoon caraway seed   1 tablespoon water
1½ teaspoons poppy seed

Day before making, combine sour dough, 1 cup warm water, and rye flour. Cover and let stand overnight at room temperature.

Next day, dissolve yeast in ¼ cup warm water. Add to sour dough mixture along with salt, caraway seed, poppy seed, oil or butter, sugar, and enough unbleached flour to make a stiff dough. Turn out on floured surface and knead, adding flour as needed to keep dough from being sticky, for 10 minutes. Place in greased bowl, turning to grease top. Cover with plastic wrap and let rise until doubled, about 2 hours. Punch dough down and divide in half. Shape into round loaves and place on baking sheet, sprinkled generously with corn meal. Cover with damp towel and let rise until almost doubled, about 1 hour. Heat oven to 375 degrees. Beat egg with 1 tablespoon water and brush loaves. Bake until loaves are lightly browned and sound hollow when tapped, about 30 minutes. Cool on wire rack, covered with towel to keep crust soft. Freezes well. Makes 2 loaves.

Mrs. Peterson Cavert (Mary Beth Wear)

SOUR DOUGH BISCUITS

1 cup flour
2 teaspoons baking powder
½ teaspoon salt

¼ teaspoon soda
1 cup sour dough culture
⅓ cup liquid shortening

Mix flour, baking powder, salt, soda, culture, and shortening. Add enough flour until you have a workable dough. Knead on floured board 10 times or more. Pat into ¾-inch thickness. Cut. Allow to stand 20-30 minutes before baking. Heat oven to 425 degrees and bake for 10-12 minutes. Watch, as they burn easily, and if too brown, they may be tough.

Mrs. Jan Bates (Joan Bostick)

SOUR DOUGH LOAF BREAD OR ROLLS

½ cup warm water (115 degrees)
1 package dry yeast
¾ tablespoon fat

1 cup sour dough culture
2 cups self-rising flour
(approximately)

Measure warm water into a large warm bowl. Sprinkle yeast over water and stir until dissolved. Add fat. Add sour dough. Gradually add flour. Beat until smooth. Turn dough out onto a lightly-floured board and knead until springy. Place in a greased bowl. Cover and let rise in a warm place at least 30 minutes.

For Rolls: Punch down and form into rolls of desired shape. Let rise again 30-40 minutes or until double in size. Bake at 400 degrees for 10-15 minutes.

For Loaf: Punch dough down and form into one large loaf or 2 small loaves. Put into well-greased and floured loaf pan(s). Let rise at least 1½ hours or until double in size. Bake in a preheated oven at 325 degrees about 30 minutes. Remove from pans and cool on wire rack.

Mrs. Jan Bates (Joan Bostick)

BEER BISCUITS

2 cups Bisquick
1 tablespoon sugar

¾ cup beer

Heat oven to 400 degrees. Mix ingredients together well. Batter should be like muffin batter rather than like real biscuit dough. Fill greased muffin tin ½ full of batter as if making cupcakes. Bake for 10-12 minutes, until lightly browned. Makes 12.

Mrs. David Mathews (Mary Chapman)

ANGEL BISCUITS

9 cups self-rising flour (sift before measuring)
1 cup Crisco
1 teaspoon soda dissolved in ⅓ cup water

2 cups buttermilk
½ cup sugar
2 well-beaten eggs
2 packages yeast dissolved in 1 cup warm water

Cut shortening into flour. Add soda, buttermilk, sugar, eggs, and dissolved yeast. Mix well. Store, covered, in refrigerator until needed.

To bake, preheat oven to 400 degrees. Take out as much dough as you think you will need and knead as for biscuits. Roll to ½-inch thickness and cut with a 1½-inch roll cutter for dainty biscuits (larger, if desired). Place in a greased pan and brush with melted butter. Bake until brown.

Note: Dough will keep for 2 weeks in refrigerator. Makes 5 dozen medium biscuits or 8-10 dozen 1½-inch biscuits. This recipe is excellent for "ham and biscuits."

Mrs. Guy Moman, Jr. (Anne McAliley)

BODKA CREEK BISCUITS

2 cups self-rising flour
4 tablespoons Crisco shortening

¾ cup milk

Heat oven to 400 degrees. Cut shortening into flour. Add milk. Knead. Roll out biscuits on floured surface and cut. Bake about 10-15 minutes, until brown. Yield: 2 dozen.

Mrs. William Dowling (Charlene Clary)

MIDDLE EAST BREAD WAFERS

1 cup flour, plain
¼ cup corn meal
¼ teaspoon soda
¼ teaspoon salt
1 teaspoon sugar

¼ cup butter, melted
¼ cup warm water
1 tablespoon cider vinegar
Poppy, celery, sesame, carraway seeds

Heat oven to 400 degrees. Mix flour, corn meal, soda, salt, and sugar. Add 2 tablespoons butter, water, and vinegar. Mix with fork. Shape into roll. Cut into 16 pieces. Place ¼ teaspoon seed on surface with piece of dough. Roll paper thin and place on cookie sheet. Brush tops with melted butter. Bake 5 to 7 minutes. Yield: 16 wafers.

Mrs. Max Bailey (Julie Knight)

ONION CHEESE BISCUITS

2½ cups plain flour
1 tablespoon baking powder
½ teaspoon salt
½ cup butter or margarine

2 cups shredded cheddar cheese
½ cup minced onion
1 egg
1 cup milk

Preheat oven to 425 degrees. In large bowl, with fork, mix flour, baking powder, and salt. Cut into flour mixture the butter or margarine until mixture resembles coarse crumbs. Stir in cheese and onion. In small bowl, with fork, beat egg and milk until well mixed. Stir into flour mixture just until flour is moistened. Onto greased cookie sheet, drop heaping tablespoonfuls of dough about 1 inch apart. Bake 15-20 minutes or until biscuits are golden. 18-24 large biscuits.

Mrs. Dom Elmore (Susan Rogers)

SOUR CREAM BISCUITS

2 sticks real butter
1 (8-ounce) carton sour cream

2 cups self-rising flour

Soften butter. Add sour cream and flour, and mix with spoon. Drop in small greased muffin tins. Bake at 400 degrees until brown. Yield: 24 small biscuits.

Hint: To freeze, cook until almost brown. Cool, then freeze.

Mrs. David Ellis (Patricia Mitchell)

CHEESE BREAD

½ cup milk
1 beaten egg
1½ cups biscuit mix
3 tablespoons chopped parsley
2 tablespoons minced onion

½ teaspoon seasoned salt
1 cup grated sharp cheddar
  cheese, divided
¼ cup melted margarine

Combine milk and egg. Add biscuit mix, parsley, seasoned salt, onion, and ½ cup cheese. Pour into a greased 8 or 9-inch round pan. Sprinkle ½ cup cheese and margarine over bread. Bake at 350 degrees for 30 minutes or until golden brown. Yield: 6-8 servings.

Mrs. James William McFarland (Miriam Webster)

CORN BREAD

2 tablespoons shortening or bacon
   grease
1½ cups corn meal
½ teaspoon soda

1½ teaspoons salt
1 teaspoon baking powder
2 eggs
1¼ cups buttermilk

Preheat oven to 400 degrees. Put shortening or bacon grease into seasoned 6- to 8-inch iron skillet and put pan in oven. Combine corn meal, soda, salt, baking powder, eggs, and buttermilk, and mix well. Place in *hot* corn bread skillet. Cook at 400 degrees for 12-15 minutes. Yield: 6-8 servings.

Note: 1 tablespoon instant minced onion is a tasty addition.

Mrs. John G. Hogue (Peggy Hinton)

FLUFFY SPOON BREAD

3 cups milk
¾ cup white corn meal
2 tablespoons butter

1½ teaspoons salt
1 teaspoon baking soda
3 eggs, separated

Heat milk in saucepan until tiny bubbles appear at edges. Slowly stir in corn meal and cook and stir over medium heat until consistency of mush. Remove from heat and stir in butter until melted, then salt, baking powder, and egg yolks. Cool 20 or 30 minutes. Preheat oven to 375 degrees. Beat egg whites until stiff. Carefully fold into corn meal mixture. Bake 30-40 minutes, until puffed and golden brown. Serve while hot with butter.

Mrs. Joe Sewell (Willie Veal)

SOUR CREAM CORN BREAD

2 eggs, well beaten
1 small can cream-style corn
1 cup self-rising corn meal

⅓ cup oil
8 ounces sour cream

Add oil and meal to eggs. Stir in corn and then sour cream. Mix well. Grease skillet on bottom and sides and put in 400-degree oven until hot. Pour mix in hot skillet. Bake at 400 degrees until brown on top. Cut in wedges from skillet. Serves 8.

Note: This is a salvation for people whose "regular" corn bread tastes like concrete blocks (me!).

Mrs. Larry McGehee (Betsy Boden)—Martin, TN

APPLESAUCE NUT BREAD

1 cup sugar
1 (8-ounce) jar applesauce
⅓ cup salad oil
2 eggs
2 tablespoons milk
⅛ teaspoon almond flavoring
2 cups all-purpose flour

1 teaspoon soda
½ teaspoon baking powder
½ teaspoon ground cinnamon
¼ teaspoon salt
¼ teaspoon ground nutmeg
¾ cup chopped pecans

Combine sugar, applesauce, oil, eggs, milk, and almond flavoring. Mix well. Combine flour, soda, baking powder, cinnamon, salt, and nutmeg. Add to sugar mixture; mix well. Fold in pecans. Pour into greased loaf pan.

TOPPING:
¼ cup chopped pecans
½ teaspoon ground cinnamon

¼ cup packed brown sugar

Combine pecans, cinnamon, and brown sugar. Sprinkle over batter. Bake at 350 degrees for 1 hour. Cover loosely with foil the last 30 minutes of baking time. Cool on rack. Makes 1 loaf.

Mrs. Edward M. Streit (Eleanor Gage)

CHERRY BREAD

1 (6-ounce) bottle maraschino
   cherries, drained and cut in
   pieces (about ½ cup)
⅓ cup reserved cherry syrup
¾ cup chopped pecans

1½ cups sifted flour
1½ teaspoons baking powder
¼ teaspoon salt
2 eggs
¾ cup sugar

Preheat oven to 350 degrees. Grease bottom only of 9½ x 5¼ x 2¾-inch loaf pan. Line with wax paper cut to fit bottom. Grease wax paper. Sift together flour, baking powder, salt. Beat eggs and sugar together until thick and piled. Mixing until well blended after each addition, alternately add dry ingredients in thirds and cherry syrup in halves to egg mixture. Mix in cherries and pecans. (All of this should be mixed by hand.) Turn batter into pan, spreading to corners. Bake 45 to 50 minutes. Cool 10 minutes in pan on rack. Run spatula gently around sides to loosen. Turn out. Peel off wax paper and turn top side up. Cool before slicing. Makes 1 loaf.

Mrs. Gary Loper (Nancy Tally)

CRANBERRY BREAD

¼ cup shortening
¼ cup water
2 eggs
4 cups flour
2 cups sugar
2 teaspoons salt

1 teaspoon baking soda
1 tablespoon baking powder
1 cup orange juice
1 pound cranberries, washed, stemmed, halved (do not grind)

Preheat oven to 350 degrees. Heat shortening and water together until shortening is melted. Beat eggs in large bowl. Sift flour, sugar, salt, soda, and baking powder together. Add orange juice, water, and melted shortening to eggs. Beat well. Add dry ingredients slowly. Fold in cranberries. Bake in greased loaf pans which have greased wax paper in the bottoms. Bake in preheated oven for 1 hour, or until top is brown and springs back when pressed. Makes 2 loaves.

Mrs. Peterson Cavert (Mary Beth Wear)

EASY NUT BREAD

1 egg
1 cup sugar
1 cup milk
3½ cups flour

3½ teaspoons baking powder
1 teaspoon salt
1 cup chopped pecans

Preheat oven to 350 degrees. Beat egg and sugar until light. Add milk, flour, baking powder, and salt. Beat well and stir in nuts. Bake in greased loaf pan in preheated oven for 45 minutes to 1 hour. Cool on wire rack before slicing. Makes a heavy loaf and should be sliced thin. Yield: 12-15 slices.

Ann Cox Montgomery

SUDS PUPPIES

2 cups corn meal
1 tablespoon flour
1 teaspoon soda
1 teaspoon baking powder

1 tablespoon salt
6 tablespoons chopped onion
1 egg, beaten
1 cup beer

Mix corn meal, flour, soda, baking powder, and salt. Add onion, egg, beer. Mix just until moistened. Drop by spoonfuls or make round pones with fingers and drop into hot grease. When puppies float, they are done. Drain. Makes 36-48 small puppies.

Mrs. Hugh Underwood (Ginger Puryear)

GRANDMA'S BROWN BREAD

2 cups buttermilk
2 cups molasses
1 teaspoon soda
2 teaspoons salt

3 cups whole wheat flour
2 cups raisins, dredged in white
flour
1 cup boiling water

Mix all ingredients together, adding boiling water last. My grandmother cooked this in 1-pound baking powder cans that had tight fitting metal lids. These are unavailable now, so I substitute cans covered with foil held on with a rubber band (15-ounce tomato cans are good). Fill cans ¾ full, cover and steam, standing cans upright in kettle of boiling water (kettle should have a tight-fitting lid) for two hours. Remove from cans while still quite hot. (It may be necessary to take bottom off can and push loaf out.) Cool before slicing. Makes 4 round loaves.

Mrs. Peterson Cavert (Mary Beth Wear)

Hint: Mash very ripe bananas and freeze in measuring cup. When frozen, remove and wrap in plastic bag. Use thawed in banana bread or frozen in any drink whirled in blender. As it has the shape of the cup, there is no question about the amount. Usually, 2 bananas equals 1-1½ cups mashed.

HEAVENLY BANANA BREAD

1½ cups sugar
2 eggs
1 teaspoon vanilla
¼ cup buttermilk
2 cups all-purpose flour

¾ teaspoon soda
½ teaspoon baking powder
½ teaspoon salt
3 large ripe bananas, well
mashed

Preheat oven to 350 degrees. Beat sugar and eggs together. Add vanilla and beat on high speed for 1½ minutes. Add buttermilk and beat well. Sift together flour, baking powder, soda, and salt. Add dry ingredients to egg mixture alternately with bananas. Scrape sides of bowl often while mixing. Grease a loaf pan, line bottom with wax paper, and grease wax paper. Turn batter into prepared pan. Bake for 1 hour or until it begins to turn loose from sides of pan. Serve plain or with whipped cream. Good toasted for breakfast. Makes 1 loaf.

Mrs. Jimmy Gamble—Tuscumbia, AL

PUMPKIN BREAD

1 cup oil
⅔ cup water
4 eggs
2 cups mashed, cooked pumpkin
3⅓ cups flour
1½ teaspoons salt

1 teaspoon nutmeg
2 teaspoons soda
1 teaspoon cinnamon
3 cups sugar
1½ cups raisins
½ cup chopped nuts

Preheat oven to 350 degrees. Mix oil, water, eggs, pumpkin in small bowl. Add remaining ingredients. Pour into 3 greased and floured loaf pans. Bake for 1 hour. Freezes well.

Note: Baked in cans, (1-pound coffee cans, soup cans, etc.,) muffin pans, or anything you can grease and flour, this makes a wonderful gift! Delicious with cream cheese.

Mrs. Richard Shelby (Annette Nevin)

STRAWBERRY BREAD

2 (10-ounce) packages frozen
  strawberries
4 eggs
1¼ cups vegetable oil
3 cups flour

1 teaspoon baking soda
1 teaspoon salt
3 teaspoons cinnamon
2 cups sugar
1 cup chopped nuts

Stir together thawed strawberries, eggs, and vegetable oil. Mix together the flour, baking soda, salt, cinnamon, sugar, and nuts. Add to strawberry mixture and stir until blended. Pour into 2 greased and floured loaf pans. Bake at 350 degrees for 1 hour, or until done.

Mrs. William Tucker (Harriet Belle Little)

CARAMEL BREAKFAST RING

4 tablespoons butter or margarine,
  melted
2 tablespoons brown sugar
¼ cup chopped nuts
10 maraschino cherries

⅓ cup sugar
1 teaspoon cinnamon
2 tablespoons chopped nuts
1 (7.5-ounce) can refrigerated
  biscuits

Heat oven to 400 degrees. Melt butter. Place 2 tablespoons butter in bottom of 7- to 8-inch tube pan or ring mold. Sprinkle brown sugar and ¼ cup chopped nuts over butter. Arrange cherries on top. Mix sugar, cinnamon, and 2 tablespoons chopped nuts. Dip each biscuit into butter, then into sugar mixture. Place coated biscuits in pan. Bake 25-30 minutes. Immediately invert on serving plate. Makes 10-12 servings.

Peggy Bishop—Tuscaloosa County Home Agent

ORANGE BUTTER COFFEE CAKE

1 package dry yeast
¼ cup warm water
1 cup sugar, divided
1 teaspoon salt
2 eggs

½ cup sour cream
½ cup melted butter, divided
2¾ cups all-purpose flour
1 cup pecans, divided
2 tablespoons grated orange rind

ORANGE GLAZE:
¾ cup sugar
½ cup sour cream

2 tablespoons orange juice
¼ cup butter

Soften yeast in warm water in mixing bowl. Stir in ¼ cup sugar, salt, eggs, sour cream, and 6 tablespoons butter. Gradually add flour to form stiff dough, beating well after each addition. (For first additions of flour, use mixer on medium speed.) Cover and let rise in warm place (85-90 degrees) until light and doubled, about 2 hours.

Combine ¾ cup sugar, ¾ cup nuts and orange rind. Knead dough on well-floured surface about 15 times. Roll out half of dough to a 12-inch circle. Brush with 1 tablespoon melted butter. Sprinkle with half of sugar-pecan mixture. Cut into 12 wedges. Roll up, starting with wide end and rolling to a point. Repeat with remaining dough. Place rolls, point down, in 3 rows in a well-greased 13 x 9-inch pan. Cover and let rise in warm place until light and doubled, about 1 hour. Bake at 350 degrees for 25-30 minutes, until golden brown. Leave in pan. For glaze, combine sugar, sour cream, orange juice, and butter in saucepan and boil 3 minutes, stirring occasionally. Pour glaze over hot coffee cake. Sprinkle with ¼ cup nuts. Serve warm or cold.

Mrs. William H. Darden (Caroline Sullivan)

GRILLED PINEAPPLE SANDWICH

1 (8½-ounce) can pineapple slices
French dressing
1 cup shredded cheddar cheese
¼ cup finely chopped green
  pepper

¼ teaspoon chili powder
2 tablespoons mayonnaise
4 slices bread
Butter
4 slices baked or boiled ham

Drain pineapple; brush slices lightly with French dressing. Combine cheese, green pepper, chili powder, and mayonnaise. Toast bread. Spread with butter and arrange on baking sheet. Layer ham, pineapple slices, and cheese mixture on bread. Broil until topping is melted and golden brown; be careful not to burn. 4 servings.

Mrs. James Hodo Walburn (Dean Frank)

GLAZED PINEAPPLE COFFEE CAKE

1½ cups Wesson oil
2 cups sugar
4 eggs, separated
2½ cups self-rising flour
1 (8-ounce) can crushed pineapple,
  undrained

2 tablespoons hot tap water
2½ teaspoons cinnamon
1½ teaspoons nutmeg
1 cup chopped nuts

GLAZE:
Juice of 1 orange plus water to
  equal 1 cup

⅔ cup sugar (granulated)

Beat egg whites until stiff and save. Mix Wesson oil and sugar. Add egg yolks, flour, pineapple, water, cinnamon and nutmeg, reserving 1 tablespoon flour. Mix the 1 tablespoon flour with nuts and add. Fold in egg whites. Bake at 325 degrees for 1 hour in Bundt pan. Let cool 45 minutes. Bring orange juice, water and sugar to a boil and pour over cake.

Mrs. Julian Reed (Peggy Ethridge)

COCONUT COFFEE CAKE

2 cups sugar
1½ sticks butter
6 eggs
1 (12-ounce) box vanilla wafers,
  crushed

1 (7-ounce) package Angel Flake
  coconut
½ cup milk
1 cup nuts

Cream butter and sugar. Add eggs. Add vanilla wafers, coconut, milk, and nuts. Pour into tube pan. Bake at 325 degrees for 1 hour and 15 minutes.

Mrs. James E. Shotts, Jr. (Camille Brignet)

PIMIENTO CHEESE

1 pound sharp cheese, grated
1 small onion, grated
¼ cup diced pimiento (small jar)
1 tablespoon chili powder

Salt to taste
Pepper to taste
½ to ¾ cup mayonnaise
½ to ¾ cup Durkees sauce

Mix all ingredients together in a medium bowl. If mixture is too thick, add more mayonnaise and Durkees. Cover and store in refrigerator. Will keep for weeks. For variety, add pickle relish or chopped olives.

Mrs. Thomas W. Moore (Stella Hillard)

NEW ORLEANS SANDWICH SPECIAL

4 slices bread   Margarine to cook bread
2 eggs   2 chicken breasts
½ cup milk   2 slices Swiss cheese

WHITE SAUCE:
2 tablespoons margarine   1 cup milk
2 tablespoons flour   1 tablespoon Dijon mustard

Cook chicken breasts in small amount of water, seasoning with salt and pepper to taste, until chicken is tender. Cool chicken and remove the bones. Cut chicken into slices. Make white sauce by melting margarine in small heavy saucepan, over low heat. Add flour until well mixed. Slowly add milk, stirring constantly. Cook sauce until it thickens (about 5 minutes), stirring well to keep from scorching. Add mustard and mix well. Keep sauce warm until sandwich is made.

Mix eggs and milk in small bowl. Melt margarine to cook toast in heavy skillet over medium heat. Dip bread in egg mixture, coating both sides. Fry bread in skillet until brown on one side, turn, and start cooking other side. Place sliced chicken on two pieces of the toast and top with cheese. When toast is done, remove to plates and cover with second slice of toast. Pour white sauce over sandwich and serve. Yield: 2 sandwiches.

Mrs. Howard Garrison (Ashley Smith)

THRIFT SHOP PIMIENTO CHEESE

8 ounces Velveeta cheese, grated   ½ small onion, grated
8 ounces Kraft mellow cheese,   ½ large bell pepper, grated
   grated   2 hard-boiled eggs, grated
1 (4-ounce) jar pimientos,   Kraft mayonnaise (approximately
   chopped   4 tablespoons, or more if
8-10 sweet pickles, grated   desired)

Mix Velveeta and mellow cheese, pimiento, pickles, onion, bell pepper, and eggs in large mixing bowl. Add mayonnaise and beat to a spreadable consistency. Hand-held electric mixer makes it smoother and fluffier. Keep covered and store in refrigerator. Yield: 4-5 cups.

Note: Great for picnics, fishing and hunting trips. Good for stuffing in celery.

Mrs. William E. "Brother" Oliver (Sue Kelly)

CRUST FOR PIZZA

1 cup warm water (115 degrees)
1 package dry yeast
1 tablespoon sugar
1½ teaspoons salt

2 tablespoons oil
2½-3½ cups unsifted unbleached
   flour

Sprinkle yeast on warm water in large bowl. Allow to dissolve. Add sugar, salt, oil, and enough flour to make a stiff dough. Knead on floured board until smooth and elastic, about 5 minutes. Place in greased bowl, turning to grease top. Let rise until doubled, about 45 minutes. Heat oven to 350 degrees. Punch dough down and divide in half. Roll each half into a 13-inch circle. Place on ungreased 12-inch pizza pans, pressing around edges to form rim. Bake in preheated oven for 10 minutes. Cool, wrap, and freeze, or use immediately.

Suggested topping:
Tomato sauce made of tomato paste, water, seasoned with salt, pepper, oregano, basil, thyme. Top with mixed cubed (½-inch pieces) cheeses—mozzarella, cheddar, Swiss—mushrooms, onions, green pepper; and sprinkle with grated Parmesan cheese. Bake pizza at 425 degrees for 20-25 minutes.

Mrs. Peterson Cavert (Mary Beth Wear)

REUBEN SANDWICHES

FOR EACH SANDWICH:
2 slices rye bread
1 slice Swiss cheese
Generous amount corned beef,
   sliced thick or thin

2 tablespoons or more sauerkraut
   or favorite slaw, drained
Hot mustard (Dijon)
Soft butter

Butter one slice of bread on one side. Place butter side down in skillet set over lot heat. Layer on bread in order: cheese, corned beef, sauerkraut or slaw. Spread mustard on one side of other slice, butter opposite side. Place butter side up on sauerkraut. Cook until bottom is browned; then turn (carefully!) with pancake turner and brown other side. Slice in half. Serve with dill pickle.

To do a large number, reverse layers inside sandwich (cheese on top) and bake on cookie sheet at 300 degrees until bread is toasted and cheese melted. Recipes for your own rye bread, corned beef, and mustard are in this book. Impress your friends!

Mrs. Peterson Cavert (Mary Beth Wear)

TURKEY GOBBLE-UP

6 English muffins
Butter or margarine
6 slices bacon
1 large avocado
¼ cup mayonnaise
¼ cup sour cream

1 tablespoon lemon juice
Dash Tabasco
12 slices cooked turkey
12 slices tomato
1 (8-ounce) jar pasteurized
process cheese spread

Split, toast and butter muffins. Cut bacon into fourths; fry until limp but not browned. Peel, seed and mash avocado and mix with mayonnaise, sour cream, lemon juice, and Tabasco. Spread avocado mixture generously on each muffin half. Arrange 1 slice each of turkey and tomato on top of each muffin half. Spread 1 rounded tablespoon cheese on each tomato. Top each with 2 pieces of bacon. Place on baking sheet and broil 6 inches from heat until bacon is crisp and cheese bubbly, about 4 to 6 minutes. Garnish with ripe olives, drained pepperoncini and parsley sprigs if desired.

Mrs. James H. Walburn (Dean Frank)

PARTY SANDWICHES

1 (8-ounce) package cream cheese,
   softened
Mayonnaise

1 very small onion, grated
Food coloring, if desired
Grated egg yolk, if desired

Soften cream cheese in a bowl and stir in small amounts of mayonnaise to desired spreading consistency. Add grated onion and mix well. Spread on bread.

Variations:
ROSES—Cover above mixture and refrigerate to harden. Cut bread into round shapes with biscuit cutter. Color above mixture to favorite rose color. Use demitasse or infant feeding spoon and press cream cheese around edges of bread discs. Fill centers with grated egg yolks.
DIPLOMAS—Cut crust from bread. Spread softened cream cheese mixture on each slice. Roll each slice as you would a diploma and tie with ribbons of the school's colors.
OPEN-FACED—Cut bread with appropriate cookie cutter (heart for Valentine's, Shamrock for St. Patrick's Day, etc.) Color cream cheese for appropriate holiday and spread on bread.
PLAIN—Cut crust from bread. Make sandwich using 2 or 3 slices of bread. Then cut length-wise to make 3 skinny sandwiches or cut in quarters.

Mrs. Thomas W. Moore (Stella Hillard)

PUMPKIN MUFFINS

1½ cups flour
½ cup sugar
2 teaspoons baking powder
½ teaspoon ginger
¾ teaspoon salt
1 teaspoon cinnamon
¼ teaspoon cloves

½ cup golden raisins
1 egg, slightly beaten
½ cup milk
½ cup pumpkin (canned or
  cooked with salt and mashed)
¼ cup butter, melted
1 tablespoon cinnamon-sugar

Preheat oven to 400 degrees. Sift together into large bowl the flour, sugar, baking powder, ginger, salt, cinnamon, and cloves. Stir in raisins. Combine egg, milk, pumpkin, and melted butter. Add pumpkin mixture to dry ingredients all at once, mixing only until combined. Fill greased muffin tins or paper muffin cups ⅔ full. Sprinkle with cinnamon-sugar. Bake 20-25 minutes.

Mrs. Harold B. Kirby (Connie McLain)

Muffins—the name means "little muffs" to warm the fingers.

REFRIGERATOR BRAN MUFFINS

2 cups whole bran cereal
2 cups oats
2 cups shredded wheat biscuits,
  crushed
1 cup shortening
2 cups boiling water
4 cups buttermilk

4 eggs, beaten
5 cups all-purpose flour
2 cups sugar
1 tablespoon baking powder
1 tablespoon soda
2 teaspoons salt
1½ cups raisins (optional)

Combine bran cereal, oats, shredded wheat in large bowl; add shortening. Pour in boiling water and stir until shortening is melted. Add buttermilk and eggs; mix well. Stir together the flour, sugar, baking powder, soda, and salt; add all at once to cereal mixture. Stir just until moistened. Store in tightly covered container in refrigerator up to 4 weeks. Fill greased muffin pans ⅔ full. Bake at 400 degrees 24-28 minutes. (Baking time will increase the longer the batter is stored.) Yield: 13½ cups of batter; 54 average muffins.

Mrs. James A. Neville, III (Carole Gibson)

ZUCCHINI-WHEAT GERM MUFFINS

2 cups flour
1 cup shredded zucchini
¾ cup wheat germ
½ cup packed light brown sugar

1 tablespoon baking powder
¾ cup milk
¼ cup oil
1 egg, beaten

Preheat oven to 375 degrees. In large bowl mix well the flour, zucchini, wheat germ, sugar, and baking powder; set aside. In small bowl, mix milk, oil, and egg; stir into flour mixture just to blend. Do not overbeat. Spoon into 12 2½-inch muffin cups. Bake in preheated oven 20-25 minutes. Serve hot.

Bert Wear

INSTANT STUFFING

4 cups large bread crumbs
1 teaspoon instant minced onion
1 teaspoon parsley flakes
½ teaspoon leaf thyme, crumbled
½ teaspoon leaf sage, crumbled
½ teaspoon salt

¼ teaspoon pepper
2 tablespoons sesame seed
3 tablespoons butter
¼ cup minced celery
½ to ¾ cup chicken broth

Use leftover rolls, stale bread, heels and crusts of loaves of any kind (white, whole wheat, corn bread, etc.) Heat bread crumbs in a shallow baking pan in 350-degree oven until dry, about 10 minutes. Put in large bowl and mix with onion, parsley, thyme, sage, salt, pepper, and sesame seed. Cover and keep at room temperature for several weeks or freeze for longer storage.

To Use: Melt 3 tablespoons butter in small saucepan. Cook ¼ cup minced celery in butter until tender. Pour over crumb mixture in large bowl. Add ½ to ¾ cup chicken broth; stir gently. Bake in 1-quart baking dish, covered, in 350-degree oven for 30 minutes, adding more broth if desired.

Mrs. Peterson Cavert (Mary Beth Wear)

PARSLEY BUTTER

⅓ cup parsley
1 small onion

Juice of 1 lemon
2 sticks unsalted butter, softened

In food processor, with steel blade, chop parsley and onion very fine. Add butter and lemon juice and process until well mixed. Or chop parsley very fine by hand, grate onion and work into butter with lemon juice by hand. Good on bread, and try it on baked potato, broccoli, or other hot vegetables!

Mrs. Peterson Cavert (Mary Beth Wear)

YORKSHIRE PUDDING

⅞ cup flour
½ teaspoon salt
½ cup milk

2 eggs
½ cup water
Drippings from roast beef

Have all ingredients at room temperature. Approximately 1 hour and 35 minutes before serving: sift together flour and salt. Put in blender or food processor with steel knife. Add milk and process until smooth. Add eggs and process until fluffy and pale yellow. Add water and process again. Let batter stand for 1 hour.

If oven is not already hot, preheat to 400 degrees. Pour drippings from roast into 9 x 10-inch baking pan about ¼ inch deep. Heat drippings in oven until very hot. Stir batter again and pour into hot pan. Bake at 400 degrees for 20 minutes; reduce heat to 350 degrees and bake 10 minutes longer. Cut into squares and serve hot with roast beef.

Mrs. Edwin L. Minges (Pearl Mangum)

CRÊPES

1 cup cold water
1 cup cold milk
4 eggs

½ teaspoon salt
2 cups sifted all-purpose flour
4 tablespoons melted butter

Put the water, milk, eggs, and salt into the blender jar. Add the flour, then the butter. Cover and blend at top speed for 1 minute. If bits of flour adhere to sides of jar, dislodge with a rubber scraper and blend for 2 to 3 seconds more. Cover and refrigerate for at least 2 hours. The batter should be a very light cream, just thick enough to coat a wooden spoon. If, after making the first crêpe, it seems too heavy, beat in a bit of water, a spoonful at a time. The cooked crêpe should be about 1/16-inch thick.

To cook: Brush a 6½-inch skillet lightly with cooking oil. Set over moderately high heat until the pan is just beginning to smoke. Immediately remove pan, pour in 3 to 4 tablespoons of batter, and tilt pan to cover bottom. Return pan to heat for 60 to 80 seconds. Then jerk and toss pan sharply back and forth and up and down to loosen the crêpe. Turn the crêpe and brown lightly for about ½ minute on the other side. Crêpes may be kept warm by covering them with a dish and setting them over simmering water or in a slow oven. They may also be frozen. Makes about 12 crêpes for use in main dishes. (See Index for Dessert Crêpes.)

Mrs. J. C. "Bud" Miller (Presteen Sims)

THE SEBASTIAN

Butter or oleo
12 slices rye bread
⅔ cup mayonnaise
⅓ cup chopped chutney
1 tablespoon curry powder

1 teaspoon salt
3 cups shredded cabbage
1 pound cooked ham, very thinly
  sliced
6 (1-ounce) slices cheddar cheese

Butter both sides of bread. In a large bowl, mix mayonnaise, chutney, curry powder, and salt. Fold in cabbage. On each of 6 slices of bread, place equal amounts of sliced ham, about ½ cup cabbage mixture and one slice cheese. Top with remaining bread slices. Grill on both sides until golden brown. Makes 6 servings.

Mrs. James Hodo Walburn (Dean Frank)

GRANOLA

1¼ cups sesame seed
1¼ cups sunflower seed
2 cups rolled oats
2 tablespoons torula yeast
½ cup dried skim milk
3 cups raw wheat germ
1 cup soy flour

2 cups wheat bran
½ cup oil
¼ cup brown sugar or honey
1 cup raisins
Chopped nuts and/or chopped
  dried fruits (Optional)

Preheat oven to 300 degrees. Toast seed and grind. Mix other ingredients except for raisins and dried fruits. Toast for 45 minutes, stirring every 15 minutes. Add raisins. Store in refrigerator. Makes 3 quarts.

Mrs. Dean Covington (Brenda Wood)

PUFF SHELLS

1 cup water
1 stick margarine
1 cup flour
4 eggs

1 tablespoon sugar (only if puffs
  are to be used with sweet
  filling)

Bring water and margarine to a rolling boil. Turn heat off and dump in flour all at one time. Stir until a ball is formed. Remove from heat. *Add eggs, one at a time, stirring each until well blended.* Drop half the size desired on greased cookie sheet. Bake until brown and dry. *Do not underbake* (375 to 400 degrees for 25 to 30 minutes). Fill with shrimp, ham salad, chicken, tuna or sweets. Open puffs by cutting halfway to fill. Yields about 50 puffs.

Mrs. T. Griffin Stanley, Jr. (Phyllis Miglarese)

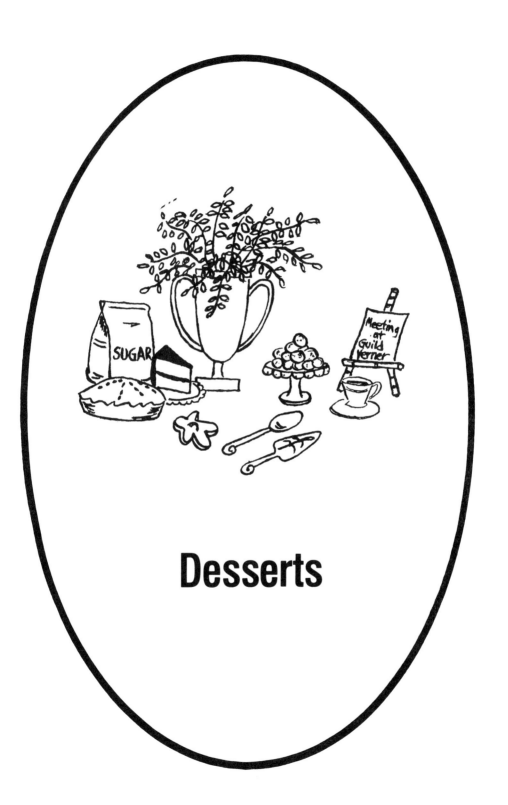

Desserts

AMBROSIA

1 ripe pineapple
6 navel oranges
½ cup confectioners' sugar

2 cups freshly grated coconut
½ cup apricot brandy

Peel and core the pineapple, and slice in thin slices. Peel the oranges and cut into sections, discarding membranes. Place in layers in a bowl with confectioners' sugar; cover with coconut and chill. Pour brandy over all and mix. Serves 6-8.

Note: Buy pineapple that is golden in color and has a definite pineapple aroma.

Mrs. James R. Shamblin (Patricia Terry)—Centre, AL

APPLE CRUNCH

5 apples, peeled
½ cup granulated sugar
1 cup flour
½ cup margarine

½ cup brown sugar
½ teaspoon cinnamon
¼ teaspoon salt

Slice apples into a lightly buttered baking dish. Sprinkle with granulated sugar. Mix flour, margarine, brown sugar, cinnamon, and salt. Cover apples with this mixture. Bake in medium oven (325 degrees) for 1 hour.

Mrs. Daniel Hoke (Gail Ford)

BLUEBERRY PUDDING

2 tablespoons butter
1 cup sugar
1 egg
½ cup milk
1½ cups sifted flour

1 teaspoon baking powder
Little salt
1 teaspoon vanilla
1½ cups blueberries

Preheat oven to 350 degrees. Cream together the butter, sugar, and egg, then beat in milk. Add the dry ingredients and beat until smooth. Fold in the vanilla and then the blueberries. Place in a 1½-quart baking dish, then put the dish in a pan of water and bake in preheated oven for 1 hour. Serve warm with Hard Sauce (See Index). Yield: 6 servings.

Mrs. E. L. Minges, Jr. (Valery Crichton)

ORANGE ALASKA

6 navel oranges
1½ pints vanilla ice cream
6 tablespoons Cointreau
2 egg whites

Pinch of salt
¼ teaspoon cream of tartar
½ cup confectioners' sugar

Cut 1-inch slice off top of orange. Scoop out pulp in one piece, if possible. If orange shell does not stand straight, cut a straight thin slice off bottom. Sprinkle inside of each orange with 1½ teaspoons Cointreau. Fill with vanilla ice cream. Sprinkle top of ice cream with 1½ teaspoons Cointreau. Cover and set in freezer.

To serve: Preheat oven to 450 degrees. Remove oranges from freezer and place them on a cookie sheet. Beat egg whites with salt until frothy and add cream of tartar. Add sugar gradually until the consistency is that of thick marshmallows. Cover top of orange with this meringue. Use a decorating bag or make a tall mound. Bake at 450 degrees for 2 to 3 minutes. Serve with garnish of orange slices and fresh mint leaves. Serves 6.

Mrs. J. C. "Bud" Miller (Presteen Sims)

CRANBERRY ICE

1 quart cranberries
2 cups water
Juice of 2 lemons

2 cups sugar
Whipping cream or half and half

Cook cranberries and water for 8 minutes. Press through sieve. Add sugar and lemon juice. Cool and freeze until mushy. Remove from freezer. Beat in cream or half and half until the desired consistency is reached. The more cream used, the smoother the ice. Cover and refreeze. Keeps well in the freezer for several months.

Mrs. E. Calhoun Wilson (Gene Henderson)

GREEN GRAPES WITH SOUR CREAM

2 pounds green seedless grapes
1 (8-ounce) carton sour cream

Brown sugar

Mix sour cream with 2 tablespoons brown sugar. Add grapes. Toss gently to coat. Place coated grapes in a dish and pack brown sugar on top. Let stand 12 hours in refrigerator.

Mrs. Daniel Hoke (Gail Ford)

STRAWBERRIES ROMANOFF

1 pint vanilla ice cream, softened
1 cup cream
9 tablespoons Cointreau, divided

1 quart strawberries, cleaned
and slightly mashed
½ cup confectioners' sugar

Whip ice cream until creamy and fold in 1 cup cream, whipped, and 6 tablespoons Cointreau. Mix strawberries with confectioners' sugar and 3 tablespoons Cointreau. Blend ice cream and strawberry mixtures quickly and lightly and serve in chilled stemmed glasses. Serves 8.

Note: Have both mixtures ready and chilled, but do not blend until ready to serve.

Mrs. James R. Shamblin (Patricia Terry)—Centre, AL

PEARS CHANTILLY

12 Bartlett pear halves
¾ cup sugar
¾ cup water
½ cup very thinly sliced oranges

1 cup whipping cream, whipped
3 tablespoons confectioners'
sugar
6 almond macaroons, crushed

Make syrup of sugar and water, add the sliced oranges (or segments) and cook until very tender and syrup is thick. Pour over pears. Chill. To serve, cover with sweetened whipped cream and top with crushed macaroons.

Mrs. Charles K. Beauchamp (Winkie Clarkson)

ANNE'S WHITE VELVET

1 cup heavy cream
1½ teaspoons unflavored gelatin
2 tablespoons cold water
¼ cup sugar

1 cup sour cream
Rum or fruit liqueur
Fruit of your choice

Heat cream over moderate heat. Soak gelatin in cold water to soften. When cream is hot, stir in sugar and gelatin until dissolved. Remove from heat. Fold in sour cream; add flavoring of rum or liqueur. Pour into individual molds, cover with plastic wrap, and chill until ready to serve. Unmold. Serve with fresh, frozen, or canned fruit or fruit sauce. Serves 4 (4-ounce servings).

Martha Moore Warner

CHARLOTTE RUSSE

2 eggs, separated
½ cup sugar
1¾ cups milk, divided

1 envelope gelatin
½ pint whipping cream
⅓ cup white wine or whiskey

Beat egg whites until stiff peaks form. Set aside. Sprinkle gelatin over ½ cup milk and set aside to soften. Mix egg yolks, sugar, and 1¼ cups milk. Cook over very low heat until slightly thickened. Add gelatin to hot mixture. Pour custard into stiffly-beaten egg whites. Set bowl in pan of ice water and keep scraping sides as the mixture thickens. Whip cream. When custard is thick, add cream and wine. Pour into dish or compotes. Serves 6.

Note: This has been in my family for many years and is hard to make but worth the effort.

Mrs. William Roscoe Johnson, III (Corella Rawls)

BAKED CUSTARD

3 cups milk
3 eggs
⅔ cup sugar

¼ teaspoon salt
1 teaspoon vanilla
Nutmeg

Heat oven to 350 degrees. Scald milk. Beat eggs and add sugar, salt, and vanilla. Beat well. Pour scalded milk slowly into egg mixture. Pour into a 1½-quart casserole, sprinkle with nutmeg, and bake in hot water bath for 45 minutes. Custard is done when knife inserted in center comes out clean. Serves 4.

Mrs. Hodo Strickland (Judy Turner)

BOILED CUSTARD

3 egg yolks
¼ cup sugar
⅛ teaspoon salt
2 cups scalded milk

1 teaspoon vanilla
½ teaspoon almond flavoring
    (optional)

Beat eggs a bit and add sugar and salt. Stir in milk and cook over low heat, stirring constantly, until it coats a spoon. Cool to warm and add vanilla. Serve cold.

Mrs. John D. Cade (Virginia Duckworth)

FLOATING ISLAND

3 eggs, separated
½ cup sugar, divided
2 cups milk
⅛ teaspoon salt

1 teaspoon vanilla
¼ teaspoon grated lemon rind
  (optional)

In a heavy saucepan, over very low heat, scald milk. At the same time, beat egg whites until they hold their shape. Gradually add ¼ cup sugar. Beat until stiff. Drop the egg white mixture onto the hot milk by table-spoons. Do not let the milk boil. Poach the "islands" for about 4 minutes, turning once. Lift them out with a slotted spoon and carefully put them on a towel. Beat egg yolks with ¼ cup sugar and salt. Slowly stir in the scalded milk. Return to saucepan and cook, stirring constantly, until mix-ture coats a spoon. Cool. Add vanilla and lemon rind. Divide among glass compotes and then place islands on top. Chill. Makes 4-5 servings.

ALMOND BALL

½ gallon vanilla ice cream
3 (3½-ounce) packages toasted
  sliced almonds

1½ cups Hot Fudge Sauce (See
  Index)

Divide ice cream into 8 equal portions and form into balls. Roll in almonds. Pour sauce over each ball and serve. Makes 8 servings.

University Club

LEMON MILK SHERBET

2 quarts milk, divided
4 cups sugar
1 (13-ounce) can evaporated milk
1 cup fresh lemon juice

2 teaspoons grated lemon rind
1 tablespoon (1 envelope)
  unflavored gelatin

Soften gelatin in ¼ cup water for 3 minutes. Heat over hot water to dissolve. Place sugar in pitcher or bowl. Stir in 1 quart milk until sugar is dissolved. Add dissolved gelatin. Pour into freezer container. Add lemon juice and rind. Fill container to fill line with remaining milk. Freeze ac-cording to freezer manufacturer's directions. Makes 6 quarts. If freezer is 1-gallon size, reduce amount of milk. Allow to ripen 3-4 hours before serving.

Note: Delicious! Great light summer dessert.

Mrs. Joe Sledge (Kathleen Johnson)

COFFEE ICE CREAM PIE

⅔ stick oleo
⅔ (6-ounce) package semi-sweet chocolate bits
½ teaspoon vanilla

Pinch salt
3 scant cups Rice Krispies
1 quart coffee ice cream

Melt oleo and chocolate bits in double boiler. Remove from heat and add vanilla and salt. Fold in Rice Krispies. Press into bottom of a greased 9-inch pie pan. Freeze. Add coffee ice cream, softened to spread, and freeze.

Note: Coffee ice cream may be made by adding 2 rounded teaspoons of instant coffee to a quart of vanilla ice cream.

Mrs. Robert Dugins (Melville Neilson)

PINK-LEMONADE ICE CREAM PIE

½ gallon vanilla ice cream, softened
2 (6-ounce) cans frozen pink lemonade, thawed

3 (8-inch) pie crusts (graham cracker or vanilla wafer)
Cool Whip and cherries for top
Red food color

Mix quickly the ice cream and undiluted lemonade, add color to reach desired shade and place in pie shells. Cover and freeze. Top with Cool Whip and a cherry when serving. Great for a "hurry-up" super-delicious light dessert for a group or several surprise desserts for your family.

Mrs. Allen Mattox (Harriet Marrs)

CHOCOLATE CHIP DESSERT

1 (6-ounce) package chocolate chips
1½ tablespoons water
4 eggs, separated

1½ teaspoons confectioners' sugar
½ cup chopped walnuts
1 cup whipped cream
1 angel food cake

Melt chocolate. Add water. Remove from stove and add egg yolks one at a time, beating after each. Cool. Beat egg whites until stiff peaks form. To chocolate mixture, add sugar, nuts, stiff egg whites, and whipped cream. Tear angel food cake into small pieces and cover bottom of rectangular shallow glass dish. Pour mixture over cake. Chill overnight. Serve with whipped cream. Serves 12.

Mrs. Edward D. Hummel (Elaine Cody)

MACAROON ICE CREAM DESSERT

2 dozen almond macaroons
2 jiggers bourbon
½ gallon coffee ice cream,
  softened

1 cup slivered toasted almonds
½ pint whipping cream

Soak macaroons in bourbon. When crumbly, mix with ice cream and almonds. Freeze in silver dish. When ready to serve, whip cream and spread on top.

Variation I: Sherry Ice Cream.
Use coconut macaroons, vanilla ice cream and creme sherry.

Mrs. Paul Bryant, Jr. (Cherry Hicks)

Variation II: Line edge of serving dish with half of the soaked macaroons.
Use butter almond ice cream and save slivered almonds to sprinkle on top
of whipped cream.

Mrs. Peyton Cochrane (Jamie Banks)

VANILLA ICE CREAM

2 cups whole milk, divided
1 tablespoon cornstarch
½ cup sugar
2 egg yolks

1 tablespoon vanilla extract (or
  bean)
2 cups heavy cream, whipped

Scald 1½ cups milk. In top of double boiler, mix sugar and cornstarch well. Add egg yolks and ½ cup milk and mix well. Add scalded milk slowly* to egg yolk mixture and cook, stirring, over simmering water, until mixture coats spoon. (If using vanilla bean, add it during cooking and remove at this point. If using vanilla extract, add after mixture has cooled.) Cool. Add whipped cream. Freeze in ice cream freezer according to manufacturer's instructions.

*Always pour hot mixture *into* egg while stirring, or egg will scramble.

Peppermint Ice Cream: Use ¼ cup sugar. Soak 1 (12- to 16-ounce) package peppermint (hard candy type) in cream to melt. This cream will not whip, so add as is.

Mrs. Thomas W. Moore (Stella Hillard)

NORTH POLE ICE CREAM PIE

CRUST:

1 (13½-ounce) package graham cracker crumbs

2 sticks margarine, melted
⅓ cup chopped pecans

FILLING:

3 pints vanilla ice cream
6 egg whites
4 tablespoons confectioners' sugar

1 (7-ounce) jar marshmallow creme

Combine graham cracker crumbs, margarine, and nuts. Line 4 pie pans with crumb mixture. Divide ice cream among the pie pans. Put in freezer while preparing topping. Preheat broiler. Beat egg whites until stiff and dry. Add confectioners' sugar and marshmallow cream. Spread over ice cream. Run pies under broiler until brown on top. Freeze immediately. Serve with hot fudge sauce. Makes 4 pies.

Mrs. Hugh Ragsdale, Jr. (Kate Webb)

VANILLA AND CHOCOLATE BOMBE

2 quarts vanilla ice cream
2 (6-ounce) packages semi-sweet chocolate chips

6 eggs, separated
4 teaspoons vanilla extract
1 cup heavy cream

Place 2½-quart mold in freezer for 5 minutes. Slightly soften ice cream. Line bottom and sides of mold with ice cream. Return to freezer for 1 hour. Melt chocolate over hot water. Remove from heat and stir in egg yolks and vanilla. Cool slightly. Beat egg whites until stiff peaks form; fold into chocolate. Beat cream until thickened; fold into chocolate. Pour into ice cream-lined mold. Freeze until firm, about 4 hours. To serve, dip mold into hot water for 30 seconds and unmold onto platter.

Guesna Bush

FREDA'S POTS DE CRÈME

¾ cup milk
1 cup semi-sweet chocolate bits
1 egg

2 tablespoons sugar
Pinch of salt

Heat milk to boiling point. Place chocolate bits, egg, sugar, and salt in blender; add hot milk. Blend at low speed for 1 minute. Pour into Pot-de-Crème cups. Chill. Serve with whipped cream on top. Makes 6 servings.

Note: Do not double recipe.

Mrs. Gene Bennett (Belle Walter)

LEMON SOUFFLÉ

1 heaping tablespoon butter
1 scant cup sugar
Pinch salt
2 eggs, separated
1 cup milk
1 heaping tablespoon flour

1 lemon, juice and grated rind
½ pint whipping cream, whipped
Grated bitter chocolate for garnish

Heat oven to 300 degrees. Set in oven a baking dish with 1 inch of water in it. Grease 4 ramekins. Cream butter, sugar, and salt. Add egg yolks, milk, flour, lemon juice, and rind. Beat well. Beat egg whites until stiff peaks form. Fold egg whites into lemon mixture. Put soufflé mixture in ramekins, set them in baking dish containing hot water and bake for 45 minutes. Top with whipped cream and garnish with grated bitter chocolate. Makes 4 servings.

Mrs. William F. Barnes, Jr. (Diane Manderson)

COFFEE MARSHMALLOW

1 cup strong coffee
1 (10-ounce) package large marshmallows
1 (8-ounce) package dates, chopped

1 cup pecans, chopped
½ pint whipping cream, whipped

Melt marshmallows in hot coffee. Add dates and pecans. Chill. When it begins to congeal, fold in the whipped cream. Pour into sherbet glasses and chill well.

Mrs. Joseph Rowland (Nancy Burch)

CHOCOLATE MOUSSE

6 ounces semi-sweet chocolate
¼ cup Grand Marnier
2 eggs

¼ cup sugar
1 teaspoon vanilla
1 cup whipping cream

Melt semi-sweet chocolate with Grand Marnier in top of double boiler. Let cool. In blender, mix eggs, sugar, and vanilla, and process at medium high speed for 2 minutes. Add whipping cream and blend 30 seconds at medium high speed. Add chocolate mixture and blend until mixed. Pour into serving goblets and chill 6 hours or overnight. Yield: 5 servings.

Mrs. Edward D. Hummel (Elaine Cody)

BRANDY SNAPS

¼ cup sugar
½ stick butter, melted
2 tablespoons golden syrup (Lyle's is best)
½ cup flour

½ teaspoon ground ginger
½ teaspoon grated lemon rind
4 tablespoons brandy, divided
1½ cups heavy cream
¼ cup confectioners' sugar

Preheat oven to 350 degrees. Heat sugar, butter, and syrup in a saucepan on low heat. Grease a cookie sheet. Mix syrup mixture with flour, ginger, lemon rind, and 2 tablespoons brandy. Drop 1 teaspoonful at a time on greased cookie sheet. Leave space between the snaps for them to spread. (See Note.) When they turn golden and are lacy, approximately 8 minutes, remove cookie sheet and quickly roll, with the lacy side on the outside, on a wooden spoon. You can make the snaps days ahead and keep dry in a tin. When ready to serve, whip cream and add confectioners' sugar and 2 tablespoons brandy. Fill a pastry bag with the whipped cream and fill the snaps with cream. Makes 16 snaps.

Note: The snaps will harden quickly, so do not try to bake and roll more than 3 snaps at a time. If you have help, you can try 6 snaps at a time.

Mrs. David Hefelfinger (Virginia Mauney)

TRIFLE

½ plain pound cake
½ cup strawberry jam
¼ cup medium dry sherry
¼ cup cognac or brandy

2 cups custard
1 cup heavy cream
¼ cup slivered toasted almonds

Cut cake into 1-inch slices and coat with jam. Place in bowl, jam side up. Combine sherry and brandy and sprinkle over cake. Let stand 30 minutes. Make custard. When cool, pour over soaked cake and chill. Just before serving, whip cream and cover custard. Add almonds to top. Yield: 8 servings.

CUSTARD:
½ cup sugar
3 eggs
1 teaspoon cornstarch

2 cups milk
½ teaspoon almond extract

Heat milk. Beat eggs until pale. Beat in sugar mixed with cornstarch. Add hot milk and stir over low heat until mixture coats spoon.

Mrs. David Cochrane (Mary B. Tompkins)

FOUR-LAYER CHOCOLATE DELIGHT

2 cups flour
1 cup chopped nuts
2 sticks oleo, melted
1 (8-ounce) package cream cheese, softened
1 cup sugar
1 (9-ounce) package Cool Whip, divided

2 (3¾-ounce) packages instant chocolate pudding
3 cups milk
Shaved chocolate and pecan halves for garnish

Heat oven to 350 degrees. For crust, mix flour, nuts, and oleo. Pat into a 9 x 13-inch baking dish. Bake for 20 minutes. Cool completely. Mix cream cheese with sugar and fold in 1 cup Cool Whip. Spread on cold pastry. Mix pudding mix and milk and let stand until thickened. Spread on cream cheese layer. Spread remaining Cool Whip on chocolate layer. Garnish with shaved chocolate and pecans. Chill. Serves 12-18.

Mrs. David M. Jones (Janet White)

Variation: Replace chocolate pudding layer with 1 (21-ounce) can of cherry, blueberry, or other pie filling.

Mrs. John B. Edwards (Becky Moore)

LEMON ANGEL FROST

2 eggs, separated
½ cup sugar
1 teaspoon grated lemon rind

¼ cup fresh lemon juice
1 cup heavy cream, whipped

Beat egg whites until soft peaks form. Gradually add sugar and whip until stiff. Set aside. Beat egg yolks until thick and lemon-colored. Fold into egg whites with lemon juice and rind. Fold in whipped cream and freeze. This is also a delicious topping when chilled and served over slices of angel food cake. Makes 1 quart.

Mrs. William A. "Butch" Miller (Jessica Frazier)

MERINGUE SHELLS

3 egg whites
Pinch salt
¼ teaspoon cream of tartar
¾ cup sugar
1 teaspoon vanilla

½ teaspoon almond extract
1 cup ground or very finely
  chopped almonds or pecans,
  blanched and toasted

Beat egg whites with salt and cream of tartar until stiff but not dry. Add sugar slowly, still beating, then add flavorings. Fold in almonds. Grease and flour a cookie sheet, or line with baking parchment. Using a bowl or cup, outline circles the desired size on cookie sheet. Mound mixture in circles, spreading to edges and making edges higher than center. These don't shrink, so make them the size and shape you want finished product. Bake until very lightly browned, 1½-2 hours at 250 degrees. When done, they release their hold on the sheet and lift off easily. Test by prying *gently*. These freeze well if wrapped heavily in plastic wrap and protected from crushing. Keep from moisture if using shortly. To use, scoop ice cream into shells and pour desired topping over, or use fresh fruit and pour boiled custard over.

Suggestions: Vanilla ice cream with hot fudge sauce, caramel sauce, fresh strawberries, peaches or other fruit, flavored with kirsch; peach ice cream with caramel sauce; peppermint ice cream with chocolate sauce; coffee ice cream with chocolate sauce. Makes six 4-inch shells.

Mrs. Peterson Cavert (Mary Beth Wear)

COMPANY CHEESECAKE

3 eggs, well-beaten
2 (8-ounce) packages cream cheese
1 cup sugar
¼ teaspoon salt
2 teaspoons vanilla

½ teaspoon almond extract
3 cups dairy sour cream
1 recipe Graham-Nut Crust
  (see Index)

Combine eggs, cream cheese, sugar, salt, and extracts; beat until smooth. Blend in sour cream and pour into Graham-Nut crust. Trim with reserved crumbs. Bake in moderate oven (375 degrees) for 35 minutes or until just set. Cool. Chill well, about 4 or 5 hours. Glaze if desired. Makes 10 servings.

Mrs. Charles S. Watson

MARCY'S DESSERT

3 egg whites
1 cup sugar
⅔ cup graham cracker crumbs
1 teaspoon baking powder

½ cup chopped pecans
Ice cream
Hot fudge, caramel, or chocolate
   sauce

Whip egg whites until foamy. Add sugar gradually and whip until stiff peaks form. Mix in crumbs, baking powder, and nuts. Pour into well-greased 9- or 10-inch pie pan. Bake at 350 degrees for 25 to 30 minutes. Cut into wedges. Scoop ice cream on each wedge, pour hot fudge, caramel or chocolate sauce on top. Serves 6 to 8.

Variation I: *12 (2-inch) saltine crackers, crumbled*
12 almond macaroons, crumbled
12 dates, chopped
½ cup chopped almonds
½ teaspoon almond extract
Add above instead of graham cracker crumbs and pecans. Top with whipped cream.

Variation II: *½ cup chopped dates*
1 teaspoon vanilla
Add above to original mixture. Top with whipped cream.

Mrs. Robert E. McCoy (Brenda Magruder)

MOCHA CREAM CRÊPES

1 cup cream cheese, softened
¼ cup sugar
4 teaspoons ground coffee (instant)
4 teaspoons instant chocolate
   drink mix

¼ cup rum
1 pint whipping cream, whipped
Shaved bittersweet chocolate

Stir the softened cheese, sugar, coffee, chocolate, and rum until smooth and thick. Spread this mixture on crêpes,* roll up, and arrange on a serving platter seam side down. Refrigerate at least 2 hours before serving. Garnish with whipped cream and shaved chocolate. Makes filling for 16 crêpes.

*Use basic Dessert Crêpe recipe.

Mrs. E. L. Minges, Jr. (Valery Crichton)

DESSERT CRÊPES

1 cup sifted all-purpose flour	2 cups milk
½ teaspoon salt	1 tablespoon rum or cognac
1 tablespoon sugar	2 tablespoons butter, melted
3 large eggs	Confectioners' sugar

Sift together into mixing bowl the flour, salt, and sugar. Beat the eggs, add the milk and rum or cognac and stir into flour mixture. Blend in the melted butter. Let batter stand 2 hours. Heat a 6-inch skillet and brush bottom lightly with melted butter. Pour in 2 tablespoons of batter. Rotate pan to spread batter evenly. Cook over direct moderate heat 1-2 minutes, until bubbles form on top. Turn and cook ½-1 minute. Sprinkle with confectioners' sugar. Stack in pancake fashion in a pan lined with a clean towel, and when all are cooked, fold ends of towel over them. Just before serving, heat the crêpes without unwrapping in a preheated moderate oven (350 degrees), only until hot (about 10 minutes). Serve sprinkled with confectioners' sugar or with honey, or spread with marmalade and roll up. Can be used in any dessert recipe calling for crêpes.

Mrs. J. C. "Bud" Miller (Presteen Sims)

HARD SAUCE

¼ cup butter, softened	1 tablespoon brandy or whiskey
¾ cup confectioners' sugar	¼ teaspoon vanilla extract

Beat butter at medium speed until fluffy. Gradually beat in sugar, brandy, and vanilla until smooth and creamy.

STRAWBERRY GLAZE FOR CHEESECAKE

Large strawberries for garnish	¼ cup cold water
1 cup crushed strawberries	Dash salt
¾ cup sugar	1 tablespoon butter
1½ tablespoons cornstarch	

Cut large strawberries in half and place cut side down on cheesecake in a decorative pattern. Combine in a saucepan the crushed strawberries, sugar, cornstarch, cold water, and salt. Boil, stirring constantly, until thick and clear. Add butter. Spoon over strawberries and cake. Refrigerate.

Mrs. Max Bailey (Julie Knight)

APRICOT-BLUEBERRY SAUCE FOR CHEESECAKE

1 (12-ounce) jar apricot jam
½ cup sugar
½ cup water

1 cup blueberries
Dash kirsch

Combine in a saucepan the jam, sugar, and water. Cook over moderate heat, stirring constantly, for 5 minutes. Strain through a fine sieve. Stir in blueberries. Cool. Add a good dash of kirsch.

Mrs. J. C. "Bud" Miller (Presteen Sims)

HOT FUDGE SAUCE

1 cup sugar
3 level tablespoons cocoa
1 tablespoon dark corn syrup
½ cup milk

1 tablespoon butter
½ teaspoon salt
½ teaspoon vanilla
¾ cup nuts

Combine in a saucepan the sugar, cocoa, corn syrup and milk, and let come to a full boil. Remove from heat. Add butter, salt, vanilla, and nuts. Makes approximately 1 pint.

Note: A tried and true recipe. Double recipe for fudge candy.

Mrs. Gene Bennett (Belle Walter)

GRANDMA'S CHOCOLATE SAUCE

3 tablespoons butter
2 squares baking chocolate
¾ cup sugar

½ cup cream (half and half will do)
1 teaspoon vanilla (optional)

Melt butter and chocolate in top of double boiler. Add sugar and mix well. Chocolate-sugar mixture will be grainy. Simmer chocolate mixture for 5 minutes, stirring occasionally. Add cream or half and half and stir until smooth as satin. Add vanilla, if desired. Makes 1½ cups.

Note: This is super sauce—very rich and not too sweet.

Mrs. Mark Bergaas (Mary Emmons)

CARAMEL SAUCE

2 cups light brown sugar
1¾ cups light corn syrup

1 stick butter
1 cup whipping cream

Combine in a heavy saucepan the brown sugar, syrup, butter. Bring to soft ball stage (234 degrees on candy thermometer). Take off heat and let cool a little. Add whipping cream.

Note: Absolutely delicious on vanilla or peach ice cream.

Mrs. Gene Bennett (Belle Walter)

FOOD PROCESSOR BUTTER PASTRY

1⅓ cups flour
1 stick butter, chilled or frozen

½ teaspoon salt
¼ cup ice water

Cut butter into eighths. Put steel blade in food processor. Add flour and salt. Turn on and off once to mix. Add butter and process until mixture has consistency of coarse meal. With machine running, pour water through feed tube and process 20-30 seconds, or until dough starts holding together above blade. Do not let ball form, as this makes a tougher crust. Wrap dough in plastic wrap and refrigerate for at least an hour, or freeze. Makes one 9-inch crust.

Hint: For a sweet pie or tart, add 1 tablespoon sugar with the flour and salt. For fruit pies, you may substitute orange juice for cold water.

Mrs. Peterson Cavert (Mary Beth Wear)

CREAM CHEESE CRUST

1 stick butter
1 (3-ounce) package cream cheese

1 cup flour

Soften butter and cream cheese. Add flour. Blend with fork or pastry blender until mixture is a ball. Chill pastry about 2 hours. Roll out on floured surface. Makes one 9-inch crust.

Note: Good crust for quiche.

Guesna Bush

GRAHAM CRACKER CRUST

1 individual packet graham
  crackers, crushed (about 1⅔
  cups crumbs)

½ stick butter, melted

Mix graham cracker crumbs and butter together and press into pie pan. If crust doesn't seem firm enough, heat oven to 300 degrees and bake crust for about 5 minutes to set. Makes one 9-inch crust.

GRAHAM-NUT CRUST

1¾ cups fine graham cracker
  crumbs
¼ cup finely chopped walnuts
  or pecans

½ teaspoon cinnamon
½ cup melted butter

Combine crumbs, nuts, cinnamon, and butter. Reserve 3 tablespoons mixture for trim, if desired. Press remainder on bottom and 2½ inches up sides of 9-inch springform pan.

Mrs. Charles S. Watson

PECAN CRUST

1¼ cups finely chopped pecans
3 tablespoons sugar
2 tablespoons butter or margarine,
  softened

¼ cup flour

Heat oven to 400 degrees. Combine pecans, sugar, butter, and flour until well mixed. Press evenly in greased 9-inch pie pan, making a small rim. Bake 8-10 minutes.

QUICK PIE CRUST

1½ cups flour
1½ tablespoons sugar
1 teaspoon salt

2 tablespoons milk
½ cup vegetable oil

Mix together the flour, sugar, and salt. Add milk to oil and whip with fork until well blended. Pour into flour mixture. Stir until mixed. Pour into pan and press to desired shape with hands. Bake at 425 degrees for 10 minutes. Makes one 9-inch pie crust.

Mrs. Wayne L. Williams (Nancy Tate)

REGULATION PASTRY

1 cup sifted flour
⅓ cup shortening

¼ cup ice water
⅛ teaspoon salt

Cut shortening into flour with pastry cutter or fork—not too fine, about the size of a small pea. First add salt to flour mixture. Next add water a few drops at a time, cutting well all the time. Pat together as lightly and quickly as possible. Put in refrigerator an hour or more. Roll thin. Bake at 400 degrees. Yield: one 8-inch crust.

Mrs. Jerry B. Ramey (Elizabeth "Ebbie" Emens)

TOASTY OAT CRUMB CRUST

1 cup quick oats, uncooked
⅓ cup finely chopped nuts
  or wheat germ
⅓ cup firmly-packed brown sugar

4 tablespoons butter or
  margarine, melted
½ teaspoon cinnamon (optional)

Heat oven to 375 degrees. Combine oats, nuts or wheat germ, brown sugar, butter, and cinnamon; mix well. Press into greased 9-inch pie plate. Bake 8-10 minutes, or until golden brown. Makes one 9-inch crust.

EASY APPLE CRUMB PIE

1 (20-ounce) can apple slices
½ cup sugar
1 teaspoon lemon juice

¼ teaspoon cinnamon
½ package white cake mix
Butter

Put apples in bottom of 9-inch square pan. Add sugar, lemon juice, and cinnamon. Mix. Pour cake mix over top of filling. Dot with butter. Bake at 350 degrees for about 35-45 minutes, until brown.

Mrs. Hodo Strickland (Judy Turner)

BUTTERMILK PIE

2 cups sugar
1 stick of butter, softened
3 eggs
1 teaspoon vanilla

½ cup buttermilk
Pinch of salt
1 tablespoon flour

Cream sugar and butter. Add eggs, vanilla, buttermilk, salt, and flour. Mix thoroughly. Pour into a deep pie shell. Bake 1 hour at 350 degrees.

Mrs. Walter Gary (Betsy Shirley)

ENGLISH APPLE PIE

1 stick margarine	½-1 cup chopped pecans
1 cup flour	4 or 5 medium apples, peeled
½ cup brown sugar	1 teaspoon cinnamon
1 teaspoon cinnamon	1 cup sugar

Mix together the margarine, flour, brown sugar, cinnamon, and pecans. Form mixture into a roll like refrigerator cookies. Chill. Slice apples and place in Pyrex dish. Sprinkle cinnamon and sugar over this. Slice refrigerator roll and place over the top. Bake 1 hour at 350 degrees.

Mrs. James G. Lee, II (Becky Thomson)

BUTTERSCOTCH PIE

2 cups milk	4 tablespoons butter
1 cup brown sugar, lightly packed	1 teaspoon vanilla
⅓ cup flour	1 baked pie shell or crumb crust
½ teaspoon salt	¼ cup sugar
3 eggs, separated	¼ teaspoon cream of tartar

Scald milk. In bowl, mix sugar, flour, and salt. Gradually stir in scalded milk. Return to top of double boiler. Cook over boiling water until mixture thickens. Add some of mixture to beaten egg yolks, then add yolk mixture to milk and cook about 2 minutes longer. Add butter and vanilla. Cool. Pour into pie shell or crumb crust. Beat egg whites at highest speed, gradually adding sugar and cream of tartar. Continue beating until egg whites stand in peaks. Heap meringue on pie, spreading to edges to seal. Place pie in 400-degree oven to brown lightly.

Mrs. Don Maughan (Danyle Christenberry)

BRANDY ALEXANDER PIE

1 graham cracker crust	½ pint whipping cream, whipped
1 (14-ounce) can sweetened	2 tablespoons crème de cacao
condensed milk	2 tablespoons brandy

Fold condensed milk, whipped cream, crème de cacao and brandy together and pour into graham cracker crust. Put in *freezer* until ready to slice and serve.

Mrs. Walter C. Densmore (Mary Kate Fuller)

CARAMEL PIE

1 (9-inch) baked pastry crust
1 (14-ounce) can Eagle Brand
   sweetened condensed milk

1 cup chopped pecans
1 (9-ounce) container frozen
   whipped topping, thawed

Prepare empty crust according to directions. Set aside. Remove label from the Eagle Brand milk and set entire unopened can in a large saucepan. Cover with cold water. Over high heat, bring the water to a boil. Reduce heat and continue boiling for 3 hours. Check periodically to see water covers the can entirely. Remove can and cool unopened for 20 minutes. Open can and spread caramelized milk in the bottom of the pie crust. Over the caramel, sprinkle ¾ cup of the chopped pecans. Pat the pecans into the caramel with open hand. Over the caramel and pecans, spread the whipped topping. Garnish with remaining pecans. Refrigerate 1 hour before serving.

Lew Worsham Voltz

CHESS PIE

½ cup butter
2 cups sugar
1 tablespoon cornstarch

4 eggs
1 (8- or 9-inch) pie shell

Cream butter. Blend together the sugar and cornstarch, add to butter, and cream again. Add eggs, one at a time, and beat well after each one is added. Put mixture in pie crust and bake in 350-degree oven until it sets, about 35 minutes.

Mrs. Samuel Payne Wright (Frances Leapard)

CHOCOLATE CHESS PIE

½ stick margarine, melted
1½ cups sugar
3 tablespoons cocoa
1 (5.33-ounce) can evaporated
   milk

2 eggs
1 teaspoon vanilla
Pinch of salt
1 (9-inch) unbaked pie shell

Heat oven to 325 degrees. Melt margarine. Mix sugar with cocoa. Add eggs, evaporated milk, vanilla, and margarine to sugar-cocoa mixture. Pour into pie shell and bake for 50 minutes. Delicious with whipped or ice cream on top. Serves 8.

Note: Quick, easy, and delicious.

Mrs. George Wright (Stella Wellborn)

BING CHERRY PIE

1 pie shell, baked
Pecans
½ pint whipping cream
¼ cup sugar
1 (14-ounce) can sweetened
   condensed milk

⅓ cup lemon juice
1 teaspoon vanilla
½ teaspoon almond extract
1 (16-ounce) can black Bing
   cherries, drained and chopped

Line pie shell with pecans. Whip cream with sugar. Mix half of whipped cream with condensed milk, lemon juice, flavorings, and cherries. Pour over pecans. Top with remaining whipped cream. Chill in refrigerator 4 hours before serving.

Note: Very easy and very good!

Mrs. Larry Howell (Mary George Hinton)

CHOCOLATE CRUNCH PIE

4 eggs, slightly beaten
1 cup brown sugar
1 cup dark corn syrup
2 tablespoons butter or margarine,
   melted

1 teaspoon vanilla extract
1 cup pecans, broken
½ cup semi-sweet chocolate
   morsels
1 (9-inch) unbaked pie shell

Preheat oven to 350 degrees. Combine eggs, sugar, corn syrup, butter, and vanilla. Mix well. Add pecans and chocolate morsels. Pour into pie shell. Bake for 45-55 minutes, or until knife inserted in center comes out clean.

Mrs. Richard L. Chaffin (Royce Woodley)

CHOCOLATE NUT ANGEL PIE

2 egg whites
½ cup sifted sugar
¼ teaspoon cream of tartar
½ cup chopped or broken pecans

¾ pound semi-sweet chocolate
3 tablespoons hot water
½ teaspoon vanilla
½ pint whipping cream

Heat oven to 275 degrees. Beat egg whites until stiff with sugar and cream of tartar. Put in buttered 9-inch pie plate and form shell. Sprinkle pecans on top. Bake for 45 minutes. Melt chocolate over boiling water and blend with hot water. Add vanilla. Whip cream and fold into chocolate. Pour into cooled meringue shell. Chill.

Mrs. John Johnson (Melissa Burrus)—Nashville, TN

COCONUT CUSTARD PIE

1 stick oleo, softened
1 cup sugar
4 eggs
2 cups milk

½ cup self-rising flour
1 cup flaked coconut
Dash vanilla

Put oleo, sugar, eggs, milk, flour, coconut, and vanilla into electric blender or food processor with steel blade in place and process for 15 seconds. Pour into a 10½-inch pie pan. (You can use a 10-inch pie pan if you don't have a larger one.) Bake at 350 degrees for 40-45 minutes. It looks as if it will spill over, but it doesn't! Very easy to make, but good. Serves 5 or 6.

Optional: Sprinkle buttered pie plate with corn meal.

Mrs. William W. Jessup (Pat Proctor)

COMPANY'S COMING PIE

18 (2-inch square) saltine crackers, crushed finely
1 cup chopped pecans
3 egg whites
¼ teaspoon cream of tartar

1 cup sugar
½ pint whipping cream
¾ cup pineapple preserves
1 cup Angel Flake coconut

Heat oven to 350 degrees. Beat egg whites with cream of tartar until stiff. Blend sugar into egg whites. Fold in cracker crumbs and pecans. Spread in greased 9-inch pie plate and bake for 25 minutes. Cool. Whip cream, fold in preserves. Pour over pie. Top with coconut. Chill before serving.

Mrs. Jay W. Anderson (Ruby Hurst)

PUMPKIN PIE

1 cup pumpkin
⅔ cup sugar
1 teaspoon cinnamon
½ teaspoon nutmeg
¼ teaspoon cloves
¼ teaspoon salt

2 eggs
1 tablespoon butter, melted
1 cup milk
2 tablespoons bourbon
1 unbaked pie shell

Preheat oven to 450 degrees. Combine pumpkin, sugar, spices, salt, eggs, butter, milk, and bourbon. Pour into unbaked pie shell. Bake at 450 degrees for 10 minutes; reduce heat to 325 degrees and continue to bake for 35-40 minutes, until filling is firm and knife inserted in middle comes out clean.

Mrs. Max Bailey (Mary Julia Knight)

GRASSHOPPER PIE

1½ cups chocolate wafer crumbs
½ cup sugar, divided
⅓ cup melted butter
1 tablespoon unflavored gelatin
1½ cups whipping cream
4 eggs, separated

Pinch of salt
¼ cup crème de menthe
¼ cup crème de cacao
Semi-sweet or mint-flavored
   chocolate for garnish

Mix chocolate wafer crumbs, butter, and ¼ cup sugar. Press into 9-inch pie plate and bake at 450 degrees for 5 minutes. Soften gelatin in ½ cup cream for 3 minutes and dissolve over hot water. Beat egg yolks and add ¼ cup sugar slowly. Add liqueurs and dissolved gelatin. Chill until the consistency of unbeaten egg white. Beat egg whites with salt until stiff but not dry. Whip remaining 1 cup cream. Fold cream, then egg whites into liqueur mixture. Turn into pie shell and chill. Garnish with shaved semi-sweet or mint-flavored chocolate.

Mrs. Peterson Cavert (Mary Beth Wear)

HEATH BAR PIE

1 graham cracker crust
2 cups (8-ounce cartons) whipping
   cream
1 cup confectioners' sugar

1 jigger bourbon
1 teaspoon vanilla
4 (1⅛-ounce) Heath bars

Whip cream. Add confectioners' sugar, bourbon, vanilla. Pour into graham cracker crust. Crush Heath bars and spread on top. Make several hours or day before serving. Chill. Divine!

Mrs. Howard Garrison (Ashley Smith)

STRAWBERRY MACAROON PIE

20 coconut macaroons
⅔ cups pecans, chopped
½ pint whipping cream

2 tablespoons confectioners' sugar
1 (10-ounce) package frozen
   strawberries, thawed

Crumble cookies coarsely and mix with nuts. Whip cream with confectioners' sugar. Fold in cookie crumbs and nuts. Fold in strawberries. Pour into pie pan. *Do not* use pie crust—makes its own. Freeze.

Mrs. W. McKay DeLoach (Marilyn Williams)

DIVINE LIME PIE

4 eggs, separated
1½ cups sugar, divided
¼ teaspoon cream of tartar
¼ teaspoon salt

⅓ cup lime juice
Green food color
1 tablespoon grated lime rind
2 cups heavy cream, divided

Make meringue pie shell: beat egg whites with cream of tartar until foamy, then add 1 cup sugar, 2 tablespoons at a time. Beat until stiff peaks form. Pour into lightly-greased 10-inch pie pan and shape into shell shape, building up sides with spatula. Bake at 275 degrees for 20 minutes, then increase heat to 300 and bake for 40 minutes more. Turn off oven and do not remove shell until oven is completely cool.

Filling: In top of double boiler, mix egg yolks, salt, ½ cup sugar, and lime juice. Cook and stir over simmering water until thick, about 10 minutes. Cool. Tint green. Whip 1 cup cream and fold into egg yolk mixture with lime rind. Pour into cooled pie shell. Whip remaining cup of cream (sweeten slightly, if desired) and spread over filling. Chill at least 4 hours.

Mrs. James Hodo Walburn (Dean Frank)

KEY LIME PIE

1 (14-ounce) can sweetened
    condensed milk
3 egg *yolks*
1½ teaspoons lime rind, grated
⅓ cup fresh lime juice
3-4 drops green food color
    (enough to make a soft green
    color)

1 (4½-ounce) carton Cool Whip
1-2 teaspoons white rum
1 baked pie shell

Heat oven to 250 degrees. Mix milk and egg yolks thoroughly. Add lime juice, lime rind, and food color and mix. Pour in shell and bake for 10 minutes or until firm. Cool at room temperature. Chill thoroughly in refrigerator. Mix Cool Whip with white rum. Top each pie slice with Cool Whip.

Note: Very rich!

Mrs. Ray Moore, Jr. (Margie Mantel)

SCRUMPTIOUS LEMON PIE

1 cup sugar
3 tablespoons cornstarch
¼ cup butter
1 tablespoon grated lemon rind
¼ cup lemon juice
3 eggs, separated

1 cup milk
1 cup sour cream
1 (9-inch) baked pie shell
¼ cup sugar
¼ teaspoon cream of tartar

Combine sugar and cornstarch in a saucepan with butter, lemon rind, lemon juice, and egg yolks. Stir in milk and cook over medium heat, stirring constantly, until mixture thickens. Remove from heat and let cool. Fold in sour cream. Place the mixture in the baked pie shell.

Prepare meringue as follows: Beat egg whites at highest speed, gradually adding sugar and cream of tartar. Continue beating until egg whites stand in peaks. Ice pie with meringue. Place pie in 400-degree oven to lightly brown it. Then chill at least 2 hours before serving.

Mrs. Carl W. Albright, Jr. (Rainer Lamar)

DEEP DISH PEACH COBBLER

5 to 6 cups fresh peaches
2 cups plus 2 tablespoons sugar,
   divided
1 teaspoon almond extract
2 tablespoons lemon juice
1½ cups all-purpose flour
½ teaspoon salt

3 teaspoons baking powder
⅓ cup shortening
1 egg, slightly beaten
1 cup milk
1 to 2 tablespoons butter
Whipped cream (optional)

Preheat oven to 400 degrees. Combine peaches, 2 cups sugar, almond extract, and lemon juice. Spoon mixture into a 2-quart baking dish, and set aside. Combine flour, salt, baking powder, and remaining 2 tablespoons sugar. Cut in shortening until mixture resembles coarse crumbs. Add egg and milk; mix well. Spread batter over peaches, and dot with butter. Bake for 45 minutes. Serve with whipped cream if desired. Yield: 8 servings.

Note: For added color and flavor, sprinkle cinnamon-sugar over the top before baking, if desired.

Mrs. Tony Smith (Susan Shirley)

PEACHES AND CREAM PIE

6 ripe peaches
½ cup sugar
¼ cup flour
1 teaspoon cinnamon, divided

¼ teaspoon nutmeg
1 cup sour cream
2 tablespoons sugar
1 unbaked pie shell

Heat oven to 450 degrees. Peel peaches by dropping them in hot water for 5-10 seconds. Put in cold water. Skins slip off easily. Halve or quarter peaches and remove seeds. Place in pie shell, cut side up. Mix ½ cup sugar, flour, ½ teaspoon cinnamon, and nutmeg. Sprinkle evenly over peaches. Pour sour cream over all. (Dilute sour cream with milk if it is too thick.) Mix 2 tablespoons sugar with ½ teaspoon cinnamon and sprinkle over cream. Bake in preheated oven for 10 minutes, then lower heat to 350 degrees and bake 30 minutes. Cool.

Bert Wear

PEANUT BUTTER PIE

1 (10-inch) baked pie shell
1 scant cup confectioners' sugar
½ cup peanut butter, plain or
  crunchy
¼ cup cornstarch
½ cup plus 6 tablespoons sugar,
  divided

¼ teaspoon salt
2 cups milk, scalded
3 eggs, separated
2 tablespoons butter
¼ teaspoon vanilla

Mix confectioners' sugar and peanut butter until it feels like corn meal. Spread half of mixture in bottom of pie shell. Mix cornstarch, ½ cup sugar, and salt. Gradually add scalded milk. Add slowly to beaten egg yolks. Cook in double boiler until thick. Add butter and vanilla. Pour into pie shell over peanut butter mixture. Cool. Beat egg whites until foamy. Add 6 tablespoons sugar gradually. Beat until stiff peaks form. Spread over filling. Sprinkle reserved peanut butter mixture over meringue. Bake at 325 degrees until light brown, approximately 15 minutes.

Mrs. Thomas Fanning (Gail Weakley)

PUMPKIN CHIFFON PIE

3 eggs, separated
¾ cup brown sugar
1½ cups pumpkin, canned or
   cooked fresh
½ cup milk
½ teaspoon salt
1 teaspoon cinnamon

½ teaspoon nutmeg
1 envelope unflavored gelatin
¼ cup cold water
¼ cup granulated sugar
1 (9-inch) baked pie shell
Cool Whip

Combine egg yolks, brown sugar, pumpkin, milk, salt, and spices. Cook in double boiler until thick, stirring constantly. Soak gelatin in cold water for 3 minutes. Stir into hot pumpkin mixture. Chill until partially set. Beat egg whites and add granulated sugar. Beat until stiff, then fold into pumpkin mixture. Pour into *baked* pie shell and top with Cool Whip. Keep refrigerated until served.

Mrs. Robert A. Drew (Jackie Atchison)

SOUTHERN PECAN PIE

1 cup white corn syrup
1 cup light brown sugar
⅓ teaspoon salt
⅓ cup melted butter or margarine

1 teaspoon vanilla
3 eggs, slightly beaten
1 heaping cup pecan halves
1 (9-inch) unbaked pastry shell

Combine syrup, sugar, salt, butter, vanilla, and mix well. Add slightly beaten eggs. Pour into pie shell. Sprinkle pecans over all. Bake in preheated 350-degree oven for approximately 45 minutes. When cool, you may top with whipped cream or ice cream.

Variation: For Southern Peanut Pie, omit salt and substitute 1½ cups dry-roasted peanuts or roasted peanuts for pecans.

Mrs. Guy E. Moman, Jr. (Anne McAlily)

LEMON CHESS PIE

½ cup melted butter
1 cup sugar
4 eggs
1 tablespoon corn meal

Juice and grated rind of 1 lemon
  (⅓ cup)
1 (9-inch) unbaked pie shell

Cream butter and sugar. Add eggs, one at a time, beating after each one. Add corn meal, lemon juice, and rind. Bake in pie shell 25 minutes at 350 degrees. Yield: 1 pie.

Mrs. James O. Parker (Yalonda Duncan)

FRESH STRAWBERRY OR PEACH PIE

4 cups fruit (sliced peaches; whole
  or sliced strawberries)
1¼ cups sugar (less if fruit is
  very ripe)
3 rounded tablespoons cornstarch
¼ teaspoon salt
Juice of 1 lemon

1½ cups water
Food color
1 (9-inch) baked pie shell
1 (3-ounce) package cream
  cheese (optional)
Whipped cream

Combine sugar, cornstarch, salt, lemon juice, and water, and cook over low heat until thick and clear. Add red color for strawberry and yellow for peach pie. Let cool. Add fruit. If desired, spread cream cheese on bottom of pastry. Place fruit with syrup in pie shell. Place in refrigerator a couple of hours before serving. Top with whipped cream.

Note: Fresh blueberries, white grapes or raspberries may also be used. To make glaze, mash enough fruit to make 1 cup and substitute for 1 cup of water. Blueberries do not require food color; use yellow for grapes.

Mrs. Jerry B. Ramey (Elizabeth "Ebbie" Emens)

SOUR CREAM RAISIN PIE

⅔ cup sugar
¼ teaspoon salt
1½ tablespoons cornstarch
3 eggs, separated
1½ cups sour cream

½ cup raisins (soaked in boiling
  water and drained)
¼ cup sugar
¼ teaspoon cream of tartar
1 baked pastry shell

In a heavy saucepan, combine ⅔ cup sugar, salt, cornstarch, egg yolks, and sour cream. Cook over low heat, stirring constantly, until thick. Stir in raisins. Pour into shell. Beat egg whites until foamy with cream of tartar. Gradually add ¼ cup sugar. Continue beating until egg whites stand in peaks. Spread over filling and seal edges. Bake at 350 degrees until lightly browned.

Mrs. Lloyd Wagner (Martha Savage)

PECAN GEMS

1 recipe Cream Cheese Crust (See Index)
½ cup pecans, finely chopped
1 egg

¾ cup light brown sugar
¼ stick oleo, melted
1 teaspoon vanilla

Preheat oven to 350 degrees. Make crust as directed, except do not roll out. Divide into 24 portions and make each into a small ball. Take each ball of dough and mash into a *tiny* muffin tin. Mix together the pecans, egg, sugar, vanilla, and oleo. Spoon into the muffin cups. Bake for approximately 30 minutes. Makes 24 gems.

Note: Any chess or custard pie filling may also be used for a variety of tarts.

Mrs. William David Smith (Jane Bandy)

FROZEN RASPBERRY PIE

1 (10-ounce) package frozen raspberries
1 cup sugar
2 egg whites at room temperature
1 cup whipping cream

Dash salt
1 tablespoon lemon juice
¼ cup chopped almonds
2 (8- or 9-inch) baked pie crusts

Thaw raspberries and combine in mixer bowl with egg whites, sugar, lemon juice, and salt. Beat for 15 minutes or until stiff. Whip cream. Fold raspberry mixture into whipped cream. Mound into pie shells. Sprinkle with chopped almonds. Freeze.

Mrs. Louis Payne (Catherine "Woodie" Murphy)

Hint: Buy almonds in the shell when they are on sale (usually in January). Freeze unshelled, or shell them (easy!) and freeze. To blanch: drop shelled almonds in boiling water for 1 minute. Drain and rinse with cold water. Brown skin slips off easily. To toast: spread on baking sheet and bake in 300-degree oven for 20 minutes. Easy to do and much better than prepared ones. One pound almonds in shell yields 1-1½ cups nutmeats.

WEIDMAN'S BLACK BOTTOM PIE

14 gingersnaps (1⅔ cups when
  rolled fine)
5 tablespoons butter, melted
2 cups milk
4 eggs, separated
1 cup sugar, divided
2 squares unsweetened baking
  chocolate, divided

1 teaspoon vanilla
1 tablespoon (1 envelope)
  unflavored gelatin
4 tablespoons water
¼ teaspoon cream of tartar
2 tablespoons whiskey
1 cup heavy cream, whipped
4 teaspoons cornstarch

Heat oven to 300 degrees. Roll gingersnaps fine and add butter. Pat crumb mixture evenly in 9-inch pie pan. Bake 10 minutes. Cool.

Scald milk in top of double boiler. Beat egg yolks. Combine ½ cup sugar and cornstarch. Pour a little of the hot milk into the egg yolks, then pour yolks back into hot milk. Add sugar mixture and cook, stirring occasionally, for 20 minutes, or until mixture coats a spoon. Remove from heat. Pour out 1 cup of custard. Add 1½ squares chocolate to 1 cup custard and beat. As chocolate custard cools, add vanilla. Pour into prepared crust. Put in refrigerator to chill. Sprinkle gelatin on water. Let stand 3 minutes. Add to remaining hot custard. Let cool but not thicken. Beat egg whites with cream of tartar until foamy. Add remaining ½ cup sugar gradually and beat until it will hold stiff peaks. Add whiskey. Fold into custard. As soon as chocolate layer sets, add this on top. Chill until set. Spread whipped cream on top. Garnish with remaining ½ square of chocolate, shaved and sprinkled on whipped cream.

Mrs. Harry Marrs—Hueytown, AL

AUNT MARY'S WHISKEY CAKE

½ pound butter
2 cups sugar
6 eggs
1⅓ cups whiskey

4 cups flour
1 (10-ounce) box currants
1 (15-ounce) box white raisins
1 quart pecan halves

Cream butter with sugar. Beat in eggs, one at a time. Add whiskey alternately with 2 cups of the flour. In another large bowl, mix currants, white raisins and pecans with the remaining 2 cups of flour. Combine mixtures. Bake in greased and floured bundt pan or 2 loaf pans for 3½ hours at 275 degrees. Place foil loosely over the cake the first hour and then uncover for remaining baking time.

Mrs. David M. Cochrane (Mary B. Tompkins)

APPLE DAPPLE CAKE

1½ cups oil	3 cups fresh yellow apples—
2 cups sugar	peeled, cored, and in pieces
3 eggs	1½ cups pecans, chopped
2 teaspoons vanilla	1 cup brown sugar
3 cups plain flour	¼ cup milk
1 teaspoon salt	1 stick oleo
1 teaspoon soda	

Heat oven to 325 degrees. Mix together oil, sugar, eggs, vanilla, flour, salt, soda, apples, and pecans. Bake in a 9 x 13-inch pan for 1 hour and 20 minutes. Remove from oven and make glaze. Pour glaze over while cake is still hot.

For glaze, combine in a saucepan the brown sugar, milk, and oleo. Boil for 3 minutes. Serve with Cool Whip if desired.

Mrs. Rodney P. Wilkin (Susan Strong)

Hint: Always cream butter, margarine, or solid shortening with sugar or other dry ingredients with your hands, as the warmth of your hand makes it blend much more thoroughly than by mixer or other method.

BRAZIL NUT FRUIT CAKE LOAF

2 cups chopped pecans	¼ pound dates, chopped
*1 pound Brazil nuts (2 pounds in shell), chopped	1 (3½-ounce) can flaked coconut
½ pound candied pineapple, chopped	1 (14-ounce) can sweetened condensed milk
½ pound candied cherries, halved	¼ teaspoon salt
	1 teaspoon vanilla

Combine pecans, Brazil nuts, pineapple, cherries, and dates. Mix with coconut and milk. Add salt and vanilla. Pack in loaf pan and bake in 250-degree oven until brown (about 1¾ hours). Mixture may be divided into two smaller loaf pans and baked at 250 degrees for about 1 hour.

*Note: Freezing the nuts in the shell makes them easier to crack.

Mrs. Milford Espey, Jr. (Becky Flowers)

BLACKBERRY JAM CAKE

½ cup shortening
1 cup brown sugar
3 eggs, separated
1¾ cups flour
½ teaspoon cloves

1 teaspoon cinnamon
1 teaspoon nutmeg
1 cup blackberry jam
3 tablespoons milk
¾ cup chopped raisins

Cream shortening and sugar; add egg yolks. Beat until fluffy. Sift flour with cloves, cinnamon, and nutmeg. Add to shortening mixture alternately with jam and milk; add raisins. Fold in stiffly beaten egg whites. Place in angel food pan and bake at 375 degrees for 1 hour 15 minutes.

Mrs. Phillip R. Jenkins (Linda Sullivan)

BLUEBERRY CAKE

1 angel food cake (either
   homemade or bought)
1 (21-ounce) can blueberry pie filling
1 package Dream Whip
1 (8-ounce) package cream cheese

½ cup confectioners' sugar
½ cup granulated sugar
1 teaspoon vanilla extract

Split cake into 3 layers. Spread pie filling between layers. Reassemble the layers and frost.

For frosting, make Dream Whip as directed on package. Blend in cream cheese, confectioners' sugar, granulated sugar, and vanilla extract. Frost sides and top of cake. Makes plenty of frosting. Yield: 12 servings.

Mrs. Jerry L. Carnes (Burns Levy)

CARROT CAKE I

3 cups grated carrots (not fine)
2 cups plain flour
2 cups sugar
1¼ cups vegetable oil
1 cup chopped pecans

4 eggs
2 teaspoons cinnamon
2 teaspoons baking powder
2 teaspoons baking soda
1 teaspoon salt

Grease and flour three 9-inch cake pans. Preheat oven to 350 degrees. Mix eggs, sugar, oil, and flour. Beat well. Add chopped nuts, carrots, cinnamon, baking powder, baking soda, and salt. Mix thoroughly. Pour into cake pans. Bake for about 30 minutes. Do not let cake bake until dry; it should be moist. Frost when cool with Cream Cheese Frosting (See Index).

Mrs. Mickey M. Petty (Donna Davenport)

CARROT CAKE II

2 cups sifted flour
½ teaspoon salt
2½ cups sugar
2 teaspoons soda
2 teaspoons cinnamon
1 cup cooking oil
3 eggs

1½ teaspoons vanilla
2 cups grated carrots
1-2 cups chopped nuts
1 (8-ounce) can crushed
    pineapple
1 cup chopped dates

Heat oven to 325 degrees. Sift together into large bowl the flour, salt, sugar, soda, and cinnamon. Add oil, eggs, and vanilla. Mix well. Add carrots, nuts, undrained pineapple and dates. Pour into greased and floured 10-inch tube pan. Bake for 1 hour 15 minutes. Do not open oven door until this time is up. May take another 15 minutes. Top will spring back when touched, and cake is lightly browned when done.

Mrs. W. McKay DeLoach (Marilyn Williams)

CHERRY JUBILEE CAKE

1 (18.5-ounce) box Duncan Hines
    Cherry Supreme cake mix
1 cup apricot nectar or pear nectar
½ cup oil
½ cup sugar

½ teaspoon cherry flavor (or 1
    teaspoon juice of maraschino
    cherries)
3 drops red food color
4 eggs

Heat oven to 350 degrees. In a large bowl, blend cake mix, nectar, oil, sugar, flavoring, and food color. Beat at medium speed for 1 minute. Add eggs, one at a time, beating at medium speed for 1 minute after each addition. Spread batter in a greased and floured 10-inch tube pan. Bake for about 45 minutes, or until cake tests done with a toothpick. Cool right side up for 15 minutes, then remove from pan.

GLAZE:
1 cup confectioners' sugar
6 maraschino cherries, chopped
    fine

2 tablespoons juice from cherries

For glaze, mix sugar, cherries, and juice. Pour over cake while still warm.

Mrs. Maurice Tidwell

CHEW CAKE
(Favorite of Paul "Bear" Bryant)

2 eggs, beaten
1 cup flour
1 teaspoon baking powder

½ pound brown sugar
1 cup nuts, broken
½ stick butter, melted

Preheat oven to 350 degrees. Grease and flour a 9 x13-inch pan. Mix eggs with flour, baking powder, brown sugar and melted butter. Add nuts and spread a thin layer in pan. Bake for 30 minutes. Cool in pan and spread with topping.

TOPPING:
¾ cup sugar
½ cup milk

½ stick butter
½ teaspoon vanilla

Mix sugar, milk, butter, and vanilla. Cook in a heavy saucepan until it forms a soft ball (234 degrees F.). Cool, beat until thick, and spread on cake in pan.

Mrs. Paul (Bear) Bryant (Mary Harmon)

CHESS CAKE

1 (18.5-ounce) box yellow cake mix
2 eggs

1 stick oleo

TOPPING:
2 eggs
1 (8-ounce) package cream cheese

1 (1-pound) box confectioners'
   sugar

Mix together the cake mix, eggs, and oleo. Press into a greased 9 x 13-inch pan. Mix together the eggs, cream cheese, and confectioners' sugar (use steel blade in food processor, if desired). Pour over cake. Bake at 350 degrees for 30 to 40 minutes.

Mrs. Richard Linderman—Nashville, TN

CREAM CHEESE POUND CAKE

3 sticks butter
1 (8-ounce) package cream cheese
3 cups sugar
6 eggs

3 cups all-purpose flour
Pinch of salt
3 teaspoons vanilla

Cream butter and cheese. Add sugar and cream well. Add eggs, one at a time, and beat well. Stir in flour and salt. Add vanilla. Bake in 10-inch tube or bundt pan. Start in *cold* oven, and bake at 300 degrees for 2 hours.

Mrs. James J. Jenkins (Carol Sue Schwerdt)

WORLD'S BEST CHOCOLATE CAKE

¾ cup Crisco
½ cup sour cream
2 cups sugar
2 eggs
2 cups sifted flour

1 teaspoon soda
½ teaspoon salt
3 tablespoons cocoa
1 cup boiling water
1 teaspoon vanilla

Cream together the Crisco, sour cream, and sugar. Add eggs, one at a time, beating well after each. Sift together flour, soda, salt, and cocoa four times. Add gradually to egg mixture, beating well. Add water and vanilla; mix well. Grease, flour, and line cake pans with wax paper. Bake on bottom rack in two 9-inch cake pans at 350 degrees for 30-35 minutes; or bake in one 9 x 13 x 2-inch pan for 40-45 minutes.

FUDGE FROSTING: (Double for layer cake!)
1½ cups sugar
¼ cup butter
1 tablespoon light corn syrup
2 tablespoons cocoa

7 tablespoons milk
¼ teaspoon salt
2 teaspoons vanilla

Combine sugar, butter, syrup, cocoa, milk, and salt in a saucepan. Bring to a full, rolling boil over medium heat, stirring constantly. Boil briskly 1 minute. Add vanilla and beat until thick enough to spread over cake. This will ice one sheet cake; double for layer cake.

Mrs. Tony Smith (Susan Shirley)

ROULAGE (CHOCOLATE ROLL CAKE)

1 cup confectioners' sugar
1 pint whipping cream
5 eggs, separated
1 cup sugar

2 tablespoons cocoa
1 tablespoon flour
1 teaspoon vanilla
Sifted cocoa

Whip cream and sweeten with confectioners' sugar. Chill. Heat oven to 375 degrees. Beat egg whites until stiff and set aside. Beat egg yolks and sugar until fluffy. Add cocoa, flour, and vanilla. Fold in egg whites. Pour into 12 x 14-inch pan lined with wax paper. Bake in preheated oven for exactly 15 minutes. Cool in pan for 5 minutes, then turn onto wax paper dusted with cocoa. Spread with chilled whipped cream mixture. Roll up jellyroll fashion. Refrigerate for 6-8 hours in dusted wax paper roll. Slice and serve. Yield: 6-8 servings.

Mrs. James O. Parker (Yalonda Duncan)

DENTIST'S CHRISTMAS CAKE

½ pound margarine
1 cup sugar
4 eggs
2½ cups sifted flour

2 teaspoons baking powder
1 teaspoon soda
½ pint sour cream
1 teaspoon vanilla

Cream margarine and sugar thoroughly. Add eggs, one at a time, beating well after each egg. Sift flour, baking powder, salt, and baking soda. Add to creamed mixture alternately with sour cream. Add vanilla.

FILLING:
6 tablespoons butter
1 cup firmly packed brown sugar

5 teaspoons cinnamon
1 cup chopped pecans

For filling, mix butter, sugar, cinnamon, and pecans until soft. Spread half of cake batter in 10-inch tube pan greased and lined with wax paper. Sprinkle half of filling mix over batter. Add rest of batter, and sprinkle rest of filling mixture on top. Bake at 350 degrees for 40-50 minutes.

Note: Freezes well.

Mrs. Sidney Tarwater (Susan Foster)

FIG CAKE

2 cups plain flour
1½ cups sugar
1 teaspoon salt
1 teaspoon soda
1 teaspoon cinnamon
1 teaspoon nutmeg

¼ teaspoon cloves
1 cup oil
3 eggs
1 cup buttermilk
1 cup fig preserves
1 tablespoon vanilla

GLAZE:
½ stick butter
½ cup sugar

1 tablespoon light corn syrup
¼ teaspoon soda

Heat oven to 325 degrees. Mix flour, sugar, salt, soda, spices, oil, eggs, buttermilk, preserves, and vanilla together well. Pour into 9 x 13-inch greased cake pan. Bake for 45 minutes. Make glaze by mixing butter, ½ cup sugar, syrup, and soda together, and boil for 3 minutes. Pour over cake while cake is warm. May serve with Cool Whip.

Note: Applesauce may be substituted for fig preserves. Good for breakfast or brunch.

Mrs. Max Bailey (Julie Knight)

LIBBA'S JAPANESE FRUIT CAKE

2 cups sugar
3 cups flour
3 teaspoons baking powder
½ teaspoon salt
1 cup shortening
1 cup milk, divided
4 eggs
1 teaspoon vanilla
1½ cups chopped pecans
1 teaspoon cinnamon
½ teaspoon nutmeg

1 cup white raisins
2 oranges, juice and grated rind
1 lemon, juice and grated rind
1 heaping tablespoon flour or
    cornstarch
2 cups sugar
1 cup water
1 (12-ounce) package frozen
    grated coconut (unsweetened)
    or 1 fresh coconut, grated

Preheat oven to 350 degrees. Sift together into large mixer bowl the sugar, flour, baking powder, and salt. Add shortening and ½ cup milk. Beat thoroughly, then add remainder of milk and beat 2 minutes. Add eggs, one at a time, beating well after each. Divide batter into ⅔ and ⅓. To the ⅔ portion, add vanilla and pecans. To the ⅓ portion, add cinnamon, nutmeg, and raisins. Mix both portions thoroughly. Pour batter into three 9-inch cake pans, dividing ⅔ portion between 2 pans. Bake for approximately 30 minutes, or until cake tester inserted in center of cake comes out clean. Cool in pan. When assembling cake, the raisin-spice layer should be in middle.

Into a large heavy saucepan, put flour. Gradually add juice and rind of oranges and lemon, whisking well so flour does not lump. Add sugar and water and bring to a rolling boil. Boil until syrup is clear, about 5 minutes. Remove from heat. Add coconut and mix well. Put on top and sides of cake while still slightly warm. Leave cake open overnight until filling has soaked into the layers, then cover.

Mrs. Jimmy Gamble—Tuscumbia, AL

Hint: Opening a coconut is easier if it is placed in a preheated 325-degree oven for 15 minutes (no longer). Let it cool until it can be handled, wrap in a towel and tap gently with a hammer. Have a bowl ready to catch the liquid. Use a potato peeler to remove brown skin. Grate or chop in blender, food processor or by hand. Freeze any extra grated coconut for later use.

MILLIE'S CHOCOLATE POUND CAKE

½ pound oleo
½ cup Crisco
3 cups sugar
5 eggs
3 cups plain flour

½ teaspoon baking powder
5 tablespoons cocoa
½ teaspoon salt
1 cup milk
1 teaspoon vanilla

Cream shortening and sugar, then add 4 eggs, one at a time, beating after each. Sift together flour, baking powder, cocoa, and salt, and mix into egg-shortening mixture alternately with milk. Add vanilla and then add 1 egg at the last. Turn into your favorite tube pan and bake in a 275-degree oven for 45 minutes. Then raise oven temperature to 325 degrees and bake for 30 more minutes.

Mrs. William Roscoe Johnson, III (Corella Rawls)

POUND CAKE

1 cup butter
1½ cups sugar

5 eggs
2 cups flour

Preheat oven to 350 degrees. Cream butter and sugar. Beat in eggs, one at a time. Fold in flour. Bake in greased and floured small tube pan for 1 hour.

Note: ¾ teaspoon mace may be added for a classic flavor.

Mrs. Richard Shelby (Annette Nevin)

RED VELVET CAKE

2½ cups plain flour
1½ cups sugar
1 teaspoon salt
1 teaspoon cocoa
1 cup buttermilk
1½ cups cooking oil

2 eggs
1 teaspoon vanilla
1 (1-ounce) bottle red food
   color
1 teaspoon vinegar
1 teaspoon soda

Heat oven to 325 degrees. Grease and flour three 9-inch cake pans. Sift flour, sugar, salt, and cocoa together. Add buttermilk, oil, eggs, and vanilla to dry ingredients. Mix well. Blend in red food color. Finally, mix vinegar and soda together and blend into other mixture. Mix only until well blended. Pour into pans and bake for 30-35 minutes. Cool. Frost with Cream Cheese Frosting (See Index), adding 1 cup broken pecans. Great Holiday addition!

Mrs. Larry Satterwhite—Birmingham, AL

ORANGE SLICE CAKE

2 cups chopped pecans	1 pound chopped dates
1 pound chopped orange slices	1½ cups sugar
1 cup butter	1 teaspoon soda
1 (3½-ounce) can coconut	½ cup buttermilk
4 eggs	2½ cups flour, divided

Mix well the dates, pecans, and orange slices. Add coconut and mix with ½ cup flour. In separate bowl, cream butter, eggs, and sugar. Add flour and buttermilk in which soda has been dissolved. Mix coconut, dates, pecans, and orange slices with creamed mixture. Bake in a well-greased tube pan at 350 degrees for 2 hours. Place a small pan of water in oven with cake. Let cake cool in tube pan and then turn out.

Note: Good with boiled custard poured over each slice.

Mrs. David Matthews (Mary Chapman)

OLD-FASHIONED LANE CAKE

1¼ cups butter or oleo	2 cups sugar
6 egg whites (save yolks for filling)	1 teaspoon soda
3 cups flour	1 cup buttermilk

Heat oven to 350 degrees. Grease and flour four 9-inch cake pans. Cream butter and sugar. Add 1 egg white at a time and 2 tablespoons flour alternately. Then add buttermilk, using last ¼ cup milk to dissolve soda. Bake until straw comes out clean. There will be four thin layers.

FILLING:

6 egg yolks	1 (4-ounce) can coconut
3 whole eggs	1 quart chopped nuts
2 cups sugar	½ cup bourbon
1 stick butter or oleo	
1 (12-ounce) box seedless raisins (grind, if desired)	

Combine yolks, eggs, sugar, and oleo in double boiler. Cook over simmering water until thick enough to spread. Add raisins, coconut, nuts, and bourbon. Cook a little longer and spread between layers. Yield: 1 9-inch cake.

Note: This recipe has been in the family for over 100 years.

Mrs. Ronald W. Laycock (Debbie Barton)

MAMA KATE'S GINGERBREAD

½ cup sugar
½ cup shortening
½ cup molasses
1 egg
1½ cups flour

1 teaspoon soda
1 teaspoon cinnamon
1 teaspoon ginger
1 teaspoon nutmeg
¾ cup boiling water

Preheat oven to 350 degrees. Cream sugar, shortening, and molasses. Add egg. Mix soda, cinnamon, ginger, and nutmeg with flour. Add to liquid mixture. Add boiling water last. Pour into 8 x 8-inch pan. Bake 25 minutes. Serve warm with lemon sauce.

LEMON SAUCE:

1 cup sugar
½ cup milk

½ stick butter
1 teaspoon lemon extract

Cook sugar, milk, and butter at low boiling for 5 minutes. Add lemon extract. Serve hot over gingerbread.

Mrs. William Dowling (Charlene Clary)

BUTTERMILK POUND CAKE

3 cups sugar
3 cups flour
1 cup butter
¼ teaspoon soda
1 tablespoon almond, rum, or
   lemon flavoring

½ teaspoon salt
1 cup buttermilk
6 eggs
1 tablespoon vanilla

Preheat oven to 325 degrees. Cream butter and sugar. Add eggs, one at a time, beating after each. Combine flour, soda, and salt, and add to creamed mixture alternately with buttermilk and flavorings. Bake 1½ hours in bundt pan.

Tip: Do all beating before adding flour, or cake will be tough.

Mrs. Alvin Michael Sella (Mary Lyle)—Birmingham, AL

Variation I: Sour Cream Pound Cake. Substitute 1 cup sour cream for buttermilk, omit almond, rum or lemon flavoring, if desired. Bake at 300 degrees for 1½ hours.

Variation II: Whipping Cream Pound Cake. Substitute 1 cup whipping cream for buttermilk and omit soda; omit almond, rum or lemon flavoring, if desired. Start cake in cold oven set at 325 degrees. Bake 1 hour 20 minutes.

Mrs. Paul Guthrie, Jr. (Donna Gortney)

MILKY WAY CAKE

8 Milky Way bars (for a total
  of 15-ounces)
½ cup melted butter
1½ cups sugar
½ cup softened butter
4 eggs

1 teaspoon vanilla
1¼ cups buttermilk
½ teaspoon soda
3 cups flour
1 cup chopped pecans

Combine candy bars and ½ cup melted butter in saucepan. Place over low heat until candy melts. Cream sugar and softened butter. Add eggs and beat well. Add vanilla. Combine buttermilk and soda, and add to creamed mixture alternately with flour. Beat well. Stir in candy and pecans. Pour batter into a greased and floured 10-inch tube pan. Bake at 325 degrees for 1 hour 20 minutes. Let cool in pan 1 hour.

MILK CHOCOLATE FROSTING:
2 cups sugar
1 cup evaporated milk
½ cup melted butter
1 (6-ounce) package semi-sweet
  chocolate bits

1 cup marshmallow creme
Milk

Combine sugar, milk, and butter in heavy saucepan. Cook over medium heat until a small amount dropped in cold water forms a soft ball. Remove from heat. Add chocolate and marshmallow and stir until melted.

Mrs. James Allen Randall (Kathleen Powers)

ITALIAN COCONUT CREAM CAKE

1 cup buttermilk
1 teaspoon soda
5 eggs, separated
2 cups sugar
1 stick oleo

½ cup shortening
2 cups flour
½ cup pecans
1 teaspoon vanilla
1 (4-ounce) can coconut

Heat oven to 350 degrees. Combine soda and buttermilk and set aside. Beat egg whites until stiff and set aside. Cream sugar, oleo, and shortening. Add egg yolks one at a time, beating after each. Add flour and buttermilk alternately, beginning and ending with flour. Add vanilla. Fold in egg whites gently. Fold in chopped pecans and coconut. Bake in three 9-inch pans or tube pan for 40 minutes. Ice with Cream Cheese Icing (See Index), adding ⅓ cup chopped nuts, if desired.

Mrs. Richard O. Jones (Cissie Roberts)

BOURBON PECAN CAKE

2 cups (1 pint or 16 ounces) whole
    red candied cherries
2 cups white seedless raisins
2 cups bourbon
2 cups (1 pound) softened butter
    or margarine
2 cups sugar

1 pound dark brown sugar
8 eggs, separated
5 cups sifted all-purpose flour
4 cups pecan halves
1½ teaspoons baking powder
1 teaspoon salt
2 teaspoons ground nutmeg

Combine cherries, raisins, and bourbon in large mixing bowl. Cover tightly and let stand in refrigerator overnight. Drain fruits and reserve bourbon. Cream butter well. Add sugar and brown sugar gradually. Add egg yolks and beat. Combine ½ cup of flour with pecans. Sift the rest of the flour with other dry ingredients. Add 2 cups of this to butter mixture, then add remainder alternately with bourbon. Beat well. Beat egg whites until stiff and fold in. Add drained fruits and floured pecans. Grease a 10-inch tube pan and a small loaf pan. Line with wax paper and grease and flour wax paper. Pour batter to 1 inch from top. Set oven at 275 degrees. Cook loaf cake 2 hours and tube cake 4½-5 hours. Test with toothpick. Cool in pan on rack 2-3 hours. Wrap in bourbon-soaked cheese cloth and foil or plastic wrap. Store in tightly covered container in refrigerator several weeks. Freezes well. Excellent for gifts.

Mrs. Max Bailey (Mary Julia Knight)

WHITE CHOCOLATE DESSERT

4 egg whites
1⅓ cups sugar
30 Ritz crackers
1 pint whipping cream

¼ cup confectioners' sugar
1 teaspoon vanilla
1 or 2 blocks white chocolate
    for garnish

Preheat oven to 325 degrees. Beat egg whites stiffly. Add sugar slowly and add crackers which have been crumbled by hand. Butter and flour a 2-quart casserole. Line casserole with egg white mixture. Bake for 25 minutes. Cool 2 hours. Whip cream, confectioners' sugar, and vanilla. Pour in cooled crust. Grate white chocolate over top and refrigerate overnight. Serves 8.

Mrs. Clarence Rice Baxter (Gin Jordan)

BANANA SPLIT À LA SPECIAL

5 bananas
3 sticks oleo
2 cups graham cracker crumbs
2 eggs
2 cups confectioners' sugar
1 (20-ounce) can crushed
   pineapple, drained

1 (13½ ounce) container Cool
   Whip
1 cup pecans
1 (6-ounce) jar cherries, chopped

Melt 1 stick of oleo and add to crumbs. Pat in bottom of 9 x 13⅓ Pyrex dish to make crust. Beat 2 sticks of oleo, sugar, and eggs in mixer for 15 minutes. Pour onto crumbs. Slice bananas over mixture. Pour pineapple over bananas. Spread with Cool Whip, sprinkle with pecans, and top with cherries. Chill several hours.

Note: Best to use this same day.

Mrs. Tony Smith (Susan Shirley)

EASY CHOCOLATE LAYER CAKE

4 ounces unsweetened chocolate
1 cup boiling water
2 cups sifted cake flour
2 cups sugar
1½ teaspoons salt

1 teaspoon baking soda
½ cup shortening
½ cup buttermilk or sweet milk
2 eggs

Preheat oven to 350 degrees. Pour boiling water over chocolate in large mixing bowl. Stir until melted. Sift flour, sugar, salt, and soda into bowl with chocolate. Add shortening. Beat until smooth. Add milk and egg and beat again. Grease and flour two 8 x 8-inch pans. Divide batter between pans and bake for 35-45 minutes, or until done. Cake pulls away from sides of pan slightly. Frost with Granny's Chocolate Icing or Fluffy Peppermint Icing (See Index).

Bert Wear

ORANGE DATE CAKE

1 cup butter
2 cups sugar
4 cups flour
1 teaspoon soda
4 eggs

1⅓ cups buttermilk
2 tablespoons grated orange rind
1 cup dates, chopped
1 cup pecans, chopped and lightly floured

Cream butter and 2 cups sugar. Sift flour and soda together. Add eggs, one at a time, to butter and sugar. Add buttermilk and flour alternately. Add 2 tablespoons orange rind. All this in mixer. By hand stir in dates. Add pecans to mixture. Bake in one loaf or bundt pan, or use 3 bread pans, greased and floured. Bake in 350-degree oven for 50 minutes (if 3 small pans) or 60 minutes (if bundt pan). Remove from oven and pour glaze over cake.

GLAZE:
½ cup orange juice
1 cup sugar

1 teaspoon orange rind

Mix orange juice, 1 cup sugar, and 1 teaspoon orange rind. Boil to dissolve and cool.

Mrs. George S. Shirley (Betty Bailey)

MY MOTHER'S WHITE FRUIT CAKE

¾ pound butter, softened
2 cups sugar
10 eggs
1 cup self-rising flour
3 cups cake flour, divided
1 teaspoon vanilla
2 tablespoons wine

2 pounds white raisins
1 pound crystallized pineapple, cut up
½ pound crystallized cherries, cut up
4 cups chopped pecans
1 cup wine

Heat oven to 250 degrees. Cream butter and sugar. Beat in eggs, one at a time, then add self-rising flour and 2 cups cake flour. Add vanilla and 2 tablespoons wine. Mix together the raisins, pineapple, cherries, and pecans and coat well with 1 cup cake flour. Add to creamed mixture. Mix well and pour into 10-inch tube pan which has been greased and lined with wax paper. Bake 2 hours 45 minutes, then raise heat to 300 degrees and bake 15 minutes longer. Cool in pan and then pour a cupful of wine over cake. Keeps well.

Mrs. Joseph Rowland (Nancy Burch)

FUDGE CAKE I

1 stick oleo
2 (1-ounce) squares unsweetened
chocolate
1½ cups sugar
2 eggs

1 cup flour
⅛ teaspoon salt
1 teaspoon vanilla
1 cup pecans, chopped

Melt margarine and chocolate; pour over sugar. Add eggs and mix. Add flour, salt, vanilla, and pecans. Spread into a 9 x 13-inch cake pan or two 9-inch round cake pans. Bake at 350 degrees for 35-40 minutes. Cut into squares. Yield: 18 squares.

Note: Unique—similar to a chewy brownie or delicious served with vanilla ice cream and chocolate sauce as a complete dessert.

Mrs. Frank E. Spell (Bell Searcy)

FUDGE CAKE II

1 cup oleo or butter
2 cups sugar
4 eggs
1⅓ cups flour
1 cup chopped pecans
3 (1-ounce) squares baking
chocolate

Pinch salt
1 teaspoon vanilla
1 (10-ounce) bag small marshmallows

For cake, melt oleo and chocolate together. Add sugar and beat well. Beat in eggs, one at a time. Add flour, nuts, and vanilla. Beat well. Pour into greased 9 x 13-inch pan. Bake at 350 degrees for 25-30 minutes. While warm from the oven, spread marshmallows on top and press onto cake with hand. Cool, then frost.

ICING:
1 stick oleo
2 (1-ounce) squares chocolate
1 teaspoon vanilla
1 (1-pound) box confectioners'
sugar

¼ cup evaporated milk (or
more)
1 cup toasted salted pecans

Melt oleo and chocolate. Add vanilla, sugar, and evaporated milk. Mix to consistency to spread. Spread over marshmallows and sprinkle with pecans.

Mrs. Ward McFarland (Frances Morrow)

PINK LEMONADE CAKE

1 2-layer size yellow cake mix
1 quart vanilla ice cream, softened
6 drops red food color
1 (6-ounce) can frozen pink lemon-
    ade concentrate, thawed, divided

1 cup whipping cream
2 tablespoons sugar

Prepare cake mix and bake in two 9 x 1½-inch round cake pans. Cool cakes. Stir ice cream to soften; quickly stir in red food coloring and ½ cup of lemonade concentrate. Spread ice cream mixture evenly in foil-lined 9 x 1½-inch round cake pan. Freeze 2-3 hours, until firm. Place one cake layer on serving plate, add ice cream layer, and top with second layer cake. Return to freezer. Whip cream with remaining lemonade concentrate and sugar until stiff. Then frost sides and top of cake. Return to freezer at least 3-5 hours. Yield: 12 servings.

Mrs. Joseph Vengrouskie (Mary Lucius Lunsford)

PLUM CAKE

2 cups self-rising flour
2 cups sugar
1 teaspoon cinnamon
1 teaspoon nutmeg

2 (4½-ounce) jars plum baby food
1 cup oil
3 eggs, beaten
1 or 2 cups chopped pecans

Preheat oven to 350 degrees. Mix together the flour, sugar, cinnamon, and nutmeg. Add plum baby food, oil, and beaten eggs. Add nuts. Just mix cake; do not beat it. Pour into a greased and floured 10-inch tube pan. Bake for 1 hour.

TOPPING:
½ stick butter or margarine
1 cup confectioners' sugar

Juice of 1 lemon

For topping, melt butter and mix together with sugar and lemon juice. Pour half on cake before removing from pan. Remove and pour remainder over top of cake.

Mrs. Carl Adams, Jr. (Jean Anders)

PRUNE CAKE

1¼ cups sugar	1 teaspoon nutmeg
1 cup oil	1 teaspoon cinnamon
3 eggs	1 teaspoon baking powder
1 cup buttermilk	1 teaspoon soda
2 cups flour	1 cup cooked prunes
1 teaspoon salt	1 cup chopped pecans

Heat oven to 350 degrees. Mix sugar, oil, and eggs. Sift flour, salt, nutmeg, cinnamon, baking powder, and soda together, and add to egg mixture alternately with buttermilk. Add prunes and pecans. Pour into greased and floured 9 x 13-inch pan. Bake 30-35 minutes. Ice while hot.

ICING:

½ cup buttermilk	1 tablespoon white corn syrup
1 cup sugar	½ stick oleo
½ teaspoon soda	1 teaspoon vanilla

Mix buttermilk, sugar, soda, corn syrup, and oleo and cook to a soft ball (234°F) stage. Remove from heat. Add vanilla and beat until thick enough to spread. Pour over hot cake.

Mrs. William Morris Abernathy (Gayle Snow)

NUT CAKE

1 cup sugar	¼ teaspoon salt
4 eggs	1 teaspoon vanilla
1 cup cake flour	1 pound chopped dates
1 teaspoon baking powder	1 quart chopped pecans

Preheat oven to 325 degrees. Grease brown paper; line 10-inch tube pan with the paper. Beat sugar and eggs until fluffy. Sift together flour, baking powder, salt. Add alternately with dates and pecans. Add vanilla. Pour into lined tube pan and bake for 1 hour.

Mrs. Eric Lee Wilson (Margaret Marshall)

SPICE CUPCAKES

1 pound seedless raisins
2 teaspoons baking soda
1 teaspoon nutmeg
¼ teaspoon allspice
2 teaspoons cinnamon
¼ teaspoon salt
3 cups sifted flour

1 cup raisin water
1½ cups sugar
½ cup solid shortening
2 eggs
1 teaspoon vanilla
1 teaspoon lemon extract
1 cup chopped nuts

Boil raisins with 3 cups water for 20 minutes, so that you end up with 1 cup raisin water. Heat oven to 350 degrees. Sift together soda, spices, salt, and flour. Cream shortening, then add sugar. Beat in eggs. Add flour combination alternately with raisin water. Add flavorings, nuts, and raisins. Bake for 15 minutes, or until done. Use paper muffin cups in muffin tins, filling them ½ to ¾ full.

Mrs. G. Locke Galbraith (Suellen Ridgely)

BIRTHDAY CAKE ICING

1 pound confectioners' sugar,
   sifted
½ cup Crisco (no substitute)
¼ teaspoon salt

2 or 3 drops butter flavor
1 teaspoon vanilla flavor
4 tablespoons milk or water

Combine sugar, Crisco, salt, flavors, and milk or water in a large mixer bowl. Beat at medium speed for at least 5 minutes, or until creamy. This frosting may be kept refrigerated for up to 6 months in an airtight container. To use, bring to room temperature and stir. Makes enough for a 2-layer cake.

Mrs. Thomas Fanning (Gail Weakley)

CREAM CHEESE FROSTING

1 (8-ounce) package cream cheese,
   softened
1 stick oleo
1½ (1-pound) boxes confectioners'
   sugar

1 teaspoon vanilla
⅓-1 cup broken or chopped
   pecans (optional)

Beat cream cheese, oleo, sugar, and vanilla until well mixed. Add nuts, if desired.

Mrs. Joe F. "Skip" Cannon (Diane Stansell)

FLUFFY WHITE ICING

⅓ cup water
1½ tablespoons light corn syrup
1½ cups sugar
½ teaspoon cream of tartar

⅛ teaspoon salt
2 egg whites
1½ teaspoons vanilla

Place in a saucepan or wide-bottomed tea kettle with pouring lip the water, corn syrup, sugar, cream of tartar, and salt. Stir over medium heat until sugar is completely dissolved. Put egg whites in large mixer bowl. Use whip attachment, if mixer has one. Beat on highest speed until egg whites begin to hold their shape. Continuing on high speed, pour hot syrup gradually into bowl in a fine stream (takes about 1-1½ minutes). Add vanilla and continue beating about 5 minutes or until frosting loses its sheen and will stand in stiff peaks. Frost cake immediately. Enough for three 8- or 9-inch layers.

Variations:
FLUFFY PEPPERMINT ICING: Crush enough peppermint stick candy to make 1 cup. Fold into icing before frosting cake.
FLUFFY LEMON ICING: Use 6 tablespoons water and add 2 table-spoons lemon juice and ¼ teaspoon grated lemon rind.

Mrs. Peterson Cavert (Mary Beth Wear)

SEAFOAM ICING

2½ cups brown sugar
½ cup water
2 egg whites
⅛ teaspoon salt

1 teaspoon vanilla
½ cup pecans, halves or
   chopped (optional)

In a heavy saucepan or wide-bottomed tea pot with pouring lip, mix brown sugar and water. Stir until dissolved and cook over medium heat to soft ball stage, 238 degrees on candy thermometer. In large mixer bowl, beat egg whites with salt until frothy. Pour the syrup over the egg whites in a thin stream, beating constantly. Add vanilla. Place bowl containing icing over boiling water. Beat until icing will hold a point. Spread between layers and on top and sides of two 9-inch layers. Sprinkle or place nuts in a decorative pattern on the top.

Variation: For **MOCHA ICING**, *add 1 teaspoon instant coffee to brown sugar-water mixture, or substitute brewed coffee for water.*

Elizabeth Overton Cravens

OLD FASHIONED CARAMEL ICING

3 cups sugar, divided
1 cup evaporated milk
2 sticks oleo

Pinch salt
1 teaspoon vanilla

Heat in a large boiler 2½ cups sugar, milk, oleo, and salt. Put ½ cup sugar in iron skillet. Stir this on low heat until it melts and turns brown. Then add this to contents in large boiler, stirring constantly. When well mixed, test with a cup of cold water by dropping small amount in water. Keep cooking and stirring until there is a soft ball in water than can be picked up (238 degrees on candy thermometer). Then remove from heat and add vanilla. Beat until right consistency to spread. Will ice sheet cake or 2-layer 8-inch cake.

Mrs. David McGiffert (Betty Jane Price)

LEMON CHEESE ICING OR FILLING

3 tablespoons cornstarch
¾ cup cold water
¼ cup freshly-squeezed lemon
  juice

1 cup sugar
2 egg yolks
2 tablespoons butter
Grated rind of 1 lemon

Mix cornstarch with water to make smooth paste. Cook in double boiler until thick, stirring constantly. Add lemon juice and continue cooking. When thick and smooth, add sugar which has been thoroughly mixed with egg yolks. Cook 3 minutes longer. Add butter and rind and beat until smooth. Cool. Spread on layers; will cover a 2-layer cake.

Mrs. Harry E. Marrs—Hueytown, AL

GRANNY'S CHOCOLATE ICING

2 cups sugar
½ cup milk
2 squares chocolate or 4 tablespoons cocoa

1 teaspoon vanilla
1 stick butter or margarine

Mix all ingredients in a boiler. Let come to a slow boil, stirring constantly. Then boil hard for 1 minute. Remove from heat and beat until it reaches spreading consistency. If desired, when using to frost a sheet cake, add 1 cup chopped nuts.

Mrs. Guy E. "Buddy" Moman, Jr. (Anne McAliley)

REAL BUTTER COOKIES

½ pound real butter, softened   2 cups plain flour
1 cup confectioners' sugar

In a large mixer bowl, combine butter, sugar, and flour. Beat well. Make one large or 2 small rolls, wrap in wax paper and refrigerate until cold enough to slice about ¼-inch thick. If dough gets too cold to slice well, let stand at room temperature about 10 minutes. Preheat oven to 350 degrees. Place sliced cookies on an ungreased cookie sheet and bake for about 10 minutes. Watch carefully, because butter burns easily.

Note: I have never served these that someone didn't want the recipe.

Elizabeth Overton Cravens

NANNA'S TEA CAKES

1 stick butter   3 cups plain flour
1 cup sugar   2 teaspoons baking powder
2 eggs   ¾ teaspoon salt
1 teaspoon vanilla

Cream together butter and sugar. Add eggs and vanilla and beat well. Sift together flour, baking powder, and salt and add to mixture. Refrigerate. Divide into three or four portions and roll quite thin. Cut with cookie cutter and bake at 375 degrees for about 12 minutes. Yields about 4 dozen 2½-inch cookies.

Mrs. Robert McCurley (Martha Ann Dawson)

TEA CAKES

1 stick butter or oleo, melted   ½ cup buttermilk with 1 tea-
1 cup sugar   spoon soda dissolved in it
1 egg   4-5 cups sifted flour
1 teaspoon nutmeg

Beat together butter or oleo, sugar, egg, nutmeg and buttermilk. Knead with flour until dough is stiff enough to roll out. Roll out ¼-inch thick and cut on floured surface. Bake in 325-degree oven until golden brown, about 12 minutes. Makes about 4 dozen 2½-inch tea cakes.

My grandmother had these at her grandmother's house, so it's truly an old recipe.

Mrs. Ronald W. Laycock (Deborah Barton)

BUTTER BRICKLE CRUNCH COOKIES

1½ cups sifted flour
½ teaspoon baking soda
½ teaspoon salt
½ cup butter
¾ cup brown sugar, packed

1 egg
1 teaspoon vanilla
1 (7.8-ounce) package Heath
 Brickle
⅓ cup chopped pecans

Sift flour, soda, and salt together. Cream butter. Add sugar, egg, and vanilla. Mix until smooth and creamy. Stir in dry ingredients, then blend in Heath Brickle and pecans. Drop by tablespoonfuls 2 inches apart onto greased baking sheets. Bake in 350-degree oven for 12-15 minutes. Remove from baking sheets; cool. Makes 3 dozen.

Note: Heath Brickle Chips are hard to find. Look for them with chocolate, butterscotch, and peanut butter chips. These are worth the search!

Mrs. Phil Graves (Leska Turner)

HOLIDAY COOKIES

1 pound butter (no substitutions)
1 cup sugar
1 egg

2 teaspoons vanilla
4½ cups flour, sifted

Cream butter and sugar. Add egg and vanilla. Gradually add the flour. Wrap dough in plastic wrap and refrigerate 2 hours.

Preheat oven to 375 degrees. Roll dough, one quarter at a time, to ⅛-inch thickness. Cut with cookie cutters in seasonal shapes. Bake on cookie sheets 6 to 8 minutes, or until very lightly browned. Let cookies cool, then frost.

ICING:
2 egg whites
¼ teaspoon cream of tartar
Pinch of salt

2 teaspoons vanilla
3 cups confectioners' sugar
Food color

Beat egg whites until stiff with salt and cream of tartar. Add vanilla. Add confectioners' sugar gradually. Beat until peaks form. Divide into 5 bowls; color 4. Ice cookies, using colored sugar, silver dragees, coconut, chocolate sprinkles, etc., as desired. Let dry. Store in airtight containers.

Note: Cold dough is extremely brittle, due to all the butter. Beat it with a rolling pin to soften. It gets more pliable as it is worked.

Mrs. Peterson Cavert (Mary Beth Wear)

SUGAR COOKIES

½ cup butter, softened
1 cup sugar
1 egg

2½ cups sifted flour (plain)
½ teaspoon soda

Preheat oven to 350 degrees. Cream butter and sugar together; add egg. Sift flour with soda, and add to first ingredients. Chill. Roll out and cut, or press through a cookie press. Bake until edges are brown, about 8-10 minutes. Makes 4 dozen.

Note: This recipe has been passed down through the Mathews family for years. This recipe can be doubled.

Mrs. E. S. "Brother" Harris, III (Frances Mathews)

SHORTNIN' BREAD

1 cup butter
1 cup oleo
1 cup pure lard
1 (1-pound) box confectioners'
    sugar

1 egg
⅛ teaspoon soda
9 cups flour, divided

Preheat oven to 300 degrees. Cream butter, oleo, and lard. Add sugar and beat until fluffy. Add egg and beat well. Add 4 cups flour, sifted with soda. Add remaining flour and mix with hands. Press in a 12 x 16 pan until ½-inch thick. Prick with fork and bake until light brown, about 50 minutes. Cut into squares while still warm. Cool in pan. Makes 6 dozen 1½-inch squares.

Note: Flavor improves with age. May be stored in tins for many weeks.

Mrs. Ronald Sanders (Betsy McNair)

PECAN CRISPIES

1 cup sugar
1 pound butter (4 sticks)
4 heaping cups self-rising flour

2 cups pecan pieces
3 teaspoons vanilla
Confectioners' sugar

Cream butter and sugar in electric mixer. Add flour, 1 cup at a time. Add pecans and then vanilla. Shape into balls or desired shape. Bake at 325 degrees for approximately 20 minutes. While still warm, put in bag of confectioners' sugar and shake. Makes about 3 dozen.

Mrs. Downey W. Walker (Sondra O'Neal)

ORANGE COOKIES

2½ cups flour
¼ teaspoon salt
2 teaspoons baking powder
1 cup shortening
¾ cup sugar
1 egg

1 cup cooked, mashed carrots
 (5 or 6)
¾ cup milk
1 teaspoon vanilla
1 teaspoon lemon flavor

Preheat oven to 375 degrees. Sift together flour, salt, baking powder. Cream shortening and sugar. Add egg, carrots, and milk. Mix well. Add sifted dry ingredients. Add flavorings. Drop by teaspoonfuls on greased cookie sheet. Bake until firm to touch and lightly browned. Cool on rack. Frost when cool.

ICING:
2 cups confectioners' sugar
1½ tablespoons butter, melted
1 teaspoon grated orange rind

4 tablespoons orange juice (or 2
 tablespoons orange juice and 2
 tablespoons orange liqueur)

Mix ingredients together and ice cookies. Adjust consistency with more sugar or juice as needed.

Bert Wear

GRANNY'S SUGAR COOKIES

1 stick butter
1 cup sugar
1 egg
2 cups flour

2 teaspoons baking powder
½ teaspoon salt
½ teaspoon vanilla

Cream butter and sugar together. Blend in egg. Sift together flour, baking powder and salt; add to mixture. Add vanilla. Roll out on floured surface and cut ,with cookie cutters. Bake at 400 degrees for 8-10 minutes on greased cookie sheet. Glaze while hot. Makes 4 dozen.

GLAZE:
¾ cup confectioners' sugar

3-4 teaspoons water

Blend together sugar and water. Spread on hot cookies. Add sprinkles or decorations.

Comment: Great recipe for making special occasion cookies with special children.

Mrs. Frank E. Spell (Bell Searcy)

OATMEAL-RAISIN COOKIES

1 cup butter	2 cups sifted flour
1 cup sugar	½ teaspoon salt
2 eggs, beaten	1 teaspoon cinnamon
1 tablespoon milk	1 cup raisins
¾ teaspoon soda	2 cups uncooked rolled oats

Preheat oven to 375 degrees. Cream butter and sugar. Combine well-beaten eggs and milk and mix with butter-sugar mixture. Sift together soda, flour, salt, and cinnamon. Gradually blend dry ingredients with creamed. Fold in raisins and oats. Drop by teaspoonfuls onto greased baking sheet. Bake 12 to 15 minutes. Makes 3 dozen.

Mrs. Richard O. Jones (Cissy Roberts)

JELLY COOKIES

½ pound butter	2 cups flour, unsifted
1 egg yolk	1 teaspoon vanilla
Pinch of salt	Jelly (currant or red plum)
½ cup sugar	

Cream butter and sugar. Add egg yolk, flour, salt, and vanilla. Mix well. Mold into small balls with hands. Press down with little finger in center. Place small amount of jelly in center. Bake at 375 degrees about 20 minutes or until cookies are light brown around the edges.

Mrs. Daniel M. Hoke (Gail Ford)

ORANGE-ALMOND MACAROONS

½ cup sugar	1 teaspoon vanilla
½ cup confectioners' sugar	2 egg whites
1 cup almond paste	2½ teaspoons grated orange rind
¼ teaspoon salt	

Mix sugars, blend gradually into almond paste. Add salt and vanilla. Add 2 egg whites, one at a time, mixing thoroughly. Stir in orange rind. Chill. Drop by spoonfuls on ungreased brown paper laid on baking sheets. Bake in a slow oven at 325 degrees for 20 minutes or until light beige in color. Cool; wet the underside of the paper by placing on a damp cloth. Cookies will peel off easily. Store tightly covered. Makes 4 dozen.

Mrs. Hugh Ragsdale, Jr. (Kate Webb)

CRESCENTS

1½ cups confectioners' sugar,
  divided
¼ vanilla bean (optional)
½ pound butter

2 cups pecans or walnuts
2 cups sifted cake flour
1 teaspoon vanilla

Bury the vanilla bean in 1 cup confectioners' sugar, cover, and let stand several days or at least overnight. This step is optional, but the results are worth it.

Cream butter with ½ cup confectioners' sugar. Very finely chop or grind nuts and add to butter mixture along with flour and vanilla. Use fingers or wooden spoon to mix into a smooth dough. Chill dough, then pinch off pieces, about 1 teaspoonful at a time, and shape into crescents. Place on ungreased cookie sheets and bake 10 minutes at 300 degrees, then raise heat to 325 degrees and bake 10 minutes longer. Remove from oven, cool, then roll in prepared vanilla sugar. Store in an air-right box. Will keep several weeks. Makes 4 dozen.

Mrs. James Hodo Walburn (Dean Frank)

GRANOLA COOKIES

1½ cups brown sugar
¾ cup oil
6 tablespoons buttermilk
1 teaspoon vanilla
1½ cups flour
½ teaspoon salt
¾ teaspoon soda
2 cups oats (preferably old
  fashioned)

¾ cup wheat germ
¼ cup sesame seed
¼ cup chopped almonds or
  peanuts
¼ cup shredded coconut
1 cup raisins, chopped dates, or
  chopped dried fruit (apricots,
  prunes, apples, or a mixture)

Preheat oven to 350 degrees. Combine brown sugar, oil, buttermilk, vanilla, flour, salt, and soda, mixing thoroughly. Combine remaining ingredients and mix well. Add to first mixture. Shape into balls about 1 inch in diameter and flatten on greased cookie sheet. Bake in preheated oven for 10-12 minutes or until slightly browned. Remove from oven and let cool on pan for 1 minute, then transfer cookies to wire rack to finish cooling. These get even better in a few days. Oats may be substituted for any or all of the wheat germ, sesame seed, nuts and coconut; then you have oatmeal cookies. Makes 4 dozen.

Mrs. Peterson Cavert (Mary Beth Wear)

KATHLEEN MAXWELL'S FRUIT COOKIES

1 pound candied pineapple
1 pound candied cherries
1 pound dates
6 cups nuts, broken
½ pound white raisins
3 cups flour, divided
1 teaspoon cinnamon

1 teaspoon nutmeg
3 teaspoons soda dissolved in 3 tablespoons milk
½ cup sherry
1 cup brown sugar
½ cup butter or oleo
4 eggs, separated

Preheat oven to 300 degrees. Cut pineapple, cherries, and dates into fine pieces. Mix pineapple, cherries, dates, nuts, and raisins with 1 cup flour. Sift remaining 2 cups flour with cinnamon and nutmeg. Cream butter and sugar. Add well-beaten egg yolks. Add flour-spice mixture. Alternate adding soda-milk and sherry. Stir in fruit-nut mixture. Beat egg whites until stiff and fold in fruit mixture. Drop on greased cookie sheet. Bake for 20 minutes in preheated oven. Makes 20 dozen. Delicious at Christmastime.

Mrs. George Wright (Stella Wellborn)

MRS. JAMES COOPER'S FRUIT DROPS

3 pounds candied cherries, chopped
2 pounds candied pineapple, chopped
5 quarts pecans, coarsely broken
1 pound margarine
1 pound sugar (2¼ cups)
10 eggs

1 wine glass wine or orange juice (¼ cup)
2 tablespoons dark corn syrup
1 teaspoon cinnamon
1 teaspoon allspice
1 teaspoon cloves
½ teaspoon salt
5 cups flour, divided

Mix chopped fruit and nuts with 1 cup of the flour. Cream margarine and sugar. Add 1 egg at a time and beat well. Add liquid and flour alternately. Mix batter with fruit and nut mixture. Drop small amounts of mix (use an ice-tea spoon) onto a lightly greased baking sheet. Bake at 275 degrees until light brown, about 25-30 minutes. Yield: *Dozens—enough for family and for gifts.*

Mrs. Guy Moman, Jr. (Anne McAliley)

MAMA'S APRICOT BALLS

½ pound dried apricots
2 cups Angel Flake coconut
½ cup sweetened condensed milk

4 cups sifted confectioners' sugar
1 tablespoon vanilla

Grind apricots and coconut together. Add milk to fruit mixture. Add sugar, a little at a time, until mixture holds together. Shape into marble-size balls and roll in remaining confectioners' sugar. So easy! and taste great!

Mrs. Larry Satterwhite—Birmingham, AL

ICE BOX COOKIES

1 cup white sugar
1 teaspoon salt
5 cups flour, sifted twice before
　measuring
1 cup shortening, melted

1 cup brown sugar
3 eggs, well beaten together
1 teaspoon soda
1 teaspoon nutmeg
1 cup chopped pecans

Add both sugars to melted shortening. Add beaten eggs. Sift flour, soda, nutmeg, and salt together. Add pecans to flour mixture, then add these ingredients to boiler mixture. Form 2 or 3 rolls. Put in refrigerator and chill. Cut to desired thickness, then bake at 350 degrees for 15 minutes. Note: Wrapped in wax paper or foil, this cookie dough will keep for about 2 weeks. Yield: 4 to 5 dozen.

Mrs. Downey W. Walker (Sondra O'Neal)

OLD FASHIONED CINNAMON COOKIES

1 cup butter (not margarine)
1 cup sugar
1 cup brown sugar
2 eggs
3½ cups sifted flour

1½ teaspoons cinnamon
1 teaspoon baking soda
⅛ teaspoon salt
1 cup broken pecans

Cream butter and sugars. Beat in eggs. Blend in sifted flour, cinnamon, baking soda, and salt. Stir in nuts. Drop from teaspoon about 1½ inches apart onto a lightly greased baking sheet. Bake at 350 degrees for 8 to 10 minutes. Remove from sheet while warm and put on paper towel to dry out in one single layer. Turn over if other side is damp and let dry. Yield: 4 dozen.

Mrs. Peyton Cochrane (Jamie Banks)

MRS. BENNETT'S CHINESE CHEWIES

1 pound box brown sugar, light or
   dark
3 eggs
1 teaspoon vanilla
1 stick margarine, melted and
   cooled

2 cups plain flour
2 teaspoons baking powder
1 cup chopped nuts (pecans)

Beat eggs, add brown sugar, vanilla, and melted margarine. Then add a little at a time the flour, baking powder, and chopped pecans. Grease and flour a 9 x 13-inch pan. Spread batter in prepared pan. Bake 30-40 minutes at 350 degrees. Check center, and if not done, cook longer. Let cool; cut into squares. Makes about 30 squares.

Mrs. Gene Bennett (Belle Walter)

OLD FASHIONED DATE COOKIES

4 eggs
2 cups sugar
1 teaspoon vanilla
4 tablespoons flour

2 teaspoons baking powder
1 cup chopped pecans
1 cup chopped dates

Beat eggs and sugar. Add vanilla. Sift flour and baking powder together. Add chopped nuts and dates to flour and baking powder. Combine the flour mixture with the eggs and sugar. Spoon onto very lightly greased baking sheet. Bake at 350 degrees. Watch *closely* so they won't burn. Cookies will spread; be large, thin and crispy. Makes several dozen.

Mrs. Leon Sadler, III (Dana McNeill)

MARTHA WASHINGTON COOKIES

2 egg whites
¾ cup brown sugar (light)

1 teaspoon vanilla
1 cup pecan halves

Beat egg whites until foamy. Gradually add brown sugar and vanilla, and continue beating until stiff peaks are formed. Fold in pecan halves. Drop with teaspoon on lightly greased or Teflon cookie sheet. Bake 45 minutes at 250 degrees. Upon removal, place cookie sheet out of draft until cookies cool. Yield: 3 to 4 dozen.

Mrs. Victor M. Friedman (Segail Irwin)

SPRITZ COOKIES

1 cup shortening
¾ cup sugar
1 egg
1 teaspoon vanilla

2¼ cups sifted all-purpose flour
¼ teaspoon salt
½ teaspoon baking powder
1 cup nuts, chopped

Preheat oven to 350 degrees. Cream shortening. Add sugar and cream until light. Add egg and beat. Add vanilla, flour, salt, baking powder, and nuts. Drop by teaspoonfuls onto ungreased cookie sheet. Bake in preheated oven until lightly browned, about 9 minutes.

Mrs. Fred Maxwell (Kathleen Searcy)

SCOTCH SHORTBREAD

½ pound butter, softened
½ cup confectioners' sugar

2 cups plain flour

Mix butter and sugar. Gradually add flour. Mix well. Pinch dough into small balls and place on ungreased cookie sheet and flatten to about ½ inch or so. Bake at 300 degrees for 30 minutes.

Mrs. Melford Espey, Jr. (Becky Flowers)

CHOCOLATE CHIP-OATMEAL COOKIES

1½ cups flour
1 teaspoon baking soda
1 teaspoon salt
1 cup shortening (not butter or
   margarine)
¾ cup granulated sugar

¾ cup brown sugar, packed
1 teaspoon vanilla
2 eggs
1½ cups semi-sweet morsels
2 cups quick-cooking oats

Preheat oven to 375 degrees. Sift together flour, soda, and salt; set aside. Blend shortening, sugar, and vanilla. Beat in eggs. Add flour mixture and mix well. Stir in semi-sweet morsels and oats. Drop by well-rounded half teaspoonfuls onto greased cookie sheet. Bake for 10-12 minutes. Makes 8 dozen.

Ruth Tisdale Wilder

GLITTER COOKIES

1 cup margarine	4 cups plain flour
1½ cups confectioners' sugar	1 teaspoon cream of tartar
1 cup sugar	1 teaspoon salt
1 cup cooking oil	1 teaspoon baking soda
2 eggs, beaten	Colored sugar crystals
1 teaspoon vanilla	

Beat together sugars, margarine and oil until light and fluffy. Add eggs and vanilla and beat well. Sift flour, cream of tartar, salt, and baking soda together and mix well. Chill overnight. Roll into small balls and place 3 inches apart on ungreased cookie sheet. Flatten and sprinkle with colored sugar crystals. Bake at 375 degrees for 10 minutes. Makes 6 dozen.

Mrs. Winfrey Sanderson (Annette Harrison)

FUDGE SQUARES

2 sticks butter (*no* substitute)	½ teaspoon soda
4 squares of baking chocolate	1 teaspoon cream of tartar
4 eggs	Pinch of salt
2 cups sugar	1 heaping cup chopped nuts
2 teaspoons vanilla	(pecans or English walnuts)
2 cups sifted cake flour, very	Confectioners' sugar
slightly rounded	

Preheat oven to 350 degrees. Sift flour, soda, cream of tartar, and salt together. Melt together butter and chocolate at low temperature in heavy saucepan and set aside to cool. Beat eggs only until yolks and whites are thoroughly blended. Gradually add sugar. Continuing to beat, add melted butter and chocolate and mix well. Add vanilla, then fold in sifted dry ingredients. Stir in nuts with a spoon and pour the mixture evenly into a well-greased and floured cake pan. (This amount is right for a rectangular pan measuring approximately 10 x 15 inches.) Place on middle rack of oven. Bake at 350 degrees for 20 minutes. Do not overcook! Cake should be moist inside. Remove from oven and sift confectioners' sugar over top. Cut into squares immediately and place on wax paper to cool. Store in tins. Rich!—Fattening!

Mrs. Hoyt Winslett (Louise Fargason)

GERMAN CHOCOLATE BROWNIES

50 light caramels
1 cup evaporated milk, divided
  in half
1 (18.5-ounce) package German
  chocolate cake mix

¾ cup margarine
1 cup chopped nuts
1 cup chocolate chips

Combine caramels and ½ cup evaporated milk in top of double boiler. Cook over low heat until caramels melt. Combine cake mix, margarine, remaining ½ cup evaporated milk and nuts. Lightly grease 9 x 13-inch pan. Spread ½ cake mixture in pan. Bake in 350-degree oven for 6 minutes. Remove from oven. Sprinkle chocolate chips over partially-baked cake mixture. Then spread caramel mixture over chips. Drop the remaining cake mixture by tiny spoonfuls over the caramel mixture. Bake 5 minutes. Remove from oven and spread to make a top layer. Return to oven and bake 13 minutes longer. Cool before cutting.

Mrs. Eric Lee Wilson (Margaret Marshall)

CREAM CHEESE BROWNIES

2 (4-ounce) packages of Baker's
  German Sweet Chocolate
10 tablespoons butter, divided
2 (3-ounce) packages cream cheese
2 cups sugar, divided
6 eggs, at room temperature

1 cup plus 2 tablespoons unsifted
  all-purpose flour
3 teaspoons vanilla
1 teaspoon baking powder
½ teaspoon salt
1 cup coarsely chopped nuts
½ teaspoon almond extract

Melt chocolate and 6 tablespoons butter over low heat and cool. Cream remaining butter with cheese until soft. Gradually cream in ½ cup sugar. Blend in 2 eggs, 2 tablespoons flour, and 1 teaspoon vanilla. Beat 4 eggs until thick, adding remaining 1½ cups sugar, baking powder, salt, and 1 cup flour. Stir into chocolate mixture the nuts, 2 teaspoons vanilla, and almond extract. Spread *half* in greased 13 x 9-inch pan. Add remainder alternately with cheese mixture. Zigzag spatula through batters to marble. Bake at 350 degrees for about 40 minutes. Cool, cut into bars. May be frozen.

Mrs. Richard Thigpen (Mary Ann Anderson)

EASY SURPRISE BROWNIES

1 box family-size brownie mix
  (22½ ounces)
Marshmallows (enough to cover
  top of brownies)
1 stick butter or oleo
4 tablespoons cocoa

6 tablespoons milk
1 box confectioners' sugar
  (1 pound)
1 teaspoon vanilla extract
1 cup pecans

Make brownies according to directions on box. When they are done, remove from oven and stand marshmallows on top. Put back into warm oven until marshmallows are soft enough to spread. Then put on the following icing: Put into saucepan the oleo, cocoa, and milk. Bring to a boil and remove from heat. Add confectioners' sugar, pecans, and vanilla. Beat well and spread on brownies while hot. When icing sets and brownies are cool, cut into squares.

Mrs. Jerry L. Carnes (Burns Levy)

GOLD RUSH BROWNIES

2 cups graham cracker crumbs
1 (14-ounce) can sweetened
  condensed milk

1 (6-ounce) package chocolate bits
1 cup chopped pecans
Pinch of salt

Mix all ingredients together. Grease 8-inch square cake pan, put wax paper in bottom of pan, and grease again. Add mixture to pan. Bake at 350 degrees for 40 minutes. When removed from oven, take out of pan at once and cut into pieces then. You must follow directions or will be a flop. These are good, but even better a day old. Makes 36 pieces.

Variation: For Butterscotch Brownies, substitute a 6-ounce package of butterscotch bits for chocolate bits.

Mrs. Robert E. McCoy (Brenda Magruder)

BISQUICK BROWNIES

2 cups Bisquick
4 eggs
1 box light or dark brown sugar

1 cup pecans, chopped (or
  coconut or raisins)
½ teaspoon vanilla

Preheat oven to 325 degrees. Grease 9 x 13-inch pyrex pan with butter. Beat eggs and mix with Bisquick and brown sugar. Add chopped pecans and vanilla. Bake for 25 minutes. Watch, as they burn easily. Cut while hot; let cool in pan.

Mrs. Joe G. Burns, Jr. (Jo Del Laney)

CANDIED FRUIT BARS

2 cups chopped pecans
1 stick butter
1⅓ cups dark brown sugar
2 eggs, well beaten
1 cup cake flour
1 tablespoon vanilla

½ pound candied cherries, cut finely
6 slices candied pineapple, cut finely
½ pound candied orange peel, cut finely

Preheat oven to 300 degrees. Grease and flour an 8x13-inch pan. Sprinkle pecans over bottom of pan. Cream butter with sugar; then add eggs, flour, and vanilla. Pour this mixture over nuts. Mix together the cherries, pineapple, and orange peel. With wet hands, press fruit over mixture in pan. Bake in preheated oven for 1 hour. Makes 4 dozen.

Mrs. Joseph Rowland (Nancy Burch)

PEANUT BUTTER DELITE

1¼ sticks butter, softened
1 cup peanut butter
1 cup graham cracker crumbs
¾ pound confectioners' sugar

1 (6-ounce) package chocolate chips
1 ounce paraffin

Mix butter and peanut butter in 9 x 13-inch pan. Add crumbs and sugar and mix well. Pat firmly in bottom of pan. Melt chocolate chips and paraffin over hot water in double boiler. Pour over crumb mixture and spread. When cool, cut in 1-inch squares. Freezes well.

Mrs. David M. Jones (Janet White)

CHOCOLATE MINT STICKS

3½ squares unsweetened chocolate, divided
1½ sticks butter, divided
1 cup granulated sugar
2 eggs, beaten
¼ teaspoon peppermint extract

½ cup flour
Pinch salt
2 tablespoons butter, melted
1 cup confectioners' sugar
1 tablespoon cream

Preheat oven to 325 degrees. In double boiler, melt 2 squares chocolate and ½ cup (1 stick) butter. Stir in granulated sugar, beaten eggs, peppermint extract. Add flour and salt and mix well. Pour into 9-inch square pan and bake 25 minutes in preheated oven. Cool. Melt 2 tablespoons butter and add confectioners' sugar and cream. Spread over cooled cake. Melt in double boiler 1½ squares chocolate and 2 tablespoons butter. Drizzle on top. Cut into oblong pieces. Keep in refrigerator.

Mrs. John C. Boles (Donna Waters)

LYNN ADAMS' CREAM WAFERS

1¼ cup soft butter, divided
⅓ cup thick cream
2 cups sifted flour
¾ cup sifted confectioners' sugar

1 egg yolk
1 teaspoon vanilla extract
Granulated sugar

Cream 1 cup butter with cream and flour. Chill. Preheat oven to 375 degrees. Roll out ⅓ of dough at a time on floured board to ⅛-inch thickness. Cut with small round cookie cutter and place on ungreased cookie sheet. Sprinkle with granulated sugar and prick each twice with fork. Bake 7 to 9 minutes. (Don't let them get too brown.) Cool. Blend ¼ cup soft butter, confectioners' sugar, egg yolk, and vanilla extract. Put filling between two wafers. Store in tightly shut tin in refrigerator or freezer. Freezes well. Makes 4 dozen.

Mrs. Thomas W. Moore (Stella Hillard)

LEMON SQUARES

2 sticks real butter, softened
½ cup confectioners' sugar
2¼ cups flour, divided
2 cups granulated sugar

4 eggs
1 tablespoon grated lemon rind
½ cup fresh lemon juice
Confectioners' sugar

Preheat oven to 350 degrees. Mix by hand the butter, ½ cup confectioners' sugar, and 2 cups flour. Press mixture into greased 9 x 13-inch pan. Bake 20 minutes. Meanwhile, mix granulated sugar, ¼ cup flour, eggs, lemon rind and juice. Pour over crust. Bake 25 minutes longer. Sprinkle with confectioners' sugar while hot. Cool. Cut into squares.

Mrs. William H. Darden (Caroline Sullivan)

PRINCESS SQUARES

1 cup fig preserves
½ cup butter
1 cup sugar
1 egg

2 cups flour
1 cup coconut
1 cup nuts
¼ teaspoon vanilla

Preheat oven to 350 degrees. Mash fig preserves. Mix butter and sugar together, add egg and flour. Last, add vanilla, coconut and nuts. Put ½ this mixture on bottom of 9 x 9-inch pan. Add mashed figs, spreading evenly over dough. Then put on top layer of dough over figs. Bake until lightly browned, about 25 minutes. This can be served as cookie or as a pudding, topped with whipped cream.

Mrs. Ward McFarland (Frances Morrow)

KISSES

3 egg whites
Pinch of salt
¼ teaspoon cream of tartar

1 cup sugar
1 teaspoon flavor (see below)
2 cups filling (see below)

Preheat oven to 300 degrees. Beat egg whites until stiff but not dry with salt and cream of tartar. Add sugar gradually, beating, and beat until peaks form. Add flavoring. Fold in filling. Drop on greased and floured cookie sheet or on wax paper by teaspoonfuls. Bake until lightly browned, about 20 minutes. Makes about 3 dozen.

Flavor should enhance filling flavors. Suggested fillings: broken nut-meats, chopped dates, chocolate chips, crushed peppermint candy, crushed crackers, cornflakes, coconut or desired combinations. Try 1 cup broken pecans, 1 cup chocolate chips with orange flavor. Tint if desired for holiday party. Store in airtight container when cool.

Mrs. Peterson Cavert (Mary Beth Wear)

KENTUCKY BOURBON CANDY

1 stick butter or margarine,
　softened
1 pound confectioners' sugar
¾ cup finely chopped pecans

1½ jiggers bourbon
1 large package semi-sweet
　chocolate bits
1 to 1½ square inches paraffin

Saturate ¾ cup finely chopped pecans in bourbon about 2 hours in a covered jar. In a blender, blend softened butter or margarine with confectioners' sugar. Blend well. Add pecans to sugar-butter mixture. Roll into small balls and chill. Melt chocolate in top of double boiler with paraffin. Dip balls into chocolate and put into refrigerator to dry.

Mrs. Max Bailey (Mary Julia Knight)

CANDIED PECANS

2 cups pecan halves
1 cup sugar
5 tablespoons water

1 teaspoon cinnamon
¼ teaspoon salt
1¼ teaspoons vanilla

Toast pecans in moderate oven (350 degrees) on baking sheet for 5-8 minutes. Mix together sugar, water, cinnamon, and salt. Cover and bring to a boil. Uncover and cook to the soft ball stage (234 degrees on candy thermometer). Remove from heat and add vanilla and nuts. Stir until mixture sugars. Spread on wax paper. When cool, break apart. Store in airtight container.

Mrs. Mallory Burkhalter (Patty O'Neal)

TOFFEE CANDY

2 sticks butter, no substitute
1 cup sugar
1 tablespoon light corn syrup
3 tablespoons water
1½ cups chopped walnuts or
   almonds (3 3-ounce packages),
   divided

1 large Hershey milk chocolate
or 6 (1.2-ounce) bars

Slowly melt butter in heavy 2-quart saucepan. Stir in sugar gradually. Add corn syrup and water. Cook and stir over moderate heat until mixture reaches 290 degrees on candy thermometer. Add 1 cup nuts. Cook 1 or 2 minutes more, stirring constantly. Pour in pan which has been lined with wax paper. When cool, melt half of chocolate over hot water in double boiler. Spread over candy and sprinkle with half of remaining nuts. When this hardens, flip over and melt other chocolate and spread. Sprinkle with remaining nuts. When this hardens, break into pieces. Can be put into refrigerator to speed hardening.

Bert Wear

Hint: On rainy or humid days, cook candy 2 degrees higher than indicated in recipe.

DIVINITY

2½ cups sugar
⅛ teaspoon salt
⅓ cup white corn syrup
⅔ cup water

2 egg whites
1 teaspoon vanilla
Pecan halves (optional)

In saucepan or wide-bottomed tea or coffee pot with pouring spout, combine sugar, salt, corn syrup, and water. Cook over low heat, stirring until sugar dissolves. Bring to a boil. In electric mixer bowl, beat egg whites until stiff but not dry. Meanwhile, continue boiling syrup until it spins a thread when dripping the mixture from a spoon (230 degrees on candy thermometer). Then pour syrup slowly over egg whites, beating until the mixture begins to lose gloss and holds its shape. Add vanilla. Drop by teaspoon on wax paper and top with a pecan half immediately. Yield: 4 dozen.

Note: Do not make in rainy weather.

Mrs. Cary J. Williams (Jimmie Ellen Black)

STRAWBERRIES

1 (1-pound) box pitted dates
1 stick butter
1 cup canned coconut
1 cup sugar
2 eggs
Dash of salt

3 cups Rice Krispies cereal
1 cup pecans, chopped
2 teaspoons vanilla
3 (3¼-ounce) cartons red sugar
1 tube of green decorating icing

Chop dates. Melt butter. Mix butter, sugar, eggs, and salt. Add dates and coconut to butter mixture and cook over medium heat about 10 minutes, stirring constantly. Next, add cereal, pecans, and vanilla. The mixture will be thick and sticky. Remove from stove and let cool slightly. Shape into strawberries. Roll strawberries in red sugar until completely coated with sugar. Make "leaves" on strawberries with green icing. Store in an airtight container. Makes 3 to 4 dozen depending on size.

Mrs. Leon Sadler III (Dana McNeill)

PECAN CLUSTERS

1 (7-ounce) jar marshmallow
   creme
1½ pounds milk chocolate kisses
5 cups sugar

1 (13-ounce) can evaporated milk
½ cup butter
6 cups pecan halves

Place marshmallow creme and kisses in a large bowl; set aside. Combine sugar, milk, and butter in a saucepan. Bring mixture to a boil, then cook for 8 minutes. Pour over marshmallow cream and kisses, stirring until well blended. Stir in pecans. Drop by teaspoonfuls onto wax paper.

Mrs. William F. Barnes, Jr. (Diane Manderson)

PRALINES

5 cups sugar, divided
1 cup milk

1 pound shelled pecan halves
1 stick butter

Place 4 cups sugar and milk in a heavy pot and *slowly* bring to a boil. While this is coming to a boil, melt 1 cup sugar in a black iron skillet, then pour into milk and sugar mixture. Bring back to a boil. Add pecans and cook to soft ball, 238 degrees, stirring with a wooden spoon or spatula, about 10-12 minutes. Remove from heat. Add butter and beat well. Spoon out on wax paper. Make small drops, as this is very rich candy. Makes about 70.

Mrs. Gordon Miller, Jr. (Leslie Johnson) and
Lester LeBlanc, a professional Cajun cook—Baton Rouge, LA

CREME FUDGE

1 (5- to 10-ounce) jar marshmallow
creme
⅔ cup evaporated milk
¼ cup butter
1½ cups sugar

¼ teaspoon salt
12 ounces Nestle's semi-sweet
morsels
1 teaspoon vanilla
½ cup nuts

Bring to a full boil, stirring constantly, the marshmallow creme, milk, butter, sugar, and salt. Boil for 5 minutes over medium heat. Remove from heat; add semi-sweet morsels, vanilla, and nuts, and stir until chocolate is melted. Pour into greased 8 x 8 x 2-inch pan. Chill well, at least overnight.

Mrs. Harry Marrs—Hueytown, AL

ROCKY ROAD CANDY SQUARES

1 (12-ounce) package semi-sweet
chocolate morsels
1 (14-ounce) can sweetened
condensed milk

2 tablespoons butter or margarine
2 cups dry toasted peanuts
1 (10-ounce) package miniature
marshmallows

Over boiling water in top of double boiler, melt chocolate morsels with condensed milk and butter. In a large mixing bowl, combine marshmallows and nuts. Fold in melted chocolate mixture. Pour into a 13 x 9-inch glass dish *lightly* greased with butter. Chill at least 2 hours or until firm enough to cut smoothly. Cut into squares. May be kept at room temperature in a covered container.

Note: At holiday time, slice red cherries thinly and place on top for color—good, too!

Mrs. John Hunter Plott (Terria Wood)

PEANUT BRITTLE

1½ cups sugar
½ cup white corn syrup
½ cup water
2 cups raw peanuts

¼ block paraffin, scant
1 tablespoon butter
2 teaspoons soda

Cook sugar, corn syrup, water, peanuts, paraffin, and butter in a 3-quart saucepan until hard crack stage (300 degrees on candy thermometer). Mixture will be brown in color, and peanuts stop popping—about 10 minutes. Add soda and stir well. Mixture will foam. Spread on buttered pan. Cool. Break into pieces.

Bert Wear

CANDIED CITRUS PEEL

2 cups citrus peel   Granulated sugar

Run whole fruit lightly over fine grater to release flavor oils. Halve or quarter fruit and peel. Cut peel with scissors into ¼-inch strips. Measure 2 cups. Place in heavy saucepan. Cover with 1½ cups cold water. Bring slowly to the boiling point. Simmer 10 minutes (15 minutes for grapefruit peel). Drain well. Repeat boiling process 3 times, draining well each time. For each cup of peel, make syrup of ¼ cup water and ½ cup sugar. Add peel. Boil until all syrup is absorbed and peel is transparent. Let cool slightly. Roll in granulated sugar. Spread on racks to dry.

Note: Stores well in covered tin. Good for gifts—wonderful party addition.

Mrs. William J. Gibson, Jr. (Susan Swaim)

FUDGE

3 cups sugar   ½ can of water
3 tablespoons cocoa   ½ stick oleo
3 tablespoons white corn syrup   1 teaspoon vanilla
Pinch of salt   1 cup broken nuts
1 (5.33-ounce) can evaporated milk

Combine in a heavy saucepan the sugar, cocoa, corn syrup, salt, milk, water, and oleo. Bring to a boil slowly. Cook until soft ball stage or 238 degrees on candy thermometer. Add vanilla. Let cool before beating. (It doesn't have to be cold; just don't beat right off the fire.) As fudge thickens, add nuts. Beat until thick and not glossy. Pour into buttered 9 x 9-inch pan. Cut when cold.

Mrs. Charles S. Watson (Juanita Goodman)

PEANUT BUTTER FUDGE

2 cups sugar   3 heaping tablespoons peanut
½ cup milk   butter
2 tablespoons butter   1 teaspoon vanilla
3 heaping tablespoons marsh-
  mallow creme

Bring sugar, milk, and butter to a boil and boil 3 minutes. Add marshmallow creme, peanut butter, and vanilla. Beat with a spoon until stiff. Add nuts if you wish. Pour into a buttered 8 x 8-inch pan and let cool until firm enough to cut smooth.

Mrs. Mark Bergaas (Mary Emmons)

NUT CARAMELS

2 cups sugar
2 cups light corn syrup
Dash salt
½ cup oleo

2 cups evaporated milk
1 teaspoon vanilla
¾ cup chopped pecans

Combine sugar, syrup and salt in a 3-quart saucepan. Boil, stirring occasionally, until syrup is very thick, 310 degrees on candy thermometer. Add oleo and slowly stir in evaporated milk. Stirring constantly, cook rapidly to firm ball stage, 246 degrees. Remove from heat. Add vanilla. If mixture curdles, beat a minute or two. Add nuts, stir, and pour into greased 9 x 9-inch cake pan. Let stand until cold. Cut into ½-inch squares. Wrap individually with wax paper. Keeps well for 3 months. Excellent for gifts. Makes 300 + pieces.

Bert Wear

CHRISTMAS CANDY

6 cups sugar
1½ cups white corn syrup
1½ pints whipping cream

Vanilla
1 pound English walnuts, shelled
  (2 pounds unshelled)

Combine sugar, syrup, and cream in large preserving kettle and cook at a medium-high temperature, stirring constantly, until the mixture boils. Reduce heat to medium. Continue to cook without stirring until firm balls can be formed in cold water (242 degrees on candy thermometer). Let stand about 15 minutes. Add vanilla and beat until creamy. Pour over walnuts spread in large 9 x 13-inch buttered pan. Cut into pieces and wrap in waxed paper. Store in tight container and let ripen 1 to 2 weeks. Makes 5 pounds.

Mrs. Max Bailey (Mary Julia Knight)

Pickles
and
Preserves

FOURTEEN DAY PICKLES

2 gallons sliced cucumbers
(¼-inch thick)
1 gallon boiling water
2 cups pure salt (without non-
caking material or iodine added)
3 gallon crock or churn (that
hasn't ever had any fat or milk
in it) or glass or uncracked
enamelware

1 gallon boiling water
1 gallon boiling water
3 tablespoons powdered alum
1½ quarts vinegar (4 to 6%
acetic acid)
12 cups sugar
2¼ tablespoons pickling spice

Wash cucumbers and cut in ¼-inch slices. Add cucumbers, 1 gallon boiling water, and salt to crock. Weight cucumbers down with a plate or saucer and cover crock with a thin linen towel. Check each day and remove any scum if it forms, so that the top layer of pickles will not spoil or weaken the acidity of the brine. Let stay in the brine 7 days.

8th day: Remove cucumbers and pour out brine. Place cucumbers back in empty container and add 1 gallon boiling water.

9th day: Remove cucumbers and pour out water. Put cucumbers back into empty container. Add 1 gallon boiling water mixed with 3 tablespoons powdered alum.

10th day: Remove pickles from alum water. Make syrup of vinegar, sugar, and pickling spice which has been placed in a cheesecloth bag. Boil for 4 minutes and pour over cucumbers.

11th day: Pour off syrup, reheat and pour back over cucumbers.

12th day: Same as 11th day.

13th day: Same as 11th day.

14th day: *Pour off syrup. Pack cucumbers in sterilized canning jars. Boil syrup 4 minutes and pour over cucumbers in jars. Adjust lids. Process in boiling water bath canner (212 degrees F.) for 5 minutes.

Note: At this point if necessary they can be left in the crock by merely repeating the 11th day and leaving covered until you are ready several days later to process. These pickles make super gifts and are a favorite of ours to give at Christmastime. I cut a circle of red gingham with pinking shears just large enough to extend 1 inch beyond ring on each jar. Place gingham over lid and tighten ring back down. Presto! A cute packaging idea! Chill before eating.

Allen and Harriet Mattox (Harriet Marrs)

RED CINNAMON PICKLES

7 pounds large yellow cucumbers
1 cup lime
3 cups white vinegar, divided
1 (2-ounce) bottle red food
  color

1 tablespoon alum
6½ cups sugar
8 sticks cinnamon
1 large package red cinnamon
  candies

Peel and seed cucumbers. Soak 24 hours in 1 cup lime to 1 gallon water. Drain, rinse, and soak in ice water for 3 hours. Mix 1 cup vinegar, food color and alum with enough water to cover cucumbers. Pour mixture over cucumbers in pot and simmer 2 hours. Pour off liquid. In another pot, boil 2 cups vinegar, 2 cups water, sugar, cinnamon sticks and candy until candy melts. Pour over cucumbers. Let stand 24 hours. Pour off liquid into another pot and bring to boiling again. Meanwhile, pack cucumbers in warm jars. Pour syrup over cucumbers in jars and seal. Process in water bath canner (212 degrees F.) for 10 minutes.

Mrs. Carl Adams, Jr. (Jean Anders)

SWEET AND SOUR PICKLES

1 quart plain dill pickles, sliced
  (save juice)
1½ cups sugar

½ cup vinegar
½ teaspoon mustard seed

Drain juice from pickles and set aside. Place sliced pickles in a bowl and cover with sugar. Let soak overnight. Then, place pickles back in jar. Heat juice, vinegar, and mustard seed to a boiling point and pour over pickles.

Mrs. Thomas Fanning (Gail Weakley)

GARLIC PICKLE

1 gallon whole sour pickles
5 pounds sugar
1 (2-ounce) box peppercorns

1 (2½-ounce) box mustard seed
8 cloves garlic

Drain pickles and then slice them about ¼ inch thick. In the gallon jar, layer pickles, sugar, peppercorns, mustard seed, and garlic until all is used up. Pack the pickles down so they all will fit with the lid on. Turn jar over each day until all the sugar has melted. Then let sit in jar for 1-2 weeks. You can put in smaller containers which make great Christmas gifts.

Mrs. William H. Tucker (Harriet Belle Little)

MAMAW'S BREAD AND BUTTER PICKLE

1 quart onions, sliced
4 quarts cucumbers, sliced
½ cup salt
3 pints vinegar

3 cups sugar
4 teaspoons mustard seed
4 teaspoons celery seed

Put onions and cucumbers in a glass, pottery, or enamel container and sprinkle with salt. Let stand 1 hour. Drain and rinse. In enamel or stainless kettle, mix vinegar, sugar, mustard seed and celery seed. Bring to a boil and boil 5 minutes. Add cucumbers and onions. Stir. Bring back to a boil and boil 5 minutes. Pack in hot sterilized jars. Seal while hot. Process in water bath canner (212 degrees) for 10 minutes. Makes 8-10 pints.

Mrs. Hugh Underwood (Ginger Puryear)

GARLIC DILL PICKLES

Pickling cucumbers (not more
 than 5 to 6 inches long)
½ gallon white vinegar
½ gallon water
1 cup uniodized salt

1 teaspoon alum
8 flowers of dill
8 cloves garlic
8 pods of red pepper (optional)

Place cucumberss in clean container with very hot water. They should be hot through and through; add more hot water if necessary. Bring to a boil the vinegar, water, salt, and alum. In each of 8 quart jars, put a dill flower, a clove of garlic, and a pod of pepper. Fill jars with hot cucumbers and pour boiling liquid over them. Seal. Process in a water bath canner for 5 minutes (212 degrees). Makes 8 quarts.

Mrs. David Hefelfinger (Virginia Mauney)

SWEET STICK PICKLES

Pickling cucumbers
3¾ cups vinegar
3 tablespoons uniodized salt
4½ teaspoons turmeric

3 cups sugar
4½ teaspoons celery seed
¾ teaspoon mustard seed

Use fresh, firm medium cucumbers. Wash and cut lengthwise into quarters. Pour boiling water over them and let stand overnight. Next morning, pack solidly into sterilized jars. Mix in an enameled, stainless, or glass kettle the salt, turmeric, sugar, celery seed, and mustard seed. Boil for 5 minutes. Pour hot mixture over cucumbers. Seal while hot. Process in a water bath canner (212 degrees F.) for 5 minutes. Makes 6 pints.

Mrs. David Hefelfinger (Virginia Mauney)

SLICED CUCUMBER PICKLE

4 pounds fresh cucumbers
(weighed after being peeled
and sliced thin)
2 pounds sliced onions
½ gallon vinegar
3 pounds light brown sugar

6 red pepper pods, cut up
2 tablespoons mustard seed
2 tablespoons celery seed
2 tablespoons grated horseradish
1 tablespoon turmeric
6 tablespoons best olive oil

Sprinkle cucumbers and onions with salt; let stand 18 hours. Drain and rinse with cold water. In an enameled kettle, mix vinegar, sugar, pepper, mustard seed, celery seed, horseradish, and turmeric. Boil 10 minutes. Add cucumbers and onions, bring back to boil and boil 10 minutes. Remove from heat. When quite cold, add olive oil. Put in jars and seal. Process in simmering water bath canner (190 degrees F.) for 5 minutes.

Note: This is an old recipe I got from my aunt.

Elizabeth Overton Cravens

ICICLE STICKS

7 pounds large ripe (yellow)
cucumbers
2½ cups builder's lime
2 gallons water
4 ounces alum
2 gallons water
2 quarts clear, distilled vinegar

1 quart water
1 tablespoon salt
2 tablespoons mixed whole
pickling spices
5 pounds sugar (10 cups)
Red or green food coloring
(optional)

First day: Begin the process at 7:00 p.m. Use 7 pounds of very large cucumbers that have been peeled, seeded, and cut into sticks not longer than the jars you plan to use. Soak cucumbers in lime water for 24 hours. Use 2½ cups lime in 2 gallons of water.
Second day: At 7:00 p.m., take cucumbers out of lime water. Wash in clear water several times. Soak in alum water for 12 hours. Use 4 ounces of alum in 2 gallons of water.
Third day: At 7:00 a.m., remove cucumbers from the alum water. Wash thoroughly!! Soak in clear water for 6 hours. Make a syrup of vinegar, water, salt, pickling spices (tied in a cloth bag), and sugar. Bring syrup to a boil and pour over well-drained cucumbers. Let stand 4 hours. Bring to a boil and cook until pickles are transparent or clear, about 30 minutes. Remove spices. Add as much red or green food coloring as you wish. (I usually use red, since I use for gifts done up in red gingham as described under 14-Day Pickles.) Pack into pint jars and process in water bath canner (212 degrees F.) for 10 minutes.

Mrs. Allen Mattox (Harriet Marrs)

ICED THREE-DAY PICKLE

7 pounds cucumbers	1 stick cinnamon
2 cups household lime	1 teaspoon whole cloves
4 tablespoons alum	1 teaspoon ginger
5 pounds sugar	1 teaspoon celery seed
3 pints vinegar	1 teaspoon whole allspice

First day: Wash and slice cucumbers. Mix well 2 gallons water and lime. Let cucumbers soak 24 hours. Add ice to water.
Second day: Wash cucumbers well. Mix alum with 2 gallons water. Let cucumbers soak in alum water 24 hours.
Third day: Wash cucumbers well. Make syrup of sugar, vinegar, cinnamon, cloves, ginger, celery seed, and allspice. Boil 5 minutes and pour over cucumbers. Let stand 3-4 hours. Then simmer 1 hour. Pack in hot sterilized jars and seal. Process in water bath canner (212 degrees F.) for 10 minutes.

Note: Use churn or other non-metallic container for soaking pickles. Cook in enamel container. Add a little more vinegar if needed. Pickles will be clearer if spices are put into cheesecloth bag when making syrup. Ice is not absolutely necessary, but I find pickles crisper when ice is added several times a day to soaking water.

Mrs. David Mathews (Mary Chapman)

RUTH'S BREAD-AND-BUTTER PICKLES

4 quarts medium cucumbers (about 6 pounds sliced)	4½ cups sugar
	1½ teaspoons turmeric
1½ cups onion (12 to 15 small white ones, or about 1 pound sliced)	1½ teaspoons celery seed
	2 tablespoons mustard seed
	3 cups clear, distilled vinegar
2 large garlic cloves	
⅓ cup salt	
1 to 2 quarts ice, crushed or cubed	

Wash cucumbers thoroughly, using a vegetable brush, and drain on rack. Slice unpeeled cucumbers into ⅛-inch to ¼-inch slices. Add onions, garlic, and salt; cover with crushed ice or ice cubes, mix thoroughly, and allow to stand for 3 hours. Drain thoroughly and remove garlic. Combine sugar, spices, and vinegar; heat just to a boil. Add cucumber and onion slices and heat 5 minutes. Pack loosely into clean, hot, pint standard canning jars. Adjust lids. Process in boiling water bath canner (212 degrees F.) for 5 minutes. Yields 7 pints.

Ruth G. Kirkpatrick

PRESERVED BRANDIED FRUIT

10½ cups sugar
3 quarts water
½ cup orange liqueur (can substitute peach or any other you
  prefer)
¼ cup brandy
*Zest of 3 lemons, grated
3 fresh peaches, halved and
  peeled

3 fresh nectarines, halved and
  peeled
3 fresh plums, whole but prick
  in 3 or 4 places with a skewer
3 fresh Bartlett pears, halved
  and peeled (or unpeeled, as
  you prefer)
3 small clusters seedless green
  grapes

Combine sugar and water in a large heavy kettle or Dutch oven. Stir over medium heat until sugar is dissolved and mixture comes to a full rolling boil. Boil for 5 minutes more, remove from heat. Stir in liqueur, brandy, and lemon. Arrange fruit in hot sterilized quart jars and pour hot syrup over fruit. Screw lids on jars but not too tightly. Place in hot water bath and process for 25 minutes (212 degrees F.). Count processing time when water begins to boil. Remove from water bath, tighten lids and cool away from drafts. Makes 3 quarts.

Note: This can be doubled if you have a very large kettle in which to boil the syrup. What a lovely gift this makes, particularly at Christmastime when good fruit is hard to find. This is lovely done in old-fashioned glass canning jars with rubber rings and wire clips.

Zest refers to the colored portion of the rind only—not the white portion, as it is bitter.

Allen and Harriet Mattox (Harriet Marrs)

TABITHA HINTON'S ARTICHOKE PICKLE

1 peck Jerusalem artichokes
15 buds garlic
15 small hot red peppers
15 small or medium onions, sliced

1 gallon white vinegar
8 cups granulated sugar
½ cup uniodized salt

Pack fifteen pint jars with artichokes, cut up or whole, layered with onion rings. Add to each jar 1 bud garlic and 1 red pepper. Combine vinegar, sugar, and salt in saucepan and bring to a boil. Pour hot syrup into packed jars. Seal and process in water bath canner (212 degrees F.) for 15 minutes. Makes 15 pints.

Mrs. Hugh Underwood (Ginger Puryear)

WATERMELON RIND PICKLES

2 pounds prepared watermelon
   rind
Lime water made from 1 quart
   water and 1 tablespoon
   builder's lime
1 quart clear, distilled vinegar,
   divided

1 cup water
5 cups sugar (2½ pounds)
1 tablespoon whole allspice
1 tablespoon whole cloves
6 small pieces stick cinnamon

Trim outer green skin and pink portions from watermelon rind. Cut in desired size and soak for 2-3 hours in lime water. Drain and rinse rind. Cover it with fresh cold water and boil for 1 hour, or until tender. Drain the watermelon. Cover with weak vinegar solution (1 cup vinegar to 2 cups water), and allow to stand overnight. Discard the liquid the next morning and make a syrup of 3 cups remaining vinegar, 1 cup water, sugar, and spices. Heat syrup to simmering point. Remove from heat, cover and steep for 1 hour to extract flavor of spices. Add the drained watermelon to syrup and cook gently for 2 hours or until syrup is fairly thick. Pack in pint standard canning jars. Adjust lids and process in boiling water bath canner (212 degrees F.) for 15 minutes.

Note: Must be cooked in enamel or stainless steel or pickles will turn dark!

Mrs. Haskell Nevin (Sister Woodfin)

"B'S" PEACH PICKLES

2 gallons peaches*
4 cups sugar
1 quart clear, distilled vinegar

2 cinnamon sticks
1 tablespoon whole cloves
1 tablespoon whole allspice

Select firm fruit. Wash well. Remove the thin skin carefully and drop peaches at once into syrup made by cooking sugar, vinegar, and spices until slightly thick. Let stand overnight. Drain off liquid and boil again until slightly thick. Then add fruit. Do not stir but keep fruit under syrup until tender. Pack while hot into hot, sterilized canning jars. Cover with syrup. Adjust lids. Process in a boiling water bath canner (212 degrees F.) for 10 minutes. Yields approximately 8 quarts.

*Preferred varieties: Hiland, Cardinal, Dixie Red, Cornet or Redcap.

Hint: Peaches peel easily if dropped into boiling water for 10 seconds.

Miss Carrie B. Allen

GREEN TOMATO PICKLE

5 pounds green tomatoes	7 cups sugar
1 cup slack lime	½ small box whole stick
2 cups cold water	cinnamon
1 quart vinegar	1 teaspoon allspice

On first day, wash, core, and slice green tomatoes into plastic container. Mix lime and cold water. Pour over sliced tomatoes. Add enough cold water to cover tomatoes completely. Tilt and move container to assure mixture of lime solution and water. Cover and place in refrigerator. Soak for 24 hours.

On second day, wash well both sides of tomatoes with brush under cold running water. Place tomatoes in clean plastic container. Mix together the vinegar and sugar. Pour over tomatoes. Cover and place in refrigerator for 24 hours.

On third day, pour vinegar and sugar mixture off tomatoes into large stainless steel cooking utensil. Add sticks of cinnamon and allspice. Bring to a full boil, add tomatoes, and continue to boil slowly for 40 minutes. Arrange tomato slices in hot sterilized jars and pour syrup to the top of the jar. Seal well. Process in water bath canner (212 degrees F.) for 10 minutes. Allow to stand, as flavor increases with time.

Mrs. E. Calhoun Wilson (Gene Henderson)

PICKLED YELLOW SQUASH

8 cups yellow squash	2 cups white vinegar
2 cups onions	3 cups sugar
4 bell peppers	2 teaspoons mustard seed
¼-½ cup uniodized salt	2 teaspoons celery seed

Cut squash, onions, peppers into circles and mix with salt. Place plate on top to cover and weight it down for 1 hour. (Salt makes squash release liquid.) Drain in colander (do not rinse) and pat dry with paper towel. Mix in large kettle the vinegar, sugar, mustard seed, and celery seed. Boil and add squash, onions, and bell pepper. Then pour into sterile jars and seal. Process in water bath canner (212 degrees F.) for 10 minutes. Yield: 8 pints.

Note: Zucchini may be substituted for yellow squash. Good Christmas gifts!

Mrs. Russell "Rusty" Quarles (Paula Fink)

UNCLE JOHN'S DILLED OKRA

4 teaspoons dill seed
4 hot red peppers
4 hot green peppers
8 cloves garlic
1 quart white vinegar

½ cup uniodized salt
1 cup water
2 pounds small okra (must fit in
  jar without cutting)

Into each of 4 sterilized pint jars, put ½ teaspoon dill seed. Wash okra. Leave ¼ inch of stem on okra. Pack okra tightly in jars, being careful not to bruise. Add 1 red and 1 green pepper and 2 cloves garlic to each jar, then ½ teaspoon dill seed on top. Bring to a boil the vinegar, salt, and water. Pour hot mixture over okra in jars. Seal. Allow to stand at least 2 weeks before eating. Makes 4 pints.

Mrs. Peterson Cavert (Mary Beth Wear)

During the summer canning and freezing season, time does run so "short". Try freezing your juices for jelly- and jam-making in ice trays and drop frozen cubes in a plastic bag until later when there will be more time for jelly-making. Besides, jelly tastes better when made fresh and in small "batches". Take out just the number of cubes you will need. They thaw so much quicker than a pint or quart of juice. If you don't have enough juice (as all ice tray cubes vary in size), it only takes a few minutes for another cube or two to thaw!

PEPPER JELLY

½ cup green and red hot peppers,
  finely chopped
¾-1 cup bell pepper, finely
  chopped

6½ cups sugar
1½ cups apple cider vinegar
1 (6-ounce) bottle Certo
Food color, if desired

In a large saucepan, bring peppers, sugar, and vinegar to a *hard rolling* boil. Remove pan from heat and cool for 5 minutes. Add Certo and food color. Pour into sterilized jars. (I usually add all green, but at Christmastime I halve the mixture with red and green.) Makes about 12 baby food jars, or 4-5 half-pint jelly jars.

Note: For a clearer jelly, put peppers in a cheesecloth bag. Jalapeno peppers may be used for the hot peppers. This is a must with cornbread! Also delicious with cream cheese used as a spread on crackers.

Mrs. William E. "Brother" Oliver (Sue Kelly)

SOFT JELLY TO HARD JELLY

PER QUART OF SOFT JELLY:

4 teaspoons *powdered* pectin

¼ cup water

¼ cup sugar

1 quart of jelly

Mix pectin in water, bring to a boil, add sugar and jelly, boil rapidly, stirring thoroughly and constantly to prevent scorching. Bring to a full rolling boil over high heat, continuing to stir; boil for ½ minute. Remove jelly from heat, skim, pour into hot containers and seal.

PER QUART OF SOFT JELLY:

2 tablespoons *liquid* pectin

2 tablespoons lemon juice

¾ cup sugar

Bring jelly to boiling over high heat, quickly add the pectin, lemon juice, and sugar and bring to a full rolling boil. Stir constantly. Boil mixture hard for 1 minute. Remove jelly from the heat, skim, and pour into hot containers and seal.

USDA Bulletin #56

PEAR PRESERVES

1½ cups sugar

3 cups water

6 medium hard-ripe pears, cored, pared, and cut in halves or quarters (about 2 pounds before preparing)

1½ cups sugar

1 lemon, thinly sliced

Combine 1½ cups sugar and water; cook rapidly 2 minutes. Add pears and boil gently for 15 minutes. Add remaining 1½ cups sugar and lemon, stirring until sugar dissolves. Cook rapidly until fruit is clear, about 25 minutes. Cover and let stand 12 to 24 hours in a cool place. Pack fruit into hot canning jars, leaving ¼ inch head space. Cook syrup 3 to 5 minutes, or longer if too thin. Pour boiling liquid over fruit, leaving ¼ inch head space. Adjust lids. Process half-pints and pints 20 minutes at 190 degrees F. in simmering hot-water bath.

Variation: A piece of preserved ginger may be added to each jar when filling to make Gingered Pear Preserves.

Mrs. Haskell Nevin (Sister Woodfin)

SUE'S STRAWBERRY PRESERVES

3 cups strawberries   Water
3 cups sugar

Wash and hull (cap) firm ripe berries. Place in large heavy boiler 1½ cups of strawberries, 1½ cups sugar and add just a small amount of water to start sugar melting. Bring to a rapid boil, stirring constantly with wooden spoon. When a full rolling boil is reached, time for 1½ minutes, then add remainder of strawberries and sugar. Bring back to a full rolling boil and time for 1½ minutes more. Pour into a flat enameled pan, cover, and let stand in a cool place for 24 hours to allow berries to plump. Stir several times when passing berries during the 24 hours. Then the next day add the cold preserves to hot canning jars. Adjust jar lids. Process in boiling water bath canner (212 degrees F.) for 20 minutes.

Mrs. T. T. Pike, Sr.

STRAWBERRY-FIG JAM

4 cups figs   3 cups sugar
½ cup water
2 (3-ounce) packages strawberry
   gelatin

In a heavy saucepan, combine figs and water and boil 2 minutes. Remove from heat and mash figs. Add gelatin and sugar. Boil 2 more minutes. Pour into hot sterilized jars and seal.

Note: Easy and very good! DO NOT DOUBLE this recipe!

Mrs. William P. Patton (Pat Armstrong)

PEAR HONEY

1 pound ground pears (1½ cups)   1 teaspoon lemon juice
¼ cup canned crushed pineapple   1½ cups sugar

Wash, peel, and core fruit. Put pears through a food chopper or food processor, using coarse blade. Mix pears, pineapple, lemon juice, and sugar; heat mixture, stirring thoroughly until sugar is dissolved. Boil mixture until it is thick and clear. Pack in hot canning jars. Adjust lids. Process in a boiling water bath canner (212 degrees F.)—pints and quarts, for 10 minutes.

Mrs. Allen Mattox (Harriet Marrs)

FIG PRESERVES

1 gallon figs	2 lemons, sliced
1 cup baking soda	8 cups sugar (or 4 cups sugar and
Boiling water	1 quart honey or corn syrup)

Select only perfect figs which are ripe but not soft. They may be peeled or not, according to taste. If not peeled, sprinkle baking soda over figs, cover in boiling water, let stand 5 minutes, and drain. Place figs and sugar in alternate layers in an enamel or aluminum boiler. Let stand overnight. Next morning, lift the figs out of the syrup which formed during the night. Bring syrup to boil. Drop figs into boiling syrup a few at a time. Add lemons and cook until figs are tender, transparent, and amber colored (about 1-1½ hours). Pack while hot into hot canning jars. Adjust lids. Process in boiling water bath canner (212 degrees F.) for 10 minutes.

Mrs. Allen Mattox (Harriet Marrs)

MUSCADINE SYRUP

2½ pounds muscadines	⅓ cup corn syrup
1¾ cups sugar	1 tablespoon lemon juice

Wash and crush muscadines. Cook over low heat 10 to 20 minutes. Put through a food mill or sieve; discard hulls and seeds. Measure 1½ cups purée in a saucepan; add sugar, corn syrup and lemon juice. Bring to a full boil and boil 2 minutes. Remove from heat, remove foam and pour into hot sterilized jars, leaving ¼ inch headspace. Adjust lids. Process in boiling water bath (212 degrees F.) for 10 minutes. Makes about 1½ pints.

Note: Wonderful gift.

PLUM SAUCE

½ gallon wild plums	1 teaspoon cinnamon
5 cups sugar	1 teaspoon cloves
1 teaspoon allspice	1 cup vinegar

Cover plums with water and boil for 5 minutes. Pour off water and add sugar, allspice, cinnamon, cloves, and vinegar. Boil 30 minutes, stirring constantly. Pour into hot sterilized jars. Seal while hot. Makes 3-4 pints.

Note: Good with beef, fowl, game. Warn guests of seeds!

Mrs. William A. "Butch" Hughes (Betty Blondheim)

SPICED FIGS

3 quarts figs
6 cups sugar
1 cup cider vinegar
1 cup water

2 tablespoons broken cinnamon
sticks
2 tablespoons whole cloves

Cover figs with water and let stand 5 minutes. Mix sugar, vinegar, water, cinnamon, and cloves (tie spices in a cheesecloth bag), and bring to a boil. Add drained figs, return to boil, and simmer 10 minutes. Let stand 24 hours. *Second day:* Bring to a boil and simmer 10 minutes. Let stand 24 hours. *Third day:* Bring to a boil and simmer 10 minutes. Remove spice bag. Pack in sterile jars. Process in a boiling water bath canner (212 degrees F.) for 10 minutes.

Note: Delicious addition to relish tray. Also good as an accompaniment to pork or venison.

MUSTARD

1 cup dry mustard
¾ cup white wine vinegar
⅓ cup water
¼ cup granulated sugar
2 tablespoons brown sugar, packed
2 teaspoons onion salt
½ teaspoon turmeric

1 teaspoon caraway seed
(optional)
⅛ teaspoon cayenne pepper
2 eggs, slightly beaten
1 tablespoon prepared horseradish (optional)

Mix mustard, vinegar, water, sugars, onion salt, turmeric, caraway seed and cayenne in top of double boiler, (use glass, enamel, or stainless steel), and let stand, covered, for 6 hours or overnight.

Bring water in bottom of double boiler to simmer. Add eggs to mustard mixture and cook over simmering water, stirring constantly, until thickened, about 10 minutes. Stir in horseradish. Pour into sterilized jars and seal. Cool. Refrigerate. Keeps 3 months or more in refrigerator.

Note: Packed in baby food jars, this and a loaf of homemade bread is a nice Christmas gift—instant turkey sandwiches!

Mrs. Peterson Cavert (Mary Beth Wear)

SHORT-CUT CHILI SAUCE

3 quarts tomatoes, peeled and
  chopped
3 cups celery, chopped
2 cups onion, chopped
1 cup green pepper, chopped
¼ cup salt

2 cups sugar
¼ cup brown sugar
1½ teaspoons pepper
1½ teaspoons mixed pickling
  spices
1 cup white vinegar

Combine tomatoes, celery, onion, green pepper, and salt. Let stand over-night. Drain in colander, but do not press vegetables. Place vegetables in a large kettle and add sugars, pepper, spices tied in a bag, and vinegar. Bring to a boil, reduce heat and simmer, uncovered, for 15 minutes. Ladle into hot canning jars. Adjust lids and process in a boiling water bath (212 degrees F.) for 10 minutes. Makes 5½ pints.

Mrs. Haskell Nevin (Sister Woodfin)

TOMATO CATSUP

1 gallon sliced very ripe tomatoes
5 tablespoons salt
½ tablespoon cayenne pepper
½ tablespoon black pepper
1 teaspoon mace
1 teaspoon allspice

1 teaspoon cinnamon
1 teaspoon cloves
2 large onions
1 quart vinegar
1 tablespoon dry mustard

Combine in a large saucepan the tomatoes, salt, peppers, mace, allspice, cinnamon, cloves, onions, vinegar, and dry mustard. Cook until all in-gredients are done and mixture is thick. Strain and pour into hot sterilized canning jars. Adjust lids. Process in boiling water bath canner (212 degrees F.) for 10 minutes.

Mrs. Thomas W. Moore (Stella Hillard)

EASY RIPE TOMATO RELISH

2 quarts ripe tomatoes
½ cup vinegar
1 teaspoon salt
1 cup sugar

1 cup onion, chopped
½ cup bell pepper, chopped
2 or 3 hot peppers, chopped

Peel and quarter ripe tomatoes. Add vinegar, salt, sugar, onion, bell pep-per, and hot pepper. Cook over low heat until the consistency of catsup, about 2 hours. Seal in hot sterile pint jars. Makes 4 pints.

Mrs. Jay W. Anderson (Ruby Hurst)

ARTICHOKE RELISH

6 quarts Jerusalem artichokes
6 pounds white cabbage
3 pounds white onions
1 cup uniodized salt
10 bell peppers
2 tablespoons black pepper
6 tablespoons white mustard seed

4 tablespoons turmeric
3 pounds light brown sugar
3 pounds white sugar
24 ounces French's mustard
4 quarts apple cider vinegar
2 cups flour

Cut the cabbage, onion, and green pepper into thin slices; soak in salt water (1 cup salt to 1 gallon water) overnight. Wash artichokes in water until clean. (May need to scrub with a soft brush.) Soak whole artichokes in clear water overnight. Make a paste of pepper, mustard seed, turmeric, sugars, mustard, cider vinegar, and flour. Bring to a boil and boil for 20 minutes, *stirring constantly*. Drain sliced vegetables and dry *thoroughly* with towels. Add vegetables to paste and cook slowly for 30 minutes, stirring often. Add thinly sliced artichokes and heat thoroughly. Seal in sterilized jars. Makes 26-28 pints.

Note: The full recipe requires a container of approximately 20 quarts. It may be divided into 2 containers, or the recipe may be halved.

Mrs. Sam Phelps (Mary Ann Peak)

INDIA RELISH

4 quarts green tomatoes
1 medium-sized cabbage
15 white onions
6 green peppers
1 cup uniodized salt
3 quarts white vinegar
4 pounds brown sugar
1 tablespoon turmeric

¼ cup (scant) ground black
  pepper
1 ounce celery seed
½ pound white mustard seed
¼ pound Coleman's mustard
1 cup olive oil
1 teaspoon curry powder
1 quart vinegar

Chop fine the tomatoes, cabbage, onions, and peppers. Mix with salt and let stand overnight. Drain and add vinegar, brown sugar, turmeric, pepper, celery seed, and mustard seed. Boil 20 minutes in large enamel kettle. Remove from heat. When cool, add mustard, olive oil, curry powder, and 1 quart vinegar. Pack in pint jars. Let stand for a month before using. Makes 15-18 pints.

Note: The above is a recipe given by an English army officer who spent many years in India.

Elizabeth Overton Cravens

JANET'S GARDEN SPECIAL

4 quarts ripe tomatoes
1 quart celery
1 quart onions
1 quart water

6 green peppers
3 tablespoons salt
2 tablespoons sugar

Peel and quarter tomatoes and reserve. Dice celery, onions, and peppers very coarsely. Add water to vegetable mix and cook for 20 minutes. Add tomatoes and seasonings. Adjust seasonings to taste. Bring mixture to a boil and pack in hot sterile jars. Process in hot water bath canner (212 degrees F.) for 30 minutes for quarts, 25 minutes for pints. Makes about 7 quarts.

Note: This is wonderful to have on hand. It's a perfect base for casseroles, soups, and stews. I make a chicken soup by cooking chicken pieces in the Garden Special and adding a handful of egg noodles. Easy and so good. It adds a new dimension to spaghetti sauce.

Mrs. Mark Bergaas (Mary Emmons)

PEAR RELISH

1 peck hard pears
6 large onions
6 red sweet peppers
6 green sweet peppers
6 hot red peppers
3 cups sugar

1 tablespoon uniodized salt
5 cups vinegar
1 tablespoon ground allspice
1 tablespoon mustard seed
1 tablespoon celery seed

Wash, peel, and core pears. Remove seeds and stems from red, green, and hot peppers. Put through food grinder or chop fine in food processor fitted with steel blade the pears, onions, red, green, and hot peppers. In a large enamel or stainless pot, mix ground vegetables with sugar, salt, vinegar, allspice, mustard seed, and celery seed. Let stand at least 8 hours or overnight. Bring to a boil and cook, stirring occasionally, for about 10 minutes. Pack in hot sterilized jars leaving ¼ inch head space. Seal. Process in boiling water bath (212 degrees F.) for 20 minutes. Makes 10-12 pints.

Mrs. Peterson Cavert (Mary Beth Wear)

HOT PEPPER RELISH

20 red hot peppers	1 tablespoon uniodized salt
20 green hot peppers	2½ cups vinegar
15 medium onions	2½ cups sugar

Put peppers, discarding seeds, and peeled onions through food chopper, or use food processor fitted with steel blade. Add salt; cover with boiling water and let stand 10 minutes. Drain liquid and discard. Add vinegar and sugar to vegetables. Bring to a boil and simmer 20 minutes. Ladle into hot canning jars; adjust lids at once. Process in boiling water bath (212 degrees F.) for 5 minutes. Remove jars from canner and complete seals. Makes 6 pints.

Mrs. Haskell Nevin (Sister Woodfin)

THELMA'S SWEET CHESTNUT RELISH

1 orange, thinly diced	½ cup walnuts, halves or pieces
1 cup raisins	¾ cup maple syrup
1 apple, diced (with skin)	1½ cups water
1 pound boiled and peeled	¾ cup brown sugar
chestnuts	1 teaspoon cinnamon

Simmer orange, raisins, syrup, sugar, water, and cinnamon together for 20 minutes. Add chestnuts, walnuts, and apple and simmer 5 minutes more. Pack in jars and seal. Makes 1½ pints.

Note: Good as a dessert sauce or with meat.

Mrs. Mark Bergaas (Mary Emmons)

EGGPLANT RELISH

2 small eggplants	1 (6-ounce) can tomato paste
2 bell peppers, chopped	1 (8-ounce) can tomato sauce
2 onions, chopped	½ cup olive oil
2 cloves garlic, chopped	1 cup wine vinegar
1 bottle salad olives, drained	⅓ cup sugar

Dice eggplants, unpeeled, and steam until soft. While eggplant is steaming, sauté onions, bell pepper, and olives in olive oil. Then add eggplant, tomato paste, tomato sauce, vinegar, and sugar and bring to a boil. Cook a few minutes. Cool. Serve cold.

Mrs. Gordon Miller, Jr. (Leslie Johnson) and
Lester LeBlanc, a professional Cajun cook—Baton Rouge, LA

FRESH GARDEN RELISH

5 medium tomatoes
1 medium onion, finely chopped
1 bell pepper, finely chopped
2 stalks celery, finely chopped
1 tablespoon horseradish
(prepared)

2 teaspoons salt
Dash pepper
¾ cup white vinegar
½ cup sugar
1 teaspoon mustard seed
⅛ teaspoon ground cloves

Peel tomatoes and seed. Chop fine. (Should have about 3 cups.) Combine tomatoes, chopped onion, green pepper, celery, horseradish, salt, and pepper. Cover; let stand at room temperature for 2 hours. Drain vegetables; stir in vinegar, sugar, mustard seed, and cloves. Cover and refrigerate for 24 hours before serving.

Mrs. Cayce Rumsey (Jan Sumners)

UNCOOKED RELISH

6 onions
6 green peppers
6 sweet red peppers
1 head cabbage
1 hot pepper

4 cups white sugar
2 pints vinegar
1 tablespoon mustard seed
1 tablespoon celery seed

Grind onions, green and red peppers, cabbage, and hot pepper fine. Salt lightly and let stand overnight. Drain and add sugar, vinegar, mustard seed, and celery seed. Put in sterilized jars cold. Wait at least 2 weeks before eating. This is good with cold meats. Makes 7-8 pints.

Elizabeth Overton Cravens

CRANBERRY CHUTNEY

1 pound cranberries
1 cup water
1 lemon, grated rind and juice
1-2 cups sugar
1 cup golden raisins
1 onion, chopped
1 cup slivered almonds

1 teaspoon salt
⅛ teaspoon cayenne pepper
1 cup chopped apple
1 tablespoon chopped crystallized ginger
½ cup orange marmalade

Combine cranberries, water, lemon juice and rind, sugar, raisins, onion, almonds, salt, cayenne, and apple in large saucepan. Bring to a boil and cook over low heat 10-15 minutes or until cranberries are tender and liquid begins to thicken. Stir frequently. Add ginger and marmalade. Chill. Makes about 2½ pints.

LEMON MARMALADE

6 lemons   6-7 cups sugar
7 cups water

Use enamel or stainless steel vessel, large enough for a high boil. Slice lemons thin, removing seeds where possible. Put in pot and cover with water. Let stand 24 hours. Bring to a rapid boil and boil over medium-high heat for 25 minutes. Measure contents (should be 6-7 cups). Add equal amount of sugar. Return to heat and boil 30-40 minutes, or until lemon slices are clear and liquid is thick. Pour into sterilized jars, and seal with paraffin, if desired.

Note: Substituting limes for half the lemons is an interesting and delicious combination. This is good for fall and winter bazaars and gift-giving, since lemons are available year round.

Mrs. Edward "Flash" Florey, Jr. (Betty Finklea)

Hint: Shave paraffin into sterilized jelly glasses. When hot jelly is poured into glasses the paraffin melts, rises to top, and hardens into an excellent seal.

JANET'S TOMATO BUTTER

9 pounds ripe tomatoes, peeled   ½ teaspoon cinnamon
   and seeded   ½ teaspoon allspice
3 pounds sugar   1 pint vinegar
½ teaspoon cloves

Combine tomatoes, sugar, cloves, cinnamon, allspice, and vinegar in a large pot and cook until mixture becomes very thick, about 1½ hours. Use low heat and stir often as mixture becomes thicker or butter will burn. When mixture reaches a spreadable consistency, bring to a boil and pack into sterile canning jars. Process in water bath canner (212 degrees F.) for 20 minutes. Makes 6½ pints.

Note: Good on baked beans and any kind of meat.

Mrs. Mark Bergaas (Mary Emmons)

Children's
Recipes

POPCORN JACKS

1 gallon popped corn (cooked in oil but not salted)
¼ cup raw peanuts (optional)
1 stick oleo or butter

1 cup brown sugar
¼ cup molasses or dark corn syrup
¼ teaspoon soda

Place popped corn and peanuts in large pan with sides. Set oven at 225 degrees. Bring margarine, brown sugar, and molasses to a boil. Boil for 1 minute. Stir in soda; mix well. Pour hot syrup over popped corn and nuts. Mix well to coat. Place in preheated oven on middle shelf. Bake for 1 hour; stir every 15 minutes to coat corn with syrup. Cool and store in container with lid. Keeps well.

Mrs. Wayne Hutton (Cherie Whetstone)

CHILDREN'S FAVORITE CHOCOLATE CAKE

1½ cups flour
1 teaspoon soda
1 cup sugar
3 heaping tablespoons cocoa

½ teaspoon salt
6 tablespoons oil
1 cup water

Heat oven to 350 degrees. Mix flour, soda, sugar, cocoa, salt, oil, and water in an 8 x 8-inch cake pan. Bake for 35 minutes. Ice cake while hot in pan.

PEANUT BUTTER ICING:
⅓ stick oleo
2 heaping tablespoons peanut butter

⅔ cup confectioners' sugar
¼ cup milk (approximately)

Melt oleo and peanut butter over low heat. Add sugar and enough milk to make spreading consistency.

Mrs. John Pradat (Laura Parker)

BISCUIT TREATS

1 package refrigerated biscuits (8-10 biscuits)

8-10 sugar cubes
¼ cup orange juice

Heat oven to 400 degrees. Place biscuits on pan. Stick a sugar cube in the middle of each one. Pour a teaspoon of orange juice over the sugar. Bake 8-10 minutes. Serve hot.

Bert Wear

MARSHMALLOWS

2 envelopes unflavored gelatin
6 teaspoons water
1½ teaspoons vanilla
2 cups granulated sugar

10 tablespoons water
Pinch salt
Confectioners' sugar

In large mixer bowl, sprinkle gelatin over 6 teaspoons water mixed with vanilla. Set aside. In large saucepan or wide-bottomed tea pot with pouring lip, mix granulated sugar with 10 tablespoons water and salt. Cook until it spins a thread, 230 degrees on candy thermometer. Pour hot syrup over gelatin and beat for 10-15 minutes, or until cool and very stiff. With hot spoon, spread in a 9 x 9-inch pan dusted with confectioners' sugar. Cut with hot knife into squares and roll in confectioners' sugar. Keep in airtight container. Makes about 1 pound.

Note: Tint if desired by adding food color to gelatin mixture, and cut with cookie cutters into interesting shapes.

Mrs. Peterson Cavert (Mary Beth Wear)

EGG FRAME-UP

2 eggs
2 slices bread

Soft butter or oleo

Butter bread on both sides. Use the top of a glass to cut a circle in the bread. Heat 1 tablespoon butter in a large skillet over medium heat. Brown the frames and the circles on one side. Turn with pancake turner. Break an egg into a cup or small bowl. Slip egg into center of bread frame. Repeat. Cover skillet and cook until whites of eggs begin to set. Uncover and lower heat until whites are firm and bottom of bread is brown. Serve eggs with circles and bacon. Makes 2 servings.

Hint: For special holidays use your cookie cutters to make hole for eggs in the shape of Christmas trees, hearts, or bunnies.

BREAD AND BUTTER WAFFLES

2 eggs
1 cup milk
½ teaspoon vanilla

8 slices stale bread
Soft butter or oleo

Heat waffle iron according to manufacturer's instructions. Beat eggs, add milk and vanilla, and beat well. Butter bread on both sides. When waffle iron is ready, dip bread in egg mixture, and place in waffle iron. Close lid. Grill until lightly browned. Serve with cinnamon-sugar or syrup.

Bert Wear

POPCORN BALLS

10 cups popped corn (about ¾-1
cup unpopped corn)
1 teaspoon salt
1¼ cups white corn syrup

¾ cup light molasses
1 tablespoon vinegar
3 tablespoons butter or
margarine

Sprinkle salt over popped corn in large bowl. Combine in a saucepan corn syrup, molasses and vinegar. Boil rapidly to hard ball stage, 250 degrees on candy thermometer. Remove from heat and stir in butter. Gradually pour hot syrup into center of the corn. With long-handled spoon and fork, toss and stir to coat corn evenly with syrup. Butter hands and gather and press corn into balls. Or grease a lamb cake mold and press popcorn in, let sit for 30 minutes and unmold. Makes 10 large or 20 small balls.

Variation: Add 2 cups shelled peanuts to the popcorn before pouring syrup on.

Hint: Popcorn will pop better if you leave it in the freezer for a full 24 hours before using.

LOLLIPOPS

2 cups sugar
⅔ cup light corn syrup
½ cup water

Food color
1 teaspoon vanilla, fruit or
peppermint flavoring

In large saucepan, combine sugar, corn syrup and water. Stir over low heat until sugar is dissolved, then raise heat and cook quickly, without stirring, to just past the hard crack stage, 310 degrees on candy ther-mometer. (Grease a cookie sheet while syrup is boiling.) Stir in a few drops desired food color and flavor. Spoon by tablespoon onto greased sheet. Press into each lollipop a wooden skewer or twisted paper loop. Remove when cold. Or, pour onto cookie sheet in a thin layer. When cold and brittle, break into chunks to resemble broken glass. Or, pour into your favorite greased lollipop molds! Insert sticks. Remove when cool. You may also wish to ask your pharmacist to pour you up some of the fruit *oils* (orange, lemon, peppermint, etc.) as they are tastier and the flavors last longer. (Use 1 teaspoon). Store on wax paper in airtight tins.

PRETZELS

1 package dry yeast
1¼ cups warm water (115 degrees)
1 tablespoon sugar
1 tablespoon salt

4 cups unsifted flour
1 egg white, beaten
1 teaspoon water
Coarse salt

Dissolve yeast in water. Add sugar, salt, and flour. Mix well. Shape pieces of dough into large fat pretzels on cookie sheet. Thin beaten egg white with water and brush each pretzel. Sprinkle with coarse salt. Bake at 450 degrees until golden brown, about 12-15 minutes.

Note: Making these will entertain your children for hours!

Mrs. Allen Mattox (Harriet Marrs)

EASY SWEET TWISTS

1 package refrigerated biscuits
   (8-10 biscuits)
2 tablespoons butter

½ cup granulated sugar
1 teaspoon cinnamon

Preheat oven to 400 degrees. Melt butter in small saucepan and pour into a salad plate. Mix sugar and cinnamon and put in second plate. Stretch each biscuit into an oblong shape. Dip in melted butter to coat evenly. Dip in cinnamon-sugar mixture to cover completely. Twist before arranging on baking sheet. Bake 8-10 minutes. Remove from pan while hot with pancake turner. Cool slightly.

Bert Wear

JACK-O'-LANTERN PIZZAS

4 English muffins, split
1 tablespoon melted butter
1 (8-ounce) can pizza sauce

8 slices mozzarella cheese (3½ inches square)

Heat oven broiler. Put muffin halves, cut or torn side up, on baking sheet and brush with butter. Broil until lightly browned. Reduce oven temperature to 400 degrees. Spread 1 tablespoon pizza sauce on each muffin. Trim the cheese slices into circles to fit muffins. Use a paring knife to cut jack-o'-lantern faces out of cheese slices. Place a cheese face on each muffin. Bake until cheese melts, 8-10 minutes. Makes 8 servings.

Optional: Furnish green pepper strips, sliced black and green olives, mushrooms, pepperoni, etc., and let each person make his own "face" on pizza.

FLOWERPOT CUPCAKES

1 (18.5-ounce) package devil's
food cake mix
1 (16.5-ounce) can frosting, green
if available (white if not, and
color with green food color)

Large marshmallows
Colored sugars and candy beads
Gum drops
10 (2½-inch) clay flowerpots

Line flowerpots with foil. Grease foil by using pastry brush dipped in oil. Shake flour around in pots to coat foil.

Preheat oven to 350 degrees. Prepare the cake batter according to package directions. Put ½ cup batter in each flowerpot or fill ¾ full. Place flowerpots on cookie sheets or in muffin pans to steady and bake 15-20 minutes, or until toothpick inserted in center comes out clean. Remove from oven (be careful!) and place on wire racks until completely cool. Frost cakes with green icing. Decorate by cutting marshmallows and gum drops into slices and dipping in colored sugar. Or use a real flower, insert stem in plastic straw, and stick straw in center of cupcake.

FRUITED SNOW

3-6 cups crushed ice
1 (6-ounce) can concentrated fruit
juice (orange, pineapple, grape,
etc.), thawed

Put ½ to ¾ cup crushed ice in bowl or cup. Top with 1-2 tablespoons fruit juice concentrate. Makes 6-8 servings.

To crush ice in food processor: Fit bowl with steel blade. Turn machine on and drop ice cubes in through feed tube.

FROZEN POPS

1 (3-ounce) package fruit-flavored
gelatin
1 (.22-ounce) envelope unsweetened fruit-flavored drink mix

1 cup sugar
2 cups boiling water
3 cups cold water

Dissolve gelatin, drink mix and sugar in boiling water. Add cold water. Pour into ice cube trays or frozen pop molds. Freeze until firm. Any combination of flavors may be used; experiment and find your own favorites. Keep any extra mix in refrigerator.

Mrs. Peterson Cavert (Mary Beth Wear)

MUFFIN SURPRISES

1¾ cups all-purpose flour
¼ cup sugar
2½ teaspoons baking powder
¾ teaspoon salt

1 well-beaten egg
¾ cup milk
⅓ cup cooking oil
Jelly or jam

In mixing bowl, stir together flour, sugar, baking powder, and salt. Make a well in the center of mixture. Combine egg, milk, and oil, and add all at once to dry mixture. Stir just until moistened. Fill well-greased muffin pans or paper bake cup-lined muffin pans ⅔ full. Top batter of each muffin with 1 teaspoon jelly or jam. Bake in 400-degree oven for 20-25 minutes. Makes 12 muffins.

CHRISTMAS WREATH COOKIES

¼ cup oleo
3 cups miniature marshmallows
1½ teaspoons green food color

4 cups corn flakes
Red cinnamon candies

Butter a cookie sheet. Combine oleo and marshmallows in a saucepan and melt over low heat, stirring constantly. Add food color. Remove from heat and stir in cereal to coat thoroughly with green mixture. Let cool until warm. Butter hands and form 2-inch balls of green mixture. Place on cookie sheet and poke a hole in the middle of the ball. Spread into wreath shape. Put candies on while still warm so they will stick better. Work quickly! Let a friend help. Cool completely at room temperature. Store, tightly covered, no longer than 1 week.

FROZEN YOGURT POPS

1 (8-ounce) carton Dannon yogurt, any fruit flavor

2 (4-ounce size) paper cups
2 wooden sticks

Stir the yogurt to distribute fruit evenly. Divide the yogurt between the two cups. Freeze until slushy, about 30 minutes. Put a wooden stick into the middle of the yogurt. Freeze until hard. To eat, peel off the paper cup. Makes 2 servings.

Hint: You may use 32 ounces of any plain yogurt with 3 to 6 ounces (depending on your taste) of any fruit flavored gelatin to make your own frozen yogurt. Add yogurt to mixing bowl, blend in fruit flavored gelatin powder with mixer. Put in freezer, stir every 15 to 30 minutes until it becomes slushy. Serve in bowls or place in paper cups or pop molds, insert sticks and return to the freezer until frozen solid.

BANANA POPS

4 medium-sized bananas
1 (6-ounce) package semi-sweet
  chocolate bits
2 tablespoons oleo

1 cup chopped peanuts, granola,
  or shredded coconut
8 wooden skewers

Peel bananas and cut in half. Put wooden skewers into cut ends of bananas; freeze until firm. Melt chocolate and oleo in small saucepan over low heat, stirring constantly. Cool slightly. Pour into a tall narrow glass. Dip each frozen banana half in chocolate mixture to coat evenly. Immediately roll in peanuts, granola or coconut. Freeze. When frozen, wrap in plastic wrap. Makes 8 servings.

Note: If bananas are too ripe, mash and freeze in 4-ounce paper cups for an hour. Insert sticks, and put back in freezer until hard. Peel off cup and proceed as before.

PEANUT BUTTER BITES

1 egg
⅓ cup of peanut butter
1 tablespoon soft butter
½ teaspoon vanilla

½ teaspoon salt
2 cups sifted confectioners' sugar
Additional confectioners' sugar

Beat egg in medium-sized bowl. Add peanut butter, butter, vanilla, salt, and sugar. Mix well. Take 1 tablespoonful of mixture at a time and roll into balls. Roll in confectioners' sugar. Chill 1 hour.

Laura Stanley

NO-BAKE COOKIES

2 cups sugar
1 stick butter or oleo
¼ cup cocoa
½ cup milk

1 teaspoon vanilla
½ cup peanut butter—crunchy
  or smooth
3 cups quick-cooking oats

In saucepan, mix sugar, butter, cocoa, milk, and vanilla. Bring to a boil and boil 1 minute. Remove from heat. Add peanut butter, and stir well. Add oats and stir. Drop by spoonfuls on wax paper.

Note: Delicious and easy.

Mrs. T. Griffin Stanley (Phyllis Miglarese)

PEAR BOAT SALADS

8 canned Bartlett pear halves
1 (6-ounce) package lime gelatin
2½ cups boiling water
1 cup pear syrup, drained from
    pears

4 square slices American or
    cheddar cheese
8 plastic straws
Fish-shaped crackers

Dissolve gelatin in boiling water. Stir in pear syrup. Pour into a bowl or flat dish and chill until firm. Chill pear halves. Cut cheese slices diagonally in half to form triangles. Slit straws and insert a cheese triangle in each to form sails. Spoon gelatin into individual serving dishes to form "waves". Place pear halves, cut side up, on gelatin. Cut straws to desired length and insert one at wide end of each pear. Garnish with fish-shaped crackers. Makes 8 servings.

Bert Wear

CINNAMON TOAST

Bread
Butter or oleo, softened

½ cup sugar
1 tablespoon cinnamon

Make cinnamon-sugar by mixing sugar with cinnamon. Put in a large salt or sugar shaker and this will last a long time. Put bread on cookie sheet and toast top by broiling in oven until light brown. Remove cookie sheet, turn bread over and spread soft butter or oleo on soft side. Sprinkle with cinnamon-sugar mixture. Return to oven and broil until tops are bubbly. Be careful taking toast off pan. It's hot!

Bert Wear

ONE CUP CAKE

½ stick butter
2 eggs, beaten
1 teaspoon vanilla
Milk

1 cup self-rising flour (sifted)
1 cup sugar
1 greased and floured 8 x 8-inch
    cake pan

Heat oven to 350 degrees. Melt butter. Pour into 1-cup measuring cup. Add beaten eggs and vanilla. Add enough milk to have 1 cup liquid. Add liquid to flour and sugar in medium bowl. Mix until well blended. Pour into pan. Bake for 20-30 minutes, or until toothpick inserted in center comes out clean. Frost as desired. Yield: 1 single layer cake.

Mrs. James O. Parker (Yalonda Duncan)

PUZZLE SANDWICHES

8 slices white bread
8 slices whole wheat bread

Desired sandwich filling

Remove crusts from bread, if desired. Use cookie cutter to cut a shape from a white slice and a whole wheat slice. Carefully push cut-outs out of slice and put white bread shape in whole wheat slice and whole wheat shape in white bread slice. Do this four times. Spread desired filling on remaining slices. Make sandwiches so that bottom slice matches cut out shape in top slice.

Animal shapes are good for children's parties, as are appropriate number and letter combinations, with peanut butter and honey filling. Adapt to a card party by using heart, diamond, etc., shapes and cream cheese combination filling, chicken or shrimp salad, or Summer Vegetable Mold.

CHOCOLATE CARAMEL APPLES

6 medium apples
6 wooden skewers
1 (14-ounce) package caramels
  (about 50)
2 tablespoons water

¼ cup semi-sweet chocolate bits
6 tablespoons chopped nuts,
  shredded coconut, crushed
  whole wheat cereal or mixture
  of all

Wash and dry apples. Put a wooden skewer into stem end of each apple. Put caramels, water and chocolate pieces in saucepan. Melt over low heat, stirring occasionally. Divide nuts, coconut, cereal or mixture into equal portions on wax paper. Remove saucepan from heat. Dip apples in caramel mixture, using a spatula to spread mixture over apples. Put each apple on a portion of the coating and turn apple until all the coating is used.

QUICK HOT FUDGE SAUCE

½ cup whole milk
1 tablespoon butter or oleo

5 packages of instant cocoa mix
  (1⅛-ounce each)

Heat milk and butter (or oleo) until butter is melted. Stir in hot cocoa mix until smooth. Simmer 5-10 minutes, until desired thickness is achieved.

Mrs. Victor Friedman (Segail Irwin)

PLAY DOUGH

1 cup flour	1 tablespoon cooking oil
½ cup salt	2 teaspoons cream of tartar
1 cup water	Food color, if desired

In a saucepan, mix flour, salt, water, oil, and cream of tartar. Place over medium heat and cook for 3 minutes, stirring constantly. The mixture will form a ball. When this happens, remove from heat and drop on wax paper. Knead the dough. Food color may be added to ingredients while in pan or after the dough has been removed from the pan. You may want to make several colors. The dough may be kept a long period of time if *tightly* covered. It will not stick to fingers and is pliable.

Mrs. T. Griffin Stanley (Phyllis Miglarese)

MOUSSE
(Children can make this)

1 (13-ounce) can Pet evaporated milk	Food coloring
⅞ cup sugar	½ pint whipping cream, whipped
2 tablespoons lemon juice	Cherries, if desired

Chill milk 24 hours before using. Whip milk in large mixing bowl. Gradually add sugar. Add lemon juice and beat until mixture begins to set. Color as you like. (I usually make it green.) Spoon into sherbets and top with dollop of whipped cream and red cherry.

Mrs. Harry Wright, Jr. (Cissy James)

FRUIT DELIGHT

1 (8¾-ounce) can fruit cocktail	1½ cups crushed ice
1 (3-ounce) package gelatin, any fruit flavor	

Drain fruit cocktail, reserving syrup. Add water to syrup to make ¾ cup. Bring to a boil. Combine gelatin and boiling liquid in blender. Cover and blend on low speed for 30 seconds, or until gelatin is dissolved. Add crushed ice. Blend at high speed until ice is melted, about 30 seconds. Pour mixture into individual serving dishes. Spoon fruit cocktail into each dish. Chill until set, about 10 minutes. Makes about 4 servings.

Mrs. Michael McCrory (Linda Smith)

SNOWBALLS

Large marshmallows   Flaked coconut, tinted if desired

Bring a large pot of water to a boil. Spread the coconut on a plate or wax paper. Using a long barbecue fork, hold marshmallows over boiling water until they are sticky. Roll in coconut. Let cool until firm.

To tint coconut: Put coconut in a jar with a few drops of food color. Shake until color is even. For tan or brown coconut, spread on a cookie sheet and toast in a 300-degree oven for a few minutes. Watch!

CAMP COBBLER

3 cups biscuit mix   2 (29-ounce) cans sliced peaches
1 cup milk   ½-1 cup sugar
2 sticks margarine   2 teaspoons cinnamon

Use a Dutch oven which has a lid that will hold coals on top and legs to hold it up out of the bed of coals. Have ready a white-hot bed of coals. Place the Dutch oven in the bed with 25 to 30 hot coals underneath, place ½ stick of margarine inside, then place 15 to 20 hot coals on the top. Leave for 10-12 minutes, until the margarine has melted and oven is about 400 degrees. Mix biscuit mix, milk, half of the melted butter, leaving the rest to grease oven. Roll out dough on a floured surface of aluminum foil or wax paper with a glass and cut dough into long thin strips. Add dough strips to Dutch oven enough to cover bottom and sides. *Quickly* add 1 can of peaches and juice, sprinkle with half the sugar and cinnamon, and dot with half the remaining margarine. Repeat a second layer of dough, peaches, juice, sugar, cinnamon, and margarine. Lay the remainer of your strips across the top. Replace the cover; check in 5 minutes. No change of crust should be visible; if there is, remove a few hot coals. Check in 10 minutes, as a light crust should be forming. Continue to cook for a total of 30-35 minutes. Check by placing a clean straw or wood splinter through dough. If it comes out clean, set aside to allow the cobbler to cool slightly (if the crust is nice and brown and appears to be thoroughly cooked).

Note: Any fruit may be used. For fresh fruit, you will need 6-8 cups of fruit and 2 cups sugar. Add water to replace juice.

Allen Mattox

Young golfers, football players, and basketball players will want to taste the following recipes!

PAPRIKA CREAMED CHICKEN

1 medium onion, chopped
4 tablespoons fat (butter, oil, or a combination)
3 pounds chicken, thighs or drumsticks
1 teaspoon paprika (sweet pepper)

2 cups water plus 2 chicken bouillon cubes, or chicken stock
½-1 teaspoon salt
2 tablespoons flour
1 pint sour cream

Brown onion in fat in deep pan. Add chicken pieces, paprika, water and bouillon cubes or stock, and salt. (Use lesser amount of salt at first.) Cook slowly until chicken is tender. In a separate bowl, mix flour with sour cream until smooth. Add to chicken just before serving. Heat for about 5 minutes but do not boil.

Rose Szolnoki (Joe Namath's Mother)

COACH'S FAVORITE CHILI CON CARNE

2 pounds ground beef
5 or 6 medium onions, minced
2 cloves garlic or ¼ teaspoon garlic powder
2 teaspoons chili powder (or more to taste)

3 teaspoons oregano
1 teaspoon paprika
Salt and pepper to taste
2 pints tomatoes
2 cups kidney beans or leftover pinto beans

Brown meat lightly; drain. Add onion and cook for 5-6 minutes. Add garlic, chili powder, oregano, paprika, salt and pepper, and tomatoes. Cook slowly 45-60 minutes. Add beans and heat through immediately before serving.

Mrs. C. M. Newton (Evelyn Davis)

CHERRY PIE CRUNCH

2 cups flour
1 cup chopped pecans
2 sticks butter, melted
1 (8-ounce) package cream cheese

1 (1-pound) box confectioners' sugar
2 (8-ounce) cartons Cool Whip
2 (21-ounce) cans cherry pie filling

Combine flour, pecans, and butter. Press into 9 x 13-inch baking dish. Bake in 350 degree oven until golden (about 30 minutes). Cool. Combine cream cheese, sugar, and Cool Whip. Pour over crust. Top with pie filling. Refrigerate.

Mrs. Jerry Pate (Soozi Nelson)

Tables

TO FEED 25 PEOPLE, YOU NEED:

10 pounds ham, beef, veal or pork loin (roasted)

6 pounds ground meat for meat loaf or hamburgers

18-20 pounds shrimp (for boiling)

9 pounds poultry for salad

15 pounds poultry for roasting

8-10 chickens for frying

4-5 heads lettuce

4 pounds cabbage, shredded

3-4 cups salad dressing

6 (1-pound) cans of a vegetable

5 (12-ounce) packages of a frozen vegetable

1 (#10) can of a vegetable or fruit

7½ pounds potatoes for salad or mashing

5-6 pounds fresh string beans

1½ gallons soup

4 dozen rolls

¾ pound butter for rolls

1 gallon ice cream

6-7 dozen cookies

4 pies, cut in 6-8 wedges each

1 gallon punch

1½ gallons ice tea

2 gallons coffee (made with 1 pound coffee)

1¼ pints coffee cream

1 pound sugar for coffee

APPROXIMATE YIELDS

YIELDS APPROXIMATELY

1 pound cheese	4 cups grated
1 pound butter, margarine, or lard	2 cups
1 cup cream	2 cups whipped
1 pound cottage cheese	2 cups
1 pound granulated sugar	2 cups
1 pound brown sugar	2⅔ cups
1 pound confectioners' sugar	2½-3 cups
1 pound honey, molasses, or sorghum	1½ cups
1 pound regular all-purpose or unbleached flour	3½ cups
1 pound cake flour	4¾ cups
1 pound Graham or whole wheat flour	3¾-4 cups
1 pound rice flour	3½ cups
1 pound rye flour	5 cups
1 pound corn meal	3 cups
1 pound rice (2 cups)	6 cups cooked
1 pound oats	6 cups
5 eggs	1 cup
8-10 egg whites	1 cup
14-16 egg yolks	1 cup
12 hard-boiled eggs	3½ cups, chopped
1 pound bread	12-16 slices
2 slices bread	1 cup soft crumbs
5 slices bread	1 cup fine dry crumbs
20 2-inch crackers	1 cup crumbs
26-30 vanilla wafers	1 cup crumbs
1 pound noodles (uncooked)	7 cups cooked
1 fresh coconut	1 cup grated
1 pound flaked or shredded coconut	5 cups
1 lemon	2 teaspoons grated rind 2-3 tablespoons juice
1 orange	2 tablespoons grated rind ⅓ cup juice
1 (4-pound) chicken	4 cups cooked diced chicken
1 pound shrimp in shell	2 cups cooked and peeled shrimp
1 pound seedless raisins	3 cups
1 pound pitted dates	3 cups chopped
1 pound almonds (in shell)	1-1½ cups nutmeats
1 pound almonds (shelled)	4 cups nutmeats
1 pound peanuts (in shell)	2 cups nutmeats
1 pound peanuts (shelled)	4 cups nutmeats
1 pound pecans (in shell)	2¼ cups nutmeats

YIELDS APPROXIMATELY

1 pound pecans (shelled)	4 cups nutmeats
1 pound walnuts (in shell)	1⅔ cups nutmeats
1 pound walnuts (shelled)	3 cups nutmeats
1 pound candied fruit or peel	1¼ cups cut up
1 pound apples (3 medium)	3 cups sliced
1 pound bananas (3 medium)	2 cups mashed
1 pound strawberries	4 cups whole, 2 cups puréed
1 pound peas in shell	1 cup shelled and cooked
1 pound limas in shell	⅔ cup cooked
1 pound tomatoes	1½ cups peeled
1 pound cabbage	4 cups shredded
1 pound carrots (7-8 medium)	4 cups chopped
1 pound celery	4 cups diced
1 pound prunes	4 cups cooked
1 pound potatoes	2 cups mashed
1 pound onions	3 cups chopped
1 small onion	¼ cup chopped
1 medium onion	½ cup chopped
1 large onion	1 cup chopped
1 cup dried red beans	2 cups cooked
1 pound zucchini	3½ cups sliced
	2 cups grated, squeezed

APPROXIMATE TEMPERATURE CONVERSIONS

	Fahrenheit	Centigrade or Celsius
Water freezes	32 degrees	0 degrees
Water simmers	115 degrees	46 degrees
Water boils	212 degrees	100 degrees
Soft ball	234-238 degrees	112-114 degrees
Firm ball	240-242 degrees	115-116 degrees
Hard ball	248-250 degrees	120-121 degrees
Slow oven	275 degrees	135 degrees
Moderate oven	350 degrees	177 degrees
Hot oven	450-500 degrees	232-260 degrees
Deep fat	375-400 degrees	190-204 degrees

To convert Fahrenheit to Centigrade or Celsius: subtract 32 and divide by 1.8.

To convert Centigrade or Celsius to Fahrenheit: multiply by 1.8 and add 32.

SUBSTITUTION OF INGREDIENTS

If recipe calls FOR: **You may SUBSTITUTE:**

1 tablespoon flour
(used in thickening)

½ tablespoon cornstarch, potato starch, rice starch, arrowroot starch, or 1 tablespoon quick-cooking tapioca

1 cup sifted cake flour

1 cup sifted all-purpose flour minus 2 tablespoons (⅞ cup sifted all-purpose flour)

1 cup sifted all-purpose flour

1 cup unsifted all-purpose flour minus 2 tablespoons (⅞ cup unsifted)

1 cup self-rising flour

1 cup all-purpose flour sifted with ½ teaspoon baking powder and ¼ teaspoon salt

1 cup whole milk

1 cup reconstituted nonfat dry milk (4 tablespoons powdered milk and 1 cup water) plus 2½ teaspoons butter or margarine
or
½ cup evaporated milk plus ½ cup water

1 cup buttermilk or sour milk

1 tablespoon vinegar or lemon juice plus enough milk to make 1 cup (let stand 5 minutes)
or
1¾ teaspoons cream of tartar plus 1 cup milk

1 cup butter

1 cup margarine
or
⅞ cup to 1 cup hydrogenated shortening plus ½ teaspoon salt
or
⅞ cup lard plus ½ teaspoon salt

1 ounce chocolate (1 square)

3 tablespoons cocoa plus 1 tablespoon fat

1 cup coffee cream (20% fat)

3 tablespoons butter plus ⅞ cup milk

1 cup heavy cream (40% fat)

⅓ cup butter plus ¾ cup milk (not for whipping)

If recipe calls FOR:	You may SUBSTITUTE:
1 teaspoon baking powder	¼ teaspoon baking soda plus ⅝ teaspoon cream of tartar or ¼ teaspoon baking soda plus ½ cup sour milk or buttermilk or ¼ teaspoon baking soda to ½ cup molasses
1 tablespoon active dry yeast	1 package active dry yeast or 1 compressed yeast cake
1 cup honey	1¼ cups sugar plus ¼ cup liquid* or 1 cup molasses
1 cup corn syrup	1 cup sugar plus ¼ cup liquid*
1 cup brown sugar (firmly packed)	1 cup granulated sugar (product will not be as moist)
1 cup sorghum syrup (molasses)	1 cup sugar (reduce baking powder; use ½ teaspoon soda to 1 cup sorghum)
1 whole egg (medium or large)	2 egg yolks (for custard) or 2 egg yolks plus 1 tablespoon water (for cookies)
2 large eggs	3 small eggs
1 tablespoon fresh herbs (generally)	½ teaspoon dried herbs
1 pound fresh mushrooms	8 ounces canned mushrooms
1 teaspoon beef extract	2 beef bouillon cubes
1 clove fresh garlic	¾ teaspoon garlic salt or ⅛ teaspoon garlic powder

*Use whatever liquid is called for in the recipe. Amounts are based on the way these products function in foods.

INDEX

Winning Seasons
P. O. Box 1152
Tuscaloosa, Alabama 35403

Please send me _____ copies of **Winning Seasons** at $16.95 per copy (plus $2.75 postage and handling per copy). Enclosed is my check or money order for $ _____ . (Alabama residents add $1.35 sales tax.)

PLEASE PRINT:

Name _____

Address _____

City _____ State _____ Zip _____

All proceeds from the sale of the cookbook are returned to the community through projects of The Junior League of Tuscaloosa, Inc.
Make checks payable to: **Winning Seasons**.

Winning Seasons
P. O. Box 1152
Tuscaloosa, Alabama 35403

Please send me _____ copies of **Winning Seasons** at $16.95 per copy (plus $2.75 postage and handling per copy). Enclosed is my check or money order for $ _____ . (Alabama residents add $1.35 sales tax.)

PLEASE PRINT:

Name _____

Address _____

City _____ State _____ Zip _____

All proceeds from the sale of the cookbook are returned to the community through projects of The Junior League of Tuscaloosa, Inc.
Make checks payable to: **Winning Seasons**.

Winning Seasons
P. O. Box 1152
Tuscaloosa, Alabama 35403

Please send me _____ copies of **Winning Seasons** at $16.95 per copy (plus $2.75 postage and handling per copy). Enclosed is my check or money order for $ _____ . (Alabama residents add $1.35 sales tax.)

PLEASE PRINT:

Name _____

Address _____

City _____ State _____ Zip _____

All proceeds from the sale of the cookbook are returned to the community through projects of The Junior League of Tuscaloosa, Inc.
Make checks payable to: **Winning Seasons**.

Re-Order Additional Copies